# Inland Waterways of France

## Volume 3 – South and West

*David Edwards-May*

Imray, Laurie, Norie & Wilson Ltd

Published by
Imray, Laurie, Norie & Wilson Ltd
Wych House, St Ives, Cambridgeshire PE27 5BT England
www.imray.com
2021

All rights reserved. No part of this publication may be reproduced, transmitted or used in any form by any means – graphic, electronic or mechanical, including photocopying, recording, taping or information storage and retrieval systems or otherwise – without the prior permission of the publishers.

First published 1956
5th edition 1984
6th edition 1991
7th edition 2002
8th edition 2010
9th edition 2021 (published in three volumes)

© David Edwards-May 2021

David Edwards-May has asserted his right to be identified as the author of this work, including all unattributed photographs, in accordance with the Copyright, Designs and Patents Act 1988.

ISBN 978 178679 308 9

British Library Cataloguing in Publication Data.
A catalogue record for this book is available from the British Library.

CAUTION
While every care has been taken to ensure accuracy, neither the Publishers nor the Author will hold themselves responsible for errors, omissions or alterations in this publication. They will at all times be grateful to receive information which tends to the improvement of the work.

Printed in Croatia by Denona

# Contents

**PREFACE** .................................................................... 1

**INTRODUCTION** ............................................................. 3

**Part I - PLANNING A CRUISE** ............................................... 9

**Part II - ROUTE DESCRIPTIONS AND MAPS** ................................. 21

**CHAPTER VI – SOUTHERN FRANCE** ........................................... 23
   54. Canal du Rhône à Sète (and Étang de Thau) ........................... 24
   55. River Lez ........................................................... 31
   56. Canal du Midi ....................................................... 33
   57. River Hérault ....................................................... 47
   58. Canal du Midi, La Nouvelle branch ('La Robine') ..................... 49

**CHAPTER VII – SOUTHWEST FRANCE** ......................................... 53
   59. Canal de Garonne .................................................... 54
   60. Canal de Montech and River Tarn ..................................... 63
   61. River Baïse ......................................................... 66
   62. Garonne crossing .................................................... 70
   63. River Lot ........................................................... 72
   64. River Garonne and Gironde Estuary ................................... 86
   65. River Dordogne ...................................................... 89
   66. River Isle .......................................................... 91
   67. River Adour and tributaries ......................................... 92

**CHAPTER VIII – WESTERN FRANCE** .......................................... 97
   68. Rance Maritime and Canal d'Ille-et-Rance ............................ 98
   69. River Vilaine ...................................................... 102
   70. Canal de Nantes à Brest ............................................ 106
   71. Canal du Blavet .................................................... 116
   72. River Loire ........................................................ 119
   73. Sèvre Nantaise and Petite-Maine .................................... 123
   74. Rivers Mayenne and Oudon ........................................... 125
   75. River Sarthe ....................................................... 130
   76. Rivers Charente and Boutonne ....................................... 133
   77. Sèvre Niortaise and connecting waterways ........................... 138

**INDEX** ................................................................... 143

*Companion volumes*
Inland Waterways of France – Volume 1: North and Centre
Inland Waterways of France – Volume 2: Northeast and Southeast

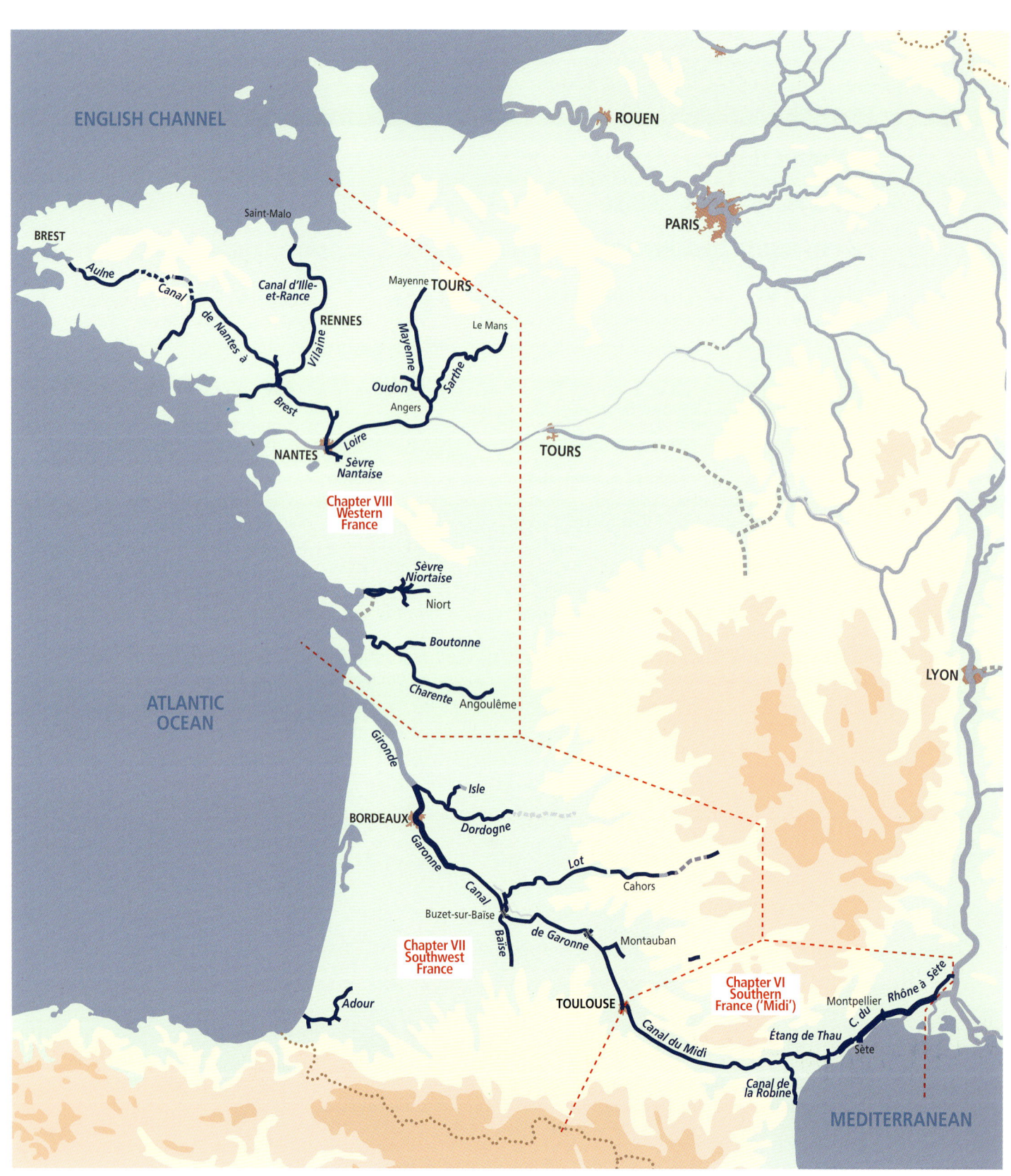

# Preface

The ways of enjoying the uniquely diverse and appealing waterways of France are changing. In this digital age, we felt that it was important to publish products that would be of greatest practical use, not only to boaters but also to all the other waterway users who are increasingly attracted to the canal towpaths and river valleys. This work was first published two thirds of a century ago as a single volume presenting nearly 80 waterways in alphabetical order. However, boat ownership, cruising habits, leisure and lifestyle choices have changed significantly over the years, and the extent of useful information has expanded.

Consequently, the 9000 kilometres of navigable waterways in France are now covered by three volumes. Volume 1 covers Northern France down to the capital region Île-de-France, central France and Burgundy. Volume 2 presents the waterways from the northeast to the southeast, hence the classic cruising itineraries from Northern Europe to the Mediterranean Sea via the Rivers Meuse, Moselle, Sarre or Rhine, converging on the 'common trunk' of the Saône and Rhône. This volume 3 brings together all the other navigable waterways, from Southern France (the 'Midi') via the rivers flowing into the Atlantic Coast, to the remarkable network of canals and canalised rivers in Brittany.

Among the reasons for expanding into three volumes is the insertion of descriptive texts – and more images – into the itineraries, to do better justice to the varied places encountered along the waterways. The new texts break up the former 'distance tables'. These texts do not pretend to replace tourist guides for the places visited, but give some context and tips, relating either to the mooring facility itself or to the corresponding town or village.

For convenience and reference, the sequence of eight chapters is continued through the three volumes. This volume includes Chapter VI, Southern France, Chapter VII, Southwest France and Chapter VIII, Western France, mainly Brittany. Each volume has its separate index. We hope that all those who love exploring the French waterways, or who are planning future adventures, will find all three of the expanded, split publications both an inspiration to extend their own travels and practical to use while actually navigating on the system.

As author I am indebted to James Newcombe for his contributions and extensive feedback from users. His website, **french-waterways.com**, reproduces much of the contents of this work, and by agreement with Imray is the place to go for updates for any specific route or waterway.

Imray's editor Jane Russell was a forensic proof-reader whose corrections and suggestions have added significant value to the guide. Both Jane and Imray's managing director Lucy Wilson gave constant guidance and encouragement during the preparation of this work, and for that the author is truly grateful.

Voies Navigables de France has given the author meaningful support for this edition, as in the past, through its Development Department and the unit in charge of waterway tourism and services to users, with special thanks to Aurélie Millot, Nicolas Delaporte and Adrien Quivoron. VNF is to be credited for its efforts to develop 'green' navigation by providing battery charging stations on the waterways of the northeast: the Canal de la Sarre and Canal de la Marne au Rhin. With significant post-pandemic recovery funding by the French Government, agreed in 2021 with the Grand Est region, it is to be hoped that the rest of the system – both the VNF network and the waterways managed by the regions and départements – will be similarly equipped as soon as possible, gradually making navigation greener and quieter.

The author is also grateful to the many contributors of photographs as well as information updates and corrections since the last edition was produced.

I would like to thank here my family and friends who have accompanied me in my own travels on the waterways in the last 10 years, Padraic Neville, who cycled with me on the towpaths from Givet to Paris in 2017, and Thierry and Catherine Eschbach, owners of the 1600-tonne *Bucentaure*, for the memorable voyage on the Seine from Tancarville to the Port of Gennevilliers in February 2019.

Finally, my thanks to all boaters, *plaisanciers* and *Sportsschiffer* – and the surviving *mariniers* in their 220-tonne barges – for their confidence and continued reference to this work.

David Edwards-May, July 2021

*For Myriam and all the family in southwest France*

# Introduction

FRANCE IS THE WORLD'S number one holiday destination, and the country's waterways have become increasingly popular with tourists from across the world. River cruise ships ply all the high-capacity (*grand gabarit*) waterways, making up one fifth of the network of around 8500 km; hotel barges offer all-inclusive cultural and gastronomic cruises on the smaller canals; comfortable self-drive boats may be hired at nearly a hundred locations. Considering the value of all these products and the €2 billion of economic activity generated annually, there is understandably a keen awareness among decision-makers – in the French Government and in the various regions concerned – of the importance of maintaining the waterway infrastructure for all these operators, as well as for the commercial traffic, their prime vocation, and providing moorings and services to meet the constantly increasing demand. While hopefully of value also to these other waterway interests, this book – since its first edition in 1956 – has been addressing the particular needs of a user that has often received less attention than the commercial waterway tourism operators: the private boat owner. This is the user category that commands respect for having started waterway tourism in France all those years ago. The boats have changed, becoming larger and more comfortable for living aboard, and the cruising practices even more so, becoming slower and more sustainable, but it is striking how the enthusiasm of boat owners for France as a destination to enjoy through her waterways seems to endure all the possible causes for discouragement. And there have been a few such causes over the years.

When the previous edition of this work was produced, the national managing body *Voies Navigables de France*, set up in 1991, had recently been instructed by the Government to concentrate its efforts on the commercially viable routes, making up less than half of the national network. The canals of Burgundy had been handed over experimentally to Burgundy Region, a move that seemingly announced the dismemberment of the national network. In fairness to the policy-makers, the principle of transfer of management or even ownership simply takes one stage further the process of devolved administration that began with the concessions to the *départements*, starting with the Brittany canals and Anjou rivers in the 1960s, continuing with the Nivernais in 1971 and the Somme west of Péronne in 1992. However, there is a fundamental difference between these concessions and the situation in the period 2010-2013. In the above examples, local authorities voluntarily accepted to manage the waterways on behalf of the State for a fixed concession period, to keep them open. The Government allocated budgets to renovate structures as required, and made available State employees through the public works administration for each *département*. In short, there was plenty of sugar to help the medicine go down. In recent years, the State has been presenting to regional or local authorities what amounts to an ultimatum: 'take over this sensitive and vulnerable infrastructure, or we close it down'! The experimental management by Burgundy Region was stopped after two years, after it was found by the regional council to be unfeasible. This is the administrative echelon with the least resources, the most recently created (1983) and with neither the organisation nor the experience required to take on such responsibilities. This created a hiatus, and concern among all parties involved in boating and development of waterway tourism. In the absence of any agreement on transfer, all progress in resolving the difficulties inevitably arising on the network was blocked.

In 2013 another significant change was made, when VNF was made an administrative arm of the State, still empowered to collect revenue but no longer a purely commercial body (*établissement public d'intérêt industriel et commercial*, EPIC). The change was brought about largely by a typically French struggle with all the accompanying industrial action and drumbeating. The thousands of public servants on the Ministry's payroll, 'made available' to the commercial body since 1991, refused to give up their *fonctionnaire* status to be employed directly by VNF. The change of status to an *établissement public administratif* enabled a return to a more unified management.

The waterways (in any country, it should be added) are under permanent threats that are more real than the consequences of any administrative and policy decisions: deterioration of the structures, under the combined effects of age and aggression by extreme climate events. This has been the case for a number of canals in recent years. The deal proposed by the Government, through VNF, to the regions and *départements* crossed by little-used rural canals was already unattractive for many while the canals were operating. Imagine how much more difficult the negotiations became after structures failed or the canals silted up, making them impassable!

The French political culture takes brinkmanship to extremes. The worst possible outcome feels certain to occur. Then, at the eleventh hour, pragmatism kicks in and all is resolved! The processes are fascinating to observe, and I have had the privilege of being involved for more than 35 years, but for the foreign boaters whose plans may be thwarted by closure of part of their intended route, the short-term picture may seem bleak.

Fortunately, in 2021, several dramatic situations have been turned round and waterways restored, and with some local nuances the show goes on. I predict that there will be a heightened appreciation of French waterways and all they have to offer as the world comes out of the COVID-19 pandemic that has changed so much in our lives. More French boaters will hopefully join the ranks of the boaters from many other countries, especially the UK, Germany, the Netherlands, Belgium and the Scandinavia, and grow the numbers of boats cruising through most of the year. After the overview of recent developments on the smaller waterways, I will come back to the main VNF network of high-capacity waterways.

## Regional and local waterways

After a series of closures of French waterways in recent years, it is heartening that two routes were reopened in 2021.

The **Canal de la Sambre à l'Oise** welcomed boats for the first time in 15 years on July 1, 2021, following a €23.5 million programme of works including the reconstruction of its two aqueducts, dating from 1836 and 1837, renovation of 25 locks on the Oise side of the summit level, and dredging to a depth of 1.60 m for the passage of recreational boats. The locks were equipped for automatic operation, and a large volume of marsh pennywort (*hydrocotyle vulgaris*) had to be removed: 30 000 m² was cleared of the weed in 2020.

This success was obtained by vigorous local campaigning and lobbying, and underlined how the future of the waterways can only be guaranteed by bringing together the widest possible partnership. VNF, under pressure from the Ministry of Finance in Bercy, would have let the canal fall into ruin without substantial co-funding of the restoration project by the Hauts-de-France region and the *département* Aisne. The lobbying by local authorities was supported by the international boating community, including DBA The Barge Association and Inland Waterways International, whose members signed an on-line petition. This took the local stakeholders by surprise, and helped them to obtain the exceptional contribution from the Government, enabling VNF to commit to three quarters of the cost.

Local bodies including *Réussir notre Sambre* designed a tourism development strategy to maximise the benefits of the restored waterway. This includes rehabilitating lock cottages to give them new use, improving tourism infastructure and developing the canalside cycleway (*véloroute voie verte*). The partners agreed to share the annual operating costs, estimated at €2.3 million, for a period of 20 years, during which it is hoped that the itinerary will become a magnet and generate economic benefits for the seven districts and the region as a whole.

The **Canal des Ardennes** was closed for a shorter period – just three years – after a lock wall the collapsed at Neuville-Day during an extreme flood on a small stream, and was reopened to navigation on May 1st 2021. Here too, the canal would have been sacrificed by the numbercrunchers in Bercy without a concerted effort by the region and Ardennes *département*. VNF signed a 'contract for the territory' with the Grand Est region in October 2020, injecting €43 million into waterway investments in the vast region over the next two years. To be eligible for part of this fund, the *département* Ardennes and the local districts (groups of communes) were required to submit a coherent tourism development plan, with services and activities that will attract tourists to the canal, both by boat and along an extension of the highly successful Trans-Ardennes cycle route, which runs 121 km from above Sedan to Givet. Again, the successful conclusion of this project demonstrates how real the risk of dismemberment of the network has been in recent years. Even before the flood damage occurred at Neuville-Day, this canal was on the list of little-used routes to be 'remaindered', to use the English word in use during the late 1960s, when the equivalent axe was poised above many English canals. Up to 20% of VNF's waterways were under threat of being no longer operated, hence the new French word *dénavigation*, which for several years was on the lips of every civil servant involved in setting VNF's budget.

The **lower River Lot** was extended in April 2021 by the opening of the restored lock at Saint-Vite. This is the eighth lock from the Garonne at Nicole, and was rebuilt in a combined investment with construction of a new adjacent hydropower plant. A grouping of local and international associations has been formed to promote restoration of the remaining missing links upstream.

*The first boat through Saint-Vite lock in April 2021*

Studies are in progress for a travel-lift solution at Fumel dam, estimated at €500 000 for the lift itself, plus €3.5 million for road access, the actual ramps down into the river above and below the dam, and cutting an approach channel to the ramp from downstream. The project would be funded 50% by the *département* Lot-et-Garonne. A lock here would cost €16 million, which it is believed would have no chance of being approved in the short term. The *tour de table* securing investment in the waterway is more complex than in the two cases examined above. Despite the spectacular progress overall (three quarters of the total length restored and navigable), there are marked contrasts between the 'grand scheme' promoted at the

# Introduction

interregional level and the agendas of each *département* involved. For several years the Lot *département* adopted a short-sighted policy, being content to reap the benefits of its 64 km long section with 14 locks opened in 1991. Downstream, Lot-et-Garonne theoretically had the advantage of being connected to the main network. This left Aveyron, upstream, in isolation. When local politicians succeeded in getting the *département* to apply for funding to start restoration at the upstream end of the 266 km waterway, this was opposed by the Lot council, its downstream neighbour! The latter was under pressure from its own local authorities to extend the navigable length, in particular on a new section around Puy-l'Évêque, and tried to divert the funds allocated to Aveyron on the grounds that navigation was not feasible upstream. Their arguments were rejected, and the first 11 km section of the river in Aveyron was opened in 2010. This inside story is only an anecdote, but it serves to underline the risks inherent in the current situation, with planning responsibilities inadequately defined and distributed. The *départements* are also continuing to refuse outright ownership of the waterway, which is maintained and operated by each of the three authorities under the legal regime of *authorisation*. The implications of the change in the river basin authority, from an *entente* to a *syndicat mixte*, are too complex and subtle to develop here; suffice it to say that the political force of the five *départements* of the Lot valley has diminished, while both the French Government and the European Commission have pulled the plug on further investments to complete the project started in 1987. *La lutte continue!*

The history of the **Roubaix Canal** restoration project is also revealing of the difficulty in securing the long-term future of canals for inland navigation. In September 2003, when the EU's INTERREG secretariat suggested that the restoration project could be submitted for funding, the local partners were willing to go ahead, but the owner VNF was reluctant to commit itself in contradiction with national policy. Instructions from the ministry were to focus exclusively on the priority network. The mayor of Roubaix succeeded in persuading VNF to be lead partner of the Blue Links project, but VNF insisted that a new owner and operator had to be identified and in place within two years. The *Région* Nord-Pas de Calais refused, which left Lille Métropole as the only 'candidate'. Here the incentive of the EU funding and the cross-border nature of the project meant that the dynamic was maintained despite this difficulty. Eventually *Lille Métropole* agreed in October 2009 to take over canal operation and maintenance for an experimental period of two years starting in May 2010. Boaters and readers of this guide played no small part in this successful outcome, by turning up in significant numbers at the highly successful 'Blue Days' rally at the Union site in Roubaix on September 19-20, 2009. The onerous tasks of operating this essentially urban canal, with its 12 locks and 8 moving bridges, and water supply by back-pumping, has forced the Lille metropolitan council to the brink of a decision to close the canal to navigation, on several occasions in recent years.

The 'northern branch' of the **Canal du Rhône au Rhin** was to be reopened by 2010, establishing a direct connection for boats between Strasbourg and Colmar, but unlike the Roubaix Canal, this project was not completed. This itinerary, avoiding the Rhine, would be open to the hire boats operating in the region. The canal had already been closed, which made it impossible for VNF to operate the completed waterway, even temporarily; it could only be project engineer for the restoration works. These started in 2006, but a year later Alsace regional council interrupted the works. The decision was motivated partly by escalation of costs; the final bill was going to be double the €7 million originally budgeted. But the main reason was that operation and maintenance were going to be entirely at the local authorities' expense, without any contribution or staff available from the French Government, through VNF. The region's intention was then to explore how the half-restored canal could be made to work as an asset without being navigable. The regional council agreed to fund the works after Colmar led a vigorous campaign, securing the support of all riparian municipalities for a sensible compromise solution: Alsace would foot the bill for the works, but the local councils together would operate and maintain the canal. This sequence of events underlined several aspects of the situation throughout the network: first, the *région* was ill-equipped to take on the management of inland waterways; secondly, the economic benefits of waterway tourism are perceived more keenly at the local than at the regional level; consequently, local authority groupings are likely to be increasingly involved in future governance models. This project is now unlikely to be completed in the near future, also because one completely new lock is required to connect the old canal with the lowered pound above lock 75, where the connecting canal from the Rhine enters.

*The sorry spectacle of lock 67 on the Canal du Rhône au Rhin in 2017, just north of Marckolsheim; The lock is fully restored while the canal itself remains impassable. Bank consolidation is required before the canal could be filled to its normal depth, but the Region Grand Est no longer wants to complete this project*

The **Brittany canals** were complex, because there was an additional level of authority between the *région*, which now owns the system, and the *départements*. Public institutions were set up in the 1960s and 1970s to operate and maintain some waterways, while others continued to be managed directly. These bodies were rendered redundant after the *Région Bretagne* took over. Prospects are now good for the system, since the regional council has recognised their importance for tourism inland, and is continuing to make substantial investments in restoration and dredging. There remains a threat to integrity of the network because of an ongoing campaign to demolish the weirs on the canalised rivers. The main advocates of weir demolition on the Aulne and the Blavet are the angling community and their representative organisations, who want to encourage migrating fish species to return to these rivers. After careful study of the impacts of weir removal, the idea was abandoned as unfeasible. Regional ownership of the waterways has been instrumental in avoiding this scenario of demolition, but the 'return to nature' movement is constantly in ambush, which means that vigilance and education are also a constant challenge. On the other hand, the region is not pursuing the project to build a bypass at the 1923 Guerlédan dam on the **Canal de Nantes à Brest**. The possible solution shown in this book is to be considered as a 'local project'. Local politicians are indeed still pushing hard, and have suggested that the bypass could be completed by about 2025, where the region's reluctance could perhaps be compensated by EDF, owner of the structure. It was EDF's duty under their original concession to ensure the continuity of navigation. In the absence of an act of parliament relieving them of that obligation, it remains in force.

The partnership needed to keep a canal properly maintained and operating, as in the above examples, can never be a foregone conclusion. One VNF waterway that has regrettably been downgraded to canoeable status is the **Scarpe inférieure** between Douai and Saint-Amand-les-Eaux. This was another closure forced by a structural failure, the lift-bridge at Lallaing, in the early 2000s. This made the newly opened *port de plaisance* at Saint-Amand-les-Eaux a *cul-de-sac*. Making the port accessible at least from the downstream junction with the Escaut was indispensable, and a practical solution was found relatively quickly in this case. Operating staff were provided by the community of communes for the Porte du Hainaut district, and are assigned during the season to the lowest two locks on the river. Saint-Amand nevertheless sees little traffic, but the authorities refuse to spend the €15 million required to dredge the waterway and restore its locks and lift bridges. In the absence of local commitment equivalent to that for the Canal des Ardennes, for example, the Scarpe inférieure remains closed. VNF continues to monitor the waterway for hydraulic continuity, and carry out minimal maintenance to ensure efficient conveyance of flood flows, and may count the occasional canoe. This is a sad destiny for the once essential industrial waterway featuring in the novels of Émile Zola.

In other parts of the network, the *départements* have been pursuing their projects without regional support. This is the case of the *Région* Centre, which does not appear to have a strategy for its historic waterways. This may be because they form a disparate and disconnected network, but it is no less regrettable. The **canalised River Cher** suffered a serious setback when the upstream *département* Loir-et-Cher stopped all works on the construction of two new gated weirs, designed to replace dangerous needle weirs. As on the Canal du Rhône au Rhin south of Strasbourg, described above, the authority was alarmed by the escalating cost of the works. A further difficulty stemmed from the local interpretation of the EU's Water Framework Directive. Civil servants, prompted by anglers and environmentalists, saw the possibility of downgrading the river from a canalised or 'heavily modified' state to a natural water body, in other words free-flowing. The downstream *département* of Indre-et-Loire has been resisting this move, supported by the Association *Les Amis du Cher Canalisé*, but negotiations are complex. The State bodies which issue authorisations for works on rivers are insisting that all weirs, old or new, should not be raised until the end of the fish-spawning season on 1st July each year, which naturally calls into question the feasibility of the weir rebuilding programme. The current situation is an unsatisfactory stalemate.

The neighbouring *département* of Loiret has made remarkable progress in restoration of the **Canal d'Orléans**, although the difficulties of water supply to the central summit level section have to date prevented completion of this valuable project. This narrow canal is expected to be opened to electrically-powered craft only, but even that now appears to be a remote prospect.

Another case where spectacular progress was made in the period 2000-2010 is the **Upper Rhône**, which remains a State-owned waterway, theoretically in the priority network for development of navigation, despite having been abandoned more than 70 years ago! Two-lock bypasses were built at the hydropower plants built by CNR at Chautagne and Belley. The Upper Rhône, like the river Loire, serves to cool a nuclear power station, and that is the argument for maintaining the 'officially navigable' status, while navigation is an optional extra to be negotiated on a case-by-case basis.

The Upper Rhône scheme faced opposition from environmentalists, whose main concern was to kill for ever any prospect of a Rhine-Rhône waterway by this route and through the Swiss lakes and the canalised river Aar to the Rhine. When the Upper Rhône project was studied in 1999-2000, the *Verts* wanted the locks to be built to smaller than Freycinet dimensions, precisely to prevent any commercial use of the waterway. Recreational boating, in their short-sighted view, could be tolerated as being intrinsically more compatible with protection of the environment. Fortunately this attempt to downgrade the project was resisted, and the new locks were built to Freycinet dimensions, like the earlier lock at La Feyssine in Lyon, built in the 1980s. Despite the lack of navigable connection with the main system at Lyon, the new locks opened up a remarkable cruising area in the heart of the Alps, extending 75 km with five locks, and this is my local waterway, with the delightful canalside village of Chanaz on the natural Canal de Savières.

Works are to start soon on construction of a new lock to

bypass the hydropower plant at Brégnier-Cordon, which will add 30 km to this navigation.

The **Upper Canal de la Somme** is another missing link in the network, which could receive funding as a spinoff from the Seine-Nord Europe Canal project, to restore the 16 km long canal with four locks through the small town of Ham. The canal became silted up and closed in 2006.

These are just a few examples of recent developments on the system. Many other stories could be told, of projects successfully completed or frustrated by political or funding difficulties, as may be experienced in any country. Overall, the situation in France is no more alarming than, say, in Germany or the UK. The risk of cuts in public spending, whether for investments or to subsidise bodies giving a public service, is universal. The main challenges are environmental: to ensure that water resources are not diverted from canal supply to other functions, and to prevent 'downgrading' of river navigations to free-flow conditions by the removal of weirs, as promoted by those who assume, often without foundation, that demolition of structures built 200 years ago will automatically make the rivers more appealing for shad, salmon and other migrators.

To conclude this overview of the smaller waterways, the fact that tourism is France's biggest export industry has justified enormous investments in waterway restoration schemes, adding hundreds of kilometres to the length of the waterway network. It is not unreasonable to predict that the institutional difficulties outlined here will eventually be resolved, as long as we users keep making our voices heard. The inevitable questioning of budget commitments at the State level, and the brinkmanship mentioned above, will doubtless lead to more scares in the future, adding to those caused by extreme climate events.

There will inevitably be some frustrations, as boaters encounter stoppages or cutbacks in service and have to change their plans accordingly. The most frequent incidents are likely to be restrictions on the use of locks across the summit level canals, even closure during extreme drought, but there can be no doubt that the waterways provide the key to enjoyment of many French regions, with all their diversity, their history and culture, their gastronomy and wines. Towns and villages alike have awoken to the vast potential, and are gradually developing boat moorings of varying configurations and size, from the landscaped quay or pontoons, generally referred to by the term *halte nautique*, to the fully-equipped boat harbour or *port de plaisance*. We use the French terms in this guide because they are are so conveniently descriptive. These facilities and the associated information, activities and services will help the boater to get the maximum enjoyment from the cruising experience.

## Integrated network for water transport

It feels strange to be heralding impending change in this edition in almost the identical terms to those used in 2010, when I referred to the 'imminent start of works on the new Seine-Nord Europe Canal' but such is the reality of the French Government's seemingly chronic hesitations regarding the waterways and the future role of inland water transport. At least now, works on the first of four sections of the 107 km long canal between Compiègne and Aubencheul-au-Bac, are genuinely taking place. Interconnecting the high-capacity (*grand gabarit*) waterways in the interests of Europe as a whole remains VNF's objective and *raison d'être*. A *société de projet* was created by Government decree in December 2016, and a parallel European Economic Interest Group for financial management including toll collection. Management of the project was transferred from the State to the region Hauts-de-France and its four *départements* in 2019. This is a strategic EU infrastructure project. The European Commission is convinced of the intrinsic value of this investment, along with others in the 'Connecting Europe Facility', justifying a 50% contribution to the total cost.

A carefully conducted process of studies and consultations had resulted in a consensus among all parties, massively in favour of the project. That was before the economic crisis, followed by the change of government in 2012. The projected cost, based on a public-private partnership, had by then increased from €4.2 to nearly €7 billion. A commission was set up to study possible savings. Its report was presented in late 2013, and suggested a route following the existing Canal du Nord for 8 km and eliminating one lock, lowering the summit level by 18.5 m. This modified route was formally adopted in 2018. The canal is divided into four distinct sections for the works and contracts, starting from the southern end. The first section along the river Oise should open in 2027, and the rest of the canal in 2028.

The link is projected to increase waterborne traffic on the Paris-Lille axis from 4 million to 13-15 million tonnes per year by 2030. Nearly all this traffic would be transferred from the A1 motorway, the busiest in France.

Implementation of the project should confirm a deep trend, which shows waterway projects as giving a greater overall return on investment than when analysis was based on freight transport alone. A major factor in gaining favour among all politicians was full consideration of the external costs of transport (including accidents, congestion and pollution), which economists and waterway lobbyists had been campaigning for since the 1960s. It was gratifying to see that the arguments were at last taken into consideration. The European Commission and Parliament have played a major role in this process, by pushing for proper accounting of these external costs, estimated at 8% of Europe's GDP.

Environmental concerns, particularly in the Somme valley, are met by routing the canal on the flank of the valley instead of along the bottom. The canal will have 5 locks, their depth ranging between 13 and 26 m, with a sixth lock (6 m rise) on the river Oise above Compiègne.

At least two other significant projects are going ahead. The first, now practically complete, is upgrading to Class Va of the **Canal du Rhône à Sète**, to improve the competitive position of the port of Sète; the second is upgrading to Class Vb of the **Upper River Seine** from Bray to Nogent.

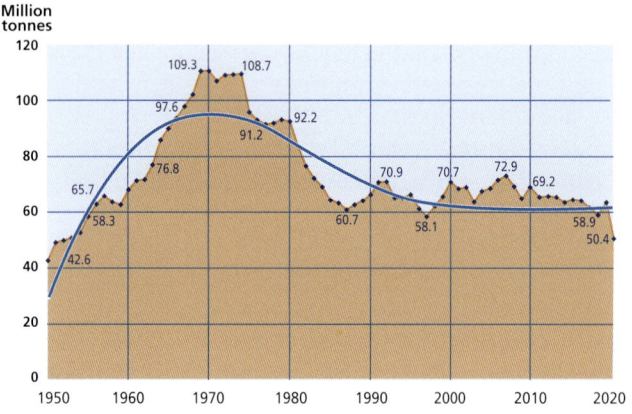

*The graph for freight traffic on French waterways, including transit on the Rhine, shows a relative stagnation since the mid-1980s: approximately 65 million tonnes transported annually, for around 8.2 billion tonne-kilometres. The boost expected from the Canal Seine-Nord Europe is now on the horizon, but 2020 showed a significant decline on account of the pandemic.*

When the entire Seine basin (a quarter of the French population and economy), already served by high-capacity waterways, is interconnected with the main European network, the mindset of politicians and industry will be radically transformed, and the climate could change for the other major project first conceived by the Roman General Vetus: the North Sea-Mediterranean link between the Moselle and the Saône. Discussions to revive this project started at the regional level a few years after the original project for the Rhine-Rhone waterway was abandoned by Environment Minister Dominique Voynet in 1997. It is premature to talk of a replacement project, because Alsace is not prepared to abandon its interest. Accordingly, the preliminary investigations of the potential for a new Saône-Moselle waterway include the possibility of a branch across the Vosges to link up with the high-capacity waterway in the Mulhouse area. This would roughly correspond to the historic Canal de Montbéliard à la Haute-Saône, which was never completed. The first timid move was made by the *Régions* Lorraine and Rhône-Alpes in 2004, when the question asked of consultants, with support from central Government and the other regions concerned (Bourgogne and Franche-Comté) was simply: is it worth studying the feasibility of a high-capacity waterway to link the Rhine and Rhône basins? The answer was yes, and the Ministry of Sustainable Development approved the subject for a national public debate which was supposed to be organised by VNF in 2012. Although the debate was cancelled, the broad vision of a French waterway system fully integrated in the European waterway network, used for bulk freight and combined transport, remains alive.

In the meantime, the bulk of VNF's investment programme concerns improvements to ageing infrastructure on the existing high-capacity network. New gated weirs have been built on the Oise and bridges are being rebuilt on the Liaison Dunkerque-Escaut to offer the new standard headroom of 7.00m, although some bottlenecks with bridges at 5.25m are likely to remain for at least 10 years.

The limited improvements made to the existing network have proved successful, contributing to a significant increase in overall traffic on the French waterways in recent years. As the graph shows, a 25% increase in tonnage transported was achieved by inland water transport between the low in 1997 and the pre-recession peak in 2007, and the industry has fared better than railway freight since then.

The owner-skippers of *péniches* carrying about 220 tonnes also continue to provide a useful service, but would like to see more maintenance of the canals they operate on. They are concerned that the current policy could gradually make commercial operation unfeasible on the smaller waterways.

On the bigger picture, the long-term trend suggests that the post-war peak of the early 1970s could be reached again by around 2030 or 2035, and the new Seine-Nord Europe Canal would make a significant contribution to this growth.

# Part I – Planning a cruise

## 9000 kilometres of cruising waterways

France has the most extensive waterway network in Europe, offering an extraordinary variety of scenery, tourist interest and cruising conditions. Water-borne transport remains the prime function over about a third of the network and remains a minority user over another quarter. That leaves almost half the above total maintained essentially for tourism and other functions not related to commercial navigation. The current situation and recent developments are described in the *Introduction*.

Recreation is accepted as one of the main justifications for maintaining the waterways, and considerable development has taken place accordingly. Harbours and attractive moorings for boats have sprung up at an astonishing rate, here as well as on all the busiest waterways: Rhine, Seine, Moselle, Saône and Rhône. In short, commercial traffic is no obstacle to safe and pleasant cruising, provided certain precautions are taken. This having been said, it is obvious that readers without previous cruising experience (or having only cruised on the English canals, for example) should study the CEVNI rules to be fully acquainted with all navigation signs and rules of the road. It is preferable to keep initially to the smaller waterways, if possible, where commercial traffic has ceased or is very slight. Inevitably mistakes will be made, but these are better made on the quiet canals of Burgundy, amongst fellow boaters, than in the centre of Paris amongst the *bateaux-mouche* and commercial barges.

## Regulations – an overview
*Notes by Tam and Di Murrell*

### (a) Registration documents

Formalities for boats entering France have been greatly simplified. Boat owners wishing to cruise in France, regardless of where and how they arrive, will need the boat's registration documents. Along with the other requirements set out on the following paragraphs, this will permit a stay without fiscal or other complications. The restriction on movements of UK citizens entering France, whose stay is now limited to 180 days, does not apply to their boats permanently moored in France.

Registration is a legal requirement. A boat takes its flag normally from either the nationality of the owner or the country of residence of the owner. Most countries have a simple register and a more complex one, which involves further checks, and tonnage and measurement surveys. In the UK, the Small Ships Register is the simple form of registration, and the Part 1 is the more involved register. Both have the same legal validity throughout the world, and they are both issued by the Registry of Shipping and Seamen in Cardiff (02920 747 333).

### (b) VAT documentation

VAT paid in one EU country is recognised throughout the EU and import can be made for an indefinite period without complication. The only conclusive proof that a boat is 'VAT paid' is the original VAT certificate, which is issued to the original owner of a new boat and subsequently passed on to future owners. However, a variety of VAT exemptions apply to boats, and it is important for the traveller to become familiar with these rules prior to going abroad. For readers in the UK, the best place to get hold of this information is from the Revenue and Customs website, where various notices are available on line and can be downloaded. The address for Revenue and Customs is **http://customs.hmrc.gov.uk**. Particularly relevant is Notice 8 *Sailing your pleasure craft to and from the United Kingdom*. This summarises the main VAT rules, including the possibility of applying for exemption from VAT in the UK if the boat is to be permanently located in the EU under the 'Sailway' scheme. Then of course VAT will have to be paid in the destination country, as well as import duty. The site also explains the rules relating to temporary importation. Owners may bring their boat into the EU and use it for up to 18 months in a 2-year period without being liable for VAT.

HMC Notice 200 gives further details on temporary import, while notice 728 now applies only to boats moved from Northern Ireland to the EU, pending the drafting of the equivalent rules for the rest of the UK as a third state.

The general rule that remains applicable is that VAT is payable either in the country of purchase at that country's rate, or at the rate applicable in country of destination.

### (c) Marine insurance

Insurance is compulsory on the inland waterways of Europe. In some cases it may be a requirement for the insurance documents to be translated. For further details refer to the relevant countries listed in the RYA's Foreign Cruising Guides, published jointly with The Cruising Association. These publications detail the regulations for European countries and list the documentary requirements of both the boat and the crew, including a section on inland waterways.

### (d) Ship's radio licence

A radio telephone ship licence is required for every British ship with radio telephonic equipment installed, intended for public correspondence use. For British registered ships, this licence is available from the Radio Licensing Centre. The user should also have an operator's licence for the appliance.

### (e) Helmsman's licence

Skippers of craft navigating inland need to hold a valid

certificate of competence, and inland waterway regulations come into effect once a vessel is upstream of the seaward limit of each estuary. The category of licence required is determined by the size of craft and the power of the engine. There is an exemption for boats less than 5m with no cabin and with a power factor T less than 1, calculated by the formula T = hp of the engine multiplied by 1.9, this sum then divided by the square of the boat's length. By this formula a 4.9 m long boat with a 12.5 hp engine just qualifies for exemption. The helmsman must be 16 or over.

### (f) International Certificate of Competence

UN Resolution 40 introduced a Europe-wide helmsman's licence, known as an International Certificate of Competence (ICC). It is issued after a test of practical ability and knowledge of the 'rules of the road', and is available for cruising with a sail boat and/or a motor-driven one, with the test being taken on an appropriate craft. To gain an ICC with coastal endorsement requires a test of knowledge of the International Regulations for Preventing Collisions at Sea (COLREGS), and for an inland endorsement a test of the CEVNI rules, which govern inland boating. In the UK the ICC is issued by the Royal Yachting Association.

In 2011 the European Boating Association and DBA The Barge Association, along with the RYA, succeeded in getting an amendment to Resolution 40. Non-EU residents can be issued an ICC by countries which have accepted the Resolution. Residents/nationals of an EU country can only get theirs from the country where they live. A valuable study book for the ICC inland endorsement is the *RYA Book of European Waterways Regulations*. This book should be carried on board, but a copy of the CEVNI rules in the language of the country one is cruising is also worth having on board, as a courtesy towards the navigation authority.

Inland boating certificates issued by non-EU countries are not generally accepted, as the CEVNI rules are specific to the interconnected European inland waterways, and differ in significant ways from the COLREGS in use at sea. The study book for the ICC Inland endorsement is the RYA Book of *European Waterways Regulations*, which will also satisfy the requirement that a copy of the CEVNI rules is carried on board.

### (g) French Certificates of Competence

French helmsman licences were reorganised in 2008. There are two categories of inland licence for recreational craft: a *Permis Plaisance* for craft between 5m and 20m, and an *Extension Grande Plaisance* for craft 20m and over. They can be held by persons of any nationality. The *Permis Plaisance* requires brief practical instruction on a small craft, and then a computerised multichoice test of knowledge of the CEVNI rules, in French. A person requiring the Extension Licence, whether for a larger craft or as a first step to a commercial licence for taking passengers on board, *must* first gain the small craft licence. There is then a minimum of nine further hours demonstrating ability to carry out common boating manoeuvres on an appropriate-sized vessel, plus instruction on various safety matters. The minimum age for holders of an Extension licence is 18.

A special temporary certificate called *Carte de Plaisance* is issued by the boat hire firms to all clients not in possession of one of the above, for cruising on waterways that are considered relatively safe. The hire firm is obliged to spend sufficient time with each client to explain the boat's operation and handling.

### (h) Community Inland Navigation Certificate (ES-TRIN, formerly TRIWV))

This originates with the 2006 and ongoing UN Resolution No. 61. Various countries previously had their own rules for construction and equipping craft, and the ES-TRIN are intended to harmonise standards throughout the jurisdiction of the ECE, now including the Rhine. All craft over 20m on European inland waters must have a Certificate of Conformity, which will be issued by authorised bodies of any of the countries concerned (this does not have to be the country of registry).

### (i) Boat licences – péage plaisance

Licences were introduced when Voies Navigables de France (VNF) was set up in 1991. The *péage* is payable by all boats for use of the waterways managed by VNF, per day of navigation, with or without passage through locks. Boats are divided into four categories, defined by length. (Regrettably, this penalises English narrow boats.) The table below gives the rates in € applicable in 2021 for each licence period: liberté or freedom, corresponding to the former annual licence, loisirs or monthly (30 days), 7 days and 1 day. The facsimile reproduced here shows the current vignette, which where the category, year and date of validity are clearly displayed.

The vignette is now easily purchased online – **vnf.fr/vnf/services/acheter-sa-vignette** – and printed at home, entering the boat owner's name and address, the boat's name and draught, length overall, the boat's registration number, or failing that, its serial number, the category of *vignette* required and the corresponding start date (for the *Loisirs*, 7-day and 1-day *vignettes*), a scan of the navigation permit, sea permit or French registration certificate, as well as proof of engine capacity. Payment is by debit or credit card. It is also possible to acquire the vignette at one of

## VNF LICENCE RATES (VIGNETTE) 2021

| Categories | I <br> <8m | II <br> 8<11m | III <br> 11<14m | IV <br> ≥14m |
|---|---|---|---|---|
| Liberté [1] | 8.90 x L + 89.00 | 8.90 x L + 205.90 | 8.90 x L + 392.10 | 8.90 x L + 511.80 |
| Loisirs [2] | 7.80 x L + 28.60 | 7.80 x L + 41.60 | 7.80 x L + 54.40 | 7.80 x L + 69.50 |
| 7 days [3] | 4.20 x L + 15.90 | 4.20 x L + 24.00 | 4.20 x L + 31.90 | 4.20 x L + 39.70 |
| Per day [4] | 3.20 x L + 11.70 | 3.20 x L + 17.60 | 3.20 x L + 23.10 | 3.20 x L + 28.70 |

1 Issued for the calendar year (1st January to 31st December)
2 Issued for 30 consecutive days
3 Issued for 7 consecutive days
4 Issued for any specified day

The amount is calculated according to the duration of navigation and the vessel's length. It is rounded up to the nearest decimal point. The calculation of the price of the vignette includes a variable part depending on the length of the boat (as indicated on the certificate of registration) and a fixed lump-sum part.
A discount of 17% is applied to the «Liberté» vignette only, if acquired before March 31.

VNF's 31 designated customer service offices, which often correspond to the local offices listed in this guide.

The formalities indicated above are a small price to pay for the freedom enjoyed while cruising through the French waterways. Occasionally, generally at a lock, a boat owner will be asked for his ship's registration papers in order to furnish basic information; the boat's name, number and port of registry, and ownership details. He may also be asked to show his vignette.

The distinction between time spent navigating and time spent at a long-term mooring is important. The licence gives the right to moor free of charge for up to 48 hours anywhere on the network, or until asked to move on (a very rare occurrence, although charges are made at harbours leased to a public or private operator).

Long-term moorings are subject either to the charges applied by the harbour concessionary, or to a mooring lease or *autorisation d'occupation temporaire* (AOT) to be obtained from VNF.

## Mast unstepping

A common experience seems to be that boatyards that offer this may be friendly and know how to operate a crane, but are not in business to provide a 'de-rigging' service. You may (as we were) be expected to undo and generally prepare everything, then they will attach a strop to the mast, lift it up and lay it onto the supports you have provided on the boat. In that respect they do not 'look after one' as one might hope. A shame, since for most of us unmasting does not happen often and is a worrying event – problems at the time maybe and maybe problems stored up for the future. We taped the positions of all our shroud and stay bottle-screws and took photographs of all the critical bits of our rig, hopefully to reassemble it correctly in the future.

## Trailer sailing

Owners of trailed craft will find it much easier than in the past to launch on the French waterways. Facilities for boats have mushroomed, and the *ports de plaisance* are usually equipped with a slipway or crane suitable for most trailed boats. Hire firms also welcome private boats to make use of their facilities, except out of season or at weekends when they are busy turning round their own boats. Generally speaking, boat harbours with slipways are encountered more frequently on river navigations than on canals. Most facilities are indicated in the route descriptions, but reference may also be made to the individual waterway guides listed under *Guides and publications*.

If you are planning on trailer-sailing, the maximum authorised dimensions of vehicle and trailer without special permission and documentation are as follows: height, no restriction (but 4m is the practical maximum); overall width, 2.50m; overall vehicle length 12m, and overall trailer length, 12m. The vehicle/trailer combination should not exceed 18.5m. The RYA legal department publishes a booklet on trailer sailing.

## Boat transport

An increasingly popular method of having a vessel delivered to the continent is by truck and trailer using a haulage firm with experience in transporting heavy, oversize loads, especially boats to continental Europe. The haulier arranges competitive ferry prices, selects the appropriate route and obtains the necessary transport permits and *Convoi Exceptionnel* documents and escorts where required. Documents to be supplied to arrange the transport of privately owned vessels are (a) documentation showing the vessel's VAT paid, or exempt, status and (b) a copy of the registration documents. This method of relocating your boat has a number of advantages. There is not the wear and tear of a Channel crossing, there are no forced delays waiting for favourable weather, and the cruise starts where you want, avoiding the occasionally awkward first week's navigation from a busy commercial port through high-capacity waterways shared with heavy inland shipping. For example, the normal delivery time from the UK to Laroche-Migennes is 48 hours.

## Hire boats

A convenient way of discovering France through her waterways is to hire a comfortable cruiser (*houseboat* in French), ideally suited to inland navigation. There are about 100 hire bases operating on the French waterways, belonging to 50 separate companies, with a total of about 1800 boats. It is thus now possible to plan a week's cruise virtually anywhere on the network. Only the waterways between the Seine basin and north-eastern France remain poorly represented.

Listing all hire firms is a risky exercise, for changes occur from one season to the next, but it worth setting out all the details, for hire bases are such an important part of the French waterway scene. Bases are listed in alphabetical order by region. These include a number of relay bases which are operated mainly to allow clients to cruise one-way only. The possibility of one-way cruises is indicated.

Compared with the situation 10 years ago, there has been significant contraction and reorganisation of the hire fleet. The two largest firms, Crown Blue Line (itself the result of a merger) and Connoisseur, merged under the name Le Boat. The table also shows the base at Nieuwpoort in Flanders, Belgium, because it gives access to the waterway network of northern France.

There is no point in contacting the individual bases of the bigger firms for reservations, which are all centralised. These companies, which have bases throughout France, are listed under the first heading 'Central reservation offices'. Their web sites are not repeated under the individual entries.

Many of the smaller firms can offer high-quality boats at reasonable prices. Generally speaking, where lower prices can be obtained for a boat with the same number of berths, clients will get less for their money (older, smaller, less well-equipped and less comfortable boats).

Given the considerable choice of cruising areas, decide first which waterway and which region appeal to you most, and then consult the web sites or ask to be sent the brochures of the various firms operating in the area. Study carefully the characteristics of the boats and their equipment, and compare the dimensions of boats rather than taking for granted the spaciousness apparent in the wide-angle photographs.

### Central reservation offices

| Name | Tel | Website | Details |
| --- | --- | --- | --- |
| FPP Travel | 03 85 53 76 70 | fpp.travel | agency for a network of several small French operators |
| Le Boat | 04 68 94 42 80 | leboat.com | combines former Crown Blue Line and Connoisseur |
| Locaboat Holidays | 03 86 91 72 72 | locaboat.com | 14 bases throughout France |
| Nicols Locations | 02 41 56 46 56 | nicols.com | 8 bases throughout France, and agent for others |

### Midi

| | | | |
| --- | --- | --- | --- |
| Arolles Marine (aff. Nicols) | Bellegarde | camargue-fluvial.com | on the Rhône-Sète near Nîmes |
| Canalous Plaisance | Agde | canalous-plaisance.com | Midi, Rhône-Sète and one-way to Carcassonne |
| Canalous Plaisance | Carcassonne | | Midi and one-way to Agde |
| Canalous Plaisance | Carnon | | Camargue, one-way to Homps |
| Canalous Plaisance | Colombiers | | Midi, Robine branch |
| Canalous Plaisance | Homps | | Canal du Midi |
| Constance Location (aff. Nicols) | Aigues-Mortes | constancelocation.fr | Rhône-Sète and Camargue |
| France Fluviale | Capestang | francefluviale.com | middle of the Canal du Midi long pound |
| Le Boat | Castelnaudary | | base on the Midi, also head office for reservations |
| Le Boat | Castelsarrasin | | Canal de Garonne (Moissac and Montauban) |
| Le Boat | Homps | | Canal du Midi, one-way to Port Cassafières |
| Le Boat | Narbonne | | La Robine branch of the Midi |
| Le Boat | Port Cassafières | | on the Midi, one-way to St Gilles or Castelnaudary |
| Le Boat | Saint-Gilles | | Rhône-Sète, one-way to Port Cassafières |
| Le Boat | Trèbes | | Midi and one-way to Homps |
| Locaboat Holidays | Argens-Minervois | | end of the long pound, one-way to Bram or Lattes |
| Locaboat Holidays | Négra | | only base near Toulouse, one-way to Argens |
| Locaboat Holidays | Bram | | Canal du Midi, one way to Négra or Argens |
| Locaboat Holidays | Lattes | | on the canalised river Lez, one-way to Argens |
| Minervois Cruisers | Le Somail | minervoiscruisers.com | Midi (no one-way cruises) |
| Navicanal | Port-Lauragais | navicanal.com | Midi near the Naurouze summit level |
| Nicols Midi | Le Somail | | Canal du Midi at junction of the branch to Narbonne |
| Nicols Midi | Port-Lauragais | | Midi near the Naurouze summit level |
| Péniches de Thau | Sète | location-peniches.com | Etang de Thau, Canal du Midi and Rhône-Sète |

# Introduction

## Southwest

| Company | Location | Website | Description |
|---|---|---|---|
| Aquitaine Navigation (aff. Nicols) | Buzet-sur-Baïse | aquitaine-navigation.com | Garonne latéral, Lot and Baïse |
| Babou Marine | Cahors | baboumarine.com | long-established boat dealer with fleet on the Lot |
| Canalous Plaisance | Luzech | | River Lot |
| Le Boat | Douelle | | attractive base and village on the Lot |
| Le Boat | Le Mas d'Agenais | | near the Canal de Garonne/Baïse junction |
| Locaboat Holidays | Agen | | middle of Canal de Garonne, one way to Baïse |
| Locaboat Holidays | Cahors | | middle River Lot, 75km from Luzech to Larnagol |
| Locaboat Holidays | Valence-sur-Baïse | | at the end of the Baïse, one-way to Agen |
| Lot Navigation | Bouziès | lot-navigation.com | the spectacular River Lot |

## Anjou rivers, Charente and Sèvre, Cher and Canal de Berry

| Company | Location | Website | Description |
|---|---|---|---|
| Anjou Navigation (aff. Nicols) | Sablé-sur-Sarthe | anjou-navigation.fr | Sarthe and one-way to Laval |
| Anjou Navigation (aff. Nicols) | Laval | anjou-navigation.fr | Mayenne and one-way to Sarthe |
| Anjou Plaisance | Grez-Neuville | anjou-navigation.fr | Mayenne |
| Canalous Plaisance | Chenillé-Changé | | Mayenne and Sarthe, with several relay bases |
| Canalous Plaisance | Cognac | | Charente |
| Canalous Plaisance | Daon | | for Mayenne, Sarthe and Oudon |
| Canalous Plaisance | La Suze-sur-Sarthe | | Sarthe, one-way to Chenillé-Changé |
| Inter-Croisières | Sireuil | intercroisieres.com | Charente |
| Le Boat | Jarnac | leboat.com | Charente (no one-way cruises) |

## Brittany

| Company | Location | Website | Description |
|---|---|---|---|
| Aulne Loisirs Plaisance | Châteauneuf-du-Faou | aulneloisirs.com | Aulne, isolated waterway in western Brittany |
| Bretagne Fluviale (aff. Nicols) | Glénac | bretagne-fluviale.com | one way Vilaine, Erdre and Canal de Nantes à Brest |
| Bretagne Fluviale (aff. Nicols) | Sucé-sur-Erdre | bretagne-fluviale.com | one way Erdre, Canal de Nantes à Brest, Vilaine |
| Cris'Boat Croisières | Dinan | crisboat.com | Canal d'Ille-et-Rance, one-way to Redon |
| Canalous Plaisance | Redon | | at Brittany's waterway hub in Redon |
| Le Boat | Dinan | leboat.com | Canal d'Ille-et-Rance, one-way to Messac |
| Le Boat | Messac | | river Vilaine, and one-way cruises to base at Dinan |
| Le Boat | Nort-sur-Erdre | | Erdre, Canal de Nantes à Brest |
| Locaboat Holidays Bretagne | Saint-Martin-sur-Oust | locaboat.com | Vilaine and Canal de Nantes à Brest |

## Navigable dimensions

The waterways of France may roughly be divided into three categories.

### High-capacity (grand gabarit) waterways (Class IV or larger)

These are the Seine and Oise, the Liaison Dunkerque-Escaut and lower Escaut, the Moselle, the Rhine, the Rhône and the Grande-Saône, as well as the maritime navigations in the Loire and Gironde estuaries.

Navigable dimensions obviously present no constraint for boats and barges on these waterways, which offer lock dimensions of at least 144m by 12m, a minimum navigable draught of 2.50m and a minimum air draught of 4.50m (generally much more).

### 'Freycinet' waterways, including Canal du Nord and the lower river Yonne (Classes I and II)

Most of the waterways come into this category, offering standard dimensions established in 1879 by the Minister of Public Works Charles Louis de Saulces de Freycinet. Here too, the dimensions are ample for most boats, with minimum lock dimensions of 38.50m by 5.10m, minimum navigable draught of 1.80m and a minimum air draught of 3.40m (generally 3.50m). It must be noted, however, that the available depth on many canals is far short of the theoretical 2.20m, and that barges are increasingly forced to waste valuable energy ploughing their furrow through the thick layer of sediment that has deposited on the bed over the years. The remaining commercial carriers are even forced off the routes restored for recreational navigation, where the funding was agreed for dredging for a loading depth of 1.60m instead of the historic 1.80m. This reduced draught also of course excludes many recreational craft, especially yachts.

### Smaller waterways (Class 0)

Here dimensions are more critical, especially for barges or deep-keeled yachts. A glance at the table of maximum authorised dimensions in metres will show whether or not the proposed itinerary is feasible (see table left).

*The owners of large motor yachts and barges will regularly be nudging through low bridges like this one on the Canal d'Ille-et-Rance in Brittany.* © PHILIP COOK

### Rules of the road

The rules of the road are relatively easy to comply with, and the ability to handle one's boat precisely and confidently is just as important as theoretical knowledge of the waterway code. The rules to be observed by boaters are documented thoroughly in the RYA *Book of European Waterway Regulations* by Tam Murrell, but some of the main points are summarised in the following paragraphs.

#### Priority to commercial traffic and other barges

Smaller boats must at all times leave room for barges to proceed on their course and to manoeuvre. Barges must never be forced by small boats to steer clear. Skippers of boats must constantly bear in mind this priority to working boats, including trip boats. They must also steer well clear of all craft under way, dredgers and other maintenance vessels, and any work sites on the waterways.

#### Meeting other craft (croisement)

Boats may pass each other only when the channel is wide enough, taking into account local circumstances and other traffic movements. Boats whose respective courses are such that there is no risk of collision must not alter their course or their speed in a manner likely to cause a risk of collision. Boats meeting must normally keep to the right (passing port to port). There is an exception to this rule (more important for barges than for small boats) on wider river navigations, where it is normal practice for boats heading upstream to keep to the inside of the channel in bends to take advantage of the slacker water, while boats heading downstream keep to the middle of the channel. This practice is covered by the international 'blue flag' rule, under which the upstream-bound barge wishing to keep to the left makes its intention clear by displaying a blue flag or panel on the right-hand side of the wheelhouse (or by night, a flashing white light). The barge heading downstream acknowledges by displaying its blue flag or flashing white light, and adopts the corresponding course. If the skipper of the first barge fears his intention has not been understood, he sounds two short blasts (to pass on the left), and this signal must be acknowledged. (Similarly, one short blast confirms the intention to pass normally on the right, and must be acknowledged.) Small craft are not bound to observe this rule, but being aware of it makes it that much easier to comply with the number one rule of priority to commercial craft.

On French river navigations, there are certain sections where all craft are forced by these conventional signs to cross over or keep to the 'wrong' side of the channel and pass oncoming boats starboard-to-starboard. Here too, the blue flag is normally displayed. At points where the course thus changes sides it is the boat heading downstream which has priority, the upstream-bound boat slowing down or stopping as necessary. Where there is insufficient width for two barges to pass abreast, this prohibition sign is often displayed. On encountering this sign, a boat must not proceed until the skipper has satisfied himself that the channel in the restricted section is not occupied. Barge skippers communicate by radio at such locations, using the ship-to-ship channel 10; boaters should proceed cautiously, sounding a long blast on their horn as appropriate. Generally speaking, it is the boat heading downstream which has priority over that heading upstream.

#### Overtaking (dépassement or trématage)

Overtaking normally takes place on the left. Only on wide river navigations may overtaking on the right be envisaged. The skipper of the overtaking boat must strictly indicate his intention by displaying a blue flag at the bow. If the overtaken vessel has to modify its course or speed to facilitate this manoeuvre, the overtaking one shall sound two long blasts followed by one short one to signal he is overtaking to starboard, or two long blasts followed by two short ones for overtaking to port. Boaters must not accelerate momentarily for the exclusive purpose of passing another boat or barge, and should bear in mind that it is forbidden to overtake (a) whenever it is not certain that the manoeuvre can be effected safely, (b) within 500m from a lock and (c) wherever these prohibition signs are displayed. Generally speaking, never try to overtake a barge on the 'Freycinet' canals unless invited to do so by the barge skipper, since this can be a dangerous manoeuvre. If no such invitation is forthcoming, and the boat skipper is certain that there is time to get far enough ahead of the barge before the next lock is reached not to cause any delay (in practice, this means that the next lock must be at least 2 or 3 kilometres away), he may signal his intention to overtake by sounding two long blasts and two short (to overtake normally to port). It is then permitted to overtake unless the barge skipper sounds one short blast, meaning that he would prefer to be overtaken to starboard, or five short blasts, meaning that he considers it unsafe or inappropriate to be overtaken at this point. However, only experienced navigators with loud horns should indulge in such dialogue; it is simpler, especially on a heavily-locked canal, to moor when the opportunity arises and let the barge get well ahead.

# Introduction

## LIGHTS AT LOCKS

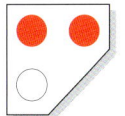    

Wait | Wait (lock in operation) | Wait, lock is being prepared | Enter the lock now | Lock not operational

## OTHER LIGHTS

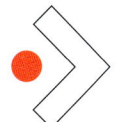

No entry to basin or channel indicated by white arrow

## MANDATORY & WARNING SIGNS

No entry | No overtaking | No meeting or overtaking (i.e. single lane) | No mooring or anchoring | No anchoring | No mooring | No turning (winding) | Do not create wash | Motor boats forbidden

Proceed in direction indicated | Stop | Speed limit | Make a sound signal | Unspecified hazard | Major waterway ahead | Headroom limited | Width of passage or channel limited | Keep this distance from bank

Make radio contact with waterway staff* | Cross channel to pass boats starboard to starboard | Cross channel to pass boats port to port (normal) | Keep to port | Keep to starboard | Channel moves to port | Channel moves to starboard | No passage outside marked limits

\* Note that channel 10 is the ship-to-ship channel on inland waterways throughout the continent.

## OTHER SIGNS (RECOMMENDATORY OR INFORMATIVE)

Weir | Ferry | Chain ferry | Side turning | Tributary waterway | Priority waterway | Berthing permitted | Anchoring permitted | Making fast permitted | Turning

Recommended direction | Electricity cable | End of prohibition or restriction

## SIGNS ON BRIDGES

Keep within limits (green) | Recommended channel (in both directions) | Passage only in direction indicated (other direction prohibited)

## SOUNDS

```
—         Attention
•         I am moving (or holding) to starboard
• •       I am moving (or holding) to port
• • •     I am going astern
• • • •   I am incapable of manoeuvring
• • • • • •   (6 very short) Imminent danger of collision
— — — —   (repeated) Distress signal
— •       I am turning to starboard
— • •     I am turning to port
```

## Part I

### Turning (virement)
When a boat wishes to turn to head in the opposite direction, notice of the intention is to be given by one prolonged blast on the horn, followed by one short blast if swinging to the right and two short blasts if swinging to the left.

### Navigation signs
The most common navigation signs are shown opposite.

### Speed limits
The special regulations for each waterway (*règlement particulier de police de la navigation intérieure*) lay down speed limits, and the owner of any boat exceeding the authorised limit renders himself liable to prosecution. Throughout the smaller canal network the limit is 6km/h (3.7 miles/hour) for barges and pleasure boats displacing more than 20 tonnes, reduced to 4km/h for the passage of movable bridges and navigation at night (where allowed). The limit is eased to 8km/h and in some cases 10km/h for boats of less than 20 tonnes. One of the uses of the tables, with distances precise to within 100m, is to allow speed to be checked. In practice, however, speed in the smaller canals should constantly be adapted to local conditions, the basic rule being to ease off whenever the boat causes wash to break on the banks, as well as when passing moored boats and anglers, thus avoiding damage in the first case and unpleasantness in the second.

On canalised rivers, higher speeds are authorised in river sections than in lock-cuts or canal sections. For example, the limits are respectively 15km/h and 6km/h on the Marne, on the Saône above Auxonne and on the Yonne, while the maximum on the smaller river navigations is 10km/h.

On the large-scale waterways, much higher limits are applied, generally 15km/h in canals or lock-cuts and up to 35km/h in open river sections. Speeds higher still, up to 60km/h, are allowed on specified short reaches for the practice of water-skiing and small power boating only. It must be underlined that local restrictions may be applied on any waterway, and indicated by the conventional speed limit sign shown in the section on navigation signs.

## Locks
Different recommendations must be given for negotiating locks according to the four main types of lock encountered on the network.

### High-capacity (grand gabarit) waterways
The big locks on these waterways (as defined under navigable dimensions) are all controlled by lock-keepers, normally from a control tower located midway in the lock basin on one side or the other. The automatic lock filling or emptying sequences (and corresponding light displays for navigators) are subordinated to the lock-keepers' decisions, based on the observed or announced traffic situation. A boat navigating singly may thus be kept waiting for 20 minutes or longer if the lock is ready for a barge announced in the other direction. This is allowed for by the regulations, so do not be surprised if the double red light display persists for that time. In case of doubt, moor at one of the dolphins providing access to the bank and approach the lock-keeper to announce your arrival. Alternatively, a VHF radio call number is listed in the route descriptions for locks on these large-scale waterways, and lock-keepers may be called on VHF for an inquiry or to announce your arrival time. A single red or red and green lights side by side mean that the lock is being prepared. Wait until the double green light is displayed before entering the lock. If there are barges or other craft queueing at the lock, take your place in the queue, but in any event when the double green light shows, allow all barges to enter the lock first. When traffic is heavy, the lock-keeper will generally wave or use a loud-hailer to call boats into the spaces remaining in the lock chamber. Avoid coming close to a barge's stern until she has stopped in the chamber, in case there is an unexpected last-minute use of reverse at high revs causing pronounced turbulence for some distance behind the prop. The deepest locks have floating bollards or a series of bollards set in the wall vertically at intervals of one or two metres. These are referred to as 'step bollards' and require a certain amount of juggling with the bow and stern lines as the water level rises or falls. The recommended procedure here is to have two lines available or one lengthy line with an eye at each end at both bow and stern. This allows use of the 'one on - one off' method as you rise or fall. It is forbidden to make fast to the rungs of a ladder between two sets of bollards. It is sometimes more convenient to come alongside a barge (with the skipper's permission) and make fast to its bollards.

*Don't forget to put on your lifejackets when passing locks on the high-capacity waterways!*

### Automated locks on smaller waterways
To reduce operating costs on the smaller canals and canalised rivers (for example, the Canal de Garonne, the Canal du Centre, the Canal de la Marne au Rhin, the upper Saône), a large number of locks have been equipped for fully automated or semi-automatic operation. These locks, often grouped together and referred to as a *chaîne* or flight, are equipped with lights, with the same meanings as above: red = wait, red plus green = lock in preparation, and green = proceed into lock. A system of advanced detection registers the boat's arrival some distance before the lock. This system may be automatic (radar) or will involve using

a remote control supplied by the lock-keeper at either end of the flight. Some canals still have the simple device of a pole suspended above the water, which needs to be given a quarter turn.

A flashing orange light near the detector, or the red plus green light display at the lock, means that the boat has been detected. When the green light is displayed, proceed slowly into the lock. Some locks have a chamber entry/exit detector, either a photoelectric sensor or on older locks a horizontal pole to be pushed forwards by your boat for at least 5 seconds. Once the boat is safely moored in the chamber, raise the blue rod situated on the edge of the lock, to start the automatic lock filling or emptying sequence. It will take a few seconds for the command to be registered. The red rod is be pulled in a case of emergency only. This not only stops the sequence, but shuts down the entire system, and requires intervention by waterway staff to set it up again. If it is an actual case of emergency requiring a rapid response you should also call on the interphone to advise someone of this, or your problem will simply be treated as a lock out of action, and an itinerant lock keeper will come to repair it in due course. At the end of the cycle, the gates open automatically. It is important to clear the chamber promptly. It should be noted that a group of boats locking together should pass the radar detector in close file. If the lock fails to start or fails in mid-sequence, use the telephone (interphone) outside the lock cabin.

Once in a flight it is important to maintain a constant speed between locks, and if it is decided to stop, if only for lunch, before the flight is completed, the lock-keepers must be notified of this intention. They are normally stationed at each end of the flight. In an emergency or in case of breakdown, they can be also be contacted by two-way telephone outside the small control cabinet beside each lock. If conditions are extremely difficult (strong wind or heavy rain, for example), the section lock-keeper will often be seen on the towpath on his scooter ascertaining that all is well.

### *Locks operated by lock-keepers*

Staff cutbacks everywhere – on the VNF network and on the other waterways – combined with the cheap technology available for mechanal operation, whether automated or not, mean that there are now precious few locks on the 'Freycinet' network that are still operated by lock-keepers. It is not usually necessary to warn the lock-keeper of your arrival, but a short, polite beep on the horn may be required if there is no sign of any activity. Be sure not to do this during the lunch break, however! No action is necessary if other traffic is moored up waiting to lock through. In any event, it is advisable to make a complete stop 50m from the lock, to wait until the lock-keeper signals permission to enter, or until the gates are completely open. While waiting, if it is preferred not to moor up to the bank, care should be taken not to obstruct the passage of any boat which may emerge from the lock when the gates are opened. On entering the lock (at low speed), arrange for one of the crew to alight on the side opposite the lock-keeper, normally the towpath side, or whichever side he is not working. Having attended to the boat's lines it is customary to assist in working the lock (closing one of the gates when the boat has entered the lock, possibly working the gate paddles and opening the gate on the same side when the lock is ready). Some of the older locks on the Seine and Yonne have sloping sides, requiring particular caution, especially when descending. It is often possible and preferable to pass your mooring lines to the lock-keeper as you enter these particular locks. Be ready to bear off with boat-hooks, preferably one forward and one aft. Many of these sloping-sided locks have been upgraded in recent years, with a floating pontoon inside the chamber. This facility is suitable only for smaller vessels, unfortunately!

A recent development which is changing the practical arrangements for passing locks on considerable lengths of canal is the complete reorganisation of waterway personnel, the numbers of permanently-posted lock-keepers being drastically reduced (by non-replaced departures or transfers to maintenance staff). Locks on designated sections are thus attended by mobile teams, which follow boats through successive locks, in some cases only two but perhaps as many as 20. This makes the boater a little less free to move as he pleases, for the team's movements obviously have to be programmed, and a spontaneous decision to stop between two locks will create confusion and perhaps even delay commercial traffic. Boaters are thus requested to cooperate by giving reasonable notice of their movements and stops.

Finally, it is worth noting that tipping the lock-keepers is not normal practice. Lock-keepers are State or local authority employees and are paid a fair salary for their job. On the other hand, they often do more than is strictly required of them, and in such cases the navigator should use his discretion and imagination in judging the best way of showing appreciation. In some cases a euro will suffice, or perhaps a cool drink on a hot day? Cash will obviously be appreciated if water is supplied from the lock-keeper's private tap, say €1.50 or €2, but water is generally provided by VNF at locks as part of the service paid for by the licence fee.

### *Unmanned locks on the smaller waterways*

'Do-it-yourself' lock operation has become the system on a number of waterways that are used only by tourist traffic. This is the case on the western section of Canal de Nantes à Brest, the Charente, the Seille and the Lot, for example. In all cases the lock operating gear is already installed, and a leaflet of instructions on lock operation is issued to navigators.

## Observations by a seasoned canaller

The reflections by the late Robert Somerville that were included in previous editions of this work remain relevant today. The increasing popularity of the canals and rivers of France means an increased responsibility for all users, not just the long-term, perhaps retired, year-round navigator who will tend to know the ropes, the waterway etiquette, not to mention half of the entire family of seasoned canallers, but also the first-time family vacationer hiring a self-drive vessel for the first time, or perhaps the navigators passing through the system from or to the Mediterranean with their motor yacht or sailing boat for the one and only time.

Why have you been moored to that quay for three weeks? One should not expect to stay moored indefinitely to a public quay, usually where the services are superior and possibly free. A stay of two or three days is normally tolerated but by then it is time to move on and allow others to enjoy those same facilities, the sights and sounds that have kept you staying for as long as you have. Especially if others are being turned away daily! Have you considered breasting up? Perhaps the extended stay should be made in a privately-managed port. There are suitable facilities at or near most popular locations, and by paying the going rates you acquire the right to stay as long as you wish.

Why have you got your screwdriver out, to pry open the security door on the service panel? A charge of €2 for water is not excessive, nor is €3 for a nightly power hook-up. Once the services have been vandalised to save some small change, in all likelihood they will be unusable for the next user and probably will not be serviceable at all the following year.

Why are you moored in the middle of the quay? Snuggle up to the boat ahead of you or to one of the ends of the pontoon and leave some room for others who are certain to come along later. If the most recent arrival is having difficulty getting a line ashore and securing their vessel – take a minute or two to assist in securing the vessel – being careful not to trip over your own lines which may have been carelessly coiled on the pontoon!

Why are you cruising so fast? More importantly you're on holiday. Take a moment and have a look at your bow wave and behind at your wake! All canals and rivers have speed limits. They are designed to preserve the banks, respect the speed limit and the waterways' navigable depths will not be rapidly reduced as a result of collapsing banks.

Why is that other vessel owner yelling at you? Have you raced ahead to get to the next lock first? Have you overtaken in a dangerous location? Have you had too much to drink? There are 'rules of the road'; know what they are and follow them, but more importantly, respect your fellow boater!

On a completely different issue which I have found to be critical, canal guides make frequent reference to the concept of a *bassin* or canal basin. They come in various shapes and sizes and are normally found downstream of a lock, close to a small village or town, a loading quay or silo, or for no apparent reason in the middle of nowhere. In the past they were an important part of the commercial life on the canal and river system. They allowed *péniches* to turn around and proceed in the opposite direction to load or unload cargo or to return to a favoured port without having to travel great distances in the opposite direction to do so. Where situated in the middle of nowhere, their function was often to allow barges to moor while waiting for a new load. The biggest were given the more important title of *gare d'eau*.

Unfortunately, with the decline of commercial traffic these basins fell into varying degrees of disrepair. Many became silted up, overgrown with weed or worst of all served as a dumping ground for abandoned vessels or even cars. Consequently, a number have been staked off or have signs to indicate that entry is neither possible nor recommended. However, the majority have no indication of their suitability for turning or mooring.

This means that if it is contemplated to use a basin it is advisable to approach with extreme caution and expect the worst! Proceed slowly, bow first, ideally with a person up at the bow paying special attention to what is ahead. That stone quay just inside might look very inviting but in all likelihood there are no services and the risk of damage to your vessel is just not worth it. Look for a more suitable turning location or mooring a little further on.

## Hours of navigation

It is as well when planning a cruise to realise that for all practical purposes there is no navigation after dark or, during the lighter months of the year, after 19:30. Locks are generally open between 06:30 and 19:30 in summer, and the working hours progressively shorten as the nights close in. However, now that many waterways are being handed over to regional councils or other local bodies, it is to be expected that operating hours will vary much more widely than in the past. Councils are known to be seeking to reduce the financial burden of operating costs, so boaters should expect some disappointments in the coming years. While it is possible to run between locks during the dark hours (the proper navigation lights being shown and the regulation reduction in speed being observed), there is little advantage for boats in doing so, except in an emergency.

## Time of year

The season suitable for pleasure cruising extends from March to November, depending on how comfortable and well heated your boat is. The weather in France, being of the continental type, tends to be more settled than that of the British Isles, and long periods of high temperature are not infrequent in the summer. Before about the end of April, cold weather and night frosts may occur. Moreover, it is always colder on the water than on the land and, owing to the higher humidity, it feels colder. The weather is often fine in September and October, when the autumn colours make the scenery particularly beautiful. However, morning mists on the canals and rivers will often delay a planned early morning departure.

In the late autumn and winter, the intrepid navigator must be prepared for floods (from November to March, but often also in the spring months through to May) and also for icing (December to February). Bear in mind that some of the canals rise to a considerable height above sea level, and with the increase in altitude the fall in temperature is accentuated. Such severe conditions do not usually extend beyond the month of March.

Seasonal restrictions in the coming years will not be a question of climate, but of canal operating conditions, as indicated in the previous paragraph on hours of navigation. Some authorities will want to close their canals completely during the winter months, and some vigorous campaigning is likely to be required, before new waterway authorities will accept to pay for more staff time. The cause will be difficult to defend, since the resulting additional traffic will seem not to have been worth the effort.

Out-of-season cruising has become a genuine trend on the Canal du Midi, where it is seen by private boat-owners as the ideal way to enjoy the canal's charms without having to struggle with the large numbers of hire boats on the busiest sections of the canal.

## Mast lowering

One important aspect of planning to enter the inland waterways, for sailing yachts, is mast lowering or stepping. This will benefit from some preparatory work. The marinas at Dunkerque, for example, whilst helpful and able to provide craneage, may not be as familiar with the techniques as the yard at Rouen. They cannot be relied on to know and do everything required. It might be advisable to talk to an experienced yard in your home country about the practicalities and the sequence: disconnecting electrics, the order in which shrouds and stays and their bottle screws should be loosened and released, how and where the lifting strop on the mast should be attached (to avoid the wrongly balanced mast tipping end over end), and how the mast should actually be lifted and laid down.

## Planning a cruise

The following through routes are commonly used:

### Bordeaux to Sète via Canal du Midi
503km, 139 locks
This route joins the Atlantic to the Mediterranean and is formed east of Toulouse by the Canal du Midi, the first canal in the world to be designated a World Heritage site by UNESCO, in 1996. This has become the most popular cruising waterway in France, the climate no doubt being a significant factor, and some delays at locks are to be expected during the summer season.

### English Channel (St-Malo) to the Atlantic
239km, 63 locks
For boats drawing no more than 1.40m, this is a useful short cut through Brittany to the west coast of France, avoiding the long, open sea passage and strong tides round the iron-bound coast of Ushant. At Redon the Vilaine is crossed by the Canal de Nantes à Brest, which offers two alternative routes to the Atlantic, (a) via Nantes and the Loire estuary (total route length 352km, 78 locks), (b) via Pontivy and the Canal du Blavet (total route length 370km, 178 locks).

## Guides and publications

Much of the basic data for the route descriptions, particularly the kilometre distances or *points kilométriques*, was originally taken from the *Guide de la Navigation Intérieure*, a comprehensive two-volume guide published by Berger-Levrault in Paris in 1965. This continues to be my favourite reference work, at least where there has been no change in basic configuration of the waterways since that date. Imray's general map of the waterways of France, Belgium and the Netherlands, scale 1:1.500.000, produced by the author, is useful for cruise planning and for the overview it gives of the network in the three countries. Jane Cumberlidge has prepared a map broken down into regions in another Imray publication – *Waterway Routes Through France*. Éditions du Breil also offers a good French waterways map.

Another useful and popular map is the *European Waterways Map and Concise Directory* (sixth edition, 2021), compiled by the author and now also published by Imray (the previous editions were published by the author's publishing and consultancy firm Euromapping, then Transmanche Consultants). The map now becomes one of the 'family' of waterway publications. It covers the whole of Europe at scales of 1:3 800 000 (for the overview from Portugal and Ireland to the Caspian Sea) and 1:1 500 000 (for the main network from Dublin to Bratislava), and is accompanied by a 64-page directory with brief descriptions for each country.

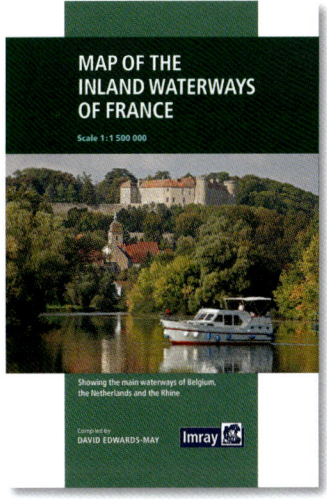 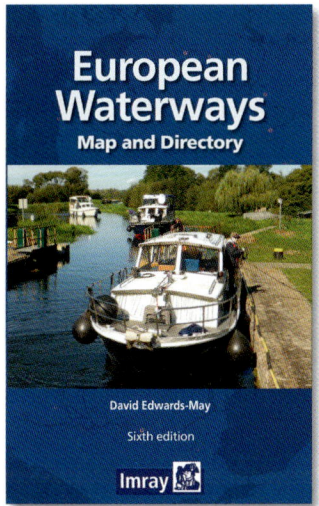

A prime source of information is the online version of the present publication, included, by agreement with Imray, within the website **french-waterways.com**. The 'hands on' (or practical navigation) section of the website contains valuable guidance and recommendations, complementing those set out in this introduction, while the descriptions of each waterway or each chapter may be downloaded as pdfs, as well as compilations of through routes. We hope that boat owners will appreciate having the actual book at home or on board, despite the availability of much of its content in digital format! The site also sells the Imray, Éditions du Breil and Fluviacarte publications.

For a wealth of detailed information on navigable conditions, sites to visit, restaurants and practically everything else you might need to know while cruising,

# Part I

there is a choice of specialist guides. The most thoroughly researched and best-documented are those published by Éditions du Breil, the company founded by John Riddel in 1997.

### Éditions du Breil

The maps in these guides are at 1:50 000 for canals and 1:25 000 for rivers, with the exception of the Saône (1:40 000) and the Charente (1:12 500).

No. 1    Bretagne
No. 5    Lot
No. 6    Charente
No. 7    Midi/Camargue
No. 10   Pays de la Loire
No. 12   Aquitaine
No. 14   Sèvre Niortaise
No. 16   L'Estuaire de la Gironde

503, chemin Notre-Dame, 11400 Castelnaudary, France +33 (0)4 68 23 51 35  **editionsdubreil.com**

### Fluviacarte

*Fluvial*, the French monthly waterways magazine, publishes a useful *Guide du Plaisancier* every two years. It is like a condensed version of the present guide, and gives up-to-date information on nearly 700 mooring locations and more than 100 boatyards. Their *Fluviacarte* series includes the following guides covering waterways in the present volume:

No. 4    Canaux du Midi – Camargue
No. 5    Canal de Garonne – Garonne
No. 12   Bretagne
No. 13   Pays de la Loire
No. 25   La Charente, de la Rochelle à Angoulême
No. 27   Le Lot amont, de Luzech à Larnagol
No. 29   La Sèvre Niortaise, de La Rochelle à Niort

Marina Del Rey - Bât. A, 2 rue des Consuls - CS 30031, 34973 Lattes Cedex  **fluvialnet.com**

The above guides have English and German texts alongside the French. They are available from specialised bookshops, from **imray.com** and from **french-waterways.com**. Inland Waterways International also has a useful online shop selling the main titles, but not the individual waterway guides: **inlandwaterwaysinternational.org**.

### Other sources

The DBA website **barges.org** has a wide range of information for cruising on the continent, including a mooring guide and updates on current legislation, much of it available to non-members.

The Cruising Association **cruising.org.uk** also publishes *Cruising the Inland Waterways of France and Belgium*, compiled by Gordon Knight. This is an invaluable publication, formerly edited by Dr Roger Edgar. Now in its 25th Edition, the 216-page guide is regularly updated via reports from members actively cruising the waterways.

It supplements rather than replaces the above publications. Described as their 'Bible' by regular users and yacht skippers planning routes to and from the Mediterranean, the guide contains a wealth of information on cruising routes, cruising preparations, supplies, equipment, licences and documents, useful addresses, books and websites as well as listing around 250 mooring places throughout France and Belgium, with comments upon facilities (including where fuel may be obtained either alongside or within easy jerry can distance), depths, prices, closest shops and restaurants and nearby attractions.

Included in the guide is a 25 per cent discount offer on first year of membership to purchasers applying online for CA membership during the year. Cost: free for members, £25 for non-members, in pdf or print versions.

The Cruising Association, CA House, 1 Northey Street, Limehouse Basin, London E14 8BT, +44 (0)20 7537 2828

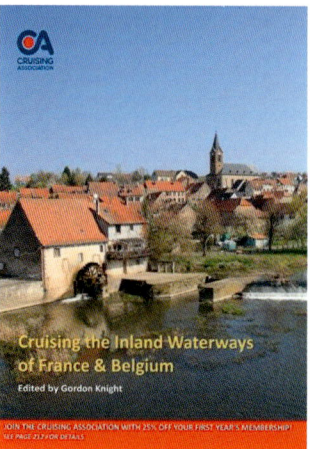

For approaching the French waterway system from the coast the following publications are available:

*Mediterranean France and Corsica Pilot*
   Rod and Lucinda Heikell (Imray)
*Cruising Almanac*
   The Cruising Association (Imray)
*Mediterranean Almanac*
   Rod and Lucinda Heikell (Imray)
*Atlantic France*
   Royal Cruising Club Pilotage Foundation (Imray)

# Part II – Route descriptions and maps

The route descriptions and accompanying maps and plans are designed to be of use both for planning and during the actual cruise. Distances are given precisely to within 100m, and possible mooring places are highlighted in bold type. The distance from the mooring to the centre of the locality is also indicated. This is not to be interpreted as a guarantee that mooring will be practicable at this point, but may be useful in emergency situations, as well as for all users of the towpath or riverside cycle itinerary. Junctions are readily identifiable by the use of a distinctive style with white text on a blue background. The route descriptions include sections that are not navigable, either because restoration is in progress or at least envisaged, or for continuity of the cycling itinerary where feasible.

The abbreviations u/s and d/s are used for upstream and downstream, and r/b and l/b for right bank and left bank. These abbreviations are also used on canals, the downstream direction being implicit in relation to the summit level or parallel river. On summit levels or tidal waters, geographical directions are used instead, to avoid confusion.

Boat harbour entries (*ports de plaisance*) will be valuable for users of this guide, and have been researched in detail. Changes take place rapidly, however, so readers are invited to take the information as indicative only. 'Fuel' means that both diesel and petrol are available. The price indicated for visitor moorings is the average charge per night in season, for a boat 10m in length. Prices will of course change over time. In most cases the local *taxe de séjour* will be charged, usually between 20 and 50 cents per person on board.

The index map shows the position of the waterway in the network, and the strip map, which is precise despite the relatively small scale, enables immediate identification of the boat's position in relation to the overall route, and to the towns and villages where it may be proposed to stop. Partial distances on these maps are shown between pin markers, with the number of locks in italics.

Most junctions and locations where alternative routes are possible are covered by detailed plans at a scale of approximately 1:15 000. These distinguish navigable and unnavigable water areas and give route indications, positions of moorings, main sites of interest and other useful information.

Details of the engineers responsible for each waterway – the local *unité territoriale* or *subdivision* – are given, and in case of specific enquiries or difficulties en route, they may be contacted. Otherwise the regional headquarters listed here will forward any queries to the appropriate office. For the waterways that are not managed by VNF, we have tried to be as explicit as possible, distinguishing the managing authority and the agency in charge of operation and maintenance.

## *VNF Regions*

### VNF Rhône Saône
2 rue de la Quarantaine, 69321 LYON CEDEX 05
04 72 56 59 00    **dt.rhonesaone@vnf.fr**

### VNF Sud-Ouest
2 port Saint-Étienne, BP 7204, 31073 TOULOUSE CEDEX 7
05 61 36 24 24    **dt.sudouest@vnf.fr**

### VNF Bassin de la Seine
18 Quai d'Austerlitz, 75013 PARIS
01 83 94 44 00    **dt.bassindelaseine@vnf.fr**

*The River Loire is administratively attached to this VNF region.*

## *Head office*
Voies Navigables de France
175 rue Ludovic Boutleux
B.P. 820, 62408 BÉTHUNE CEDEX
03 21 63 24 24

## *Paris office*
156, rue du Faubourg Saint-Denis, 75010 PARIS
01 44 89 65 00

## *Brittany Waterways*
Conseil régional de Bretagne
Service des Voies Navigables
283, avenue du Général Patton
CS 21101, 35711 RENNES CEDEX 7
02 99 27 10 10 bretagne.fr

*For the canals of Brittany (since 2010, excluding the section of the Canal de Nantes à Brest in Loire-Atlantique).*

# CHAPTER VI – SOUTHERN FRANCE ('MIDI')

This section covers the enormously popular waterway that crosses southern France from the Rhône to Toulouse. The route breaks down into three separate waterways.

The first is the Petit-Rhône, which leaves the Rhône at Fourques just north of Arles. The second is the Canal du Rhône à Sète, which will be followed for 69km (with no locks) from Saint-Gilles to Sète. Navigation is then in the Étang de Thau over a distance of 17km. After this long and fascinating *hors d'œuvre*, it will be time to attack the *plat de résistance*, the famous Canal du Midi, which is 240km to Toulouse. The Canal de Garonne, which begins in Toulouse, could have been part of this same section, but in Toulouse there is a clear transition from the Midi to South-West France. The entire route is just under 350km long.

After the multiple choices heading down through France, the *plaisancier* has a single itinerary to follow through to Toulouse, enjoying a remarkable diversity of landscapes, traditions, food and wines, and countless sites to visit, both on the main route and on the many branches to explore on the way.

Allow at least three weeks to make this transit, including the branches to Lattes (for Montpellier) and Narbonne. The branch to Beaucaire will mainly be of interest to those who plan to leave their boats there in the popular *port de plaisance*.

This is a thoroughly compelling cruising region, despite the reservations expressed by some *plaisanciers* on account of the heavy traffic of unpredictable hire boats during the peak season in May and June, with possible delays at some locks. Throughout the rest of the year, even during July and August, the canal experience fully lives up to its reputation, and even the most disgruntled *plaisancier* will return with renewed enthusiasm once his reservations have been put into perspective.

Some changes in management of the canal may be expected in the coming years, following creation of the *Groupement d'Intérêt Public*, bringing together VNF and the regional and local authorities, which has the responsibility of producing the Management Plan for the Canal du Midi as a UNESCO World Heritage Site.

*Répudre aqueduct on the Canal du Midi, PK 159*

# VI – Southern France ('Midi')

## 54. Canal du Rhône à Sète and Étang de Thau

THE INLAND WATERWAY CONNECTING THE RHÔNE to the port of Sète and the Canal du Midi extends 98km from Beaucaire to Sète, followed by the crossing through the Étang de Thau, a further 17km. However, the works on the Rhône resulted in closure of the entrance lock to the canal at Beaucaire, so that through navigation uses an improved length of the Petit Rhône and a short length of canal at Saint-Gilles, to enter the Canal du Rhône à Sète at PK 29. Accordingly, the through route is now 69km long, and the 29km section to Beaucaire is a dead end. Despite this handicap, the basin in Beaucaire has been attractively developed as a *port de plaisance* and is well worth the detour. The project to re-establish the direct route involving restoration of Beaucaire lock and a new lock bypassing the weir on the Rhône has been shelved. The port in Beaucaire is already overbooked, so it has little interest in creating additional demand.

*This canal joined up several smaller canals linking up the coastal lagoons, some dating back to Louis IX in the 14th century. It is the continuation of the Canal du Midi, or rather its link with the Rhône. Riquet's heirs started it in the 18th century. It had a curved lock to join the Rhône at Beaucaire, which limited size to 37m by 6.66m. To increase capacity, a new lock was built at Beaucaire around 1900, for 700t craft. The Rhône canalisation led to blocking of this lock around 1980, and a new lock was built to replace it at Saint-Gilles, down the Petit Rhône, where a 4km canal connected nearly midway with the earlier line. Various improvements and short cuts enabled craft around 1200t to use it, and presently there are further works in hand to raise bridges and deepen the canal for barges carrying up to 2000 tonnes.*

The canal crosses two rivers on the level, the Vidourle at PK 55 and the Lez at PK 75. At times of flood the canal has to be isolated from the river by closure of the movable gates on either side of the crossing and navigation is interrupted. Both rivers may be used by smaller boats to reach the Mediterranean, although the main points of access to the

| Key dimensions* | (m) |
|---|---|
| Length | 38.50 |
| Beam | 5.45 |
| Draught | 1.80 |
| Air draught | 4.10 |

\* The dimensions apply to the section from Beaucaire to the junction at Saint-Gilles

# Canal du Rhône à Sète/Étang de Thau

sea are via the Canal Maritime from Aigues-Mortes (PK 51) to the modern resort of Le Grau-du-Roi and via the basins of the port of Sète, reached by crossing part of the Étang de Thau from the western end of the canal. The Canal de la Peyrade, which provided a sheltered route to the port of Sète from the main canal at PK 96, has been filled in where it is crossed by a road near its junction and is no longer available for through navigation.

Improvements have been made to the canal in recent years, to allow Rhône barges to navigate from the Rhône to the port of Sète (and 500-tonne barges through to the Étang de Thau). In particular, new sections have been opened to bypass Aigues-Mortes to the north and Frontignan to the south. The upgrading has been completed through most of the length.

The canal borders the Camargue and crosses extensive sea water lagoons, offering superb views across to the foothills of the Cévennes. The near views are often partially obstructed by high banks, which nevertheless offer the advantage of some protection against the frequent strong winds. Distances are shown here following the original route via Aigues-Mortes, a beautiful walled city closely associated with the history of the Crusades and Louis X.

At Sète the canal enters the **Étang de Thau**, a large sheltered sea water lagoon. The through route across the lake is 18 km in length, from the point where the canal enters the eastern part of the lake, known as the Étang des Eaux Blanches, to the lighthouse on the mole at Les Onglous, marking the entrance to the Canal du Midi. The navigable outlet to the Mediterranean is at Sète, through the Canal Maritime (see plan), giving access to this busy port. There are harbours on the northern shore of the lake at Marseillan and Mèze. The northern side of the lake features many square hectares of oyster beds as well as the fishing villages and *ports de plaisance* of Marseillan, Mèze and Bouzigues.

## Navigation

The canal is easy to navigate, the only difficulties being the relatively frequent cross-winds and the less frequent cross-currents at the river crossings. The rockfill banks built as part of the upgrading works make it difficult to stop outside the 'official' mooring places. A number of concrete quays have been provided along the length, but were not intended for pleasure craft. A curious decision has been made by VNF to continue the Rhône kilometre markers along the Petit Rhône and throughout this canal to Sète. The original distances, starting at PK 0 in Beaucaire, are retained here.

Crossing the **Étang the Thau** may take as little as 1.5 hours if conditions are good, but should be avoided in bad weather. Conditions are particularly dangerous when a strong north-westerly wind is blowing. Because the *étang* is relatively shallow (roughly 5m in the centre, but large areas around the fringes are 3m or less) a strong wind can easily and very quickly kick the surface into a chop. The geography is flat and open, and strong breezes and winds are very common. Most of the time this warning will seem completely irrelevant, the surface flat and calm, but it would be wise to check that the boat and her crew are up

*The disused lock into the canal from the Rhône at Beaucaire* © F-W

to the task of coping with a side or head wind and some unsettling motion.

There is a buoyed channel across the *étang* from the Roquérols mark (situated about midway between two promontories, Pointe de Barrou to the south and Pointe de Balaruc to the north) to Les Onglous. Here there is a breakwater with port and starboard marks, and a small lighthouse; it is wise to approach from a northerly direction, there are shallows to the east.

## Locks

There is one lock on the bypassed section of the canal at Nourriguier (PK 8), which fell into disrepair in 2020 but is expected to be restored by 2022. It is 80m long and 12m wide, and automatically operated (follow the instructions for boats). A second lock at Aigues-Mortes (PK 50), designed to prevent sea water from penetrating inland, never had to be used and in 1955 the gates were removed. It should be noted that the maximum navigable width is less than the width of Nourriguier lock (see under Bridges).

*The port de plaisance in Beaucaire* © F-W

# VI – Southern France ('Midi')

## Draught
The maximum authorised draught has been increased by the recent improvement works from 1.80m to 2.20m (except on the dead end section to Beaucaire).

## Headroom
The fixed bridges offer a minimum headroom of 4.10m, although this figure is gradually being increased to 5.00m or more on the through route. Several bridges offer a reduced width by comparison with the lock at Nourriguier. The least width at the bridges in Beaucaire is 8.70m, the railway bridge at Saint-Gilles is 10.80m wide, the gate structures on either side of the Lez crossing are 10.00m wide and the railway bridge at PK 97 offers a navigable width of 9.60m. The bridges on the Lez down to the sea at Palavas offer severely limited headroom: 2.40m above normal water level, reduced to as little as 2.00m when the Lez is in flood. It should be noted that the lift bridge at Frontignan (PK 92) is opened for boats at certain times of the day only. For opening times, 04 67 48 65 29.

## Authority
VNF Rhône Saône, Subdivision Grand Delta:
- 1 quai de la Gare, 13200 Arles 04 90 96 00 85 (PK 118-310)
  *subdi.granddelta@vnf.fr*
- Pointe Caramus, 34110 Frontignan cedex
  04 67 46 65 80 (PK 51-98)

## Route description

### Canal du Rhône à Sète (Beaucaire to Saint-Gilles junction)

PK **0.6** **Beaucaire** basin and extensive *port de plaisance*, 230 berths, 10 visitor moorings, limit of navigation, 04 66 59 02 17, email *port@beaucaire.fr*, night €32, fuel on request, water, electricity, showers, crane, slipway, town centre with restaurants on north side

Popular and frequently overbooked *port de plaisance* and interesting town. Many of the 230 berths are occupied by boats that are moored permanently or semi-permanently during the winter. Some may find the density of population in this basin and the bustling quaysides slightly forbidding, for Beaucaire is a lively market town and has been since its fair attracted countless merchants in the Middle Ages. The canalside buildings reflect the prosperity that trade brought to the town. The lock that originally gave access to the canal from the Rhône could be restored but an additional lock would be needed to bypass the weir built as part of the Beaucaire works on the Rhône in the 1970s.

| PK | |
|---|---|
| **0.9** | Footbridge |
| **1.3** | Bridge (Porte Vieille), narrow passage |
| **1.5** | Le Boat hire base, moorings l/b |
| **2.2** | Railway bridge and private bridge, narrow passage, industrial quays d/s r/b |
| **2.9** | Pipeline crossing |
| **3.4** | Bridge (Charenconne) |
| **4.0** | Bridge (D90, Beaucaire and Tarascon bypass) |
| **7.7** | Lock 2 (Nourriguier), drop 4m, automated, basin d/s r/b |
| **7.9** | Bridge (Nourriguier) |
| **13.1** | Bridge (D6113) |

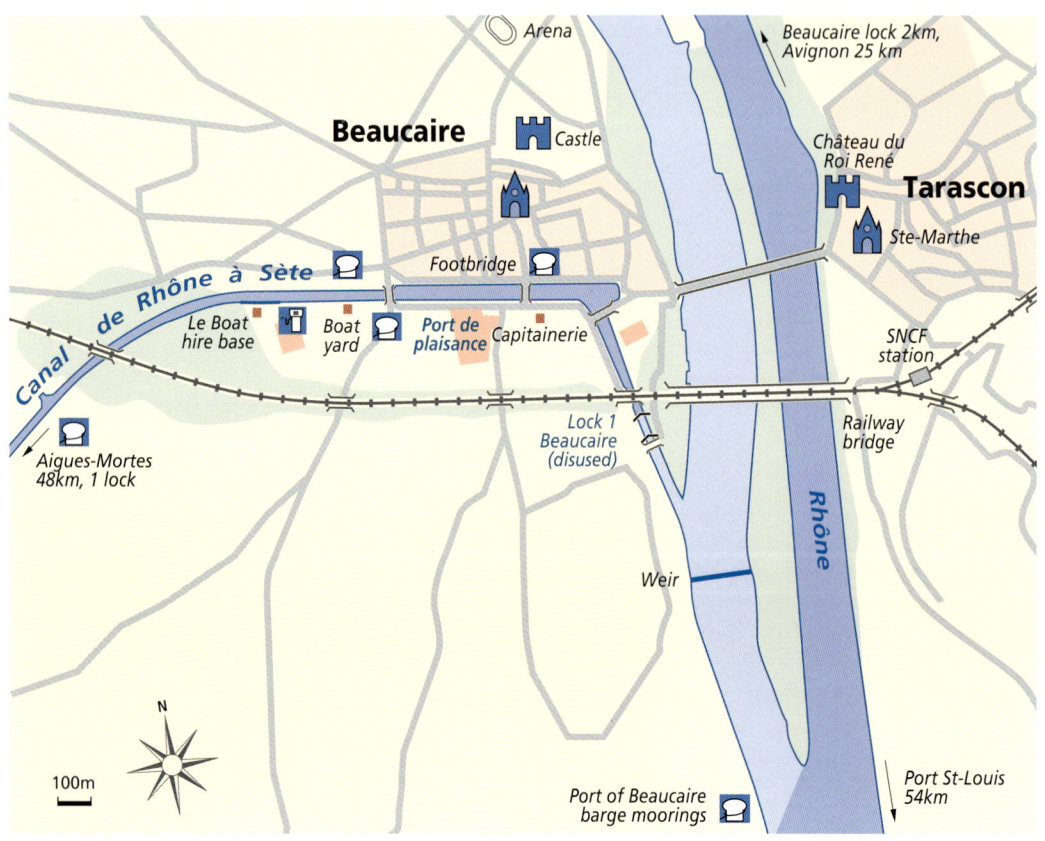

# Canal du Rhône à Sète/Étang de Thau

PK **13.2** **Bellegarde** bridge (Pont d'Arles), narrow passage, *port de plaisance* d/s, 04 66 59 02 17 or 06 70 56 81 71, 70 berths, 8 visitor moorings, night €32, fuel on request, water, electricity, showers, pump-out, wifi, restaurant, Arolles Marine hire base, village 1200m r/b

This attractive port has its own little *capitainerie* but is effectively managed by the 'mother' port of Beaucaire. It offers all facilities, a short walk from the village. Possible over-wintering.

PK **16.6** Bridge (Broussan)
PK **17.2** Motorway bridge (A54)
PK **24.0** Footbridge, aqueduct
PK **24.2** **Saint-Gilles** basin, *port de plaisance* and Le Boat hire base, 06 71 22 88 54, 89 berths, night €23, water and electricity included, showers, wifi, mobile pump-out, slipway, small town, restaurants r/b

Moor bow or stern to the quay, using a buoy. The quayside moorings are nearly always taken. Distillery opposite. Saint-Gilles is named after the saint who founded the abbey in the 7th century. It became a place of pilgrimage for medieval Europe and a stopping place on the Via Tolosana to Santiago de Compostela in northern Spain. Today the town is less glamorous, but authentic and charming. Good market, shops in the centre, supermarkets and *brico* store to the west from the southern end of the port.

*The* port de plaisance *at Saint-Gilles*  © F-W

**Nîmes** is easy to reach by bus from Saint-Gilles, for the airport (regular flights to the UK) and railway station, and the town itself with its famous Roman amphitheatre, Maison Carrée Roman temple and Sir Norman Foster's Carre d'Art library/gallery. Hire a car in Nîmes to see the Pont du Gard, the stunning Roman aqueduct.

PK **24.6** Bridge (Saint-Gilles), D6572
PK **24.9** Railway bridge, narrow bridge

## Canal du Rhône à Sète (through route)

PK **29.0** Junction with Canal de Saint-Gilles (Petit Rhône) and through route of navigation from the Rhône to Sète l/b
PK **29.7** Bridge (Espeyran)
PK **35.1** Bridge (Franquevaux)

PK **39.2** **Gallician** bridge, *halte* d/s r/b, 38 berths, 10 visitor moorings, 06 27 30 21 82, night €21.40, water, electricity, showers, wifi, pump-out, village and restaurant 400m

Bows-to mooring. *Capitainerie* and café beside a small village. Alongside bollards have been removed for a cycle path, but there is good depth.

PK **43.0** Bridge (Tourradons), narrow passage
PK **47.3** Junction with canal de dérivation d'Aigues-Mortes

The modern cut to the right bypasses Aigues-Mortes, but will be of little interest to *plaisanciers*. It was built in the 1980s as part of the upgrading of the canal to Sète.

PK **48.0** Bridge (Soulier), D58
PK **49.9** Stop lock 3 (permanently open)
PK **50.8** **Aigues-Mortes** bridge, medieval fortified town l/b
PK **50.9** Railway swing bridge

The available headroom under the bridge in the closed position is 2.80m.

PK **51.0** Junction with Canal Maritime l/b, access to *port de plaisance*, 06 19 96 21 23, 35 visitor berths (maximum length 17m), night €25.50, water and electricity included, showers, pump-out, wifi
PK **51.6** Access to private marina (Port du Roy)
PK **51.9** Main road bridge (D62)
PK **53.2** Junction with canal de dérivation d'Aigues-Mortes

The modern cut comes in from the right.

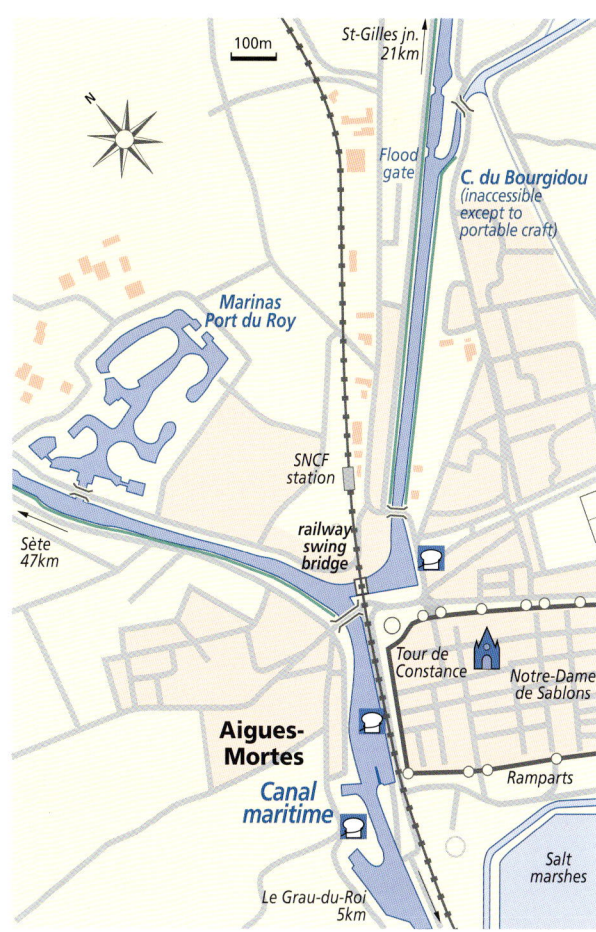

# VI – Southern France ('Midi')

*The* port de plaisance *at Aigues-Mortes is located just outside the town's fortifications.* © STEFANO INCERPI

*The Vidourle crossing* © F-W

*Improvised mooring to the rough bank at Grand Travers* © F-W

*Looking west towards Sète at the four-way junction, PK75. Left (through the bridge) lies a fully-equipped* port de plaisance. *Right is the River Lez, giving access to Port Ariane and Montpellier.* © F-W

PK 55.0  **Vidourle crossing** (the river may be navigated by shallow-draught vessels only to Le Grau-du-Roi), footbridges on the sluice-gate structures either side of crossing

Along the canal by-passing Aigues-Mortes there are a number of wooden pontoons near the Tour Carbonnière. They are in various states of repair, but are good, free moorings compared to the expensive *port de plaisance*. A passenger boat regularly makes the circular excursion through the floodgate and the Vidourle, and may appear without warning.

PK 58.9  Main road bridge (D61)
PK 59.0  Junction with Canal de Lunel, r/b (disused)
PK 61.7  **La Grande-Motte** mooring l/b, resort 1.5 km
PK 64.8  Grand Travers

It is just about possible to find a spot to moor bankside, between the jagged fallen stonework and the gravelly shallows, with the lagoon just across the grass, flamingos and all. Magic atmosphere from early evening to early morning, but passing commercial traffic could be a problem.

PK 70.0  Main road bridge (D62)
PK 70.7  **Junction with canal du Carnon** (Canal du Hangar), marina, Canalous hire base and *port de plaisance*, 04 67 50 81 19, 30 boats, night €15, water, electricity, showers, fuel, pump-out, access to Mediterranean for small boats only  **carnon@lescanalous.com**
PK 70.7  **Carnon** bridge, resort 1 km

To the north of the bridge runs a very short channel, the Port de Pérols; it is difficult to turn at the end, and there is a risk of running aground. To the south of the bridge a channel goes through to a small marina and the sea, air draught only 1.20m. West of the bridge there is a good quay with bollards, ideal for lunch in a restaurant and taking on provisions.

PK 75.1  Bridge
PK 75.2  **Junction with canalised river Lez** Palavas-les-Flots *port de plaisance* south of junction (see under Lez, p.32)

There are footbridges over sluice-gate structures on either side of the junction, giving access seaward to the *port de plaisance* Pierre Paul Riquet for boats with less than 2.40m air draught, 04 67 07 73 48, and inland to **Port Ariane** (see under Lez).

PK 75.3  Bridge (Quatre-Canaux), D986, quays d/s
PK 78.6  **Maguelonne Abbey** on mound, l/b

Walk to the gorgeous sandy beaches, to the adjacent historic abbey (or take the little tourist train, in season) and to the nearby (3km) village of Villeneuve-les-Maguelonne. At PK 78.5, although there are three idyllic timber pontoons it is extremely shallow. Further south there is a long length of stone quayside; much better draught but usually crowded. Between the two there is a floating footbridge, pivoting at one end and powered by an outboard motor at the other. Sound the horn to request it to open.

PK 86.6  New road bridge (replacing former pedestrian swing bridge), D114
PK 91.2  **Junction with access to Sète harbour**

This link was built for commercial traffic (barges of 1000 tonnes) to reach the port of Sète, and is forbidden to recreational craft.

# Canal du Rhône à Sète/Étang de Thau

*The lift bridge at Frontignan, PK 92* © F-W

PK **91.7**  Bridge (D612, Frontignan bypass)
PK **92.1**  Railway bridge
PK **92.2**  **Frontignan** lift bridge, *port de plaisance* d/s, 30 places on 220m quay, mooring free for 3 days, 06 79 73 23 05, water €2/100 litres, electricity €5 for 5 kWh, pump-out, showers, crane, slipway, restaurants, town centre r/b

The lift bridge opens each day at 8:30 and 16:00 for a very short period. In July and August there is a third opening at 13:00. A harbourmaster's assistant is on hand every day to assist and orient *plaisanciers* before and after passage through the raised bridge, for mooring, using the pump-out facility, or for general information. Frontignan, famous for its *muscat* or mellow yellow wine, is a pleasant town on a medieval circular grid pattern.

PK **96.1**  Bridge (D600)
PK **96.2**  Former junction with Canal de la Peyrade, l/b (entrance infilled)
PK **97.3**  Railway bridge, narrow passage (9.60m)
PK **97.3**  Bridge (D2)
PK **98.0**  *Outfall in Étang de Thau* navigation continues in Étang de Thau, Sète *port de plaisance*, 04 67 74 98 97, 25 visitor berths, night €30 (€35 in high season), water and electricity included, showers, wifi, *sete.port.fr*

For Sète, enter the *étang*, turn to port and (keeping the safe depth marks to port) head southwest. For the Canal du Midi (i.e. crossing the *étang*) head west-northwest towards the two yellow marks. Access to/from Sète is governed by the lifting railway and road bridges, which open for a short time only twice a day, at 10:00 and 19:00. Boats with an air draught of up to 2.30m will pass under the bridges when closed.

## Branches of the Canal du Rhône à Sète

### Canal de dérivation d'Aigues-Mortes

This short cut for barges is of little interest for *plaisanciers*. It cuts 2.3km from the old line via Aigues-Mortes. The Rhône kilometre numbering and corresponding posts follow this bypass canal.

PK **0.0**  *Junction with through route* (PK 47.3)
PK **0.7**  Bridge (D46)
PK **1.9**  **Aigues-Mortes** road (D979) and railway bridge
PK **3.6**  *Junction with through route* (PK 53.2)

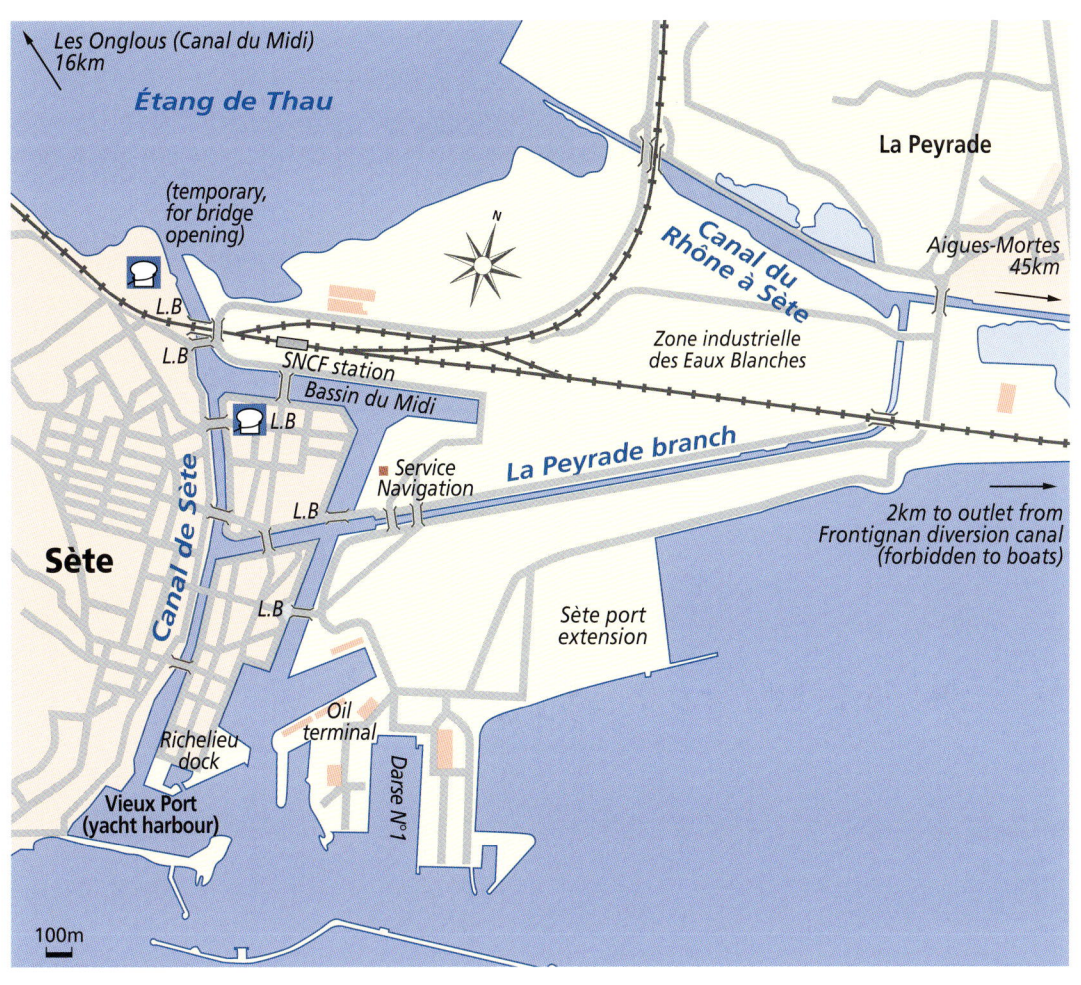

# VI – Southern France ('Midi')

## Canal Maritime

- PK **0.0** Junction with Canal du Rhône à Sète at PK 51.0
- PK **0.1** Bridge
- PK **0.4** **Aigues-Mortes** *port de plaisance*, see above
- PK **5.2** Bridge
- PK **5.3** Confluence with Vidourle, navigable by shallow craft only to the crossing on the main canal at PK 55.
- PK **5.5** **Le Grau-du-Roi** *port de plaisance*, 04 66 51 10 45, 100 berths, night €34, water, electricity, showers, wifi (at Maison du Nautisme), fuel, pump-out, slipway, wintering   *capitainerie@portcamargue.com*

*The Canal maritime reaches the Mediterranean at Le Grau-du-Roi.*

## Étang de Thau

*(Note: distances relate to the straight line across the étang)*

- PK **0.0** Entrance to the étang from the Canal du Rhône à Sète
- PK **0.3** Navigation crosses dredged channel to industrial quays on the eastern shore at Balaruc-les-Bains
- PK **2.3** Roquérols lighthouse, **Bouzigues** harbour, north side, 04 67 53 39 84, 10 berths, night €18 (€24 in season) including water, electricity, showers, wifi, crane 4t, slipway, pump-out
- PK **6.5** **Mèze** harbour, north shore, 04 67 43 58 94, 30 berths, night €14.62 (up to €37.35 in high season), water, showers, crane, slipway, pump-out, repairs
- PK **16.0** **Marseillan** harbour, north side, 04 67 77 34 93, 22 berths, night €39.90, water and electricity included, showers, wifi, pump-out, crane 5t, slipway, repairs, restaurants
- PK **17.0** Les Onglous lighthouse, entrance to Canal du Midi

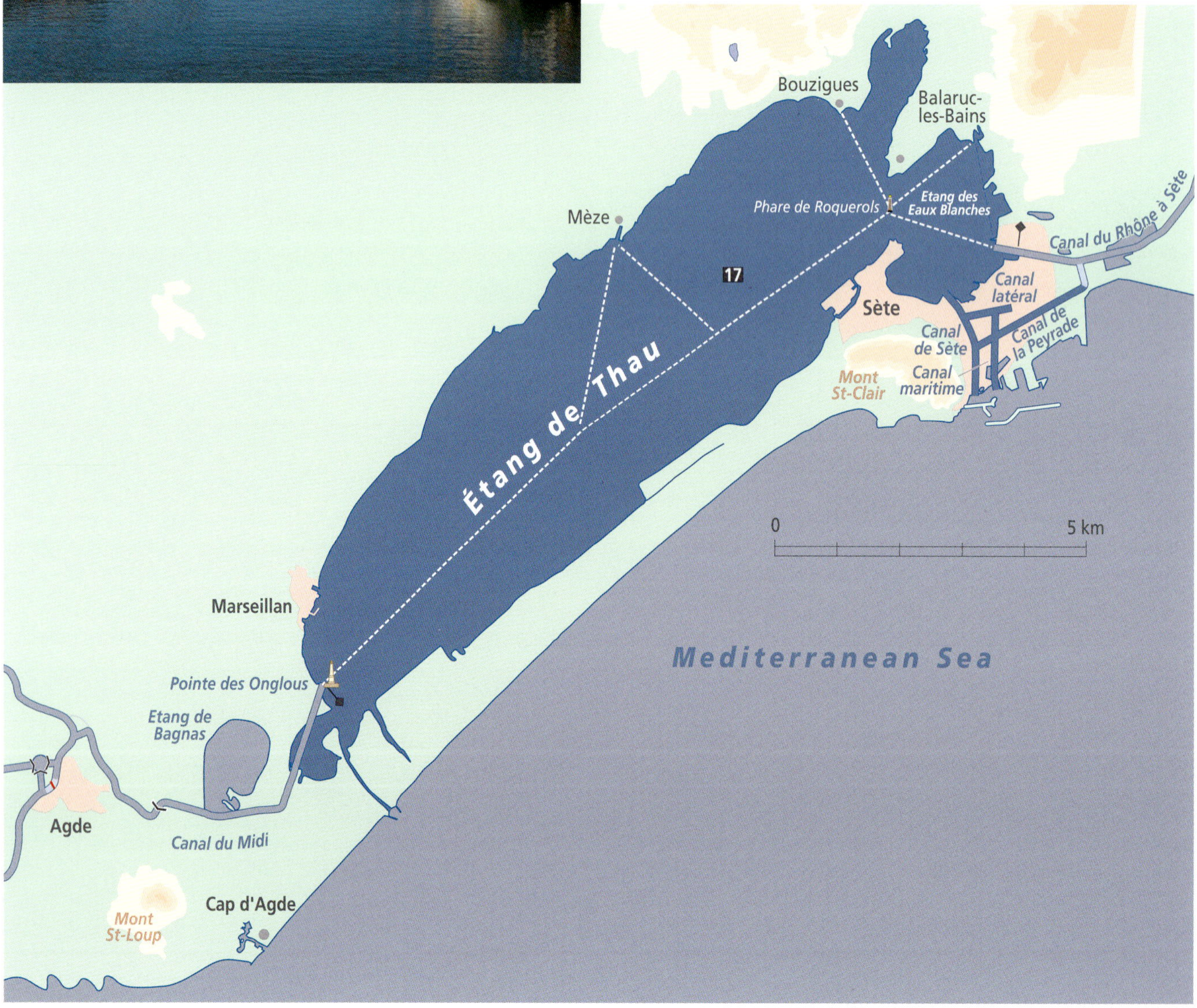

# 55. River Lez

The river Lez, a short and unpredictable Mediterranean torrent, was restored to navigation in the 1980s over a length of 5 km from the Canal du Rhône à Sète at PK 75.2 to the Port Ariane marina at Lattes, just south of the city of Montpellier. The architect Ricardo Bofill had planned to develop a harbour at the historic limit of navigation, restoring three original locks, but practical considerations, especially the incompatibility between flood protection and navigation, thwarted this ambition.

Over the first two kilometres, the river winds between the lagoons and is lined by countless boats, many of them half abandoned and some even sunk. Then the river is enclosed between high flood embankments, with no possibilities for mooring, until the lock is reached. After Méjean bridge, the entrance to the marina is clearly marked, with a light showing red when the flood gate has to be closed. This excursion from the Canal du Rhône à Sète is recommended for the excellent mooring in the marina, managed by Locaboat, with all services (except fuel) and for convenient access by tram to the centre of Montpellier.

*Works to make the Lez navigable inland to Montpellier were envisaged as early as the 12th century by the bishop of Maguelonne. Canalisation with three locks was planned by The Marquess François de Solas in 1666 and Royal assent was obtained in 1675. Works were completed in 1695. The waterway was extended to Palavas in 1719. It was acquired by the State in 1878, and closed in 1942. It was conceded to the commune of Lattes in 1980, allowing the restoration works to take place, and transfer of ownership is expected to take place in the near future.*

and calm in summer, in the winter the river Lez can flood dramatically. Port Ariane has very large flood gates that are closed each night, even in summer.

| Key dimensions | (m) |
|---|---|
| Length | 26.00 |
| Beam | 5.05 |
| Draught | 1.50 |
| Air draught | 3.30 |

## Navigation
For much of the short journey up from the Canal du Rhône à Sète the river is twisty, narrow and bounded by reeds and small home-made pontoons (for day boats). Keep to the centre, or the marked channel (there are buoys at places). From half-way along there are high embankments; benign

## Locks
There is one 17th century oval lock, monitored from the harbourmaster's office at Lattes and operated automatically, although there is often a technician on site. Maximum authorised dimensions are 26.00m by 5.05m.

## Draught
The Lez normally offers a minimum depth of 1.50m.

## Headroom
The maximum authorised air draught is 3.30m.

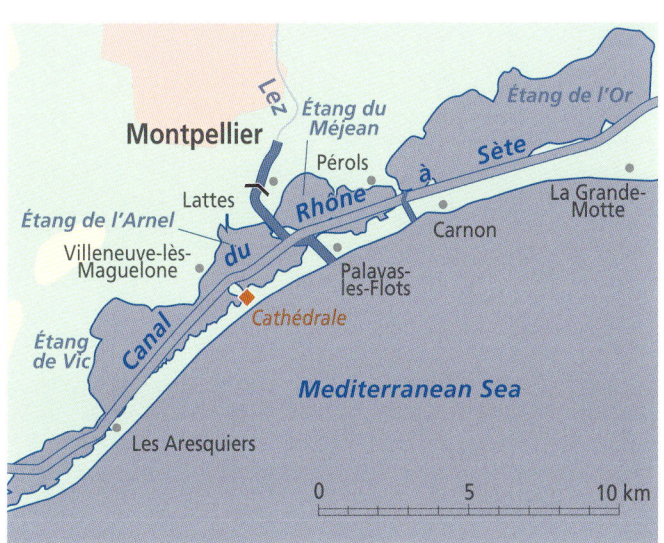

## Towpath
There is a rough path throughout most of the length on the left bank, set back from the river in the lower reaches, to bypass the fishermen's huts.

## Authority
Ville de Lattes, 1 avenue de Montpellier, 34970 Lattes
04 67 99 77 77

## VI – Southern France ('Midi')

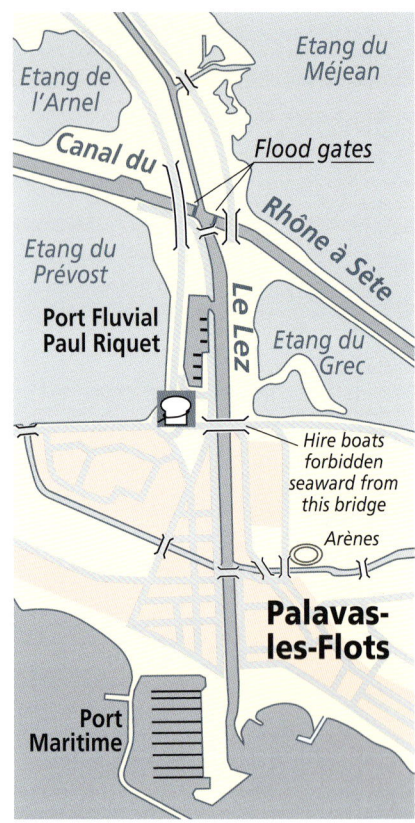

*The approach to the lock at PK 4.4, and the excellent* port de plaisance *in Lattes* © F-W

## Route description

**PK 0.0** **Junction with Canal du Rhône à Sète** (PK 75.2) access to **Palavas-les-Flots**, *port fluvial* Paul Riquet 300m d/s, 04 67 07 73 45, 15 visitors' berths, night €26, water, electricity, showers, wifi, slipway

See plan for access south to the *port fluvial* Paul Riquet. The first section of the route heading north is narrow, with many small boats tied to the bank or to ramshackle home-made pontoons (for day boats).

**PK 0.4** Channel l/b to Étang de Méjean (small craft only)
**PK 0.8** Short quay, 12m long, r/b

Supermarket with fuel immediately adjacent to the quay.

**PK 1.4** Footbridge (Les Quatre Vents)

This is the lowest bridge (3.30m)

**PK 1.7** Large boatyard 'Les Quatre Vents' for small craft, r/b, pontoon 60m long, private
**PK 2.2** Mas des Salins huts l/b
**PK 2.8** Camarguais restaurant and campsite r/b, pontoon

There are many pontoons along the Lez but they are often damaged by the winter floods.

**PK 4.4** Lock (Troisième Écluse)

The pontoon before the lock can be used to stay overnight if arriving too late. The lock is controlled via CCTV from Port Ariane's *capitainerie*. There is an intercom on the control building by the lock, otherwise call 04 67 81 86 07 or 06 26 98 55 82.

The lock is open from 8:00 to 12:15 and from 14:00 to 17:30, the same opening hours as the *capitainerie* at Port Ariane. The oval-shaped lock has vertically dangling chains to attach to. From the lock proceed upstream and under the bridge, turn right past the *capitainerie* building into the port. Visitor pontoon (fingers of varying length) immediately to the right.

**PK 5.3** Bridge (Méjean), D132
**PK 5.5** **Lattes** marina (Port Ariane) entrance l/b, 5 visitor moorings, 04 67 81 86 07, night €27, Locaboat hire base 04 67 20 24 12, water and electricity included, showers, slipway, pump-out, shops, restaurants
*port.fluvial@ville-lattes.fr*

The sockets on the service units have an unusual, non-standard pin arrangement. **Montpellier** is very easily accessible by tram from the terminus of Line 3 at Lattes Centre. It is an easy walk down to the shopping centre in Lattes, which has a big market on Sunday mornings. Launderette and a small Carrefour.

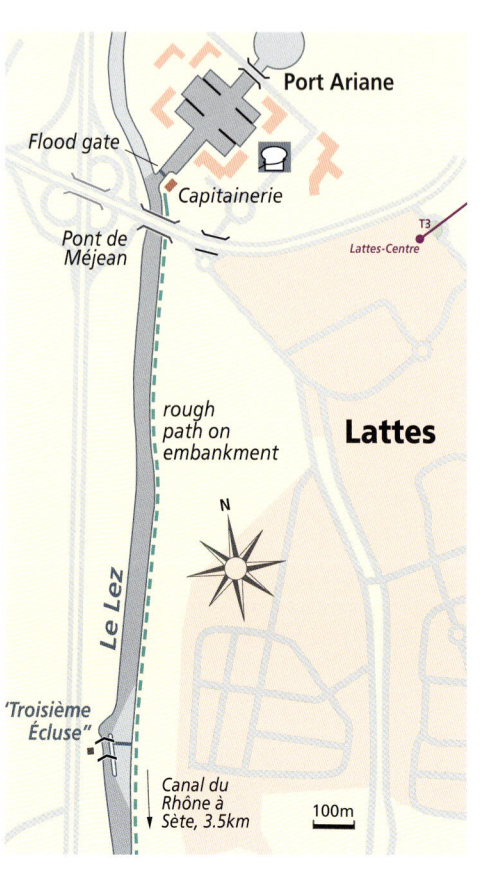

# 56. Canal du Midi

THE CANAL DU MIDI, DESIGNED AND BUILT by Pierre-Paul Riquet in 1662-1681, is a remarkable work of engineering, justifying its inclusion in the Unesco world heritage list in 1996, and one of the most popular cruising waterways in France. 2021 marked the 340th anniversary of opening of the canal, and the 25th anniversary of the world heritage listing. The canal runs 240km from the Étang de Thau, a sheltered lagoon behind the Mediterranean port of Sète, to Toulouse, where it connects with the Canal de Garonne. Its green waters twist and turn through the countryside, following the contours, bordered by an avenue of thousands of plane trees whose exposed roots interlock at the water's edge, reinforcing the banks. Although many have been cut down to limit the spread of the deadly canker stain, a minute blue fungus, the characteristic landscape remains in many sections, and the newly-planted trees will gradually recreate the majestic presence of their predecessors. The canal passes through a great number of wine-growing areas, including the Hérault, the Aude, Minervois and Corbières, as well as many fields of sunflowers and corn. These dominate the more pastoral landscape after the canal leaves the Mediterranean climate west of Carcassonne.

From its entrance at Les Onglous, marked by a charming small lighthouse, the canal cuts across the coastal plain to Agde, where it crosses the river Hérault behind a weir, then enters its lowest pound at the round lock in Agde. It leaves sea level at the lock in Portiragnes, and soon reaches Béziers, where the canal crosses the river Orb, this time on an aqueduct. Here starts the 'heavy engineering' of this truly unique canal, where nature forms a constantly delightful backdrop to all manner of staircase locks, aqueducts, siphons, spillways, feeders and one tunnel.

At Fonserannes the six- (formerly eight-) lock staircase lifts boats to the 'long pound' (*grand bief*) which follows the 31.50m contour for no less than 54km to Argens-Minervois. This includes the world's first canal tunnel, at Malpas, with a length of 161m and a width of 6.45m

at water level. From Argens the canal climbs again in earnest through Carcassonne then Castelnaudary. A few hours after leaving Castelnaudary and its extensive basin, the summit level is reached at the Col de Naurouze, at an altitude of 190m. Here it is worth stopping, where the feeder enters, to visit the former octagonal basin and the imposing obelisk erected in Riquet's memory.

*France's most famous canal was born, like many great projects, from a meeting of men with uniquely converging motivations and capabilities. Tax collector Pierre Paul Riquet saw the value of the canal crossing the watershed, connecting Toulouse to the Mediterranean. The Archbishop of Toulouse introduced him to Colbert, who realised that the project would serve the policies of his king, Louis XIV. The concession was given to Riquet, and works began in 1662. The fascinating story of the canal's construction is told by Tom Rolt\* in* From Sea to Sea. *The canal was ceremonially opened in October 1681, 10 months after Riquet died, ruined after investing his entire fortune in the works. Vauban made a number of improvements in the 1690s, but was understandably impressed by the boldness of the project completed by Riquet and his engineers.*

*\* Co-founder of the Inland Waterways Association in the UK.*

*The plane-trees of a new disease-resistant variety planted by VNF at Trèbes. In the background is the Le Boat hire base.* VNF

# VI – Southern France ('Midi')

*Sailing boats are much less common on the canal than in the early days of waterway tourism, when sea-to-sea transits accounted for the majority of movements on the canal. Laval lock (PK 37.5)* ©JACQUES NOISETTE/VNF SUD-OUEST

*Deyme bridge is one of the characteristic arched bridges which were raised in the late 1970s when the canal was upgraded to 38.50 m 'Freycinet' dimensions.* ©JACQUES NOISETTE/VNF SUD-OUEST

It was to the summit that Riquet succeeded in bringing a more-than-adequate supply of water by an ingenious feeder system, the main components of which are the Saint-Ferréol reservoir, still efficient after more than three centuries of operation, the *Rigole de la Montagne*, 24km long, and the *Rigole de la Plaine*, 35km long. The large-scale development of irrigation from the 1970s, combined with maintenance problems and the resulting wastage of precious water, and a series of exceptionally dry years, stretched this system beyond its limits, but additional resources were made available (a new reservoir at Montbel supplying the Ganguise reservoir by gravity), so that all the canal's functions are in principle guaranteed even in the driest summers. From the summit level the canal descends through the rich cereal-growing plain of the Lauragais to Toulouse, the suburbs and the procession of cyclists and walkers on the towpaths becoming increasingly present from Ramonville (PK 11).

A short branch, the Descente dans l'Hérault maritime, leads from the round lock at Agde to the river, thus giving alternative access to the Mediterranean. East of Agde lock, the canal uses the course of the Hérault for 1km.

## Navigation

The Midi has just cause to be popular. During the season hundreds of hire boats cruise to and fro, not always completely sure of what they are doing, particularly in

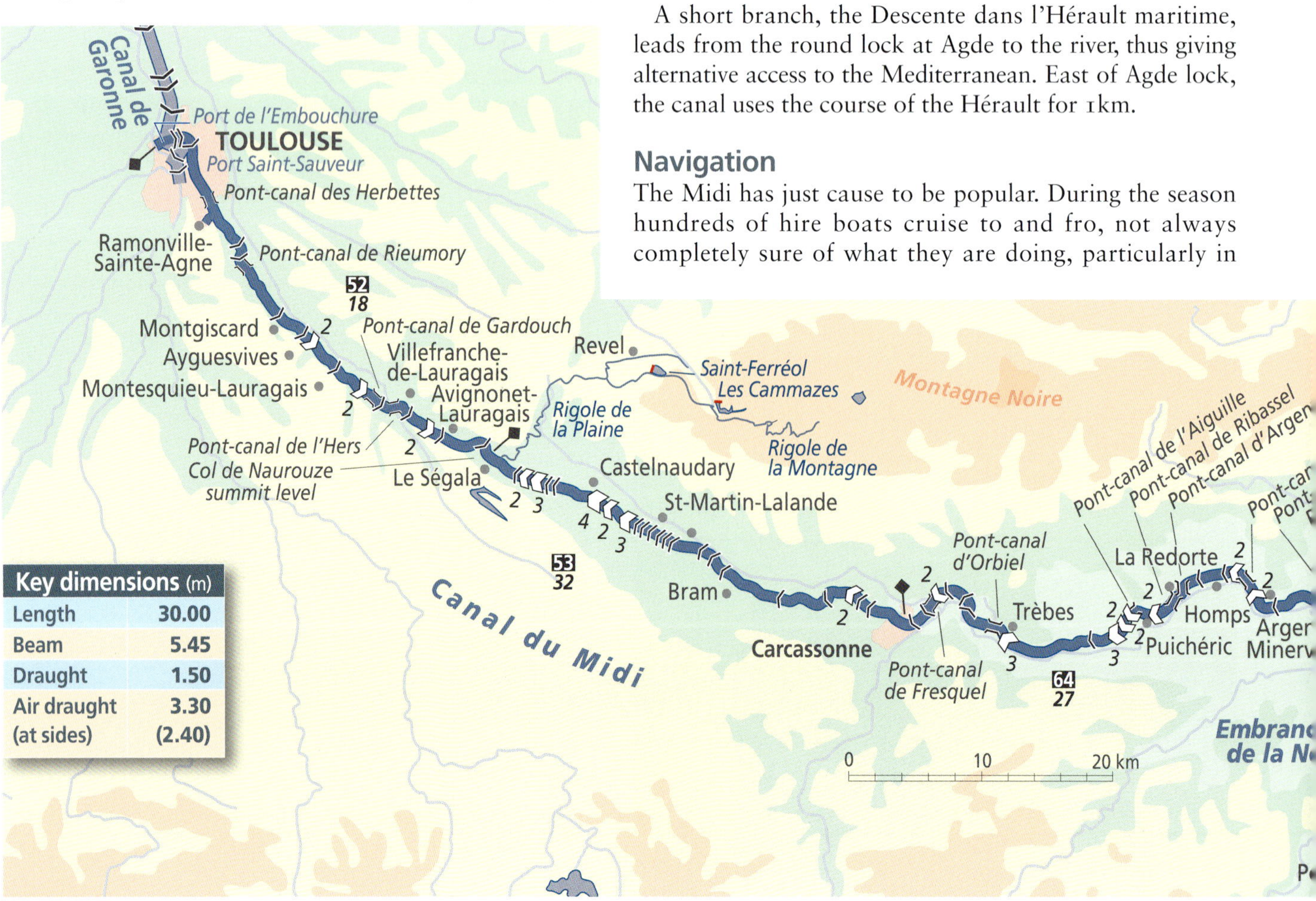

| Key dimensions (m) | |
|---|---|
| Length | 30.00 |
| Beam | 5.45 |
| Draught | 1.50 |
| Air draught | 3.30 |
| (at sides) | (2.40) |

the locks (tricky enough for more experienced boaters). These are subject to a perpetual overflow waterfall noisily cascading over the upper gates. It pays to be somewhat on guard when sharing a lock with hire boats. The quantity of hirers naturally increases during the *grandes vacances* in July and August. Thefts from this tempting array of targets are not unusual, so boats should always be locked up.

## Locks

Discounting the two locks down to the Garonne in Toulouse (buried) and the stop lock east of the Hérault that is normally open, there were formerly 64 locks on the canal, 48 rising from the Mediterranean to the summit and 16 falling towards the Garonne. With 19 double staircases, four triple, one quadruple and one sextuple, the number of separate chambers to be negotiated was 99 (75 and 24 respectively). Minimum lock dimensions are 30.00m by 5.50m. In the late 1970s the canal was modernised over a certain length at each end (like the Canal de Garonne in the early 1970s), to make it navigable by the 38.50m long *péniche*, loading up to 250 tonnes. The works consisted in lengthening the existing lock chambers, from Toulouse to Bazièges (PK 28) and from Argens (PK 152) to the Étang de Thau, including the entire branch to Port-la-Nouvelle. Five new deep locks were built at the Toulouse end of the canal, and two at Béziers, replacing former double staircase locks, so that there are now 15 locks and 18 chambers between Toulouse and the summit. The most significant change east of the summit was construction of the water slope to bypass the Fonsérannes staircase, opened in 1989 after protracted court action following failure of the traction unit when the water slope first opened in 1984. In 1990, the prospects for a revival of water transport were seen to be negligible, even for 250-tonne barges, and in 1996 the canal became a World Heritage site, protected by UNESCO. The section of the Canal du Midi which retains its original structures will thus remain as it is, a relief for all those who were concerned that Riquet's heritage would be desecrated beyond recognition. Heading west from the Étang de Thau, the number of locks is 48 (73 chambers) to the summit level.

In conclusion, the maximum authorised length is 30m, beam 5.45m. The locks have an unusual oval shape on plan, but the walls are vertical. The double, triple, quadruple and sextuple staircases are electrically-operated, and can be negotiated in a relatively short time. Most of the locks west from Castelnaudary are now user-operated, and have been automated. There is a control panel at the lockside with buttons. Crew must be let off in advance of the lock in order to press the appropriate button to prepare and open the lock-gates before a boat can enter. Once moored, another button is pressed to start the lock cycle. In the high season there may be queues of boats waiting to pass through locks.

## Draught

The maximum authorised draught is 1.50m. This is the norm, but actual depths vary according to conditions. There may be some shallower spots at downstream lock entrances, at least until the current 10-year dredging programme is completed. Some stretches are highly prone to either silting or to falling leaves forming a soft bed that can be ploughed through but which certainly reduces the actual water depth. As on most waterways, the given depth is the middle of the channel. The sides may be noticeably less deep and this may affect coming alongside, especially if one has twin bilge keels or twin propellors. The final factor is that on the downstream side of a lock the outgoing water scours a depression immediately outside the gates but then deposits that silt a short way beyond, forming a bar.

## Headroom

The bridges leave a minimum clear headroom of 3.25m in the centre line of the arch and 3.00m at the sides.

*A tight squeeze for this large hire boat under the bridge at Capestang* ©F-W

# VI – Southern France ('Midi')

## Towpath
There is a good towpath throughout, except over the first 22km from Les Onglous to Portiragnes lock.

## Authority
VNF Sud-Ouest
Subdivision de Haute-Garonne:
— 115 bis, rue des Amidonniers, 31000 Toulouse, 05 62 15 11 91
subdi.languedoc-est@vnf.fr (PK 0-76)
Subdivision Languedoc-Ouest:
— Port du Canal, 11000 Carcassonne 04 68 71 74 55
subdi.languedoc-ouest@vnf.fr (PK 76-151)
Subdivision Languedoc-Est:
– Pont Rouge, avenue du Prado, 34500 Béziers 04 67 11 81 30
subdi.languedoc-est@vnf.fr (PK 151-240)

## Descente dans l'Hérault
The Descente dans l'Hérault maritime leads from the round lock at Agde (PK 231) to the port of Agde on the Hérault. The cut is about 500m long and includes a railway bridge offering a minimum headroom of 4.22m. The maximum authorised draught is 1.80m. (See also under Hérault in the next section, 57).

## Route description

*The Étang de Thau from the outlet of the Canal du Midi at Les Onglous lighthouse.* © JACQUES MORAND

PK **240.1** Les Onglous lighthouse, *entrance from the Étang de Thau*
PK **239.8** Quays (Les Onglous)

This is a Glénans sailing school base located in the former stable and other buildings for the teams that hauled boats through the canal. There are a few areas of quayside available for visitors. Interesting and peaceful spot to stay for a day or so by the *étang*, but also quite near the big beaches to the south at Marseillan-Plage.

PK **238.5** Bridge (Les Onglous)
PK **235.3** Lock (Bagnas)

The first or last lock on the Midi, operated by a lock-keeper.

PK **234.1** Bridge (Saint-Bauzille)
PK **233.2** Bridge (Prades)
PK **232.9** Stop lock (Prades)
PK **232.7** *Canal enters Hérault*

Turn south and go downstream for 800m (past possible bankside river moorings) until within sight of the Agde weir, then turn right into the canal. The grassy banks are high but there are timber posts to tie up to outside the round lock at Agde. Entering the river, it is possible to turn north and cruise up to Bessan (see under river Hérault).

PK **231.9** *Canal leaves Hérault*
PK **231.4** Round lock (three-way), *junction with branch (Descente dans l'Hérault)*

The lock is no longer round since it was altered to accommodate longer *péniches*. It is more difficult than it looks: if the wind is blowing, you can become trapped on one quadrant or another, unable to get off and make the turn out through the gate. Bear this in mind when choosing where to tie up. Some places are subject to quite a lot of turbulence as the lock fills. The lock is manned (04 67 94 10 99). To the left of the lock lies the spur canal that also connects with the river Hérault, below the weir, that provides a route to the sea.

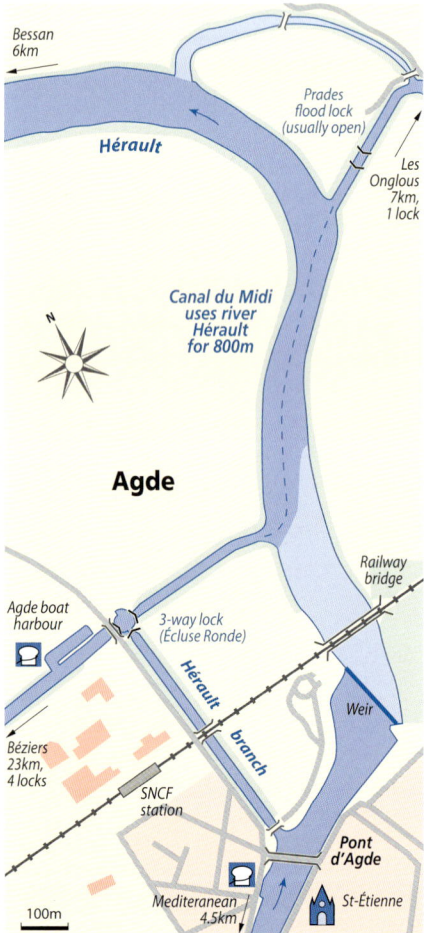

PK **231.3 Agde** bridge, Canalous Plaisance hire base, basin, quay u/s r/b for 15 boats, water, town centre 800m r/b

Public quayside mooring to the left, possible bankside on the right before the long series of hire boats starts. Agde is a picturesque and historic town, well worth visiting – about 15mins walk south from the lock.

# Canal du Midi

*The round lock at Agde. Left is the little-used branch down to the Hérault. Beyond the bridge, to the right, is the harbour basin* © F-W

PK **229.7** Three-arched bridge
PK **229.2** Railway bridge
PK **229.0** Bridge (Pont Neuf, Vias), D912
PK **228.2** New road bridge (D612, Agde bypass)
PK **226.4** **Vias** bridge (Pont Vieux), *halte* d/s r/b, 04 67 21 76 25, moorings for 8 boats, free (maximum 72 hours), water, electricity, wifi at tourist office, village 1200m l/b

Quayside mooring by the bridge, close to the beach at La Tamarissière.

PK **226.3** Bridge (D137)
PK **225.2** Libron crossing, narrow passage, bridge
PK **222.0** **Port Cassafières** basin r/b, Le Boat hire base, 04 67 90 91 70, 80 berths, night €20 (except weekends), diesel, water and electricity included, showers, pump-out, wifi, restaurant, Redoute-Plage 1800m
*cassafieres@leboat.com*

A major hire boat base with facilities potentially available for outside use: repairs, crane, etc, as well as diesel. Some spaces available for visitors, or moor bankside nearby. The sandy beach of La Redoute-Plage is close by.

PK **221.6** Bridge (Roquehaute)
PK **218.3** Lock (**Portiragnes**), bridge, village 400m l/b
PK **216.5** Bridge (Caylus)
PK **215.5** **Cers** bridge, village 800m l/b
PK **214.9** Bridge (D64)
PK **213.5** **Villeneuve-lès-Béziers** *halte* l/b, campsite Les Berges du Canal, visitor moorings for up to 6 boats, 04 67 39 36 09, night €6, water, electricity, showers and wifi at campsite

A good place to moor for a day or two, the village has an excellent wine cooperative. This friendly and well run camp-site has a small restaurant, bar, and all facilities. Phoning ahead to reserve a mooring is advised. Alternative moorings are just before the lock: the public quay with water on the south bank (*jetons* supplied by the adjacent tourist office), or in front of the pizzeria on the north bank.

PK **213.8** Lock (Villeneuve), bridge, **Villeneuve-lès-Béziers** r/b, public quay d/s r/b, water, f
PK **212.7** Motorway bridge (A9)
PK **212.5** Lock (Ariège)
PK **210.5** Bridge (Capiscol)

PK **210.0** Former lift bridge on industrial railway siding
PK **209.5** Bridge (Saint-Pierre)

*Moorings at Villeneuve-lès-Béziers. Since this picture was taken all the plane trees have been felled and new trees planted.* © F-W

PK **208.8** Flood gate (Sauclière), bridge and footbrige, quay d/s l/b
PK **208.5** Bridge, junction with Canalet du Pont Rouge r/b
PK **208.4** Deep lock (Béziers)

Timber waiting pontoons ahead of the lock. The short canal spur off to the left provided access to the River Orb via a lock. Possible bankside mooring, but the spur has completely silted up. This manned lock is straight-sided and deep (more than 4m). Vertical poles to moor to and slide up or down. It will only be possible to loop round one pole, as they are spaced for *péniches*, not smaller craft.

*View of Bézier's Pont-Neuf and Saint-Étienne cathedral from the Orb aqueduct.*

PK **208.1** **Béziers** basin, *halte nautique* l/b, 04 67 36 80 08, 16 visitor moorings, night €15, water, electricity, fuel delivered to order, cameras for security, town centre 500m l/b beyond railway *brice.vacquier@ville-beziers.fr*

A historic town dating back beyond Roman times to the Neolithic. It became a stronghold of the Cathar sect, forcibly supressed in 1209 when the population (15 000–20 000) was massacred in its entirety by Catholic forces. The town is very pleasant to walk up to from the port, to sit in the main square by the statue of Paul Riquet, born in Béziers. The port (local VNF office 04 67 11 81 30) is spacious and modern (see plan p.38).

# VI – Southern France ('Midi')

*View looking down the Fonserannes staircase. The whole site has been redeveloped and landscaped, and land visitors now exclusively approach the site from upstream.* © FRANCE VÉLO TOURISME - J. DAMASE

*The impressive rush of water from the gate paddles one basin up from where boats are made fast; this mode of operation accelerates the locking cycle.* © F-W

**PK 208.0** Deep lock (Orb), bridge

Straight-sided and more than 6 m deep. Again, there are vertical poles.

**PK 207.6** Aqueduct (Orb, length 240m)

The aqueduct takes the canal over the River Orb. Before this was built in 1858 craft had to descend to the river, travel along, and then come back up to canal level. Conditions often meant this was not possible. The plan shows the Port Notre Dame (below Fonserannes) and its lock, unused since then and slowly sinking into picturesque decay. It is to the credit of the original builders that it is still so well preserved.

**PK 207.0** New cut r/b to water slope (disused)
**PK 206.9** Six-lock (formerly eight-lock) staircase (Fonserannes)

There were once 8 locks, plus Notre Dame, to get up from the river Orb. Now there are just six in operation rising from the aqueduct level. The ascents and descents are according to a timetable – up 10:00-11:45 and 16:00-18:45, down 8:00-9:30 and 13:30-15:30. An ascent takes about an hour. It is always time for an *apéritif* at the top and one is entitled to expect appreciative applause. The locks are invariably shared with other boats of differing sizes and crew abilities, often quite tightly packed in. It is best to be at the back, but beware of the gates closing on the stern. If at the front the bow may be worryingly close to the rushing water, but a secure line taken to the upper bollard, at the top or foot of the steps, will keep the boat safe. The controlling lock-keepers do this all day every day, so they know what they are doing, but they tend to want to take things at a gallop. There are usually lots of spectators enjoying what they see as fun, but the recent development and landscaping of the whole site now keeps them at a safe distance, which is a relief for boaters. Going up, the basic technique is to have crew on the lock-side with the bow line. Moving between lock-chambers, they lead the boat with the line, walking up the steps whilst the skipper attempts to keep the boat under control, go through the gates and then tuck into the curved lock-wall. Crew takes a couple of turns of the bow line around the forward bollard and then darts back to take the stern

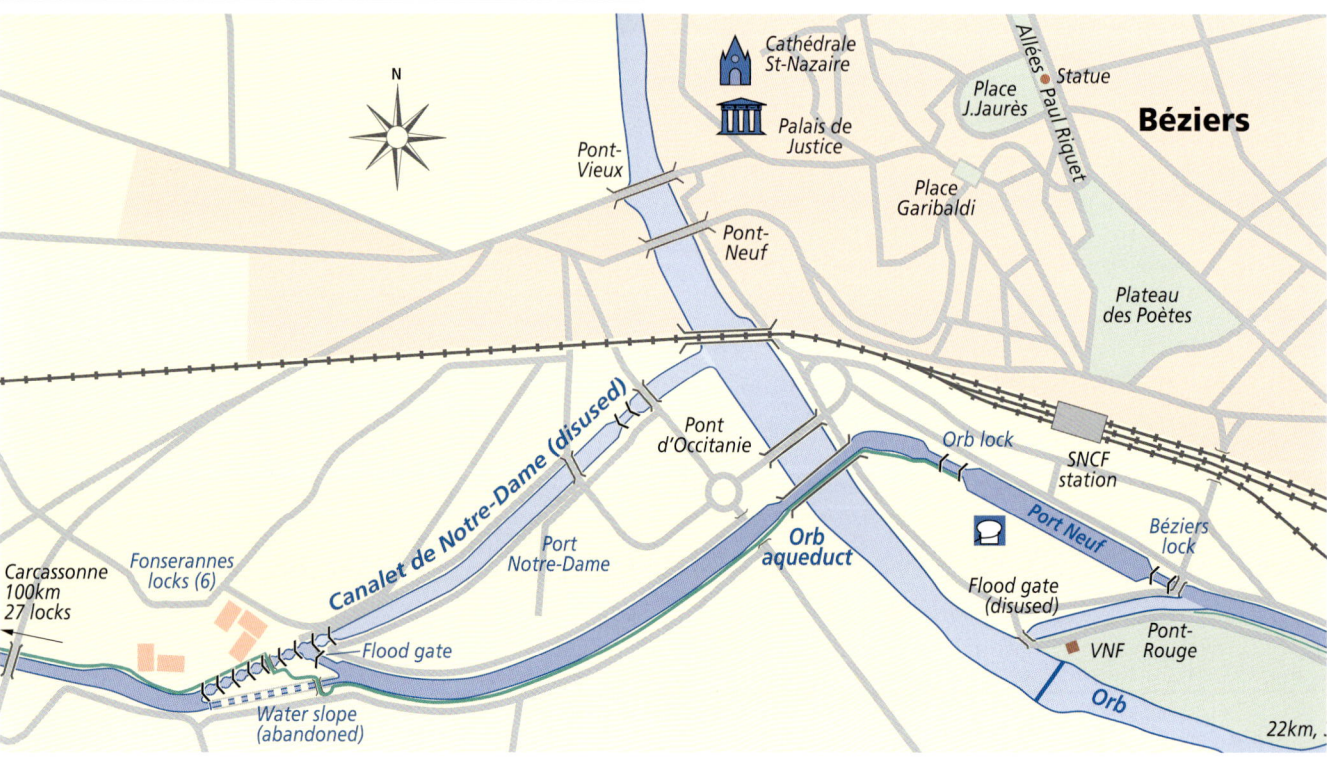

# Canal du Midi

line from the skipper, around the aft bollard, back to the skipper and then forward to pick up the bow line and control the bow.

There are two situations where this does not work. Going into the first (lowest) chamber the configuration means that the crew will not be able to walk in, bow line already in hand. It may be difficult to lasso the necessary bollards from the boat. Secondly, half-way up there is a footbridge that means crew also cannot lead the boat here. The skipper may have to throw the lines to the crew.

PK **206.6** Bridge over third lock
PK **206.5** End of staircase, former entrance r/b to water slope

From here, heading west, there are no locks for 53km.

PK **205.9** Bridge (Narbonne), D609, quay u/s r/b
PK **205.4** Bridge (D64)
PK **204.4** Bridge (Gourgasse)
PK **204.0** End of narrow section
PK **203.8** Second passing place
PK **202.7** First passing place
PK **202.0** Canal narrows, one-way traffic (except for small boats)
PK **200.5** **Colombiers** bridge, marina and Canalous Plaisance hire base, d/s r/b, 04 67 11 86 00, 12 visitor berths, 2 nights €21, water €2/300 litres, electricity (metered), showers, wifi, slipway

Hire boat base (travel-lift and yard) in a harbour off the river. Apparently, free water and electricity for the first night. Colombiers has its regular customers, who have left their boat there for the winter. The port can be a little noisy.

PK **198.8** Malpas tunnel (length 161m), Oppidum d'Ensérune ruins 1.5 km l/b

The oldest canal tunnel in the world; quite short but the tunnel and the approaches are narrow (single passage) so hooting loudly to warn oncoming traffic is advisable. Above, the Oppidum d'Enserune is an ancient hill settlement, occupied for 500 years up to 100AD – magical, but a stiff walk up from the canal. It overlooks the Étang de Montady, once a swamp but drained in 1247, with spectacular radial fields and ditches.

*The narrow approach to Malpas tunnel from the eastern end.*

PK **196.3** Bridge (Régimont)
PK **194.2** **Poilhes** bridge, quay moorings r/b for 7 visiting boats, night €7, 06 12 57 45 34, water €2/300 litres, electricity €2/30 minutes, village r/b

Poilhes is a delightful village that spans the canal with two bridges connecting the halves. There are bollards along a short stretch of quayside before the road bridge, and for 500m beyond it, but mooring off the old washing-place opposite is no longer allowed. Small shop/boulangerie, restaurants, and a justifiably proud *Mairie* overlooking the canal.

PK **194.1** Footbridge (Poilhes)
PK **191.7** Bridge (Trézilles), D11
PK **188.5** Bridge
PK **188.3** **Capestang** bridge, quay and moorings d/s l/b, France Fluviale hire base, 06 12 57 45 34, 18 visitor berths, night €22, water, electricity, showers, wifi, diesel (to order, for minimum 300 litres), pump-out, restaurant

Capestang is a good village, with facilities including supermarkets. There are plenty of bankside moorings either side of the bridge, as well as a hire boat base. The bridge has the reputation of being the lowest on the canal; it is not, but it is the most awkward because of its shape.

*Approaching the notoriously tricky bridge at Capestang, PK 188* ©F-W

PK **180.6** Bridge (Malviès)
PK **178.3** Bridge (Pigasse)

This stretch is wide and an excellent place to moor bankside; far-reaching views to the south.

PK **176.5** Bridge (Sériège), quay u/s l/b, restaurant
PK **172.6** **Argeliers** bridge (Pont Vieux), quay u/s l/b, village 700m

Good, popular, bankside moorings with a pleasant small village nearby

PK **171.4** Bridge (Pont de la Province)
PK **168.8** Railway bridge, end of one-way section traffic
PK **168.7** **Junction with embranchement de La Nouvelle**, r/b, moorings

# VI – Southern France ('Midi')

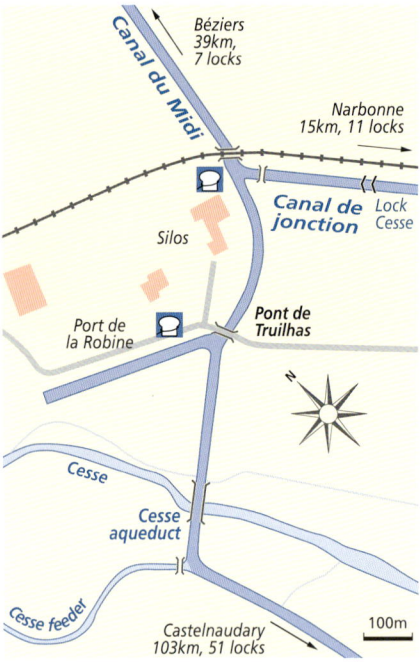

*La Répudre aqueduct, as completed by Riquet in 1679, which made Vauban green with envy when he visited the site.* © SILVA

**PK 168.3** Bridge (Truilhas), **La Robine** basin u/s l/b, 350m long, Cathare Marine, 06 84 52 55 31, 45 berths, 2 visitor moorings on pontoon at entrance (before movable footbridge), night €25, water (€4/500 litres), electricity, diesel, showers €3, slipway (at end of branch), wifi

The moorings off the canal are well secured behind a sliding footbridge, while the pontoon at the entrance welcomes visiting boats and offers the basic services including diesel. There may be some noise and dust from the adjacent factory. It is a very pleasant walk or bike ride down the Canal de Jonction towards Narbonne to the pretty village of Sallèles d'Aude for provisions. (See following section.)

**PK 168.0** Aqueduct (Cesse)

The little *halte* beside the bridge over the River Cesse offers a stone quay but no services. The river is worth a look at, or even to scramble down and paddle in. A fairly thin stream running between gravel banks, you will surely be taken aback by the plaques on the south side of the bridge recording winter flood heights – 10 m above the summer low water level.

**PK 167.7** Canal narrows, one-way traffic (applies only to large vessels)
**PK 165.9** **Le Somail** bridge (Pont Vieux), Nicols hire base, *halte* d/s for 35 boats, night €20, water and electricity included, showers (during office hours), wifi, pump-out, village and restaurants both banks   **somail@nicols.com**

Very pretty village and bridge. Visit the stunning, very large antiquarian bookshop, 'Le Trouve Tout du Livre'. Several restaurants.

**PK 165.4** Bridge (Pont Neuf), D607
**PK 162.7** Bridge (Saint-Nazaire)
**PK 160.9** **Ventenac d'Aude** bridge, quay u/s l/b, village l/b

Good quaysides immediately outside a huge wine 'cave'.

**PK 158.8** Aqueduct (Répudre)

The aqueduct over the river Repudre (1676) is the oldest in France, probably the world.

**PK 157.6** **Paraza** bridge, *halte* for 5 boats on quay u/s l/b, free, water, village l/b
**PK 154.8** **Roubia** bridge, quay d/s l/b, water, village l/b
**PK 152.3** Lock (Argens), beginning of long pound
**PK 151.1** **Argens-Minervois** bridge, *port de plaisance* (Port Occitanie) in basin d/s l/b, Locaboat hire base, 04 68 27 03 33, night €20, water and electricity included, wifi, shower, crane 10t, picnic area

A very attractive village, with an ancient and seemingly untouched château set on the hill above. Down at canal level things have moved on, with the large hire boat base. There are also bankside moorings alongside the path where the locals play *pétanque*.

*Pechlaurier double staircase lock, PK 150.* © JACQUES MORAND

**PK 149.8** Double staircase lock (Pechlaurier)
**PK 147.5** Bridge (Ognon), D11
**PK 147.2** Stop lock (Ognon), footbridge
**PK 147.1** Double staircase lock (Ognon), aqueduct d/s
**PK 146.4** Lock (Homps), bridge
**PK 145.8** Bridge

# Canal du Midi

PK **145.5 Homps** footbridge, basin u/s, quayside moorings for 30 boats, 04 68 91 18 98, night €18.90 (first night free), water €2/300 litres, electricity €2 per 10 kWh, shower, restaurant, wifi, village r/b   *lechai-portminervois@orange.fr*

The village has some fine buildings including the Knights Tower – in the Middle Ages Homps was one of the most important sites of the Templar Order of Jerusalem. On the edge of the village is a service station and convenience store. There are long quays with services). Big hire boat base with craned lift-out. A bike ride away is the much larger village of Olonzac.

PK **144.0** Bridge (Jouarres)

By the bridge, a romanesque arch and colonnade fronts a vineyard estate. Closer to Homps, what was obviously intended to be a *port de plaisance*. Two entrances with an island between that would make an excellent, safe overnight mooring, but this is a fenced-off property development.

PK **142.7** Lock (Jouarres)
PK **141.4** Bridge (Métairie du Bois)
PK **141.0** Argent-Double aqueduct
PK **140.5** Bridge (Pont Neuf), D11
PK **139.6** Aqueduct (Ribassel)
PK **139.5 La Redorte** bridge (Pont Vieux), *halte* d/s l/b for 18 boats, free, water and electricity by credit card, €3/one hour, €5 for 4 hours, €10 for 24 hours, €20 for 48 hours, restaurant, village 500m l/b
PK **136.4** Double staircase lock (Puichéric)
PK **136.0** Bridge (disused)
PK **135.0** Bridge (Rieux), **Puichéric** 800m r/b
PK **133.7** Aqueduct (Aiguille)
PK **133.4** Double staircase lock (Aiguille), bridge

A brilliant collection of witty sculptures made from bits of wood and *objets trouvés*. The lady on the bike pedals if you approach. Down by the lock overflow channel is a wooden alligator.

*A unique benefit of cruising on the Canal du Midi is the presence of lock-keepers, in an age which seems to dictate automatic operation as the only way to operate a canal.*

*In the lower chamber at Saint-Martin lock, PK 132*

PK **131.6** Double staircase lock (Saint-Martin), bridge
PK **130.4** Triple staircase lock (Fonfile)
PK **127.2** Lock (Marseillette), bridge
PK **126.2 Marseillette** bridge, village 200m r/b

A number of bankside moorings, also a timber pontoon with water.

PK **122.2** Bridge (Millegrand)
PK **121.0** Bridge (Millepetit)
PK **119.4** Bridge (Saint-Julia)
PK **118.0** Triple staircase lock (Trèbes), bridge
PK **117.3 Trèbes** bridge, quay u/s l/b, Le Boat hire base, 04 68 78 73 75, night €20, water, village r/b

A busy place. Hire boat base, bankside moorings, shops and restaurants.

PK **116.7** Aqueduct (Orbiel)
PK **116.4** Orbiel feeder enters l/b

This pretty feeder canal is well worth exploring on foot up to its intake at the Orbiel diversion weir, 700m upstream.

*Passelis diversion weir on the river Orbiel and intake to the canal feeder (left),* PK *116.* © ROSELINE TARBOURIECH

PK **116.2** Bridge (Rode)
PK **113.4** Lock (Villedubert)
PK **112.6** Lock (Evêque), bridge
PK **110.6** Bridge (Méjeanne)
PK **109.3** Bridge (Conques)
PK **109.0** Lock (Fresquel)
PK **108.8** Double staircase lock (Fresquel), quay d/s l/b

# VI – Southern France ('Midi')

*Moorings downstream of Carcassonne lock* © F-W

PK **108.7** Aqueduct (Fresquel)
PK **108.0** Lock (Saint-Jean), bridge (Friedland), very low (3.30m)

The bridge headroom here (and at Carcassonne lock upstream) is at the 3.30m canal minimum.

PK **107.9** Bridge (D118)
PK **105.6** Les Canalous hire base r/b
PK **105.4** Railway bridge (main line Toulouse-Narbonne)
PK **105.3** Lock (Carcassonne), bridge, very low (3.30m)
PK **105.0** **Carcassonne** basin, *port de plaisance* in town centre and 1.5 km from La Cité, 04 68 25 10 48, 67 berths, night €16, covering water, electricity, showers, crane on request, slipway, pump-out, repairs

Spectacular, world-renowned and unmissable, Carcassonne comprises a very large, complete and intact ancient fortified town (the *Cité*) and a 13th century 'new' town. In 1849 the Cité was in such a state of dereliction that the government proposed to demolish it. This caused a national outcry and Viollet-le-Duc started the comprehensive restoration – somewhat inauthentic in places. There are plenty of facilities within an easy and pleasant stroll from the *port de plaisance*, as well as a main-line station. Moorings are divided between the bows-to port in the basin and the alongside quay below the lock (photo above). Both have water and electricity; the *capitainerie* (also the local VNF office) is by the port. It is advisable to make contact in advance of arrival, as this is a much sought-after mooring.

PK **104.8** Bridge (Pont de la Paix)
PK **104.6** Footbridge
PK **104.4** Bridge (Iéna)
PK **103.6** Railway bridge
PK **102.3** Bridge (D6161, Carcassonne ring road)

Quayside outside an old canal building. When first built, the Canal du Midi bypassed Carcassonne (the cost of going though the town was more than the town, impoverished by plague, could bear) and this is where that old canal emerged. Later on, soldiers captured from the Franco-Prussian war were used to dig the revised 'through' route, in particular the extremely deep cutting immediately above the *port de plaisance*. There is now practically nothing to show of the old canal, but some masonry of the at least one of the locks survives.

PK **99.9** Lock (Ladouce)

*Delightful lockside restaurant La Rive Belle, at Herminis lock.*

PK **98.5** Lock (Herminis), bridge
PK **98.2** Double staircase lock (Lalande)
PK **95.9** Bridge (Rocles), Pezens 1.5 km l/b
PK **94.1** Bridge (Caux-et-Sauzens), quay d/s r/b
PK **93.4** Lock (Villesèque)
PK **91.2** **Villesèquelande** bridge, village 600m l/b

Excellent grassy bank moorings under the trees, pretty bridge and picturesque village nearby.

PK **89.1** Bridge (Saint-Eulalie)
PK **87.9** Aqueduct (Espitalet)
PK **85.9** Lock (Béteille), bridge
PK **84.7** Bridge (Diable)
PK **83.9** Railway bridge (through route Toulouse-Narbonne)
PK **83.6** Aqueduct (Rebenty)
PK **80.8** **Bram** bridge, basin and quays d/s r/b, Locaboat hire base, 04 68 13 02 38, visitor moorings on 100m quay, night €20, water and electricity included, diesel (on request), showers, crane, slipway, repairs, restaurant

*Another attractive lockside restaurant at Bram*

PK **80.3** Lock (Bram)
PK **79.0** Lock (Sauzens), bridge
PK **77.4** Lock (Villepinte)

Good bankside moorings above the lock near the small village; a lovely location albeit with some background traffic noise from the nearby main road.

# Canal du Midi

PK 76.5  Pumping station, concrete quay under a tree
PK 76.0  **Villepinte** bridge, village 1 km l/b
PK 73.6  Lock (Tréboul), bridge
PK 73.4  Tréboul aqueduct
PK 72.2  Lock (Criminelle)
PK 71.7  Lock (Peyruque), bridge
PK 70.6  Lock (Guerre), bridge, **Saint-Martin-Lalande** 1 km l/b
PK 69.7  Lock (Saint-Sernin), bridge
PK 69.1  Lock (Guilhermin)
PK 68.7  Triple staircase lock (Vivier), bridge
PK 67.2  Bridge (D6313)
PK 67.1  Double staircase lock (Gay)
PK 65.6  Quadruple staircase lock (Saint-Roch), water

The latest time for passage through this four-chamber staircase is 20 minutes before the usual lock closing time, in other words 11:40 before the lunch break and 18:40 (earlier out of season).

PK 65.4  Bridge (Saint-Roch)
PK 65.2  Basin (Grand Bassin), Le Boat hire base r/b, short-stay mooring only (a few hours), 04 68 94 52 94, water, showers €2.50

The 'Grand Bassin' is a 5-hectare reservoir feeding the locks. The Le Boat hire base is on the south side, with showers and moorings available to *plaisanciers*. Dry dock. The port de plaisance is along the quaysides west of the bridge closer to the centre. *Capitainerie*. Good town with all facilities. The home of the legendary bean and pork *cassoulet* baked in goose-fat.

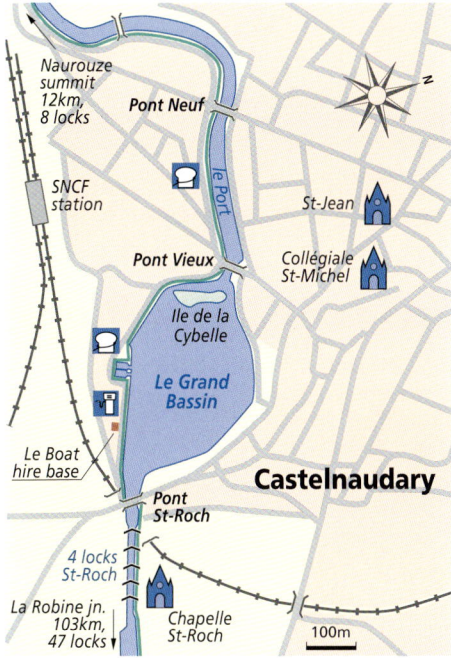

PK 64.8  Bridge (Pont Vieux)
PK 64.6  **Castelnaudary** port de plaisance both banks, moorings for 51 boats, 06 24 08 00 48, night €12 water, electricity (16A), shower, slipway, pump-out, wifi, town l/b
PK 64.5  Bridge (Pont Neuf)
PK 64.1  Footbridge
PK 60.9  Lock (Laplanque), bridge
PK 59.7  Lock (Domergue)
PK 58.7  Triple staircase lock (Laurens), bridge
PK 57.5  Double staircase lock (Roc)

PK 56.6  Lock (Méditerranée), bridge, beginning of summit level
PK 53.8  **Le Ségala** bridge, quay south bank.

The watershed or summit level. Quayside moorings by the small village.

PK 52.1  **Naurouze** feeder enters canal

A beautiful place; Riquet's feeder canal enters the canal in a wonderful octagonal parkland setting and around an avenue of plane trees. The avenue leads up to a small hill, on top of which is an obelisk commemorating the canal's crossing the watershed 'between the two seas' and celebrating Riquet.

PK 51.6  Lock (Océan), bridge, end of summit level
PK 50.6  Railway bridge (through route Toulouse-Narbonne)
PK 50.2  Bridge (A61, Autoroute des Deux Mers)
PK 50.0  **Port Lauragais** marina adjacent to motorway services and Pierre Paul Riquet visitor centre, 05 62 80 14 88, 30 berths, night €13, water and electricity included (or short-stay services water €4.50, electricity €5), slipway, restaurant, Navicanal hire base, repairs, 06 75 28 60 83

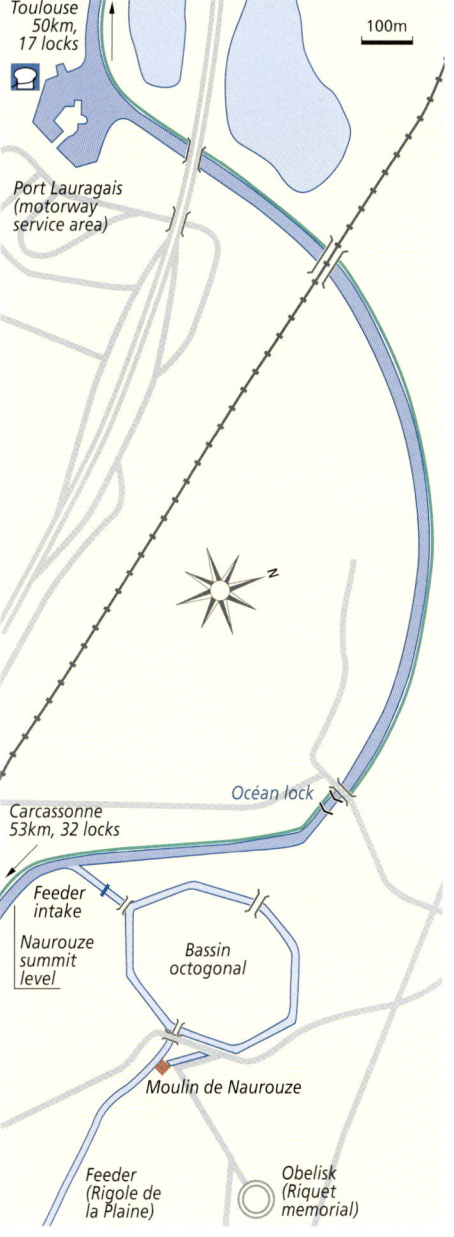

# VI – Southern France ('Midi')

*A boat passes the point where the elaborate feeder system designed by Riquet enters the canal. In the foreground the former Méditerranée lock up to the octagonal basin was converted into a control valve, just one of many adaptations of the centuries-old infrastructure.*

Between the rail bridge and the motorway bridge, a delightful bankside mooring complete with sculptural concrete recliner chairs, next to a lake. The trains are quite frequent, but easily ignored. Immediately west of the autoroute, a *port de plaisance* that is part of its spacious parkland rest area. It is much quieter and more peaceful than one might expect. The adjacent A61 autoroute is an inescapable factor for the next 35km. Most of the time there is merely a background buzz, sometimes it is lost entirely, but in a couple of places it is close and very noticeable.

| | |
|---|---|
| PK 49.5 | Bridge (Maraval) |
| PK 47.5 | Lock (Emborrel), bridge, **Avignonet-Lauragais** 1.5 km r/b |
| PK 45.9 | Double staircase lock (Encassan), bridge |
| PK 43.0 | Lock (Renneville), bridge, small village 400m l/b |
| PK 41.0 | Aqueduct (Hers), Villefranche-de-Lauragais 2 km r/b |

At PK 40, on the south bank, a good, quiet, bankside mooring. north bank – further good, quiet, bankside moorings at PK 35.5 and 33.

| | |
|---|---|
| PK 39.0 | **Gardouch** *halte* l/b managed by VNF, 4 boats, free, water, electricity, village 600m |
| PK 38.9 | Lock (Gardouch), bridge |
| PK 38.5 | Aqueduct (Gardouch) |
| PK 37.5 | Double staircase lock (Laval), bridge |
| PK 35.0 | Bridge (Vieillevigne) |
| PK 34.6 | Motorway bridge (A66) |
| PK 33.3 | Lock (Négra), bridge, **Montesquieu-Lauragais** 1 km l/b |
| PK 33.1 | Locaboat hire base l/b, 05 61 81 36 40, water, electricity, shower |
| PK 31.5 | Bridge (Enserny) |
| PK 29.6 | Double staircase lock (Sanglier), bridge |
| PK 28.1 | Deep lock (Ayguesvives), footbridge |

This lock has been modernised into a single (oval shape, plus a straight-sided 10m 'add-on') from the old double; it is quite deep (more than 4m). Coming down (towards Toulouse) long ropes will be needed if using the bollards. The position of the alternative bollards inset in the lock wall is not obvious. Going up they can be seen but bow and stern lines will have to be passed round the same one. There are 'sliding poles' but they are positioned at the extreme ends of the lock, close to the gates.

| | |
|---|---|
| PK 28.0 | New road bridge (D813) |
| PK 26.9 | Bridge (Baziège) |
| PK 25.0 | **Montgiscard** quay l/b, village 300m beyond main road |
| PK 24.9 | Deep lock (Montgiscard), footbridge |

Similar to the lock at Ayguesvives, but not as tricky or deep. Short length of quay above the *écluse*, good for lunch or overnight. *Boulangerie* in the village, up the hill. Also a pizzeria and bistrot opposite the quay.

| | |
|---|---|
| PK 24.8 | Bridge (Montgiscard) |
| PK 22.7 | Bridge (Donneville) |
| PK 19.8 | Bridge (Deyme) |
| PK 18.4 | Aqueduct (Rieumory) |
| PK 17.4 | Lock (Vic), bridge |
| PK 15.7 | Deep lock (**Castanet**), bridge, village 2 km l/b |
| PK 15.3 | Bridge (route de Labège) |
| PK 12.4 | Ramonville centre 1 km |
| PK 12.1 | Bridge (Madron) |
| PK 11.5 | **Ramonville** marina r/b, with dry dock, 05 61 75 07 64, 90 berths, night €15, water and electricity included (or services only, €5), shower €2, pump-out, diesel |

A full service *port de plaisance*, including fuel. The port is managed by the municipality of Ramonville, which has recently rehabilitated and enhanced facilities.

| | |
|---|---|
| PK 11.4 | Footbridge (Ramonville) |
| PK 10.6 | Canal basin r/b (*port technique*), 05 62 88 32 89, including dry dock for 38.50m péniches, craneage by contractor to order, repairs |

A large maintenance and repair yard, including a *péniche*-size dry dock.

| | |
|---|---|
| PK 10.5 | Road bridge (avenue de Latécoère) |
| PK 9.1 | Bridge (pont Giordano Bruno, university campus) |

Aérospatial space research centre. Science areas. University of Toulouse.

| | |
|---|---|
| PK 8.6 | Footbridge |
| PK 8.1 | Aqueduct (Herbettes, Toulouse ring road A620) |

*Les Herbettes aqueduct over the Toulouse ring road*

| | |
|---|---|
| PK 7.1 | Footbridge |
| PK 6.4 | Bridge (Demoiselles) |
| PK 6.1 | Basin l/b (Basin de Radoub) |
| PK 6.0 | Railway bridge |

# Canal du Midi

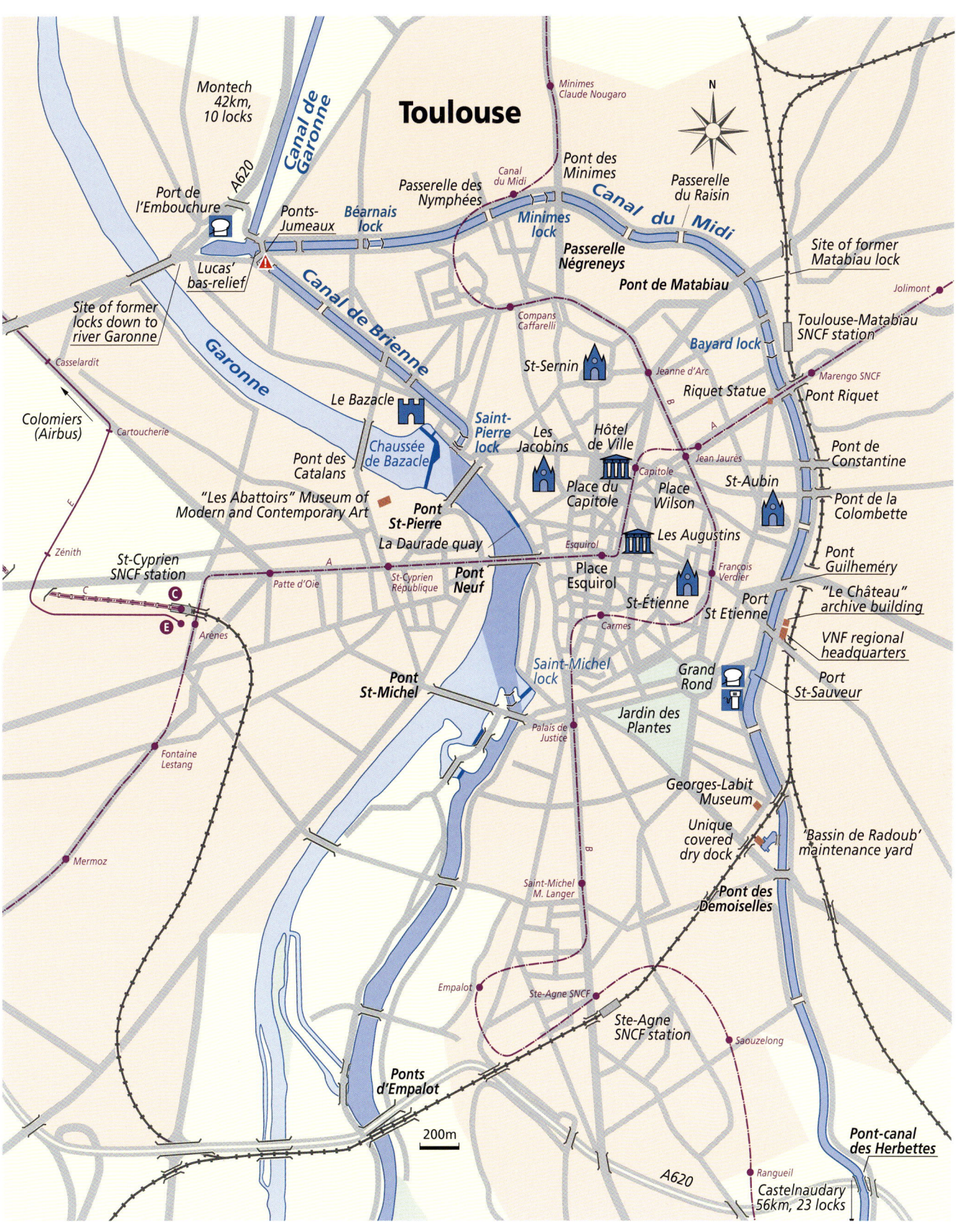

PK 5.6 Footbridge (Soupirs)

PK 5.2 **Toulouse** *port de plaisance* (Port Saint-Sauveur), moorings 800m from city centre, 05 61 22 22 17, *port-saintsauveur@mairie-toulouse.fr*, 40 berths (in practice less, since the catways are not optimised), night €13.80, water, electricity, wifi, showers, slipway, diesel, pump-out

Such a great place to stay, it is tempting to winter here. The harbour is run by friendly municipal staff. Excellent, spotless services and complete security. The port is very popular; phone or email ahead to book. Toulouse is one of France's biggest cities; there's a great deal to see and do, good shops and all facilities, including the Jardin des Plantes just by the *port de plaisance*. The shaded towpath south from the port is very pleasant but beware of the cyclists, some of whom pass at breakneck speed.

# VI – Southern France ('Midi')

*The Port Saint-Sauveur in Toulouse during a boat rally organised as part of the World Canals Conference in September 2013; the* capitainerie *is the curved roof building on the right.*
© SYLVAIN BLANCHARD

| | | |
|---|---|---|
| PK 5.1 | Bridge (Saint-Sauveur or Montaudran) |
| PK 5.0 | Basin (Port Saint-Étienne) |
| PK 4.9 | Bridge (Guilheméry) |
| PK 4.4 | Bridge (Colombette) |
| PK 4.2 | Bridge (Constantine) |
| PK 4.2 | Footbridge |
| PK 3.9 | Bridge (Riquet) |
| PK 3.6 | Deep lock (Bayard), bridge, SNCF Toulouse station r/b |

Notes on the three locks in Toulouse: Bayard (more than 6m) and Minimes (more than 4m) have been converted from double locks and are deep. They have poles (near the ends) to which bow and stern lines need to be attached. All three are automated but there will normally also be a lock-keeper at Béarnais, the nearest to PK 0. Coming up from the port de l'Embouchure (junction with the Canal de Garonne) it may be necessary to tie up at wooden pontoon downstream of Béarnais lock and go to report to the lock-keeper. Coming from the other direction, Bayard is operated via a suspended pole or *perche*.

| | |
|---|---|
| PK 3.3 | Bridge (Matabiau), narrow passage (former lock) |
| PK 3.0 | Footbridge (Raisin) |
| PK 2.6 | Footbridge (Négreneys) |
| PK 2.1 | Bridge (Minimes) |
| PK 2.0 | Deep lock (Minimes) |
| PK 1.5 | Footbridge (Nymphée) |
| PK 1.1 | Lock (Béarnais), bridge |
| PK 0.4 | Bridge |
| PK 0.3 | Bridge (Ponts Jumeaux) |

PK 0.2 **Junction with Canal de Garonne and Canal de Brienne**

The Canal de Brienne gives access to the river Garonne in Toulouse, but is accessible only to passenger boats.

PK 0.0 Toulouse basin (Port de l'Embouchure), former locks down to Garonne filled in for ring road, moorings, water

Cruise into the terminal basin and turn round to appreciate the unique view of the 'twin bridges'. There are now three, but the name stuck. Through the right-hand bridge is the short Canal de Brienne which takes water from the Garonne behind the Bazacle weir. The middle bridge is the one you have just come through. The left-hand bridge is on the connecting Canal de Garonne (see South West France). The inspired white marble bas-relief is between the first two: the Mediterranean and the Atlantic personnified together with canal building cherubs busy with picks and shovels. The turn between the two canals is quite tight; you might want to go further into the basin and take a wider approach. There are quayside moorings here, but it is bounded by busy roads.

# 57. River Hérault

THE RIVER HÉRAULT IS NAVIGABLE over a distance of 12km from Bessan to the Mediterranean at Le Grau d'Agde. It is a river navigation over a distance of 7km upstream of Agde, the last part of this course being used by the Canal du Midi. Below the weir at Agde the Hérault is a maritime waterway. The weir is bypassed by a short length of the Canal du Midi, the round lock at Agde and the branch to the Hérault maritime.

*A Mediterranean river with a steep gradient, the Hérault was never a carrier of trade. It was exploited from the Middle Ages for milling, and its history as a navigation is entirely related to the Canal du Midi, which created this navigable length.*

## Navigation

The river Hérault is split into two very different waterways by the weir in Agde, necessarily bypassed by the Canal du Midi and its Hérault branch. From Agde to the sea is a maritime channel, like many of the others along the Mediterranean coast, lined with fishing, sailing and all kinds of boats for working on or enjoying the *Grand Bleu*. Above the Canal du Midi junction at the Prades flood lock, it becomes another of those streams (like the Petit-Rhône or the Lez) with an Amazonian feel to it, with no channel markings and care required in case of hidden branches or other obstacles.

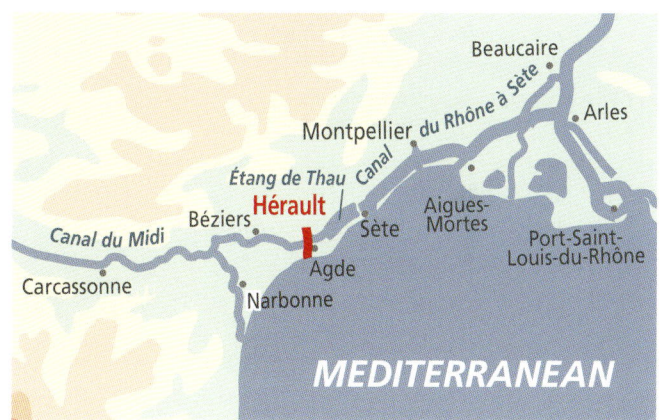

## Locks

None. Agde weir is bypassed by the round lock (see plan).

## Draught

There is a substantial depth in the river, normally 2.90m, but this is reduced to 1.50m in the Canal du Midi and its branch to the Hérault maritime.

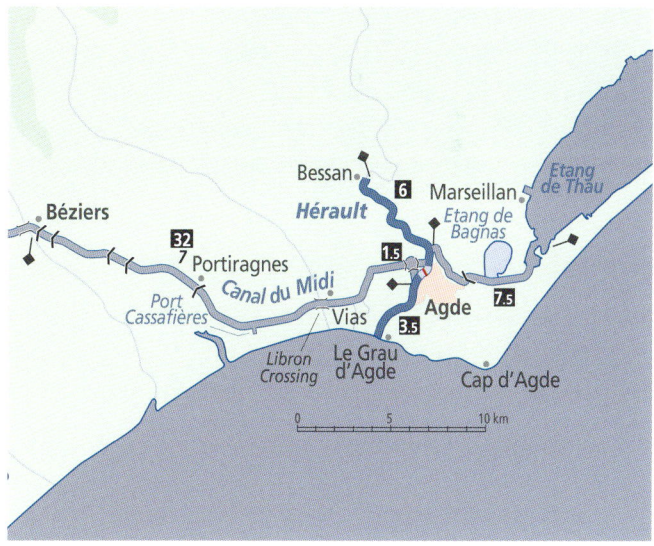

*The spur canal, looking southwest towards the river from the round lock on the Canal du Midi. A large trip boat uses the lock and the canal, and should be given as much room as possible. The boat here is waiting for the lock to open, which it does at set times.* © F-W

*Looking south-west towards the sea from the town bridge. There are moorings along the river on both sides but most are occupied or private.* © F-W

# VI – Southern France ('Midi')

## Headroom
The bridges give a minimum headroom of 5.70m above normal water level. The railway bridge over the branch of the Canal du Midi has a headroom of 4.20m.

## Authority
VNF Sud-Ouest,
– Pont Rouge, Avenue du Prado, 34500 Béziers 04 67 11 81 30

## Route description

Bessan has pontoon moorings and café, and a Roman bridge nearby. Hotel barges occasionally reach Bessan and turn round here.

| | |
|---|---|
| PK 0.0 | **Bessan** bridge, head of navigation, municipal *halte* at restaurant 'La Guinguette' r/b, pontoon for 3 boats, free, water, electricity, slipway, village 700m r/b |
| PK 0.7 | Private quay r/b |
| PK 5.6 | Backwater l/b, not navigable |
| PK 6.0 | Junction with Canal du Midi (towards Les Onglous and Sète), l/b |
| PK 6.8 | Turn into Canal du Midi (towards Béziers and Toulouse), r/b, to bypass the weir on the river |
| PK 7.2 | Round lock at Agde |

To return to the Hérault, turn in the lock to exit through the south-facing gates into the Hérault Maritime branch of the Canal du Midi (see plan).

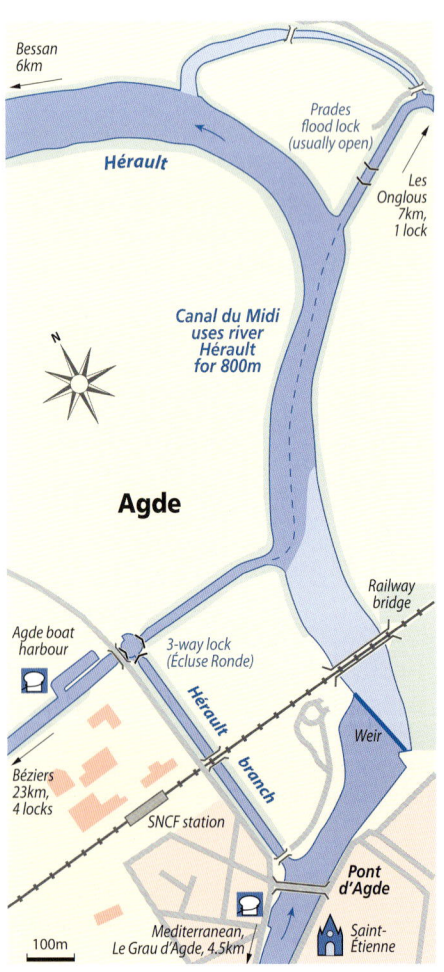

| | |
|---|---|
| PK 7.5 | Railway bridge |
| PK 7.7 | Hérault maritime branch of the Canal du Midi rejoins the Hérault, footbridge |
| PK 7.8 | **Agde** bridge, quay and town centre d/s l/b |

Historic town founded by the Greeks, it was an archbishopry from the 5th century. The striking fortified cathedral of Saint-Étienne dates from the 12th century. The town lives and breathes by the river Hérault, with countless boats, small and large, lining the quays on both banks, making a colourful scene.

| | |
|---|---|
| PK 9.6 | New road bridge (D612, Agde bypass), air draught 12m |
| PK 11.5 | Boatyard Constructions Navales J. Allemand l/b, 04 67 94 24 19 |

One of the best-known boatyards in the Midi. The yard builds boats, undertakes repairs and maintenance, has a travel-lift big enough for small *péniches* (cost approximately €370 each way for a 24m barge) and a large hardstanding area. The yard steps and unsteps masts (cost €32 per quarter hour), and has a well-stocked chandlery 'La Boutique Marine'. Its reputation is such that they are always busy and booking ahead is advisable.
**chantier-allemand.com**

*The Allemand boatyard* © F-W

| | |
|---|---|
| PK 12.4 | **Le Grau d'Agde**, river reaches the Mediterranean |

Agde's coastal harbour is an excellent place to enter or leave the waterway system. Good facilities. The harbour entrance itself is a short sea voyage from one of Europe's biggest marina complexes, Cap d'Agde, where many marine services are available. Many boaters prefer to use the river boatyard, but it is also possible to step and unstep masts at Cap d'Agde and – providing conditions are reasonably calm and the mast secured – make the short voyage to and from Grau d'Agde with the mast down.

# 58. Canal de la Robine (La Nouvelle branch)

This important waterway is officially a branch of the Canal du Midi, the La Nouvelle branch. The popular name is misleading, however, because it refers only to the third of three sections of this waterway. The first section leaving the the main canal at Cesse, north of Sallèles-d'Aude (PK168) is the Canal de Jonction, 5km long, leading down to the river Aude. The second section is a short length (600m) of the river Aude. The Canal de la Robine (32km long) is a diversion canal, taking some of the flow of the river Aude and cutting across the coastal plain to serve Narbonne, and on to the Mediterranean at Port-la-Nouvelle. The entire 'branch' was upgraded to the 250-tonne barge standard in the 1980s, in an attempt to maintain the competitiveness of water transport, especially for wine unloaded at Port-la-Nouvelle or produced in the region. However, this policy was ill-founded, and commercial transport disappeared on this 37km waterway, as on the Canal du Midi throughout.

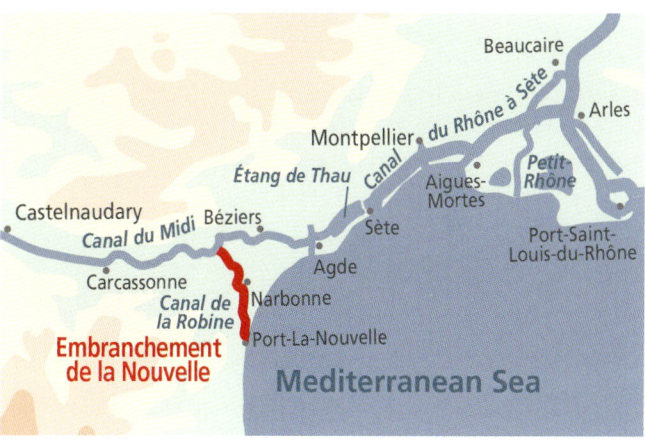

*The earliest part of this canal was prefigured by the ship channel built under the Roman governor Agrippa across the Sigean lagoon which was then the outflow of the river Aude. After the Aude changed its course, bypassing Narbonne to the north, a feeder canal ('La Robine') was built to bring drinking water to Narbonne. After the Canal du Midi opened in 1681, this feeder was enlarged for navigation, but it was not until 1787 that the missing link, the 'Canal de Jonction', was opened. This followed pressure from the Archbishop of Narbonne on Pierre-Paul Riquet's successors to add the link to the Canal du Midi, thereby increasing its traffic, but also its water consumption, hence the additional reservoir, the Lampy, in the Montagne Noire.*

## Navigation

Conditions are similar to those on the Canal du Midi itself, but are varied throughout the 37km by the nature of the terrain and the canal's unusual configuration. The Aude crossing may be tricky if the river is in flood, and care is required negotiating the tight twisting channel in Narbonne above and below the lock. Wind may be a problem in the section passing through the lagoons south of Narbonne, and the outflow from Sigean lagoon can cause a treacherous current in the right-angle bend in Port-la-Nouvelle. Speed limit is 8km/h, and 3 km/h when passing moored boats.

## Locks

There are seven closely-spaced locks on the Canal de Jonction and six locks on the Robine, all oval-shaped. Their dimensions are 40.50m by 5.85m. That at Sallèles-d'Aude is the deepest (replacing a former two-lock staircase) and trickiest (ascending). All the locks are automated. Crew will generally need to go on ahead to press the appropriate buttons on the lock-side control panel. The traditional hour-long break from 12:30 to 13:30 does not apply here.

## Draught

The maximum authorised draught of 1.80m, supposed to be provided when the locks were lengthened, has in fact never been available, and the target draught today is 1.60m. Thanks to the dredging works undertaken in recent years, the maximum effective draught should now be 1.50m. In periods of exceptional drought, this depth may not be available on the crossing of the river Aude.

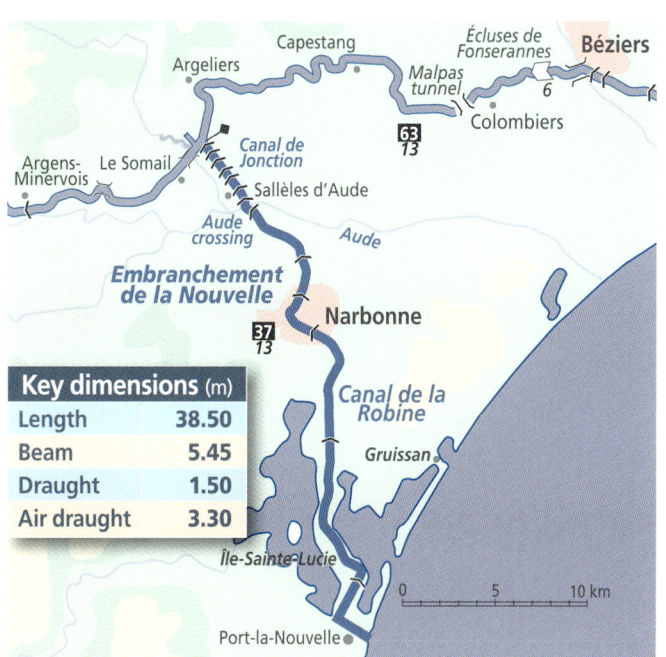

| Key dimensions (m) | |
|---|---|
| Length | 38.50 |
| Beam | 5.45 |
| Draught | 1.50 |
| Air draught | 3.30 |

# VI – Southern France ('Midi')

## Headroom
The fixed bridges leave a minimum headroom of 3.30m. The two lowest bridges are downstream of Gailhousty lock and the Pont des Marchands covered bridge in Narbonne. There is a retracting footbridge across Sainte-Lucie lock.

## Towpath
There is a towpath throughout, except for the crossing of the river Aude. The only practical solution here for walkers is to scramble up to the railway viaduct (see plan). This is no doubt illegal, and we cannot accept any responsibility, but it is a tourist railway (Autorail Touristique du Minervois) and sees very few trains, none at all on weekdays.

## Route description

**PK 0.0** Junction with Canal du Midi at PK 168.7

Lock and footbridge at the junction with the Canal du Midi. See under Canal du Midi for moorings and services.

**PK 0.1** Footbridge (Cesse), quay d/s r/b
**PK 0.3** Lock (Cesse)
**PK 1.0** Lock (Truilhas), bridge
**PK 1.6** Lock (Empare)
**PK 2.3** Lock (Argeliers), bridge
**PK 3.0** Lock (Saint-Cyr)
**PK 3.4** **Sallèles-d'Aude** footbridge, quays d/s, village r/b

Pretty village with quayside moorings (04 68 46 92 09) and a range of facilities. There is also the European patchwork centre and Amphoralis, a museum of ancient pottery that holds regular firings in the traditional manner.

**PK 3.7** Deep lock (Sallèles), pizzeria r/b

The lock is deep and tricky, coming up (poles at the extreme ends).

**PK 3.8** Bridge (Sallèles)

*Gailhousty Lock and dry dock*

**PK 4.9** Lock (Gailhousty), bridge, dry dock managed by VNF, 04 68 46 92 09, €15/day plus €180 to drain the dock, €25/day after 15 days.

A beautiful lock and building group, classified as being of historic and architectural importance and built in 1780 not only as a lock, lock-keeper's house and administrative offices, but also as a spillway and sluice in connection with the Étang de Capestang, although the works were not completed before the Revolution forced a halt. To one side is a dry dock, which is popular and booked many months ahead.

*Looking upstream from Moussoulens lock; the entrance to the Canal de Jonction is beyond the railway viaduct to the right.* © F-W

*Looking downstream from the railway viaduct to the entrance to Moussoullens lock (right); keep clear of the weir, left.* © CODINA RAMON

**PK 5.1** End of junction canal, navigation enters river Aude

It is important not to cut the corner to or from the canal entrance, as there are shallows.

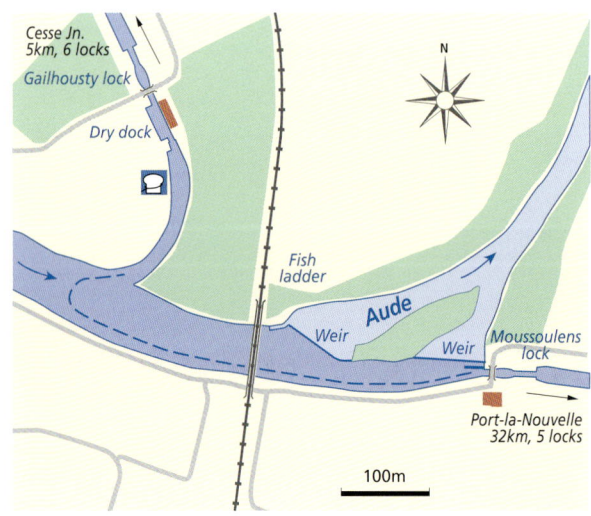

## La Robine (La Nouvelle branch)

| | | |
|---|---|---|
| PK **5.4** | Railway bridge | |
| PK **5.7** | End of Aude crossing, navigation enters Canal de la Robine r/b | |
| PK **5.8** | Lock (Moussoulens), bridge | |
| PK **6.4** | Bridge (Pont Vieux, Moussoulens) | |
| PK **9.8** | Lock (Raonel), bridge, **Cuxac d'Aude** 1800m l/b | |
| PK **13.0** | Bridge (D6009, Narbonne bypass) | |
| PK **14.2** | Lock (Gua), footbridge, quay d/s r/b | |

Below the lock there is a long stretch of (quiet and safe) quayside moorings with water and electricity. Hire boat base. Although slightly out of town (5-10 minute walk), this is a more comfortable location than along the busy town quays 1.5km further on.

| | | |
|---|---|---|
| PK **14.6** | Footbridge, quay d/s l/b | |
| PK **14.9** | Footbridge, quay d/s r/b | |
| PK **15.1** | Railway bridge | |
| PK **15.1** | Bridge (Escoute) | |
| PK **15.2** | Bridge (Carmes) | |
| PK **15.2** | Bridge (Voltaire) | |
| PK **15.3** | Lock (Narbonne), footbridge and weir | |

From this lock quaintly squeezed into the town centre the canal passes under a unique bridge (*Pont des Marchands*) with buildings on top – the arch looks smaller than it actually is (3.30m air draught).

| | | |
|---|---|---|
| PK **15.5** | Bridge (Marchands), with shops on top | |
| PK **15.6** | Footbridge, Le Boat hire base l/b | |
| PK **15.7** | **Narbonne** *port de plaisance* managed by Chamber of Commerce on quays both banks in town centre, 04 68 90 30 20 or 06 11 71 27 19, 20 visitor moorings on Quai des Barques, €15.80, water, electricity, showers, wifi (1 hour) | |

Narbonne has an ancient history and was an important seaport until silting effectively pushed the coastline ever further away. It has long had river and/or canal access to the sea, since the 17thC this has meant the Canal de la Robine (the canal's Roman name). It is a very pleasant and significant town, with all facilities including a main-line railway station. The author recommends a visit to the Archbishop's palace and its tower. It is consequently a popular place for *plaisanciers* to visit and stay at, especially over the winter; temperatures remain warm although the occasional strong winds can be less pleasant.

| | | |
|---|---|---|
| PK **15.8** | Bridge (pont de la Liberté) | |
| PK **16.1** | Footbridge | |
| PK **16.4** | Bridge (pont de l'Avenir) | |
| PK **17.7** | Motorway bridge (A9, Languedocienne) | |
| PK **24.1** | Lock (Mandirac), bridge, quay d/s r/b | |
| PK **25.4** | Quay (Gruissan) r/b | |
| PK **34.3** | Lock (Sainte-Lucie), moving bridge, quay d/s l/b | |
| PK **36.9** | Railway bridge and pipeline crossing | |
| PK **37.3** | **Port-la-Nouvelle**, bridge (D6139), canal enters harbour basins, 04 68 27 06 09 or 06 45 34 30 79, VHF 9, capacity 290 boats, 18 visitor moorings, night €22, fuel, water, showers, pump-out. Mediterranean 2.5 km down entrance channel, town r/b *pln.plaisance@aude.cci.fr* | |

*Looking from Narbonne lock towards the Pont des Marchands. The bypass comes in from the left, and the guide on the right is useful when approaching from downstream.*

*Early morning light on the calm waters of La Robine, the Pont des Marchands and Narbonne cathedral.*

### Entering the canals from the Mediterranean

Port-la-Nouvelle is the most south-westerly of the possible exit points from the waterways into the Mediterranean (or vice versa), the closest to the Spanish border. Its use is restricted by the depths both of the canals; the officially available depth is 1.50m, obtained by an extensive campaign of dredging. An un-masting/re-masting service is available from the chandlery/mechanic along the southern quayside.

*The stunning landscape of the coastal lagoons skirted by the canal north of Sainte-Lucie island and nature reserve.*

# CHAPTER VII – SOUTHWEST FRANCE

## From Toulouse to the Atlantic

The southwest is a favourite destination in France, not only for navigators but for the countless expatriates, many of them British, who have chosen to live there. There is amazing diversity both on the waterways and among the various sub-regions within what the French often refer to as the *Grand Sud-Ouest*. Toulouse, at the end of the Canal du Midi, is the gateway to the Garonne and its navigable tributaries.

The first section of the Canal de Garonne north from Toulouse is often described as uninspiring, and it is true that the feeling of being in the outer suburbs of a modern metropolis lingers for a few hours as one drops through the first few locks, but the canal and its many *haltes* and other mooring places are consistently charming, in a way that is less ostentatious and more genuine than along the Canal du Midi.

The cruising experience in this region will typically be an alternation of canal sequences, enjoying the qualities of the finely-engineered Canal de Garonne with its splendid aqueducts and good hard quaysides in most towns and villages, and navigation in navigable rivers. The first to be encountered is the river Tarn upstream of Montauban. This is reached through the Canal de Montech (a branch of the main canal). The Tarn is also accessible for a short length in Moissac, behind the dam at Golfech. Continuing west, after Agen, come the twin *pièces de résistance* of this region: the river Baïse leading south from Buzet-sur-Baïse, and the River Lot, heading east towards the Massif Central. The author has spent many years in the region and will continue to promote the extraordinary River Lot. Christian Bernad, president of the *Association pour l'Aménagement de la Vallée du Lot* was right to initiate restoration of this 270km long waterway back in 1973, but development is seriously hampered by the restricted conditions of access to the river via the Garonne crossing. This will have to be addressed in the near future, to ensure that the huge investments – not only restoration but the construction of new deep locks or travel-lift solutions to bypass the hydropower dams – bring the projected return in tourist income.

At Castets-en-Dorthe, the *plaisancier* locks out into the tidal river Garonne, and a series of different experiences beckons, playing the tides on the rivers Garonne, Dordogne and Isle, and eventually in the Gironde estuary.

The tidal river Adour and its tributaries are an isolated but delightful and little-used cruising waterway in the heart of the Basque region in the far southwest.

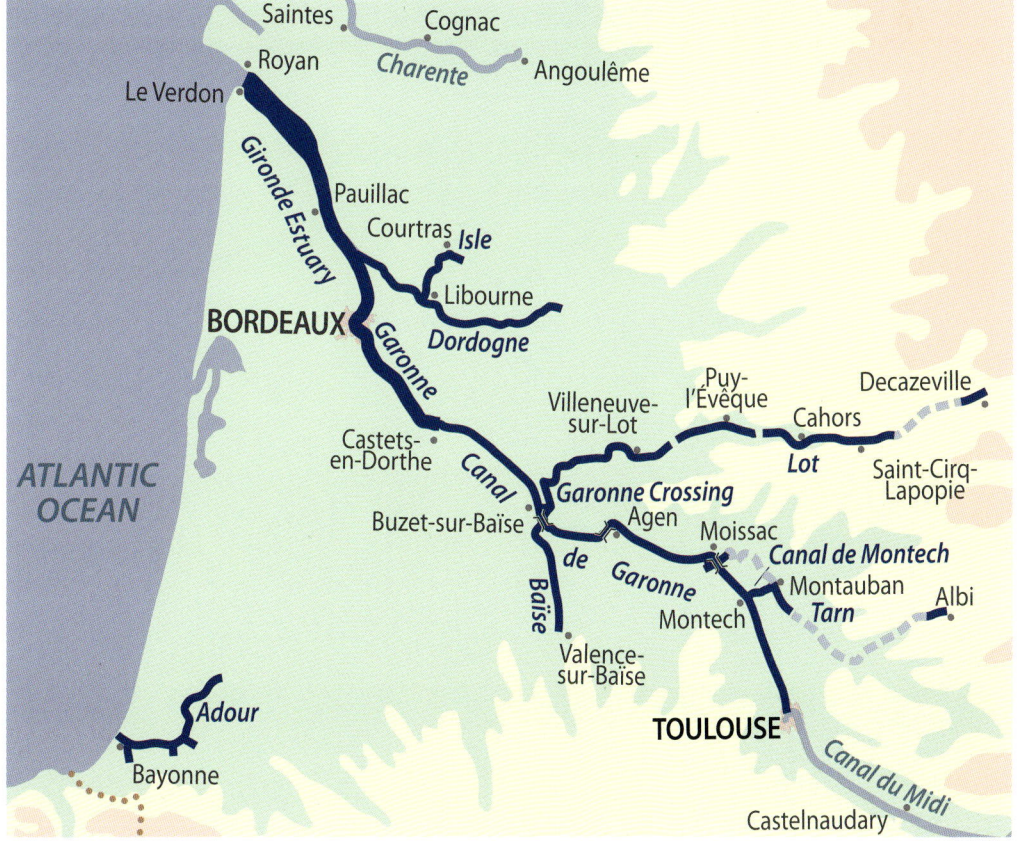

*Lustrac lock delightfully hemmed in between a château and a mill on the River Lot, PK 68*

## VII – Southwest France

# 59. Canal de Garonne

THE CANAL DE GARONNE WAS OPENED in 1856 to bypass the unpredictable river Garonne over a distance of 194km from Toulouse, where it connects with the Canal du Midi, to Castets-en-Dorthe, where it falls into the tidal river. It thus forms an important link in the 600km route across southern France from the Atlantic to the Mediterranean, as well as becoming a cruising waterway in its own right, connected to the rivers Lot and Baïse at Buzet-sur-Baïse.

There are four branches off the main canal. The **Canal de Brienne** is 1.6km in length from the Port de l'Embouchure to the Garonne upstream of the Bazacle diversion weir in Toulouse. This branch serves for the canal's water supply, and is regularly used by trip boats, but the lock giving access to the Garonne is not operated for pleasure craft. There is no basin below this lock. The second, 11km in length, is the **Canal de Montech**, which leads to Montauban and the **River Tarn** (see following entry, p. 339). The other branches are via double staircase locks from the through route down to the River Tarn at Moissac and to the River Baïse at Buzet-sur-Baïse, called respectively the **Descente en Tarn** and the **Descente en Baïse**.

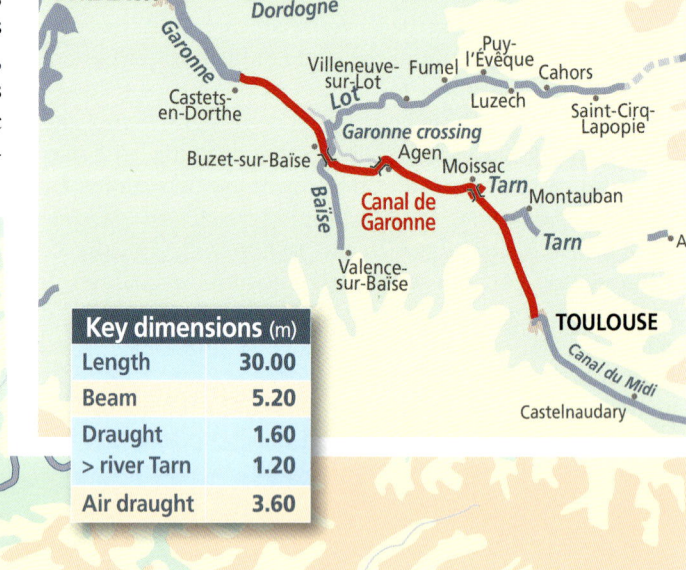

| Key dimensions (m) | |
|---|---|
| Length | 30.00 |
| Beam | 5.20 |
| Draught | 1.60 |
| > river Tarn | 1.20 |
| Air draught | 3.60 |

The canal was first envisaged by Vauban in the late 17th century as a 'logical' extension of Riquet's Canal du Midi, to bypass the unpredictable river Garonne. It was authorised by the Finance Act of July 1838, which budgeted 86 million francs for the works. It opened in 1856. It was lengthened to 'Freycinet' dimensions in 1968-1974, but without increasing the available draught. This encouraged a handful of operators to set up on the canal with 38m barges, but the decline in traffic had already set in, and the canal is now almost exclusively used for tourism.

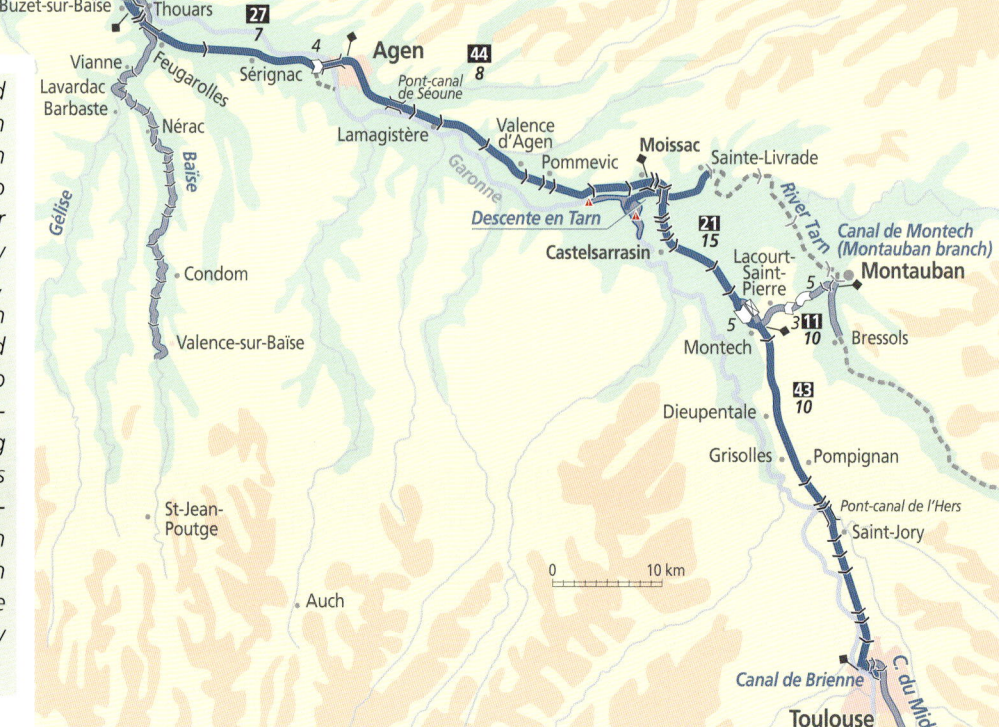

# Canal de Garonne

The canal has some impressive structures, notably the aqueducts over the Tarn near Moissac and over the Garonne at Agen. In 1974, the world's first water slope was built to bypass the flight of five locks at Montech, but has now been abandoned, its traction unit pulled half way up the slope to serve as a tourist attraction.

Unlike the Canal du Midi, built nearly two centuries earlier, the Canal de Garonne is an example of rational 19th Century civil engineering. There are many straight sections that some find uninspiring. The canal is a favourite for its unpretentious quietness, the predominately pretty countryside – soft fruit, maize and sunflowers, and to the west the remnants of the once extensive Gitanes/Gauloise tobacco area – and the similarly pretty and historic towns and villages. This was once English Aquitaine, fought over during the Hundred Years War. There are many places to stop; at *haltes* and ports and simply by tying up to the bank wherever the mood dictates. Where once there was significant commercial traffic, mainly grain and petroleum products, today there is none, although there are initiatives to revive freight traffic in niche markets.

## Navigation
The official values given for draught and air draught may vary according to conditions. The canal is reliably supplied with water. As on most other waterways, the given depth is the middle of the channel; the sides may be noticeably less deep and this may affect coming alongside, especially for boats with twin bilge keels or twin propellers. Another phenomenon specific to this canal is that on the downstream side of a lock the outflow from the bypass channel scours a depression immediately outside the gate but then deposits that silt a short way beyond, creating a bar. Also immediately outside the downstream gates this outflow enters the canal with some force. The boat will be pushed one way on the bow and then the other on the stern.

The canal is currently subject to increasing amounts of long strand weed, particularly at its western extremity. These are predominantly invasive species that originated in fish tanks and other introduced ornamental examples that have literally gone wild.

The canal carries virtually no commercial traffic. It does, however, have a number of converted *péniche* hotel-barges.

The speed limit is 8km/h, 3km/h past moored boats.

## Locks
There are 53 locks, falling towards Castets-en-Dorthe, overcoming a difference in level of 128m. The five locks at Montech were bypassed by the water slope, 6m wide and designed for 38.50m barges, but as mentioned above this structure is no longer in use. All the other 48 locks on the through route were enlarged in the 1970s to allow navigation by barges loading 240 tonnes, and their navigable dimensions are 38.50m by 5.80m. The locks on all the branches, and the five at Montech, are of restricted length (30.65m by 5.80m).

Most of the locks are equipped for automatic operation and controlled by lights. There is usually a vertical pole suspended above the water some distance before the lock, level with a first set of lights. The pole is turned to start the sequence. In season, the manned locks are open from 09:00 to 12:30 and from 13:30 to 19:30.

## Draught
The maximum authorised draught is 1.60m.

## Headroom
All the fixed bridges leave a minimum headroom of 3.60m above normal water level.

## Towpath
The towpath has been significantly improved in recent years, and may now be walked or cycled throughout.

## Authority
VNF Sud-Ouest
– Subdivision de Haute-Garonne: 115 bis, rue des Amidonniers, 31000 Toulouse
  05 62 15 11 91   *subdi.hautegaronne@vnf.fr*   (PK 0-24)
– Subdivision de Tarn-et-Garonne: Delbessous-Sud, 82200 Moissac
  05 63 04 02 41   *subdi.tarnetgaronne@vnf.fr*   (PK 24-90)
– Subdivision d'Aquitaine: 107 avenue Général de Gaulle, 47000 Agen
  05 53 47 31 15   *subdi.aquitaine@vnf.fr*   (PK 90-194)

## Route description

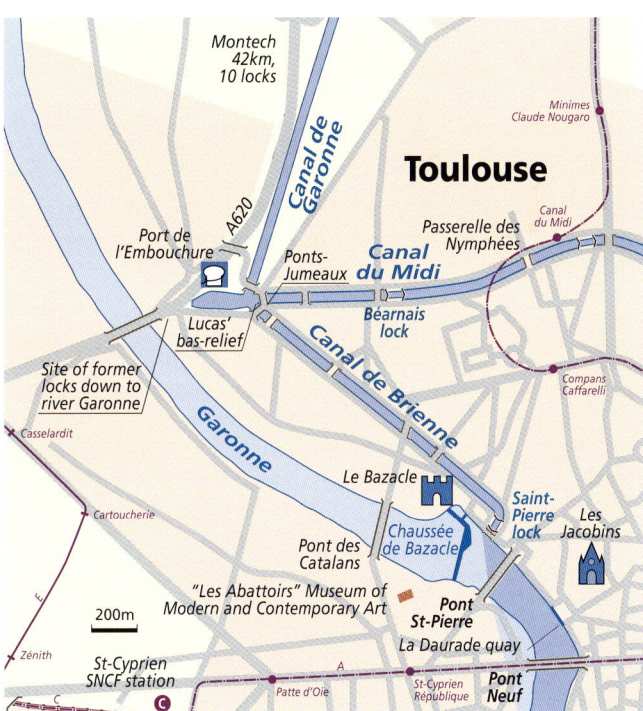

| PK **0.0** | **Toulouse**, junction with the Canal du Midi at port de l'Embouchure, and junction with the Canal de Brienne, bridge |
| PK **0.2** | Former oil terminal, quay r/b, residential barge moorings |
| PK **1.1** | Pedestrian swing bridge for access to rugby stadium, normally open (moored to l/b) |
| PK **1.4** | Road bridge (avenue d'Elche) |
| PK **2.5** | Bridge (Ginestous) |

# VII – Southwest France

*The bas-relief created by sculptor Lucas at the Ponts-Jumeaux*
© JACQUES MORAND, FROM UNESCO SUBMISSION DOCUMENT

*Bordeneuve Lock and lock-keeper's house*

Three bridges – not two, as the name of this Toulouse quarter suggests – compose an impressive stage at the northeast end of the terminal Bassin de l'Embouchure. The Canal du Midi emerges royally through the middle bridge. To the right is the short Canal de Brienne leading to the Garonne (and taking its water). Between these two bridges is the superb white marble bas-relief: the Mediterranean and the Atlantic personified together with canal building cherubs busy with picks and shovels. The bridge to the left is the entrance to the Canal de Garonne. The turn between the two canals is very tight, and it is advisable to proceed into the basin to wind round and take a better angled approach. There are quayside moorings here, but it is bounded by busy roads.

This stretch up to PK 4 is relatively unattractive, with the A62 autoroute on one side and commerce on the other. The giant Toulouse Rugby Stadium on the left has its own floating footbridge at PK 1 which cuts across the canal on match days to allow fans to access and leave the stadium. At PK 4 is a watersports school – watch out for children having fun in canoes and dinghies!

| | |
|---|---|
| PK **2.6** | Footbridge (Béziat) |
| PK **3.5** | Basin |
| PK **3.9** | Lock 1 (Lalande), bridge, basin u/s |
| PK **4.1** | Bridge (motorway spur) |
| PK **4.5** | Motorway bridge (A620, Toulouse ring road) |

PK 4- PK 11 - The canal increases in attractiveness although the railway line is hard by on the eastern side; there are large marshalling yards and a giant storage area.

| | |
|---|---|
| PK **5.1** | Bridge (Ruppé) |
| PK **6.5** | Lock 2 (Lacourtensourt), bridge |
| PK **7.6** | Lock 3 (Fenouillet), bridge |
| PK **8.5** | Bridge |
| PK **8.6** | Bridge (Latournelle) |
| PK **11.4** | Lock 4 (Lespinasse), bridge |

The canal gradually becomes more rural, more leafy.

| | |
|---|---|
| PK **11.6** | Bridge (D63) |
| PK **13.3** | Lock 5 (Bordeneuve) |
| PK **15.2** | Lock 6 (**Saint-Jory**), bridge, village 200m r/b |
| PK **18.3** | Bridge (Pont de l'Hers) |

Just before the lock, the canal crosses the River Hers in a double bend; pretty lock cottage.

| | |
|---|---|
| PK **18.4** | Hers aqueduct |
| PK **18.5** | Lock 7 (Hers) |
| PK **19.4** | Lock 8 (**Castelnau**), bridge, village 1 km r/b |
| PK **21.1** | Bridge (Bordeneuve) |
| PK **22.5** | Lock 9 (Embalens), bridge |
| PK **23.7** | Bridge (Saint-Rustice) |
| PK **24.9** | **Pompignan** bridge, small village r/b over railway |
| PK **25.9** | Bridge (Grisolles) |
| PK **26.7** | **Grisolles** bridge (Laroque), municipal *halte* u/s l/b, mooring for 10 boats, free, water, village 500m l/b |
| PK **27.6** | Bridge (D813) |
| PK **28.0** | Bridge (Saint-Jean) |
| PK **29.4** | Bridge (Villelongue) |
| PK **31.1** | **Dieupentale** bridge, quay d/s l/b, village 500m l/b |

Possible bankside mooring on the east bank, but the railway line is very close… then the canal becomes considerably more rural, passing through the Forest of Montech, offering possible bankside moorings, while the railway line moves away to the east, heading for Montauban.

| | |
|---|---|
| PK **33.4** | Bridge (Bessens) |
| PK **34.4** | Bridge (Lapeyrière) |
| PK **35.4** | Bridge (Montbéqui) |
| PK **36.6** | Bridge (Montbartier) |
| PK **38.2** | Bridge (Le Tourret) |
| PK **39.3** | Bridge (Forêt), Montech forest r/b |
| PK **41.0** | Lock 10 (Lavache), bridge |
| PK **42.7** | **Montech** bridge, basin and municipal *port de plaisance* d/s l/b, capacity 28 boats, 05 63 64 16 32 (tourist office), night €3, water €4.10 (1000 litres), electricity €1.70 (10 kWh), *capitainerie* with showers, restaurant, village 500m |

*Port de Plaisance* with *capitainerie* on the west (town) side. There are additional quayside moorings a little further on, close by the lock, but watch for depth and obstructions. Possible wintering location. A small market town with lots of facilities and the imposing brick church of Notre Dame de la Visitation (completed early 16th century). The main supermarket is a short distance east across the bridge, on the other side of the canal.

# Canal de Garonne

*The port de plaisance at Montech* © F-W

See the separate description of the charming branch canal down to Montauban and the navigable river Tarn. The adjacent water slope has been closed for many years, and has now been revamped in gaudy colours as a static visitor attraction, with the barge *Altair* positioned above the shield.

*The Montech pente d'eau before it had to be closed* © PHIL'OURS

PK 43.0 **Junction with the Canal de Montech (Montauban branch)**, r/b, and with the water slope entrance

PK 43.1 Lock 11 (Montech), entrance to branch serving former paper mills d/s l/b, quay, slipway

This extraordinary site, an improbable location for a former paper mill (closed in 1968) has seen modest development as a complementary mooring for Montech, along with a slipway.

*The entrance to the 'paper mill' branch (right)* © F-W

PK 43.8 Lock 12 (Peyrets), bridge, level with upstream end of water slope
PK 44.2 Lock 13 (Pellaborie), level with bottom of water slope
PK 44.6 Lock 14 (Escudiés)
PK 45.3 Lock 15 (Pommiès), bridge
PK 45.4 Junction with water slope downstream approach canal, r/b
PK 47.0 Bridge (Escatalens)
PK 47.4 **Escatalens** *halte* l/b, 20 boats, water, electricity

Excellent new *halte* in a delightful setting upstream of the lock.

PK 47.5 Lock 16 (Escatalens), bridge
PK 49.2 **Saint-Porquier** bridge, village 600m l/b

Grassy banks to moor to all along the north-west side, between PK 48 and PK 52. Here the village has provided a good timber pontoon adjacent to pleasant gardens.

PK 49.8 Bridge (Lavilledieu)
PK 50.6 Bridge (Saint-André)
PK 51.9 Lock 17 (Saint-Martin), bridge
PK 52.6 Bridge (Danton)
PK 53.5 Railway bridge
PK 53.7 Bridge (Gaillau)
PK 55.4 Lock 18 (Prades)
PK 56.0 Bridge (Briqueterie)
PK 56.3 Footbridge
PK 56.4 **Castelsarrasin** basin, municipal *port de plaisance* Jacques-Yves-Cousteau, 05 63 32 01 39, capacity 67 boats, night €16 including water and electricity, fuel (possible delivery), showers €2, wifi at *capitainerie*, restaurant, town centre 200m l/b

Another attractive small French town with a full range of facilities, and a popular *port de plaisance*. Railway station with services to Toulouse and Bordeaux.

PK 56.6 Bridge (Castelsarrasin)
PK 56.8 Boatyard Chantier Fluvial de Castelsarrasin r/b, 06 23 25 80 36, maintenance, repairs, crane 25t

Popular boatyard providing craneage, welding and other metalwork services, and a large shed and hard standing for winter storage.

PK 57.5 Bridge (Gandalou)
PK 57.6 Lock 19 (Castelsarrasin)
PK 58.2 Motorway bridge (A62)
PK 58.6 Bridge (Saint-Jean-des-Vignes)
PK 59.0 Lock 20 (Saint-Jean-des-Vignes)
PK 59.1 Bridge
PK 59.4 Lock 21 (Verriès), bridge
PK 59.9 Lock 22 (Artel)
PK 60.5 Bridge (Caussade)
PK 62.2 Tarn aqueduct (length 356m)

Impressive brick-arched aqueduct over the River Tarn, next to the rebuilt railway bridge; the original was swept away in the terrible flood of 1930 that also caused destruction in both Moissac and Montauban.

PK 62.6 Lock 23 (Cacor)

57

## VII – Southwest France

| PK 63.2 | Lock 24 (Grégonne) |
| PK 63.8 | Lock 25 (Moissac) |
| PK 63.9 | **Junction with locks down to the Tarn (descente en Tarn)** |
| | l/b, Tarn navigable 7.5km upstream to Sainte-Livrade |

*Approaching the only moving bridge on the entire canal, the Pont Saint-Jacques in Moissac* © F-W

The double staircase lock down to the Tarn gives access to two pontoons on the river near the junction, while mooring is also possible along the town's river quay (water and electricity). From here one can cruise downstream onto the extensive lake at the confluence with the river Garonne and a short distance up the Garonne. This lake was formed by the dam for the Golfech nuclear power plant. There are significant shallows to avoid, but also safe channels and beautiful safe anchorages. Alternatively, the Tarn may be cruised up to the first disused lock at Sainte-Livrade. The idea of reopening the upstream route through to Montauban was supported by the author's study in 1993, but there is no political momentum for it at present.

*Cruising under the railway bridge and the Canal de Garonne aqueduct in Moissac* © F-W

| PK 64.1 | **Moissac** basin, *port de plaisance*, 05 63 04 09 89 or 06 01 23 28 02, capacity 40 boats, night €9.50, fuel, water, electricity, showers €2, pump-out, wifi, town centre 300m *ceppmoissac@orange.fr* |

The *port de plaisance* is a favourite. The town is very old, has a beautiful Romanesque abbey church and cloister, a lovely brick road bridge over the River Tarn (Napoleon had promised it to the town, but fate intervened before he could deliver it), large local market on Saturdays and Sunday mornings also famed for Chasselas dessert grapes; also an unremarked suburb of small villas rebuilt following the 1930 flood destruction in authentic Art Deco styles. The canal runs straight through the centre of the town.

| PK 64.2 | Bridge (Marronniers) |
| PK 64.4 | Swing bridge (Saint-Jacques) |

The bridge opens at the same times as the locks (hoot if necessary).

| PK 64.5 | Footbridge, quay d/s r/b |
| PK 64.6 | Bridge (Sainte-Catherine) |
| PK 65.0 | Bridge (Saint-Martin) |
| PK 67.4 | Lock 26 (Espagnette), bridge |
| PK 69.2 | Suspension bridge (Coudol) |
| PK 71.2 | Lock 27 (Petit-Bezy), bridge |
| PK 73.1 | New road bridge (D26b) |
| PK 73.6 | Bridge (**Malause**), municipal *halte* on pontoon for 7 boats, 05 63 39 55 78, night €5, water and electricity included, restaurant |
| PK 74.6 | Bridge (Palor) |
| PK 75.0 | Industrial quay, turning basin |
| PK 76.2 | Bridge (Capitaine) |
| PK 76.9 | Lock 28 (Braguel) |
| PK 77.6 | **Pommevic** bridge, municipal *halte* for 3 boats, 05 63 39 56 55, free (maximum 48 hours), water, electricity, village 400m r/b |
| PK 81.1 | Bridge |
| PK 78.5 | Lock 29 (Pommevic) |
| PK 79.1 | Bridge (Gauge) |
| PK 80.3 | Lock 30 (Valence d'Agen) |
| PK 81.0 | Bridge (Auvillar) |
| PK 81.1 | Bridge (D953) |
| PK 81.5 | **Valence d'Agen** bridge, basin and municipal *halte* on pontoons for 10 boats u/s r/b, 06 19 81 28 23, night €7.60, water and electricity included, showers (in season), wifi, slipway, town centre 400m |

The village is very pleasant, with a much-photographed circular open-air wash-house. Opposite the *halte* is a remarkable 19th century *abattoir* (now an activities centre) complete with bull's head sculptures. The *halte* itself has recently been improved, with both finger pontoon and alongside moorings.

| PK 83.0 | Bridge (Roux), D813 |
| PK 83.1 | Railway bridge (through route Toulouse-Bordeaux) |
| PK 83.8 | Bridge (Coupet) |
| PK 84.6 | **Golfech** bridge, municipal *halte* for 4 boats u/s l/b, 05 63 29 42 00, night €6, water and electricity included |
| PK 85.4 | Barguelonne aqueduct |
| PK 85.5 | Bridge (Barguelonne) |
| PK 86.0 | Lac Bleu de Bergon park r/b, possible mooring |
| PK 86.7 | Lock 31 (Lamagistère), bridge, water |
| PK 87.5 | **Lamagistère** moorings in widening of canal l/b |

Delightful mooring along the tree-lined bank, but there are other spots, above lock 31 and beside the 'Blue Lake' (Lac Bleu de Bergon). The romantic hilltop village of Clermont-Soubiran overlooks the canal. South from the canal it is just a 10-12 minute walk to the stunning village of Lamagistère itself, on the banks of the Garonne. Elegant buildings date back to the time when the extensive stone quays saw 4500 vessels tie up each year, receiving and discharging cargoes of grain, wine and fruit. The quays were left high and dry by the constantly scouring and deepening river.

| PK 87.7 | Bridge (Lasparières) |
| PK 88.5 | Bridge (Saint-Pierre) |

# Canal de Garonne

- PK **90.3** Bridge (Laspeyres), D813
- PK **91.8** Bridge (Durou)
- PK **93.6** Lock 32 (Noble), bridge
- PK **94.7** Bridge (Guillemis)
- PK **95.6** Bridge (Carrère)
- PK **96.7** Lock 33 (Saint-Christophe), bridge
- PK **97.6** Bridge (Sauveterre)
- PK **98.4** Turning basin
- PK **98.8** Bridge (Ostende or Lafox)
- PK **99.4** Séoune aqueduct
- PK **99.8** Bridge (Lascarbonnières)
- PK **100.8** Bridge (Saint-Marcel)
- PK **101.5** Private quays l/b
- PK **101.7** **Boé** municipal *halte* for 11 boats r/b, 05 53 96 04 00, night €3, water €2 (15 min), electricity €2 (4 hours), shower €1.50

The *halte* has short finger pontoons, water and electricity, by a country park. Informal bankside moorings between PK 102 and PK 103, a tree-lined canal avenue with timber edgings and a small inlet at PK 102 north of the bridge. Intermarché supermarket near PK 103.

- PK **102.0** Bridge (Pourret), private quay d/s l/b
- PK **103.6** Bridge (Coupat), D813, basin u/s
- PK **104.5** Boé oil terminal, quays l/b
- PK **104.8** Bridge (Laborde)
- PK **105.6** Railway bridge
- PK **105.9** Bridge (Cahors), D656
- PK **106.3** Footbridge
- PK **107.0** Bridge (Villeneuve), basin d/s

*Agen is a large town with the significant attraction of its aqueduct across the Garonne* **1** *which is beautifully illuminated at night* © MAREEMONTI. *Good services are available at the port de plaisance Porte des Pins* **2**. *View looking back to the aqueduct from lock 34,* **3** *the first of four dropping from the aqueduct.* © F-W

- PK **107.1** **Agen** basin, *port de plaisance* and Locaboat hire base l/b, 05 53 66 00 74, night €20 including water/electricity, Monday to Thursday only, showers, crane 10t, restaurant, town centre 400m over railway

A large town – famous for its prunes – with lots of facilities, including a main-line railway station close to the *port de plaisance*, itself located in a harbour basin. The port is a clean and well-resourced hire boat base (fuel

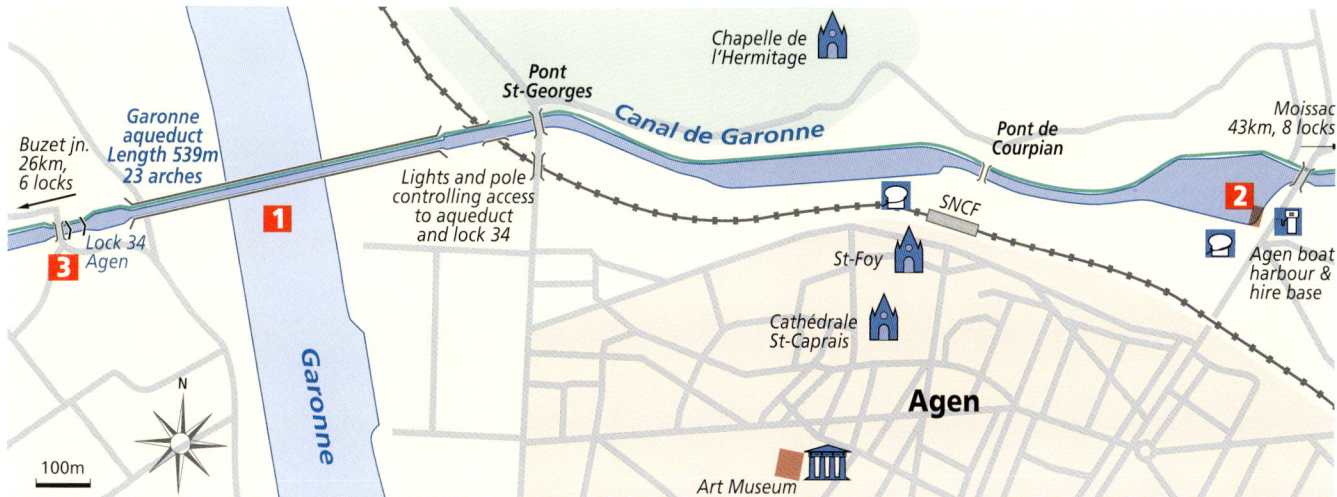

# VII – Southwest France

may be available). There are also bollards on the north side under the grassy hillside in pleasant suburban surroundings. However, the basin is surrounded by busy roads that are especially noisy in the early morning. The town is excellent for shopping.

PK **107.6** Bridge (Courpian)
PK **107.8** Moorings along quay l/b (private boat club)
PK **108.5** Bridge (Saint-Georges), D813
PK **108.6** Railway underbridge
PK **108.9** Agen aqueduct over the Garonne (length 539m)

The impressive aqueduct over the River Garonne is the longest masonry aqueduct constructed in France. It is followed by a flight of four 3-3.5m deep locks. They are easy going down, but coming up, the highest is especially difficult due to the extreme force with which the water enters the chamber. It is advisable to avoid tying up at the front near the gates, at the risk of upsetting a boat behind trying to share the lock. Allow 45 minutes to pass through the four locks.

PK **109.3** Lock 34 (Agen), bridge
PK **109.7** Lock 35 (Mariannettes)
PK **110.1** Lock 36 (Chabrières)
PK **110.5** Lock 37 (Rosette), bridge

This first/last lock of the four is by a sharp turn and the closed-off former branch that allowed descent to the river. This lock has a strong cross-current immediately outside.

PK **110.6** Former junction with feeder canal l/b (infilled)
PK **111.3** Bridge (Fressonis)
PK **113.5** Bridge (Nodigier)
PK **115.3** Bridge (Colomay), quay d/s r/b
PK **116.8** Bridge (Plaisance)
PK **118.1** Bridge (Chicot)
PK **119.1** **Sérignac-sur-Garonne** bridge, *halte* d/s r/b, 05 53 68 30 00, moorings for 14 boats, free for 3 nights, water €2 (15 min), electricity €2 (4 hours), shower, slipway, restaurant, village 500m

A delightful mooring: timber quayside with water and electricity, pleasant walks along the grassy canalside embankments. The historic 'bastide' village has a small supermarket, a restaurant, a good pizza bar, an ancient church with a twisted spire, and an excellent (seasonal) tourist office.

*Excellent mooring at Sérignac* © F-W

PK **120.0** Pipeline crossing
PK **121.1** Bridge (Madone)
PK **122.5** Bridge (Frèche)
PK **123.9** Bridge (Lapougniane)
PK **124.4** Bridge (Pages)
PK **125.1** Lock 38 (Auvignon), bridge, basin d/s r/b, Bruche 1.5 km
PK **126.6** Bridge (Saint-Martin)
PK **127.6** Bridge (Thomas)
PK **128.8** Bridge (Castelviel), disused
PK **129.7** Bridge (Feugarolles), basin u/s r/b (disused)
PK **129.8** **Feugarolles** boat moorings l/b, village 1 km
PK **130.4** Railway bridge
PK **130.7** Bridge (Thouars)
PK **132.0** Baïse aqueduct
PK **132.2** Lock 39 (Baïse)
PK **132.4** Lock 40 (Lardaret), bridge
PK **135.2** **Junction with the river Baïse** via double staircase lock (Descente en Baïse) r/b

The double staircase lock provides access from the canal down on to the river Baïse. This is the all-important junction of the Southwest France waterway network. From this point, boats head upstream along the Baïse, to Nérac, Condom and Flaran Abbey. The connection downstream to join and then cross the river Garonne to enter the River Lot (a cruising destination in itself) is currently closed to navigation.

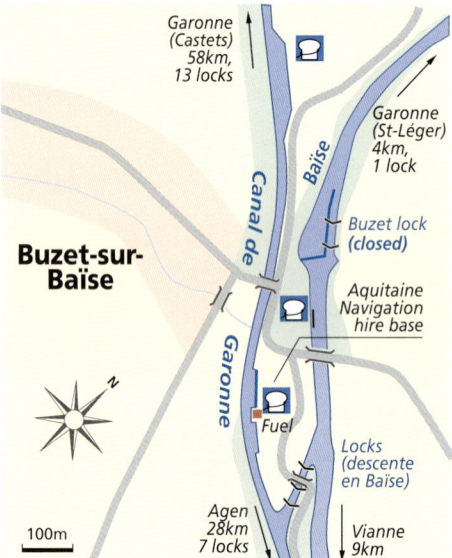

PK **135.4** **Buzet-sur-Baïse** boat harbour and Aquitaine Navigation hire base r/b, 05 53 84 72 50, 5 visitor moorings, night €13 (€25 for barges), water, electricity, showers (€2), slipway, repairs, restaurant

Good, modern, well-managed *port de plaisance*. The village is pretty and proud of its world-renowned wines.

PK **135.7** Bridge (Buzet-sur-Baïse), basin and halte d/s r/b, restaurant Au Bord de l'Eau, 05 53 84 53 31, capacity 20 boats, night €13, water and electricity included, village 700m l/b
PK **137.5** Bridge (Burrenque)
PK **138.4** Bridge (Doux)
PK **139.7** Bridge (D8 Damazan bypass)
PK **139.9** **Damazan** bridge, basin d/s r/b, long-term moorings with services managed by VNF, slipway, restaurant, village l/b

# Canal de Garonne

PK **141.9** Bridge (Lompian)
PK **142.8** Lock 41 (Berry), bridge
PK **143.6** Bridge (Maurin)
PK **144.3** Bridge (Vigneau)
PK **145.2** Bridge (Monheurt)
PK **146.2** Bridge (Lafallotte)

*Aerial view of Buzet-sur-Baïse.* © PIERRE LASVENES

PK **147.5** Lock 42 (Gaule), bridge
PK **148.4** Bridge (Labarthe), **Villeton**, *port de plaisance* for 20 boats d/s r/b, free, water €2 (15 min), electricity €2 (4 hours), shower (€2), restaurant, **Tonneins** 4500m

*Halte* with new timber quayside, water and electricity, beside the Mairie.

PK **150.2** Lock 43 (Gaulette), bridge
PK **151.1** Bridge (Jeanserre)
PK **152.2** **Lagruère** bridge (Ladonne), *halte* u/s r/b, 05 53 79 71 76, quay 30m long, free, water €2 (15 min), electricity €2 (4 hours) and shower (€2), restaurant, village l/b
PK **153.3** Bridge (Lagruère)
PK **155.4** **Le Mas d'Agenais** bridge, *halte* d/s l/b, moorings for 6 boats, free, water €2 (15 min), electricity €2 (4 hours), shower (€2) pump-out, restaurant, village l/b
PK **155.8** Lock 44 (Mas d'Agenais), bridge, Le Boat hire base u/s
PK **156.8** Bridge (Larriveau)
PK **158.6** Bridge (Larroque)
PK **160.3** **Caumont-sur-Garonne** bridge, quay for 2 boats d/s r/b, water €2 (15 min), electricity €2 (4 hours), pump-out, village l/b

*Camper vans share the facilities at Caumont, PK 160* © F-W

PK **161.2** Bridge (Église de Fourques)
PK **162.2** **Fourques-sur-Garonne** bridge, *halte* u/s l/b for 3 boats
PK **163.6** Bridge (Marescot)
PK **164.4** Bridge (Pont des Sables), *port de plaisance* Émeraude Navigation u/s r/b, 06 23 89 19 33, 4 visitor moorings, night €5, water €2 (15 min), electricity €2 (4 hours), shower (€2), slipway, crane 10t, repairs, wifi, **Marmande** 5 km r/b

Pont des Sables *port de plaisance* and Émeraude Navigation hire boat base Capitainerie website **emeraude-navigation.com**

*The Pont des Sables port de plaisance has good facilities, and is ideally located for visiting the bustling market town of Marmande, PK 164.*

PK **165.6** Avance aqueduct
PK **165.7** Lock 45 (Avance), bridge
PK **166.1** Railway bridge
PK **166.5** Bridge (Laronquière)
PK **167.4** Bridge (Rayne)
PK **168.4** Bridge (Baradat)
PK **169.2** **Marcellus** bridge, village 1 km l/b
PK **170.4** Bridge (Campot)
PK **170.9** Lock 46 (Bernès), bridge, quay d/s r/b
PK **171.7** Bridge (Tersac)
PK **172.5** Bridge (Cantis)
PK **173.4** Lock 47 (Gravières), bridge
PK **175.2** **Meilhan-sur-Garonne** bridge, basin and *halte* with moorings for 8 boats d/s r/b, 05 53 64 07 88, €7, water €2 (15 min), electricity €2 (4 hours), slipway, wifi, restaurant, village 400m l/b **contact@camping-au-jardin.com**

A beautiful leafy location for this *halte*, set under a hillside from the top of which ('le Tertre') are extensive views over the neighbouring River Garonne, where swimming is possible. Bar/restaurant adjacent.

PK **176.5** Bridge (Pimayne)
PK **177.7** Bridge (Lisos)
PK **179.0** **Hure** bridge, village l/b
PK **179.6** Bridge (Julian)
PK **180.8** Lock 48 (Auriole), bridge
PK **181.3** Bridge (Tartifume)

# VII – Southwest France

PK **182.0** **Fontet** municipal *port de plaisance* in basin off canal l/b, 06 07 62 57 85, 43 berths, pontoon for 10 visiting boats, night €11, water and electricity included, showers, wifi, slipway, **La Réole** 2.5 km r/b

The *port de plaisance* off the canal may have a weed problem during the summer. Beach and swimming pool. Museum of models made from matchsticks.

PK **182.3** Bridge (Berrat)
PK **182.8** Bridge (Fontet)
PK **183.3** Bridge (D9 Fontet bypass)
PK **183.5** Lock 49 (Fontet), bridge
PK **184.3** Bridge (Loupiac)
PK **185.5** Bridge (Gravilla)
PK **186.6** Bridge (Puybarban)
PK **187.6** Lock 50 (Bassanne), bridge
PK **188.7** Bridge (Castillon)
PK **189.5** Bridge (Noël)
PK **190.3** Bridge (Hillon)
PK **191.3** Bridge (Mazerac)
PK **192.0** Lock 51 (Mazerac), bridge
PK **192.5** **Castets-en-Dorthe** *port de plaisance*, 06 77 89 66 34, capacity 65 boats, 10 visitor moorings, night €12, water and electricity included, shower, wifi, slipway, restaurant, village l/b

A popular *port de plaisance* has recently been developed in the basin 'des Gares', Moorings are 'Mediterranean' end-to with pick-up buoys that may be difficult to pick up.

PK **192.7** Lock 52 (Gares), footbridge
PK **193.3** Lock 53 (Castets), double lock down to Garonne

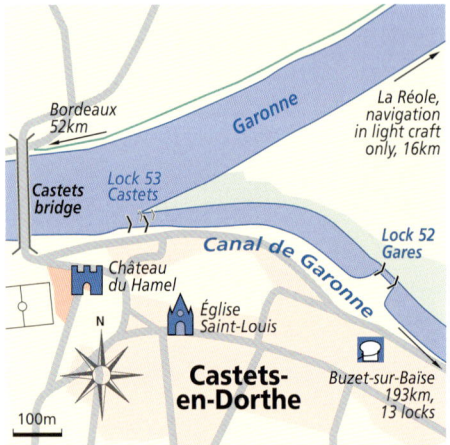

*The large and very deep double chamber lock where the canal joins the tidal river Garonne, seen at low water. The lock-keeper here is available to advise on joining the river Garonne and running down to Cadillac or Bordeaux. Local advice is valuable.* © F-W

The large lock down to the tidal river is particularly deep when the Garonne is low. Only the larger chamber (left-bank side) is used. Interestingly, when the locks were lengthened around 1970, this one was not extended by 10m but by a whole 45m! VNF vignettes will possibly be checked at this lock, coming into the system from the river. they can be purchased at the office (05 56 62 83 07) or online in advance (see VNF tariff information in Part I). The lock house entrance door is located two storeys up the face of the building, a testament to the potential height of river flooding.

PK **193.6** *Junction with River Garonne*

## Canal de Brienne in Toulouse

PK **0.0** *Junction with Canal du Midi and Canal de Garonne* in Toulouse, Port de l'Embouchure (PK 0), bridge (Ponts Jumeaux)

Note that this branch is not normally accessible to private boaters, nor is the access to the River Garonne in Toulouse (see map p. 321).

PK **0.1** Footbridge
PK **0.5** Footbridge
PK **0.9** Bridge (avenue Paul Séjourné)
PK **1.1** Bridge
PK **1.5** Lock (Saint-Pierre), bridge
PK **1.6** *Junction with River Garonne*, navigable upstream 5 km but authorisation required (not normally given to private craft)

# 60. Canal de Montech and River Tarn

THE CANAL DE MONTECH is an important branch of the Canal de Garonne, 11km long from Montech to Montauban. It was opened at the same time as the rest of the canal in 1856. In Montauban it connects with a short but popular navigable length of the river Tarn, through the recently restored double staircase lock. The canal had to be closed in 1996 because of leakage through its embankments, but was restored and reopened in 2006, and now has a well-equipped boat harbour in the canal basin at Montauban. The river Tarn is navigable 8km up to the village of Corbarieu. It is planned to continue restoration upstream to Albi, and a Syndicat Mixte was created in May 2021 for this purpose. The link with Albi is considered to hold greater potential and to be more strategic than restoring the river downstream through Montauban to Moissac. The navigable section of the Tarn in Moissac is described under the previous section as part of the Canal de Garonne. For convenience the whole length of the Tarn, 140km from the Garonne to Albi, is described below.

## Navigation
The canal is reliably supplied with water and easy to navigate, with its old 30m locks, and without the bypass channels of the main line. The canal does not see much traffic, and may be affected by weed growth. Navigability of the Tarn depends on the stage of the river, the outlet from the canal being situated just above the impressive and at times treacherous Sapiacou weir. The speed limit is 8 km/h, 3 km/h past moored boats.

## Locks
There are 10 easy locks on the canal, falling towards Montauban, maximum drop 3m. They are operated by a remote control that is available at the first lock at Lacourt-Saint-Pierre (VNF 06 62 99 48 02 or 06 62 99 49 58). The last is a double staircase lock down to the Tarn. There are no locks on the currently navigable Tarn (all 20 locks between Sainte-Livrade and Albi are disused).

## Draught
The maximum authorised draught is 1.60m. Boats drawing more than 1.20m should proceed with all due caution on the Tarn, where there is no guaranteed depth.

## Headroom
All bridges leave a minimum headroom of 3.70m above normal water level.

## Towpath
There is a good towpath throughout the canal, but not on the River Tarn.

## Authority
VNF Sud-Ouest, Subdivision de Tarn-et-Garonne: Delbessous-Sud, 82200 Moissac
05 63 04 02 41    subdi.tarnetgaronne@vnf.fr

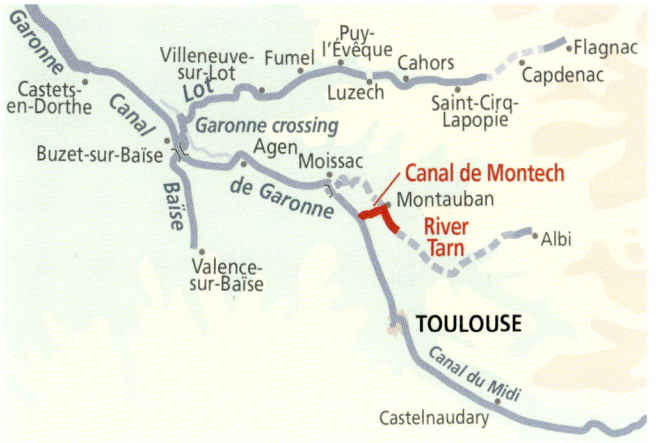

## Route description

The canal branches off from Montech just opposite the *port de plaisance* with its *capitainerie* and restaurant.

| | | |
|---|---|---|
| PK 0.0 | **Junction with Canal de Garonne** at Montech (PK 43), bridge |
| PK 1.1 | Bridge (Rat) |
| PK 2.5 | Motorway bridge (A62) |

| Key dimensions (m) | |
|---|---|
| Length | 30.00 |
| Beam | 5.20 |
| Draught | 1.60 |
| > river Tarn | 1.20 |
| Air draught | 3.60 |

# VII – Southwest France

*Good quay mooring at Lacourt-Saint-Pierre* © F-W

PK **3.4**   **Lacourt-Saint-Pierre** bridge, municipal *halte* for 5 boats, 05 63 67 49 31, night €3, water, electricity, small village l/b

A small, pretty village with an excellent quayside mooring. *Épicerie-bar* in the village. Imposing 19th century château.

PK **4.5**   Lock 1bis (Noalhac)
PK **4.7**   Bridge (Noalhac)
PK **5.0**   Lock 2bis (Lamothe)
PK **5.4**   Lock 3bis (Fisset)
PK **6.2**   Lock 4bis (Brétoille)
PK **6.6**   Lock 5bis (Mortarieu), bridge
PK **6.9**   Lock 6bis (Terrasse)
PK **7.3**   Lock 7bis (Rabastens)
PK **7.6**   Lock 8bis (Verlhaguet), bridge
PK **9.2**   Lock 9bis (Bordebasse), bridge
PK **10.6**   **Montauban** basin, moorings for 40 boats, 06 19 73 62 93, night €9, water, electricity, showers, wifi, pump-out, town centre 1km
PK **10.7**   Locks 10bis/11bis down to river Tarn
PK **10.9**   Junction with river Tarn, turn right to head upstream (see plan).

A historic and beautiful town, Montauban, the birthplace of Ingres, lies on the River Tarn, is prone to winter deluges. The Pont Vieux (completed 1335) has large arched openings above the bridge spans, to allow extreme flood

*Locks 10bis/11bis down to the Tarn in the foreground.*

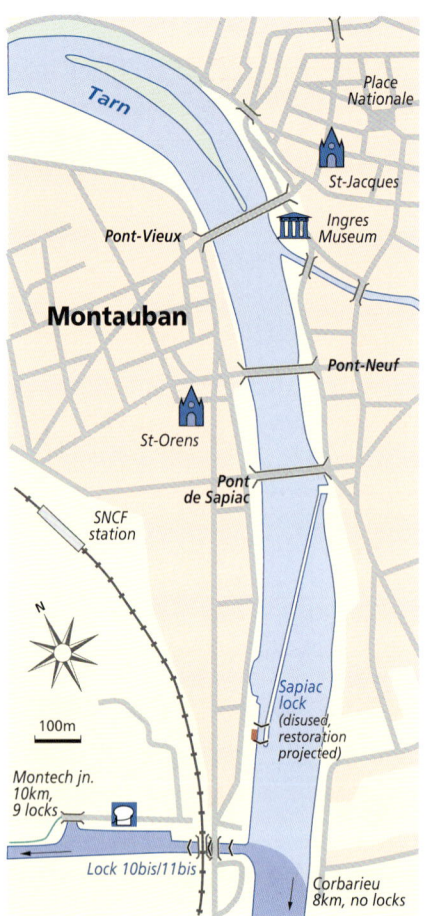

waters to pass through. In the centre of the photo, the Musée Ingres has a huge number of his paintings and was originally the castle of the English Black Prince.

The *port de plaisance* is pleasantly located, public, but feels safe. The town is an easy 10-15min walk away, but one route is through a very low and smelly tunnel under the adjacent railway line. Alternatively take the rather vertiginous stone steps by the Descente en Tarn locks, under the railway and out by the gorgeous (but peeling) Art Déco rowing club. For the nearest *boulangerie*, take the side of the lock nearest the graffiti-covered lock-house, continue along the track by the river that then rejoins the road, and then turn right. This is one of those enormous *boulangeries* occupying a former petrol station.

## River Tarn

PK **0.0**   Confluence with river Garonne, lake retained by Golfech dam
PK **3.8**   Bridge (Pont Napoléon)
PK **4.1**   Old lock (Moissac), gates removed, open passage
PK **4.4**   Junction with Canal de Garonne via double staircase lock, r/b
PK **5.8**   Moissac (Cacor) aqueduct on Canal de Garonne
PK **6.0**   Railway viaduct
PK **6.6**   Bridge
PK **12.1**   Lock 1 Sainte-Livrade, l/b

This is the upstream limit of navigation from Moissac. The following section, 24km long through three locks, is a longer-term restoration project.

# Canal de Montech and River Tarn

*The Pont Vieux and Musée Ingres in Montauban, not at present accessible by boat* © F-W

*Sapiac lock, squeezed between the ruined mill and the very long weir, needs to be restored to give access to Montauban.* © F-W

## Section not navigable (for reference)

| | |
|---|---|
| PK 12.1 | Lock 1 Sainte-Livrade, l/b |
| PK 21.4 | Lock 2 |
| PK 22.6 | Bridge D45, **Lafrançaise** hilltop village 1500m |
| PK 28.5 | Lock 3 Lagarde, l/b |
| PK 35.2 | Bridge (Montauban bypass) |
| PK 36.3 | Railway viaduct |
| PK 36.5 | Lock 4 |
| PK 37.8 | **Montauban** bridge (Pont Vieux) |
| PK 38.0 | Bridge (Pont Neuf) |
| PK 38.3 | Bridge (Sapiac) |
| PK 38.9 | Lock 5 Sapiac, l/b |

This lock remains to be restored to give access to the centre of Montauban. The Tarn is navigable for 9km from the Canal de Montech up to lock 6.

| | |
|---|---|
| PK 39.0 | **Junction with Canal de Montech** by locks 10/11, l/b |
| PK 40.7 | Bridge (Montauban bypass) |
| PK 43.5 | Bressols rowing club l/b, pontoon, slipway |
| PK 43.6 | **Bressols**, pontoon mooring 50m long l/b, village with shops 400m |
| PK 47.0 | **Corbarieu**, mooring 50m long r/b, village centre 600m |
| PK 48.2 | Lock 6 Labastide-Saint-Pierre, disused, limit of navigation |

## Section not navigable (for reference)

| | |
|---|---|
| PK 51.5 | Bridge (Reyniès) |
| PK 54.2 | Lock 7 |
| PK 56.2 | **Villebrumier** bridge |
| PK 60.4 | Lock 8 |
| PK 62.0 | Bridge |
| PK 62.6 | **Villemur-sur-Tarn** quay r/b |
| PK 62.7 | Lock 9 Villemur |
| PK 62.8 | Bridge |
| PK 68.6 | Lock 19 Escalère |
| PK 69.2 | Bridge D15 |
| PK 71.7 | **Mirepoix** bridge |
| PK 75.0 | **Bessières** bridge |
| PK 75.5 | Lock 11 |
| PK 78.3 | Bridge (Buzet-sur-Tarn) |
| PK 82.3 | Bridge (La Pointe) |
| PK 82.7 | Confluence of River Agout, l/b |
| PK 88.0 | **Rabastens** bridge |
| PK 88.2 | Lock 12 |
| PK 92.6 | Lock 13 |
| PK 93.4 | Railway bridge |
| PK 62.0 | Bridge |
| PK 98.6 | Lock 14 |
| PK 99.0 | Bridge D14, **L'Isle-sur-le-Tarn** r/b |
| PK 103.0 | Lock 15 |
| PK 106.0 | Lock 16 |
| PK 109.0 | Bridge D968 |
| PK 110.0 | **Gaillac** slipway r/b, town centre 600m |
| PK 110.3 | Bridge (D87) |
| PK 110.4 | Lock 17 Gaillac |
| PK 111.7 | Bridge |
| PK 113.2 | Lock 18 |
| PK 117.7 | Lock 19 (weir demolished to give extra head at dam u/s) |
| PK 118.2 | Rivière dam and hydropower plant, new lock or travel-lift needed l/b |

The reservoir is navigable from here to Albi

| | |
|---|---|
| PK 121.6 | **Ayguelèze** basin and port de plaisance r/b, passenger boat (*gabarre*) |
| PK 124.9 | Railway bridge |
| PK 125.8 | **Marssac-sur-Tarn** bridge (D988), town l/b |
| PK 139.0 | Lock 22 made redundant by Rivière dam, gates removed |
| PK 139.4 | **Albi** quay l/b, passenger boat (*gabarre*) |

Albi is a spectacular quay, overlooked by the towering brick cathedral of Sainte-Cécile, and with the historic mill on the opposite bank.

| | |
|---|---|
| PK 139.9 | Bridge (Pont Vieux) |
| PK 140.0 | Lock 23 Albi |

# 61. River Baïse

THE RIVER BAÏSE, A LEFT BANK TRIBUTARY of the Garonne, was restored to navigation in the 1990s over a distance of 65km, from its confluence with the Garonne at Saint-Léger to Camarade mill upstream of Valence-sur-Baïse. It was formerly navigable a further 21 km and 8 locks to the village of Saint-Jean-Poutge, a small river port serving Auch in the *département* of Gers. The Baïse is connected with the Canal de Garonne by a double staircase lock at Buzet-sur-Baïse, and with the navigable River Lot via a 5km length of the river Garonne (the 'Garonne crossing'), downstream from the outfall lock at Saint-Léger.

The navigation was abandoned in 1955 and sold to the riparians throughout most of its length, but the two *départements*, Lot-et-Garonne and Gers, invested more than €10 million in restoration of the waterway as the key to developing tourism in this rural area, redolent of armagnac and corn. The upstream limit of Valence was chosen because of the importance of the Cistercian abbey of Flaran, on the left bank of the river just before this small town is reached.

## Navigation

The Baïse is an ideal cruising river, with no particular difficulties except when the river is in flood. No vignette is required, as this is not part of the VNF network. The cruise on this tranquil shady river, steeped in history, offers a marked contrast with the long straight pounds of the Canal de Garonne.

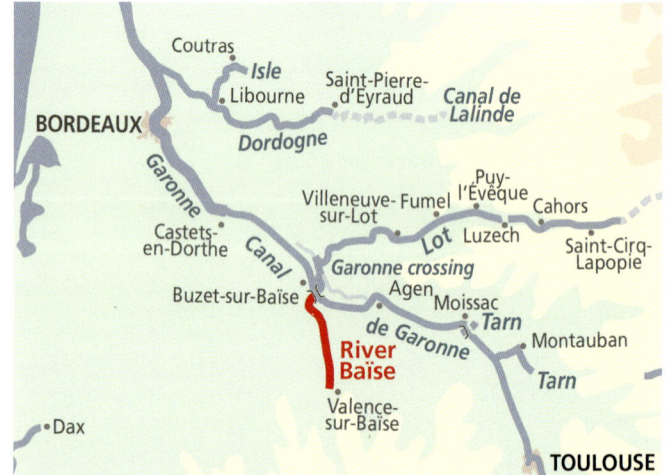

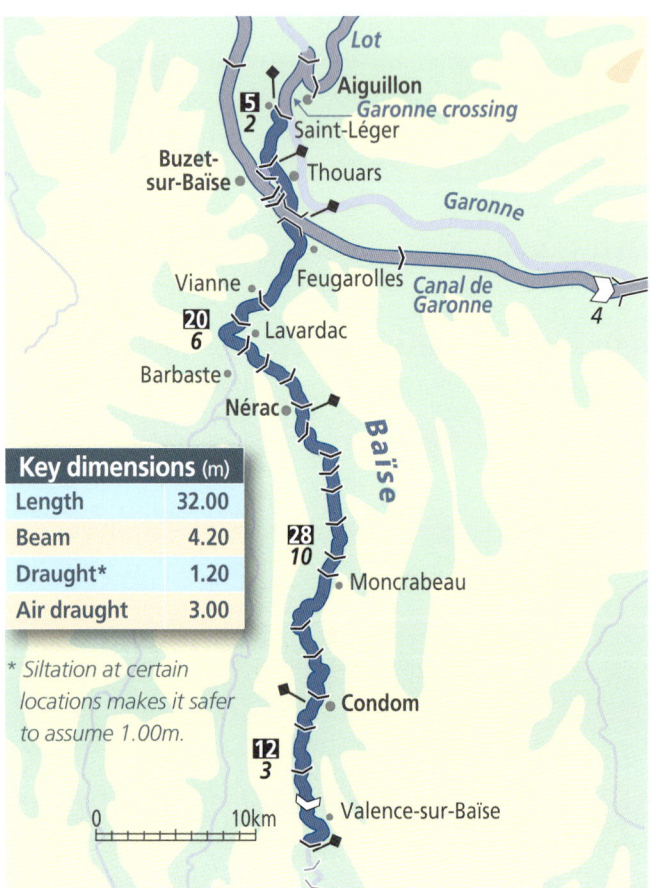

| Key dimensions (m) | |
|---|---|
| Length | 32.00 |
| Beam | 4.20 |
| Draught* | 1.20 |
| Air draught | 3.00 |

*Siltation at certain locations makes it safer to assume 1.00m.*

*The Baïse was naturally considered for possible canalisation by Henri IV, who resided in Nérac before he became king of France. It was a more regular, less challenging river than the nearby Gers. Napoleon also saw the value of canalising this left-bank tributary of the Garonne. The project was started in 1808, and completed a few years later. The waterway was closed in 1954 and removed from the list of navigable waterways in 1957, except for the section between the junction with the Canal de Garonne and the Garonne. It then became private property. Restoration works, after a study by the author in 1990-91, meant that the right to navigate had to be negotiated with the riparian (waterside) owners. This popular waterway, reopened for navigation in 1995-97, is operated by the Councils of the two départements.*

The river is attractively leafy and narrow, in some places twisting as well. In a suitable boat (including many hire boats available from Buzet or Agen) it offers a uniquely delightful cruise, surrounded by wild life including lots of kingfishers (*martin-pêcheurs*). There are several attractive, historic small towns to visit. Navigation is interrupted when the Baïse floods to a level of +0.50m on the gauge at Nérac. The speed limit is 6km/h. The banks above Lavardac are all private and mooring must be at a locks or other pontoons, or the quaysides at Nérac, Moncrabeau, Condom and Valence.

## Locks

There are 21 locks including the double staircase at Graziac. Saint-Léger lock leading to the Garonne is 40.50m by 5.20m. The route description gives the historic lock numbers, which started at Saint-Jean-Poutge, hence 29 for Saint-Léger and 9 for Flaran. The three locks up to Lavardac have the restricted dimensions of the original locks on the Midi canals: 32.00m by 5.20m. From here upstream, the locks are the same length but narrower (4.20m).

The lock-keeper, posted at the Buzet locks from June to September, issues the swipe card for operation of all locks, from 09:00 to 19:00, with the exception of Saint-Léger (access to the Garonne), and the double staircase lock at Graziac, which was not mechanised and is operated by a lock-keeper (9:00 to 18:00, with a lunch-break). The magnetic card may need to be 'jiggled' to get it to read, or *in extremis* the stop button may be given a quarter-turn to release it. Out of season, consult the canal staff or follow instructions posted at Buzet locks. Locks 29 and 28 are not currently operated, on account of polluted sediments from the cellulose factory adjacent to Lock 28 (Buzet).

## Draught

The maximum authorised draught is 1.50m downstream of the junction with the Canal de Garonne, reduced to 1.20m upstream of the junction. These official values have been reported to be optimistic in some places where siltation occurs.

## Headroom

The bridges leave a minimum headroom of 3.50m above normal water level up to Nazareth lock (upstream of Nérac), and 3.00m thereafter.

## Towpath

The towpath is of varying condition over the first 19 km up to Lavardac, and totally impracticable upstream from Lavardac following sale of the river to riparian owners.

## Authority

Conseil Départemental Lot-et-Garonne, UTI Marmande
– Coteau de Romas, 47130 Port Sainte-Marie, ✆ 05 53 77 29 00
  *webmestre@lotetgaronne.fr* (PK 0–45)
Conseil Départemental du Gers
– 19 Place du Foirail - BP 342 – 32007 Auch
  ✆ 05 62 61 53 49 (PK 45–65)

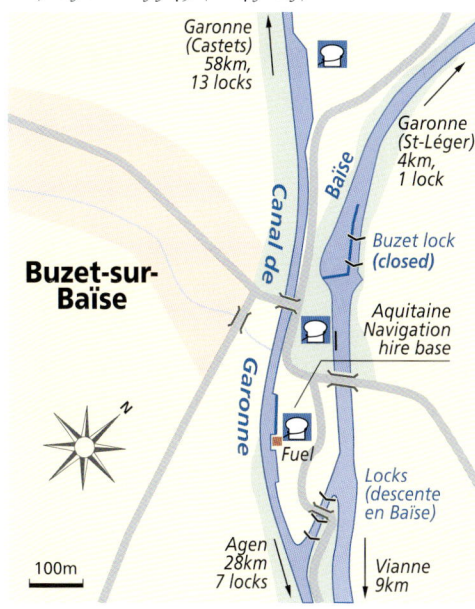

## Route description

There are waiting pontoons above and below the lock into the Garonne at Saint-Léger, but the lock is not currently operated, pending solutions for the Garonne crossing (see section 62).

PK 0.0   Lock 29 (Saint-Léger) and weir, **confluence with the River Garonne**

PK 4.5   Lock 28 (Buzet) and weir

If heading downstream from the junction with the Canal de Garonne, the weir is faced almost immediately, with the lock over on the right-bank side. There are waiting pontoons above and below the lock to land the crew who will operate the lock using the magnetic card. The pole can be very slippery. This lock is not currently operated and needs to be rehabilitated, but the works are complicated by the polluted sediments from the adjacent former Faber pencil factory.

PK 4.7   **Buzet-sur-Baïse** bridge, quay d/s l/b, village 800m beyond the canal

Good quayside mooring on the river.

PK 4.9   **Junction with the Canal de Garonne**, PK 135.2, l/b, by a double staircase lock (the *descente en Baïse*)

The locks are called 'descente en Baïse', but from the river they are of course used to lock *up* to the Canal de Garonne.

PK 8.7   Aqueduct (carries the Canal de Garonne over the river)
PK 8.9   Motorway bridge (A62, Autoroute des Deux Mers)
PK 9.9   Skew road bridge (D119)

*Coming up in the locks from the Baïse to the Canal de Garonne.*

# VII – Southwest France

PK 10.9 Railway bridge
PK 11.0 **Feugarolles** pontoon moorings, r/b, village 600m
PK 12.0 Trenquéléon château, r/b
PK 14.0 Bridge (Vianne)
PK 14.2 **Vianne** municipal *halte* on pontoon for up to 12 boats, free (maximum 72 hours), water, electricity, slipway, and turning basin d/s of weir, village l/b

Very pleasant 'bastide' walled village with gatehouses, roads on a rectangular grid pattern and a very pretty suspension bridge. The large abandoned water mill overlooks the excellent quayside moorings.

PK 14.3 Lock 27 (Vianne) r/b, and weir
PK 15.2 Skew railway viaduct
PK 16.9 Lock 26 (Lavardac)
PK 17.2 Lavardac bridge (Roman arch on r/b)
PK 17.3 **Lavardac** municipal *halte* on quay directly below village centre, r/b, mooring for 6 boats, water, electricity, slipway

A historic small town, very pleasant from the river – lock, quay and bridge. Beyond Lavardac the locks are narrower (max. 4.20m) and the river shallower (max. 1m). All banksides are privately owned.

PK 18.2 Confluence of Gélise, l/b

The stunning 13th century fortified mill of Barbaste is approached across a medieval bridge over the river Gélise, an easy 1km walk from Lavardac.

PK 18.7 Bridge (Pont de Bordes, D930)
PK 19.1 Railway viaduct
PK 19.5 Lock 25 (St Crabary) r/b, and weir
PK 20.6 Castle (Séguinot), l/b

*The delightfully located lock downstream of the medieval bridge at Nérac, PK 25* © F-W

PK 21.3 Lock 24 (Sourbet) l/b, and weir
PK 22.0 Castle (Bournac), l/b
PK 23.4 Lock 23 (Bapaume) r/b, and weir
PK 24.7 Lock 22 (Nérac) l/b, and weir
PK 24.8 Bridge (Vieux-Pont)
PK 24.9 **Nérac** quays both banks, capitainerie and trip boat departure point r/b, 05 53 65 27 75, mooring for 20 boats, night €10, water, electricity, restaurant, town centre l/b

Extremely picturesque historic town, arched Pont Vieux bridge and quaysides. One wing of Henri IV's large château survives, as do many other handsome old buildings, especially down by the quays.

*The* Prince Henri *comes out of Nérac Lock to be welcomed by an armada of hire boats moored in this attractive town, associated with the memory of the young prince Henri IV.* © CH-CAF

PK 25.0 Bridge (Pont Neuf)
PK 26.8 Lock 21 (Nazareth), lift 2.21m, in short cut l/b
PK 29.4 Lock 20 (La Saubole), lift 2.37m
PK 31.1 Accommodation bridge, entrance to lock-cut l/b
PK 31.2 Lock 19 (Récaillau)
PK 31.3 Navigation re-enters Baïse
PK 31.8 Entrance to mill-stream r/b (not navigable)
PK 34.6 Entrance to lock-cut, l/b
PK 34.7 Lock 18 (Pacheron), lift 2.54m, bridge d/s
PK 35.3 End of lock-cut, bridge, navigation re-enters river
PK 36.5 Entrance to lock-cut, l/b
PK 36.6 Lock 17 (Lapierre), lift 2.28m
PK 36.9 Accommodation bridge
PK 37.0 End of lock-cut, navigation re-enters river
PK 37.8 Bridge (D112), quays r/b, **Lasserre** village and château 2km r/b
PK 39.8 Entrance to lock-cut, l/b
PK 39.9 Lock 16 (Vialères), lift 3.01m, bridge d/s
PK 40.4 End of lock-cut, navigation re-enters river
PK 41.8 Entrance to lock-cut, r/b
PK 41.9 Lock 15 (Moncrabeau), lift 2.53m, bridge d/s
PK 42.2 End of lock-cut, navigation re-enters river
PK 42.3 **Moncrabeau** bridge, municipal *halte* on quay l/b for up to 5 boats, night €4, water, electricity, slipway, village r/b

'World Capital of Liars'. The location for the famous annual Untruth Contest (first Sunday in August) where applicants vie to tell the most unlikely stories.

# River Baïse

*Quayside mooring at Moncrabeau bridge* © F-W

*Condom bridge and former mill, PK 53, looking downstream. The town centre and Armagnac cellars are behind the right-bank quay. The entrance to the Teste lock-cut is to the right of the mill.* © F-W

PK **44.7**  Département du Gers r/b
PK **45.4**  Département du Gers l/b
PK **46.2**  Entrance to lock-cut, l/b
PK **46.3**  Lock 14 (Autièges), lift 2.55m, bridge d/s
PK **46.5**  End of lock-cut, navigation re-enters river
PK **48.4**  Entrance to lock-cut, r/b
PK **48.5**  Lock 13 (Beauregard), lift 2.86m, bridge d/s
PK **48.7**  End of lock-cut, navigation re-enters river
PK **52.3**  Entrance to lock-cut, r/b
PK **52.4**  Lock 12 (Peyrouthéou), lift 2.60m,
PK **52.8**  Bridge (Sarreméjean)
PK **52.9**  End of lock-cut, navigation re-enters river
PK **53.0**  Bridge (Barlet)
PK **53.1**  **Condom** *port de plaisance* r/b, 05 62 28 46 46, 10 visiting boats, night €10, water and electricity included, showers, slipway, restaurant, wifi, Armagnac cellars, cathedral, condom museum 300m

Another lovely historic small town – absolutely no connection with contraceptive devices, but a centre of Armagnac production.

*Flaran Abbey with the Baïse in the foreground, PK 62.* © PIERRE LASVENES

PK **53.3**  Bridge (Carmes)
PK **54.4**  Entrance to lock-cut, l/b
PK **54.5**  Lock 11 (Teste), lift 2.40m, bridge d/s, café-restaurant
PK **54.7**  End of lock-cut, navigation re-enters river
PK **57.0**  Tight bends
PK **58.4**  Entrance to lock-cut, r/b
PK **58.5**  Double staircase lock 10 (Graziac), lift 4.70m, manual lift bridge d/s

The only staircase lock on the Baïse.

PK **58.9**  End of lock-cut, navigation re-enters river
PK **62.0**  **Flaran** bridge, moorings l/b, Cistercian abbey 200m l/b

Beautifully preserved Cistercian abbey.

PK **62.4**  Entrance to lock-cut, r/b
PK **62.5**  Lock 9 (Flaran), lift 3.58m
PK **62.6**  End of lock-cut, navigation re-enters river
PK **63.3**  **Valence-sur-Baïse** bridge, *port de plaisance* d/s r/b on quay for 16 boats, 06 32 14 57 87, night €10, water, electricity, slipway, campsite and 'guinguette' restaurant

The cliff-top limit of navigation, with pleasant moorings just below the bridge. Note that the navigable channel is not guaranteed above this point.

PK **64.0**  Bridge (D571)
PK **65.1**  Moulin de Camarade, weir, effective limit of navigation

# 62. Garonne crossing (Baïse-Lot connection)

The Garonne crossing is the gateway to the navigable River Lot. The river thus provides the navigable link between the Baïse at Saint-Léger lock and the entrance to the Lot navigation at Nicole lock, 4.7km downstream. Passage is only possible when there is neither too little nor too much water in the river. The problem with low river levels is that the flow concentrated in the narrow passage becomes rapid and dangerous for all craft even if the depth is theoretically sufficient. Despite these constraints, the Garonne crossing could be planned whenever there is a reasonable expectation of sufficient flow to make it feasible (see remarks on the *Vigicrues* web site **vigicrues.gouv.fr**).

At present the connection is regrettably unfeasible because the last-but-one lock on the Baïse is out of use. As a result, the two locks down to the River Garonne are not operated. The waterway is described here for reference, pending its reopening, even if it will only be available for limited periods in the spring and late autumn.

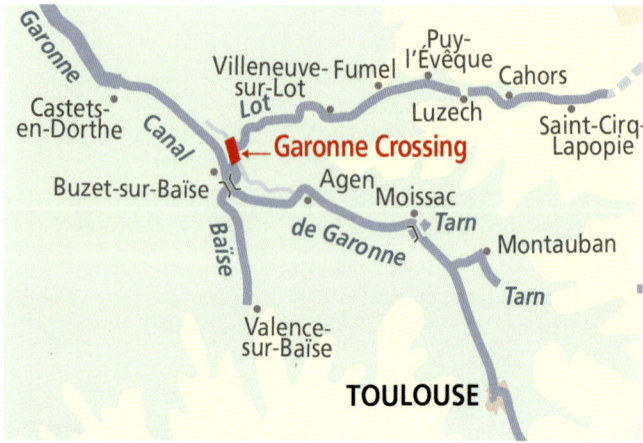

*The free-flowing River Garonne between the rivers Baïse and Lot is a recent oddity of French waterways, because historically the commercial traffic on the River Lot only used the Garonne downstream to and from port of Bordeaux. There was no traffic between the Lot and the Canal de Garonne. The connection was needed, however, to develop recreational navigation on the River Lot. Studies in 1993 (in which the author participated) led to a partial solution, clearing a narrow channel through the sill of marl above the confluence of the Lot. This was after a hydraulic scale model study had found the originally planned solution, a series of groynes to provide a 'self-scouring' channel, to be ineffective. The result, since 1995, is only a semi-navigable river, with long seasons of unavailability during low or high flows. It has been suggested that the problem should be overcome by dredging a deeper channel. Damming the river downstream from the Lot canal outlet at Nicole to maintain depth is excluded by regulations, which dictate that the Garonne must remain a free-flowing river to allow the rare Gironde sturgeon to return. The sill depth of the extra lock chamber built at Saint-Léger is another restriction. The most viable solution would be to create a completely new branch canal to join the Garonne just downstream from Nicole. This section of the Garonne is deep and steady, and navigable practically at all stages of the river.*

| Key dimensions* | (m) |
|---|---|
| Length | 30.00 |
| Beam | 5.00 |
| Draught | 1.20 |
| Air draught | 4.40 |

*The limiting dimensions are those of the lower River Lot*

## Navigation
The route to the River Lot leaves the Canal de Garonne at Buzet-sur-Baïse via the Descente en Baïse and follows the Baïse for 5km to its confluence with the Garonne. After descending onto the Garonne, the river is followed for 4.7km, downstream past the confluence of the River Lot to the 'canalet' that bypasses the last, shallow, 3km of river itself. This passage is available only at medium flows of the Garonne. During low water periods, the difficulty is not only the passage through the marl sill mentioned above but also the banks of gravel transported into the Garonne by the Lot itself. Garonne levels are further reduced at these times because water abstraction from the river by agriculture increases, compounding the problem. The Garonne river pilots were skilled and experienced and were the first point of information on the current situation, but in 2017 the service they provided was withdrawn by the *département* Lot et Garonne.

## Draught
Depths are highly variable according to the stage of the river. The advice of the lock-keeper at Saint-Léger (or Nicole if returning from the Lot) should always be heeded, but vessels drawing up to 1.50m are generally able to make the passage when the locks are operated.

## Headroom
The bridge at Saint-Léger leaves a minimum headroom of at least 6.00m above the highest navigable water level.

# Garonne crossing

*Even from a distance, the sill above the confluence and its narrow passage are clearly distinguishable.* © LALA-HERIZO-RANDRIAMIHAINGO

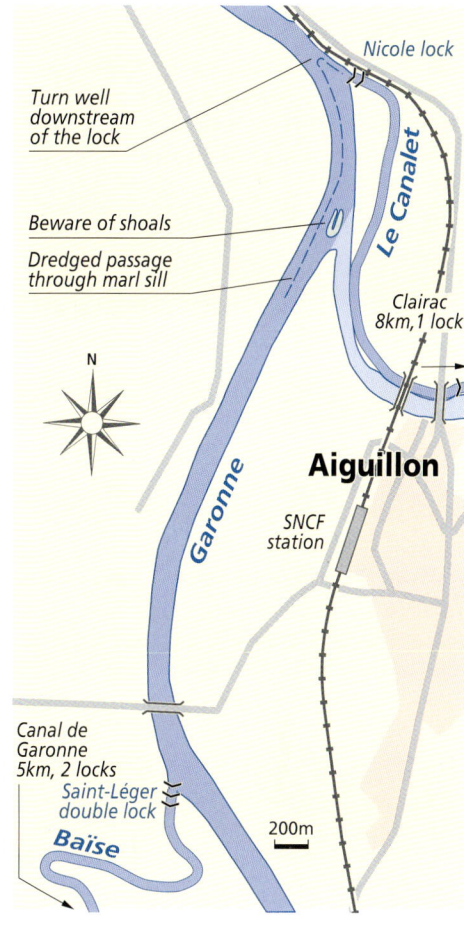

## Authority

Conseil Départemental de Lot et Garonne, Direction des Infrastructures, Transports et Logement, Service Routes et Navigation, Côteau de Romas, 47130 Port Sainte-Marie 05 53 77 29 00 (for monitoring, and the connecting locks)

VNF – Subdivision d'Aquitaine
107 avenue Général de Gaulle, 47000 Agen, 05 53 47 31 15
*subdi.aquitaine@vnf.fr* (representing the State as owner of the river, no services provided)

## Route description

| PK 0.0 | Junction with river Baïse l/b, d/s of Saint-Léger lock |
| --- | --- |
| PK 0.5 | Bridge (Saint-Léger) |
| PK 3.3 | Narrow channel through marl sill |
| PK 4.0 | Confluence of River Lot, r/b (no access) |

*The barge Zeralda leaves Nicole lock to head up the Garonne towards the Baïse. The waiting pontoon remains in place, ready to be brought back into use.* © F-W

PK **4.7** Junction with River Lot navigation, r/b, Nicole lock

Waiting pontoon downstream of the lock. When the crossing was operated, the obligatory pilotage service meant that there could be no stopping on the Garonne between Saint-Léger and Nicole.

*This tug powered boats through the gap in the natural sill on the Garonne just upstream of the confluence of the Lot, before it was sold by the Département.* © BORD À BORD.COM

# VII – Southwest France

## 63. River Lot

The river Lot has the potential to be one of the top five waterway destinations in France. Thanks to feats of engineering, both historically and in modern times, navigation potentially extends over a distance of 266 km from the Garonne at Nicole (near Aiguillon) to the village of Port d'Agrès, a few kilometres from the former industrial centre of Decazeville. Open cast mines here produced coal for steelworks and other industries throughout southwest France. The intense traffic was the reason for improving the navigation originally developed by the early 19th century, and a series of new locks and weirs was built from 1830 onwards. Later, lock-cuts were built to bypass the river's extravagant meanders at Luzech, Cajarc, Montbrun and Capdenac. Like the other river navigations in southwest France, the Lot was abandoned following the decline in commercial traffic due to railway competition. It was formally closed in 1926.

Its revival as a cruising waterway has been one of the most spectacular developments on French waterways, starting in 1985. A first 64 km length of the river was restored in 1990, from Luzech to Crégols. This section, centred on the town of Cahors, was an immediate success as a cruising holiday destination, despite difficulties due to the river's capricious flow regime, and also attracted

*The Lot is the longest tributary river in France, 481 km. From the Middle Ages onwards flat-bottomed gabares traded between Entraygues and the Garonne, a distance of 297 km. This was the only outlet for the Quercy region, and in the late 17th century Colbert ordered improvements to navigation. When the open-cast coal mines in Decazeville started supplying coal to fuel the Industrial Revolution, from 1840, 75 weirs (chaussées) and locks were built to make a viable waterway. Barge transport survived after the first railway was opened from Montauban to Capdenac in 1858. As the coal traffic increased, the railways were found inadequate and it was decided to upgrade the navigation. Canals were built to bypass the river's extravagant meanders at Luzech, Cajarc, Montbrun and Capdenac. The reprieve for river navigation was short-lived, however, since the railway line along the valley from Lot et Garonne to Cahors was opened in 1869. The decline was inevitable and the river was abandoned in 1926. An association founded by Christian Bernad in 1971 campaigned for restoration, and the author's first consultancy assignment was to assess the feasibility of developing waterway tourism on the river. This led to the first 64 km length being restored and opened in 1990.*

*Villeneuve lock, one of the modern structures built on the river, is 13 m deep.*
© FRAN BABISS

*Small-scale overview distinguishing the navigable (blue) and non-navigable (orange) sections of the river, described successively in the following pages.*

72

many land-based visitors to the otherwise neglected river. The three *départements* through which the waterway runs then agreed to seek funding for complete restoration, and the remarkably ambitious overall project was approved by the French Government in 1993, with an overall budget then estimated at €120m, including road improvements and other works.

Investments were then concentrated on the lower River Lot, and in April 2021 the *département* Lot-et-Garonne completed restoration throughout its territory, with only one missing link at Fumel dam. In recent years, the neighbouring *département* Lot, under pressure from local councils, has restored the section linking with Lot-et-Garonne, and extending up to Albas, a few kilometres short of the middle Lot. In 2006-2010, substantial works were also carried out to restore navigability of the river in the third *département*, Aveyron, and a section 11km long is open to navigation from Bouillac to Port d'Agrès.

Thus in 2021 three main sections of the river can be distinguished: the Lower, Middle and Upper River Lot. These names, and the corresponding breakdown in the following pages, are suggested here for convenience only. They are not official, and one hopes that the navigable River Lot will one day return to its former unique identity as a 266km-long navigation from Nicole to Port d'Agrès, creating an exceptional, unique, resource. This ambition is regrettably called into question by withdrawal of the Garonne crossing boat pilotage service in November 2017, depriving the river of its navigable access from the Baïse via the Garonne Crossing (see under that waterway).

The distances in the route description reach a total of 278km, corresponding to actual river kilometres as shown in the Éditions du Breil guide to the River Lot. The total of 266km given above is based on solutions to be adopted at the four meander cut-offs, at Luzech, Cajarc, Montbrun and Capdenac. There is no doubt about the latter, where the tunnel and locks are in good condition, but the other three cut-offs have been either infilled (Luzech) or converted to hydropower headrace channels.

*Passing under Masséries railway bridge, PK 181, during a survey of the river's potential in 1988. The author (at the helm) is seen here with Jean-Pierre Lagane, president of the Cahors Chamber of Commerce and Industry, and John Riddel, who later founded Éditions du Breil.*
© PIERRE LASVENES

Alignments along the cut-offs built in the mid-19th century are expected to be found preferable on environmental grounds to reusing the abandoned loops, where very substantial works would be required and unique ecosystems threatened.

## Lower River Lot, Nicole to Albas

The Lower River Lot extends from Nicole lock (the outlet lock into the river Garonne) to downstream of Albas lock and weir, a distance of 121km, although there will be an interruption at PK 78 (Fumel dam) until 2023, when a travel-lift solution is planned to be implemented. Nicole lock gives access from the Garonne to a 2.4km canal (the *canalet*) which bypasses the Lot/Garonne confluence. The channel thereafter follows the river throughout this section, which includes two deep locks built by Électricité de France (EDF) beside its hydropower plants at Castelmoron and Villeneuve-sur-Lot.

Gently undulating countryside borders the wide valley in the lower reaches, with many towns and villages of interest. The valley in this section is noted for its intensive irrigated agriculture and fruit orchards. The deep stretches retained by the EDF dams have long been used for water sports, hence the impression that this is a long-established

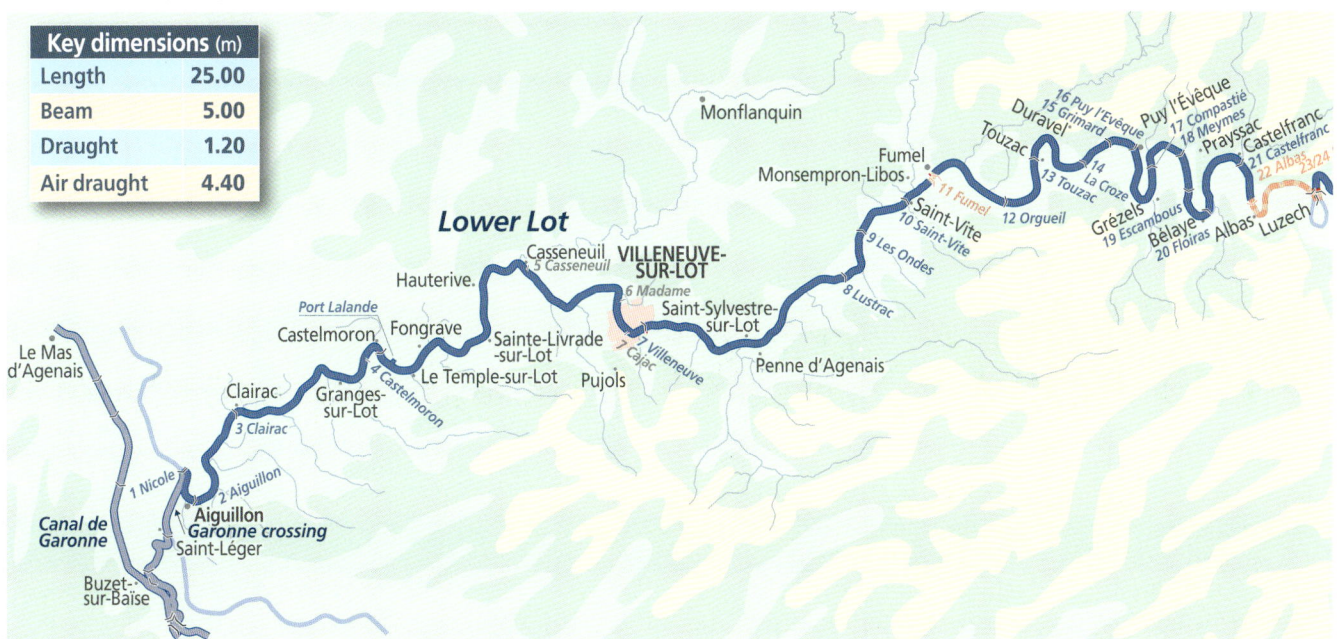

| Key dimensions (m) | |
|---|---|
| Length | 25.00 |
| Beam | 5.00 |
| Draught | 1.20 |
| Air draught | 4.40 |

# VII – Southwest France

waterway. Le Temple-sur-Lot is a rowing centre of international repute, while a length behind the dam at Villeneuve is available for power-boating and water-skiing.

Technical difficulties delayed restoration of the lock at Saint-Vite, the last before Fumel, which was opened to navigation in April 2021. Fumel dam is a greater challenge, but a travel-lift will be installed here, operating between two docks that could in the future be upgraded to conventional locks. The ramp (on a 4% gradient) will be associated with an inspection/maintenance shed and hard standing, valuable for the legal inspections of all craft on the Lower Lot. Land is reserved for continuing to provide the same functions after the future upgrading to two locks with an intermediate basin (see p. 355).

Above Fumel, the river has been restored for navigation by the Lot *département*. Nine locks have been restored, and another new lock built at Puy-l'Évêque, where the existing lock had been taken over by a hydropower plant. Despite the substantial length available above Fumel, development of recreational boating on this section will be limited until the travel-lift solution is implemented. The river and its valley become gradually more delightful heading upstream into the Lot *département*, where the Cahors wines are not the least attraction.

## Navigation

Since the River Lot is not a state-operated waterway, navigation is at the risk and peril of users, who are responsible for checking available headroom and depths according to the state of the river, which is announced and indicated by signs placed above and below the three working locks upstream of Villeneuve. Navigation is closed between November and April. Speed must not exceed 10km/h in mid-channel, and must be reduced to 6km/h in the *canalet* from Nicole to Aiguillon and within 25m of the banks. Care must be taken not to cause wash liable to damage the banks. Passenger boats have priority at the locks. Delicate passages are all in principle marked by buoys, red on the right-bank side of the channel and green on the left-bank side.

## Locks

There are 19 locks in this section. The 15 restored locks offer navigable dimensions of 30m by 5.00m. These limits also apply at the two deep locks at Castelmoron and Villeneuve, despite their slightly larger dimensions of 32.50m by 5.25m. Nicole lock is operated by the Lot-et-Garonne waterway staff, depending on the arrangements made for the transit on the Garonne through to the Baïse. The other locks (excepting Castelmoron and Villeneuve) up to the Lot *département* border are operated automatically by a T-section plastic key to be obtained from waterway staff and inserted into the terminal beside each lock. Locks may be operated from 09:00 to 19:00 (18:00 in October). Conventional signalling is in place at Castelmoron and Villeneuve locks, which are fully mechanised and operated by waterway staff. The same card works at the newly opened Saint-Vite lock. The future Fumel travel-lift will of course be operated by specialised staff. Once past the Fumel dam, the locks on this separate section are manually operated by users under their own responsibility, with gate paddle and lock-gate winding gear permanently installed, as on the middle River Lot. The last lock before reaching Luzech is at Albas. The Lot *département* is planning detailed technical and economic studies of solutions to provide the missing link through Albas and Luzech.

## Draught

The channel and all structures, especially lock sills, are designed in principle for an effective draught of 1.50m, but local siltation means that the maximum authorised draught is 1.20m.

## Headroom

The maximum authorised air draught is 4.40m, corresponding to the minimum headroom above the highest navigable water level.

## Authority

Conseil Départemental de Lot et Garonne, Direction des Infrastructures, Transports et Logement, Service Routes et Navigation, Côteau de Romas, 47130 Port Sainte-Marie 05 53 77 29 00 (PK 0–83)

Conseil Départemental du Lot, Direction de l'Éducation et de la Vie Locale, Service Sport-Tourisme-Patrimoine, Avenue de l'Europe-Regourd, BP 291, 46005 Cahors Cedex 9, 05 65 53 40 00 (PK 83–121)

*The start of a unique adventure, cruising up the magnificent River Lot, at Nicole lock, seen here from the opposite bank of the Garonne. Note the pontoon mooring below the lock.* © F-W

## Route description

**PK 0.0** *Confluence with river Garonne*

**PK 0.1** Nicole lock (lift 1.30m), navigation enters small canal ('le Canalet') bypassing confluence, footbridge, village r/b

The lock is deep (4m) but the pilots will take ropes, so the crew can stay aboard. There is a pontoon immediately through the lock, but it is adjacent to a busy, noisy road and a railway line – and there are no shops at Nicole itself. Whilst it might make a temporary, catch-your-breath, stop it is advisable to keep travelling up the *canalet*. This 3km by-pass canal is quite narrow, with fallen branches at its edges. However, you are unlikely to meet anything coming in the opposite direction, as access down onto it through Aiguillon lock will be appropriately controlled (during the limited periods of opening of the Garonne crossing, see Section 62).

# River Lot

*Approach to Aiguillon lock, beside the former mill converted into a hydropower plant, PK 3* © F-W

PK 2.2    Railway bridge (Toulouse-Bordeaux main line)
PK 2.4    **Aiguillon** bridge (Pont Napoléon, D813), town on l/b
PK 2.5    Footbridge (access to beach)

Pontoon before the lock to drop crew and magnetic card off, to operate it, then a tight channel by the large (derelict) mill building into the 2m deep lock. The water flow into the lock is quite fierce. Beach by the weir.

PK 2.6    Aiguillon lock (r/b) and weir (lift 2.00m), navigation enters River Lot
PK 7.5    **Saint-Brice** pontoon mooring and slipway l/b
PK 9.7    Camp-site and beach, r/b
PK 9.9    Clairac lock (l/b) and weir (lift 2.70m)

Pontoon below the lock for crew drop-off. This 3 metre deep lock is one of the trickiest to negotiate. The crew has to be on the lock-side to insert the key, but there is only a short section for them to use and no convenient bollard to take advantage of for the bow line. The rest of the lock becomes inaccessible when the lock gates open (for the boat to enter) since the historic mill building comes right up to the lock edge, as shown in the photo below. The lock has ropes that hang down but using them creates an unhelpful 3 metre pendulum effect. This is exacerbated by the initially fierce water inflow. Keeping a stern line short onto the ladder is advisable for control, moving this up the ladder as the lock fills. Descending is much easier.

*Detail of the awkward lock at Clairac, PK 10* © F-W

PK 10.2    **Clairac** quay r/b with moorings for 15 boats, free, water, electricity, shower, pump-out, village centre 300m

Reaching this impressive quay means continuing in the channel upstream of Clairac lock, through the bridge, then turning back through its central span. The quay is ideally situated just below the town. The capitainerie and showers are to be restored by the 2022 season. Clairac is an attractive little town., with a big sandy beach below the weir. Walk into the town by turning left above the quayside, past a historic, pretty, public spring-water source. The Carrefour supermarket just over the bridge is useful for provisions and fuel.

*The attractive quay with services at Clairac, PK 10* © F-W

PK 10.3    Clairac bridge
PK 12.7    D/s tip of island, channel in l/b arm
PK 13.0    U/s tip of island
PK 13.3    Overhead power line
PK 14.8    Piers of former railway bridge
PK 15.5    Suspension bridge (Roussanes)
PK 17.0    Mooring l/b

A long floating pontoon (no facilities, but a peaceful rural situation) for the *Musée du Pruneau*, which is fascinating.

PK 18.5    **Granges-sur-Lot** historic quay l/b, small village, shops
PK 19.0    Mooring l/b

Pontoon (floating, piles) above the village, with water and electricity. A delightful spot, a short walk along the river to the attractive little village (good small supermarket and *boulangerie*). By the village quayside (now left high and dry) is a flight of steps leading up to a garden door, halfway up which are two flood marks, very high above the current river level.

*Excellent, tranquil mooring at Granges-sur-Lot, PK 15* © F-W

# VII – Southwest France

**PK 21.3**  Site of former weir (La Chaussée), disused lock l/b, limited depths from here to Castelmoron following the lowering of this reach

The old lock and weir were demolished at this site to give extra height to the hydropower plant at Le Temple. Follow the buoyed channel through the weir. At the bend in Castelmoron the depth drops dramatically to 1.10m.

**PK 22.0**  **Castelmoron** pontoon moorings for 6 boats r/b at town hall, village with shops and facilities

Quayside moorings by the handsome Moorish building occupied by the town hall and by the impressive concrete bow-string bridge. Free water and electricity. Big sandy beach opposite, pedalos and electric whale-craft in season. Pleasant town, with an *épicerie*.

*Quayside mooring at Castelmoron, PK 22* © F-W

**PK 22.1**  Castelmoron bridge (pre-stressed concrete bow-string)
**PK 22.7**  Castelmoron lock r/b (lift 10m) adjacent to EDF hydropower plant, controlled by lock-keeper

Hydroelectric barrage with futuristic (for 1948) concrete watchtowers. The lock is 10m deep and has floating bollards. Very easy, although the initial inrush of water is noticeable, as are the two places in the lock floor where water also enters and fountains up. Crossing your lines around the bollards is a good idea, to prevent them slipping off. You may have to hoot to alert the friendly lock-keeper, to let you in. Above the lock the river is wide and open.

*Castelmoron dam and hydropower plant, with the entrance to the lock-cut in the foreground, PK 25* © F-W

*Chatting with the lock-keeper in Castelmoron lock* © F-W

**PK 23.2**  Hotel-restaurant Les Rives du Plantié, l/b

Informal bankside mooring, pleasant surroundings.

**PK 23.5**  **Port Lalande**, municipal *port de plaisance* access under footbridge r/b, moorings for 55 boats, outside pontoon for 8 boats, night €11.40, water and electricity included, showers €2, wifi, Castelmoron Nautic, 06 78 46 39 59 *castelmoron-nautic.fr*

An excellent inland harbour off the river, which means paradoxically that it dries out when the river is in flood. Port Lalande is a well maintained and safe harbour, with facilities and services including lifting-out and yard storage. Pleasant surroundings and possible additional services (laundry, swimming pool) in the adjacent holiday village. Good potential overwintering place. Adjacent to the port is the Castelmoron Nautic boatyard offering maintenance and repairs.

*The attractive basin, port and holiday village at Port Lalande, in Castelmoron* © PIERRE LASVENES

**PK 25.2**  **Le Temple-sur-Lot** boating, sailing and water sports centre l/b, municipal *halte*, free, water, village with all resources (training site for international rowing teams)

Quayside for two boats at this busy national water sports centre. Activities include rowing and kayaking, but other sports teams train here also (basketball and judo) and groups of children try their hand at various activities such as sailing in Optimist dinghies. The small village has a super-

# River Lot

market, *boulangerie*, bar, a popular restaurant 'La Commanderie' and a famous aquatic plants nursery, where Monet purchased his water lilies.

PK **26.5** **Caillac** pontoon r/b

Pontoon alongside the orchard serving a first-class farm shop (Ferme des Tuileries), visited by Rick Stein in one of his TV programmes. Friendly people and good produce.

PK **27.3** **Fongrave** pontoon r/b, free, water, electricity, slipway, small village

Timber pontoon for two boats. The village, surrounded by fruit orchards, has a post office in the *mairie* and a bar-restaurant. Farmer's market on Thursday evenings in the summer. The mooring is by the town square, next to a memorable château. It is also in a water-skiing zone: this implies some occasional rocking from the speedboats' wake. The ambience may be a little too lively when the annual village fair is held.

PK **31.4** Overhead power line
PK **32.5** **Sainte-Livrade** bridge, municipal *halte* on pontoon l/b, water, electricity, small town with all shops and services, 300m l/b

Long timber pontoon. A good small town with a big market on Friday mornings. A short walk from the pontoon is France's biggest (and presumably oldest) elm tree.

PK **35.1** **Hauterive**, pontoons, small village r/b
PK **39.1** **Casseneuil** moorings on pontoon for 4 boats d/s r/b, water, electricity, slipway, village r/b

Moorings under the willows, with a reported risk of vandalism on weekend nights. The old part of the village follows the course of the small tributary River Lède that joins the River Lot here. Ancient buildings lean and hang over the stream.

PK **48.0** Former lock (Madame) r/b, navigation through former weir
PK **49.8** Bridge (Pont de Bastérou, Villeneuve ring road)
PK **50.0** **Villeneuve-sur-Lot** municipal *halte* on quay r/b for 8 boats (below the *Mairie*), water, electricity

*The 13th century Pont des Cieutats in Villeneuve, with its curious half-timbered toll-keeper's house* © F-W

PK **50.1** Bridge (Pont des Cieutats), town centre r/b
PK **50.3** Bridge (Pont de la Libération)

PK **50.6** Former Cajac lock l/b (no difference in level following demolition of weir, narrow channel from here to lock)
PK **39.2** Bridge (D217)
PK **41.1** Overhead power line
PK **43.6** Former railway bridge (Pont du Martinet) accommodating a local road
PK **44.9** **Campagnac** pontoon moorings r/b, 4 boats

Timber pontoon in a quiet rural location, a steep walk up to the tiny village (just a few houses and a smart new *coiffeur* housed in a converted barn) past the little chapel. 5km cycle ride into Villeneuve, along a busy road.

PK **51.6** Villeneuve lock (lift 13.00m) r/b, EDF hydropower dam

*This view from downstream of Villeneuve lock and dam shows the lock entrance to be invisible from the waiting quay.* © F-W

PK **52.3** Overhead power lines
PK **53.1** Bridge (Pont de Romas, N21, Villeneuve bypass)
PK **55.0** Château Rogé sports centre, quay l/b

The imposing château on the left bank is surrounded by extensive sports and recreational facilities, including an airstrip. The quay makes a convenient mooring, except when used by the water-skiing club.

PK **56.5** **Bernoy** pontoon and slipway r/b
PK **59.6** **Saint-Sylvestre** bridge, quay u/s l/b, **Port-de-Penne** l/b, 06 31 89 60 36, 35 berths, 3 visitor moorings, night €10, water, electricity, showers (during office hours), slipway, pump-out, Penne-d'Agenais hilltop village and basilica of Notre-Dame de Peyragude 1.5km

*The quay, pontoons and slipway at Port de Penne*

# VII – Southwest France

PK **67.0**  Railway bridge (Boyer), Agen-Périgueux line
PK **67.9**  Pontoon mooring r/b
PK **68.1**  Lustrac lock (lift 1.58m), historic mill

A memorable location – a beautiful restored former mill building, a large chateau and a pretty, small, village (no facilities but there are some at Trentels, a kilometre walk away). Few boats pass the restored lock, and it is just about possible to moor at the waiting pontoon there for a night before moving on the following morning. As a longer-term alternative there is a good timber pontoon under the trees just downstream from the lock. This is a place to linger and reflect.

*One of the most spectacular sites on the lower Lot is the Lustrac, where the lock-cut squeezes between the historic mill and the château on the right bank. This chicane limits the available length to 25m, so that 30m barges visiting the Lot will have to turn back.*

PK **71.7**  Les Ondes lock (also called La Rougette) (lift 0.62m)
PK **75.7**  Saint-Vite lock (lift 2.74m)

*The first boat passes through Saint-Vite lock, on April 14, 2021*

Brand new lock with new hydropower plant on the bank side, with footbridges for access. The lock is maintained in a default position with gates closed upstream and downstream. This is part of a complex operating system designed to optimise power production except when the lock is used, when the turbined flow will be reduced. Attractive small village with *bar-tabac* and a *guinguette* beside the lock.

PK **76.0**  Bridge (D911 Fumel bypass)
PK **76.6**  Libos bridge (D102), village r/b
PK **77.6**  Site of former steel works r/b
PK **78.3**  Fumel lock l/b (lift 7.96m) adjacent to Vieille Montagne hydropower plant (travel-lift solution to be constructed)

Fumel dam will be bypassed by a travel-lift between two docks, where boats will be lifted or lowered vertically, then transferred on a constant ramp of 4%. The drawings below are based on the preliminary design.

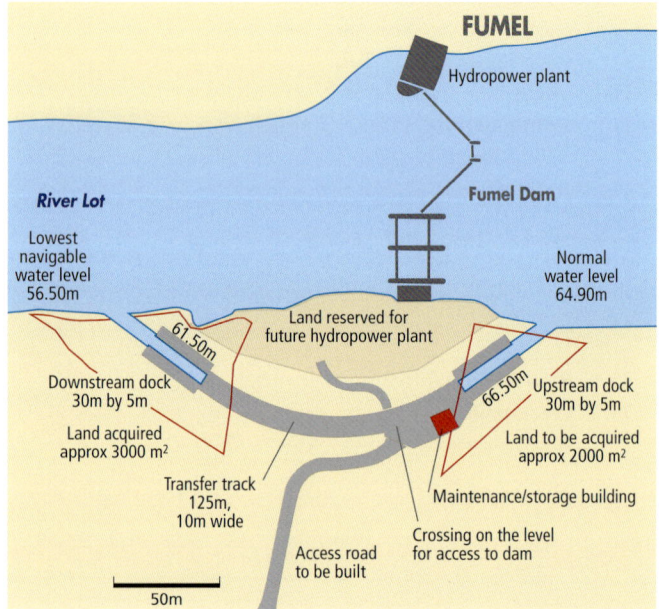

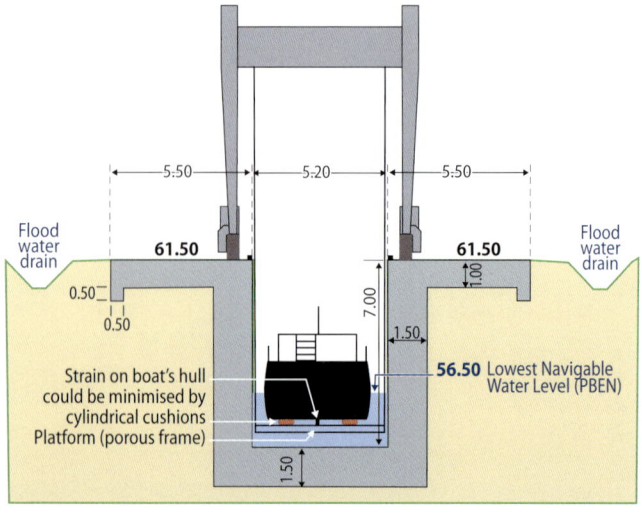

PK **78.6**  **Fumel** bridge, town centre 800m r/b
PK **81.0**  Bridge (D911 Fumel bypass)
PK **82.9**  Limit of Lot et Garonne and Lot *départements* r/b
PK **83.5**  Disused lock chamber (Fossat) r/b
PK **84.3**  Limit of Lot et Garonne and Lot *départements* l/b

# River Lot

PK **84.6**  Orgueil lock (lift 1.10m) r/b

This is the first lock in the *département* Lot, where do-it-yourself continues to be the preferred mode of operation, as adopted on the central River Lot.

PK **88.4**  **Touzac** bridge, village 400m l/b

Pleasant village but regrettably no shops or services. Best visited from mooring downstream of the lock.

PK **88.7**  Touzac lock (lift 3.15m)
PK **93.5**  Bridge (Vire-sur-Lot), D58, **Duravel** 2.5 km r/b
PK **94.6**  La Croze lock (lift 0.85m) l/b
PK **94.7**  Railway bridge (La Croze), disused
PK **96.4**  Grimard lock (lift 2.27m) l/b
PK **98.3**  Puy l'Evêque lock (lift 3.49m) l/b, adjacent to hydro-power plant
PK **98.8**  **Puy-l'Évêque** bridge, quay u/s l/b

A very attractive historic village with an authentic stone quay. From here upstream the famous Cahors vineyards become an important part of the landscape. A passenger boat offers excursions on this section of the river.

*Puy l'Évêque quay, PK 99*  © JOHN RIDDEL, ÉDITIONS DU BREIL

PK **102.6**  Former quay (port de Grézels) l/b
PK **104.5**  Compastier lock (lift 1.48m) l/b
PK **106.4**  Bridge (Pescadoires), Prayssac 2400m r/b
PK **107.7**  Meymes lock (lift 5.01m) l/b, adjacent to hydropower plant
PK **110.0**  Escambous lock (lift 0.24m) l/b
PK **112.5**  Floiras lock (lift 3.41m) r/b
PK **113.1**  U/s tip of island (d/s boats keep to r/b arm)
PK **114.1**  Suspension bridge (Juillac)
PK **117.5**  **Castelfranc** suspension bridge, village r/b
PK **117.9**  Castelfranc lock (lift 1.10m) r/b
PK **120.2**  Site of former Albas lock l/b (infilled), hydropower plant and weir, upstream limit of navigation

## Missing link

The distance from Albas lock to Luzech dam is just 7 km following the former navigation. The plan below shows the line of the short lock-cut through the centre of the village, which is also at the neck of the river's longest meander. If this option were adopted, the double staircase lock in the lock-cut would have to be associated with a new lock downstream to compensate for the lowering of the river, and a Fumel-type travel-lift to bypass the dam itself. The 5km loop of the river, originally navigable with three low-rise locks, is ruled out for restoration on environmental grounds. The Lot *département* is expected to commission new studies of this missing link in 2021, following the detailed study of four basic options completed in 1997 by the Compagnie d'Aménagement des Coteaux de Gascogne (CACG). The other two options considered in that study were a 235m-long tunnel and two locks with a combined lift of 11.35m, also shown on the plan, and a road transport solution. The Middle River Lot starts upstream of Luzech dam.

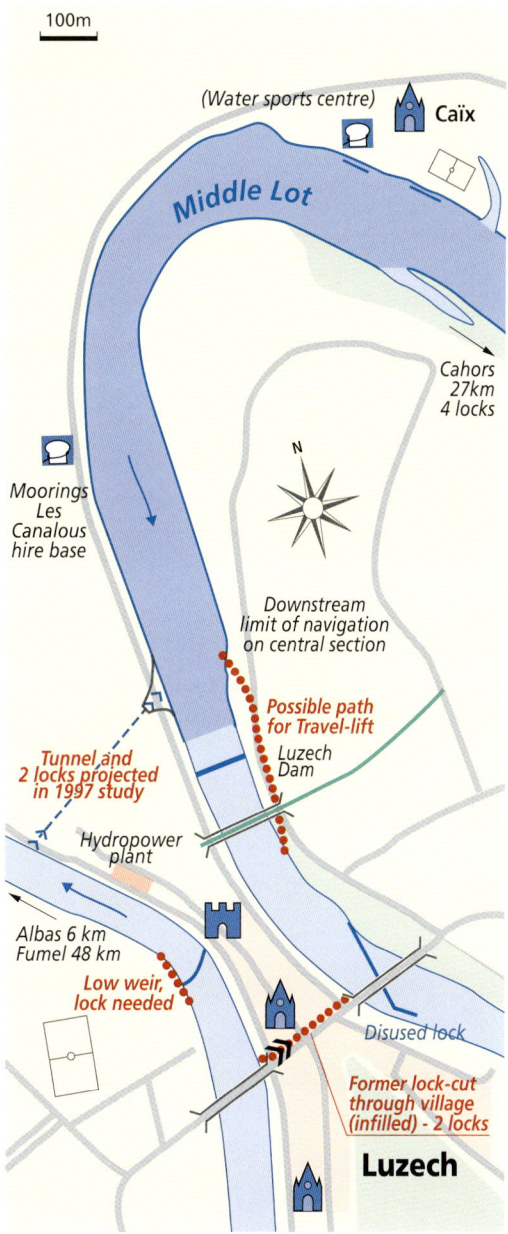

# VII – Southwest France

## Central River Lot, Luzech to Larnagol

The central River Lot is navigable over a distance of 74km, from 300m above the 6m high dam and hydropower plant at Luzech (km 128.0), to the village of Larnagol in a bypassed loop of the river. The works completed in 2006 added 10.5km to the navigable length beyond the attractive cliff-top village of Saint-Cirq-Lapopie, with two new locks and one restored lock.

This central length of the restored Lot navigation offers remarkably varied landscapes, with sheer limestone cliffs, attractive narrow lock-cuts, the Cahors vineyards, many unspoilt villages and the town of Cahors itself, remarkably located inside a long loop of the river. Because the waterway is isolated, it does not see many visiting boats, but it has four boat hire bases and three trip boat operators. It has established itself as one of the most popular waterway destinations in France.

Since the waterway was opened the *Département* has gradually improved navigable conditions at the approaches to certain locks, thus reducing the duration of interruptions to navigation on account of high water levels (see under *Navigation*).

*Entering the lock at the Pont Valentré in Cahors* © CHARLOTTE EDWARDS-MAY

## Navigation

Navigation is not authorised above a certain state of the river, indicated by signs placed above and below each lock. Each sign 'PHEN' (for *plus hautes eaux navigables*) comprises three reverse black triangles on a white background, pointing to levels marked I, II and III. When the river is below level I (discharge not specified), the navigable depth is not guaranteed. The river is navigable without restriction (albeit at the risk and peril of the navigator) between levels I and II (up to 170m³/s from Crégols to Vers bridge, 160m³/s through Vers lock, thereafter 200m³/s down to Luzech). When level II is reached, boats are required to stop at the nearest lock entrance and wait until the level drops again or until qualified staff from the hire firm or the waterway authority come to pilot the boat to a safer mooring. For this purpose there is an interphone at each lock. Security services, including convoying or pilotage, and trip boats are authorised to navigate up to level III, which corresponds to 300m³/s throughout, except through Bouziès lock (260m³/s) and through Vers lock (250m³/s). Speed must not exceed 10km/h in mid-river and must be reduced to 5km/h in the diversion canals and within 25m of the banks. Care must be taken not to cause wash liable to damage the banks, especially in the narrow lock-cuts. Passenger boats have priority at the locks.

## Locks

There are 17 locks on this section, with navigable dimensions of 30m by 5.00m, although the actual dimensions of the chambers vary. The maximum authorised length of boat is reduced from 30 to 25m for passage through the Ganil lock-cut, which is not only narrow but has a bend that is impracticable for longer boats. The wider chamber of the lock beneath the Pont Valentré in Cahors was justified in the 19th century by the intense traffic in this section.

Locks may be operated between sunrise and sunset and are worked by the users under their own responsibility, with gate paddle and lock-gate winding gear permanently installed. Only one lock is equipped for automatic operation, at the Coty mill in Cahors. A swipe card is issued to boaters for passage through this lock, which means disembarking a member of crew at the pontoon moorings installed at this site. Gate paddles can be a little tiresome to operate, the gearing being somewhat excessive, and there are some curious safety devices, which can be

| Key dimensions (m) | |
|---|---|
| Length | 25.00 |
| Beam | 5.00 |
| Draught | 1.20 |
| Air draught | 4.40 |

disconcerting when first encountered: firstly, a gate paddle has to be fully opened before opening the corresponding gate; secondly, the gate has to be closed before lowering the gate paddle; finally, a foot lever has to be pressed to start opening or closing a gate. These are minor points, however, and lock operation should be entertaining, albeit physical, for all the crew.

## Draught

The channel and all structures, especially lock sills, are designed in principle for an effective draught of 1.20m, but as a precaution the maximum authorised draught is limited to 1.00m.

## Headroom

The maximum authorised air draught is 4.40m, corresponding to the minimum headroom above the highest navigable water level.

## Authority

Conseil Départemental du Lot, Direction de l'Éducation et de la Vie Locale, Service Sport-Tourisme-Patrimoine, Avenue de l'Europe-Regourd, BP 291, 46005 Cahors Cedex 9
05 65 53 40 00

## Route description

PK 128.0 Current d/s limit of navigation, overhead power line, Luzech dam and hydropower plant 300m d/s

PK 128.4 **Luzech** (Port de Caïx) r/b, Canalous Plaisance hire base, 06 69 68 10 41, 15 boats, mooring free (maximum 24 hours), water, slipway, pump-out, Luzech village 800m *canalous.luzech@gmail.com*

See plan of Luzech on p.79.

PK 129.4 **Caïx** quay r/b, water sports base
PK 131.3 Caïx castle r/b
PK 131.4 **Parnac** municipal *halte* l/b for 3 boats, free, water, village and Cahors wine cellars 500m
PK 134.0 Langle castle r/b, former lock, alternative mooring for Parnac l/b
PK 138.7 **Caillac** mooring (no facilities) r/b, village and restaurants
PK 139.9 Disused railway viaduct (brick arches), moorings and canoeing base d/s l/b
PK 140.1 Disused lock (Douelle) l/b (earlier canalisation)
PK 140.5 Cessac lock l/b, rise 2.00m, cross-currents d/s
PK 140.6 Quay r/b and site of original hire base in restored tobacco drying shed
PK 140.7 **Douelle** pontoon mooring beneath quay l/b, Le Boat hire base 05 65 20 08 79, 3 visitor berths, water, electricity, showers, crane 10t, pump-out, attractive village with shops, restaurants *douelle@leboat.com*
PK 140.9 Douelle suspension bridge
PK 143.9 Cessac r/b
PK 146.8 Outfall of Mercuès hydropower plant, former lock, r/b
PK 147.8 Mercuès lock l/b at end of long narrow channel, rise 4.20m
PK 147.9 **Mercuès** mooring r/b, village 500m, château 1200m on hilltop (hotel and restaurant)

PK 150.2 **Pradines** *halte* on 25m pontoon l/b, free, water, slipway, shops, restaurant
PK 153.0 Bridge (D820 Cahors bypass)
PK 153.2 Labéraudie lock l/b, rise 0.70m
PK 154.5 **Cahors** boatyard (Port Saint-Mary) r/b, Chantier Naval du Lot et de la Garonne and Babou Marine/Locaboat/Nicols hire base, boat sales, 06 43 42 39 69, night 3 visitor moorings, €10 (first night free), water and electricity included, showers, crane 40t, slipway, pump-out, repairs, retaurant *baboumarine.com*
PK 154.6 Bridge (pont des Remparts)
PK 155.6 Valentré lock l/b under the 14th century Pont Valentré, rise 2.75m, **Cahors** centre 400m r/b

The lock is located dramatically under the left-bank arch of the spectacular bridge, which testifies to the rich past of the city of Cahors. Passenger boats operate from the quay just above the bridge.

PK 156.2 Railway bridge
PK 156.6 Hôtel La Chartreuse and restaurant built on former lock, l/b
PK 156.7 Cahors bridge (Pont Louis-Philippe, or Saint-Georges), D920 main road, town centre r/b
PK 157.2 Entrance to Cahors lock-cut, l/b
PK 157.3 Cahors lock (Moulin de Coty), (rise 1.30m) l/b, mechanised, controlled by swipe card on lockside control unit
PK 157.6 Bridge (Pont de Cabessut), submerged former bridge pier just d/s of middle of each arch
PK 158.2 **Cahors L'Archipel** *halte* on 74m long pontoon l/b in front of sports grounds, swimming pool, draught 1m, free (maximum 48 hours), water, electricity, pump-out, Cahors town centre 1km
PK 158.4 Cahors rowing club headquarters r/b
PK 160.8 Lacombe lock, l/b, rise 1.40m
PK 161.7 **Laroque-des-Arcs** quay in centre of village, shops, restaurant, water

*Approaching the delightful short quayside mooring at Laroque-des-Arts* © CANALOUS GUIDEMAR

PK 163.2 **Lamagdeleine** moorings on quay for 3 boats at sports ground and campsite, r/b, draught 1m, free, water, electricity, village with café and restaurant 200m

# VII – Southwest France

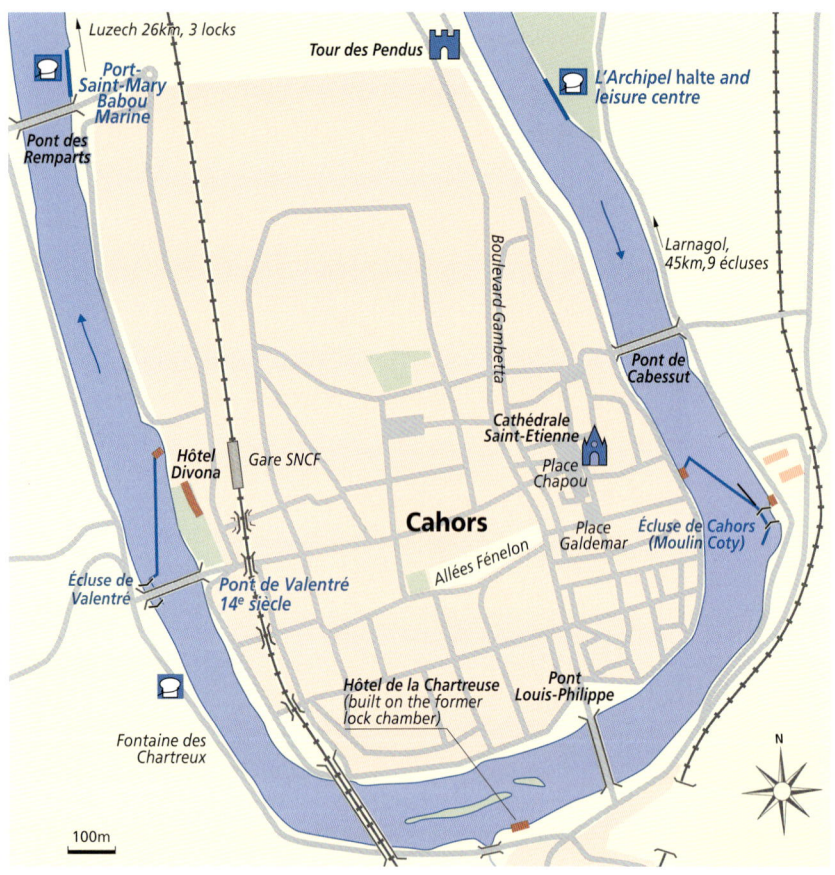

PK **173.9** Planiol lock l/b, rise 1.40m

PK **176.9** St Géry lock r/b, in lock-cut, rise 3.05m

PK **177.1** **Saint-Géry** *port de plaisance*, safe year-round moorings in lock-cut, r/b, 05 65 20 89 00, free, water, slipway, boat repairs, village centre 200m

PK **177.5** U/s entrance to Saint-Géry lock-cut

PK **178.0** Bridge (Saint-Géry)

PK **180.1** Massèries lock l/b (disused, pounds level following raising of St Géry weir, keep between buoys towards right bank)

PK **180.6** Railway bridge

PK **181.9** Island (Île aux chiens), navigation in r/b arm

PK **184.2** Bouziès lock l/b, rise 1.40m

PK **185.1** **Bouziès** bridge, municipal *halte* u/s l/b in front of Hôtel des Falaises, Lot Navigation boat hire/canoeing base, 5 visitor moorings, free, water, pump-out, slipway

PK **185.9** Railway bridge

PK **186.4** Ganil lock, l/b, rise 1.50m, navigation continue in lock-cut

PK **186.7** Confluence of Célé r/b (not visible from lock-cut)

PK **164.7** Arcambal lock, l/b, in lock-cut, rise 1.35m

PK **164.8** **Arcambal** *halte* in lock-cut, pontoon 24m, free, water

PK **165.1** U/s entrance to Arcambal lock-cut, beware of cross-currents, motorway viaduct (A20)

PK **166.1** Moorings for Savanac, r/b, Arcambal, l/b

PK **167.1** Original Galessie lock (hydropower plant), l/b

PK **167.4** Galessie new lock r/b, rise 2.80m

PK **168.7** Railway bridge (Quercyrail tourist line, closed)

PK **171.7** Vers lock r/b, rise 0.25m

PK **171.8** **Vers** bridge, *halte* u/s r/b at campsite, pontoon for 10 boats, free, water, electricity, showers €2 at campsite, slipway, all shops and restaurants in village, 200m

*Vers lock*

*The dramatic location of Ganil lock under the limestone cliffs at Saint-Cirq-Lapopie.* © PIERRE LASVENES

PK **187.3** End of lock-cut, navigation re-enters river, beware of current

PK **189.4** Saint-Cirq lock, l/b, in lock-cut, rise 1.85m

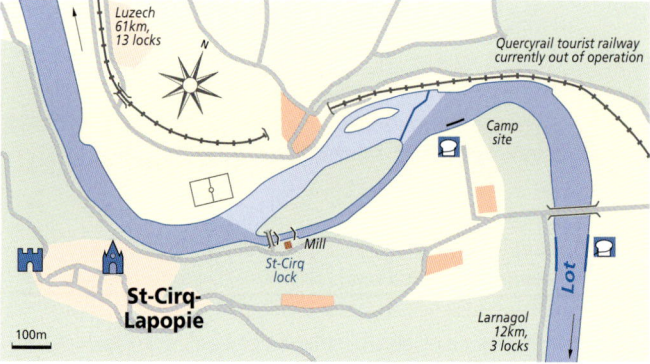

82

# River Lot

PK **189.9** End of lock-cut, navigation re-enters river, beware of current

PK **190.3** **Saint-Cirq-Lapopie** bridge, campsite, quay for up to 25 boats, 05 65 20 89 00, draught 1m, free, water, electricity, slipway, pump-out, wifi, famous cliff-top village 1km up the hill (alternative mooring below lock)

The spectacular site of Saint-Cirq-Lapopie is one of the major attractions of the central River Lot, and has for long been a tourism destination as one of the 'most beautiful villages' of France, complete with souvenir shops, art galleries, cafés and restaurants, plus the superb view from the top of the ruined château.

PK **191.7** Old Crégols lock (disused) l/b in former lock-cut
PK **192.6** New Crégols lock, r/b, village 800m l/b (no services)
PK **193.3** St Martin-Labouval lock l/b, navigation continues in lock-cut
PK **194.0** End of lock-cut, weir and hydro plant r/b
PK **197.1** Bridge (Cénevières)
PK **197.2** Railway bridge (preserved line used by Quercyrail service, currently withdrawn)
PK **199.4** Cénevières lock l/b, navigation enters short lock-cut
PK **199.5** **Cénevières** *halte* in lock-cut, 25m pontoon, free, water
PK **199.8** End of lock-cut
PK **201.5** Former Larnagol bridge, in former lock-cut
PK **202.3** **Larnagol** bridge, village r/b, current limit of navigation

*Upstream entrance to Vic lock, slightly compromised by the intake to the hydropower plant and its protective boom.* © YANN LESELLIER/LOT-46.COM

## Section not navigable, Larnagol to Capdenac

PK **202.9** Larnagol lock (presumed) l/b side of weir, adjacent to entrance to former lock-cut, used by hydropower plant, bridge
PK **207.2** Site of former Labruyère lock l/b (weir flooded by raising of lower weir)
PK **207.9** Railway bridge (disused line)
PK **210.8** Former locks used as spillway of Cajarc hydroelectric power plant r/b, navigation
PK **211.1** Entrance to lock-cut r/b
PK **211.2** Cajarc double staircase lock (rise 9.0m)
PK **211.5** Entrance to Cajarc tunnel, length 370m

Studies have suggested a compromise solution where the turbines of the hydropower plant are shut down outside peak demand periods, so that the tunnel can then be used by boats. This elegant solution to removing the Cajarc bottleneck implies a complete reconfiguration of the former double staircase lock and the intake to the power plant, because the locks were adapted to serve as the spillway.

PK **211.7** U/s entrance to tunnel, navigation reenters river 300m u/s of Cajarc hydro dam (head 6m), waterway enters *département* of Aveyron, l/b
PK **212.8** **Cajarc** bridge, pontoon moorings u/s r/b, town centre 200m, all shops and services, **Salvagnac-Cajarc** village 1000m l/b
PK **215.0** Former Cadrieu lock (chamber apparent l/b)
PK **218.6** Entrance to lock-cut r/b
PK **218.8** Montbrun lock
PK **218.9** End of lock-cut
PK **219.5** **Montbrun** village r/b
PK **220.3** Montbrun lock r/b (location to be determined)
PK **220.3** Entrance to tunnel

The Montbrun tunnel, like that at Cajarc, is used by the hydropower plant.

PK **220.6** U/s entrance to tunnel, navigation rejoins river
PK **222.2** D/s tip of island, navigation in l/b arm
PK **222.3** U/s tip of island
PK **222.5** Camboulan lock (rise 1.90m) l/b
PK **224.8** Toirac lock (rise 2.30m) r/b
PK **225.7** **Larroque-Toirac** bridge, **Saint-Pierre-Toirac** 1200m l/b
PK **228.5** Frontenac lock (rise 2.93m), r/b adjacent to power plant
PK **232.9** La Madeleine lock (rise 0.78m) r/b
PK **234.0** La Madeleine bridge, restaurant l/b
PK **235.1** Arelles lock (rise 2.0m) l/b adjacent to power plant
PK **236.6** Submerged groyne l/b, keep towards r/b
PK **237.6** Island, navigation in r/b arm
PK **240.5** Capdenac tunnel lock 1 (rise 2.00m), entrance to Capdenac tunnel (length 160m)
PK **240.6** Capdenac tunnel lock 2 (rise 2.00m) in tunnel entrance

Capdenac tunnel is another gem of waterway engineering on the Lot, with two locks inside the tunnel, fortunately easily restored since the hydropower headrace is in a separate tunnel.

PK **240.7** Navigation reenters river
PK **241.0** Vic lock (rise 2.18m) r/b adjacent to power plant

# VII – Southwest France

## Upper River Lot, Capdenac to Port d'Agrès

This upstream section, soon to be 25km in length, extends from Capdenac to the head of navigation at Port d'Agrès. This is 6km beyond the head of navigation during the industrial era, the extra distance being obtained by the dam and hydropower plant at Marcenac, and the substantial lock (5m deep) completed here in 2009. In addition to this lock, which cost approximately €4 million, three other locks were restored in this section, funded by the *département* Aveyron with contributions from the EU, the State and Midi-Pyrenees region. The resulting length of 11km was too short for substantial development. That is changing as we go to print, thanks to a new multi-purpose project at Cuzac – a new gated weir, hydropower plant and lock 3.75m deep, to be completed by 2026, which will make the two upstream locks (57 and 58 on the map below) redundant. One more lock is projected beside the hydropower plant at Assier (55), to complete the link.

This upstream section of the waterway, leading into the Massif Central, offers attractive scenery, the reddish brown rock formations contrasting with the limestone of the *Quercy Blanc*. Most of the signs of this region's industrial past have disappeared, but the few that remain contribute to the interest of this isolated section. The waterway is at present mainly used by an electric passenger boat and trailed craft, using the available slipways.

Further restoration through the Capdenac tunnel, then on to Cajarc, would open up prospects for a hire-boat holiday activity on the Upper Lot.

*Studies in the 1990s looked at the possibility of making the Lot navigable as far upstream as the Pont de Coursavy, to give access to the major tourist destination of Conques, but the free-flowing river would have lost its appeal for canoeing, and the environmental impacts would have been extensive, as the river's natural gradient becomes steeper. The proposed low dam and hydropower plant at Saint-Parthem was also abandoned.*

*The 5m-deep lock at Marcenac will be the last (numbered 62) in our sequence when the navigable Lot has been fully linked up.*

*View downstream towards the village of Laroque-Bouillac, nestled under its reddish-brown cliffs, from Laroque lock, viewed here before restoration*

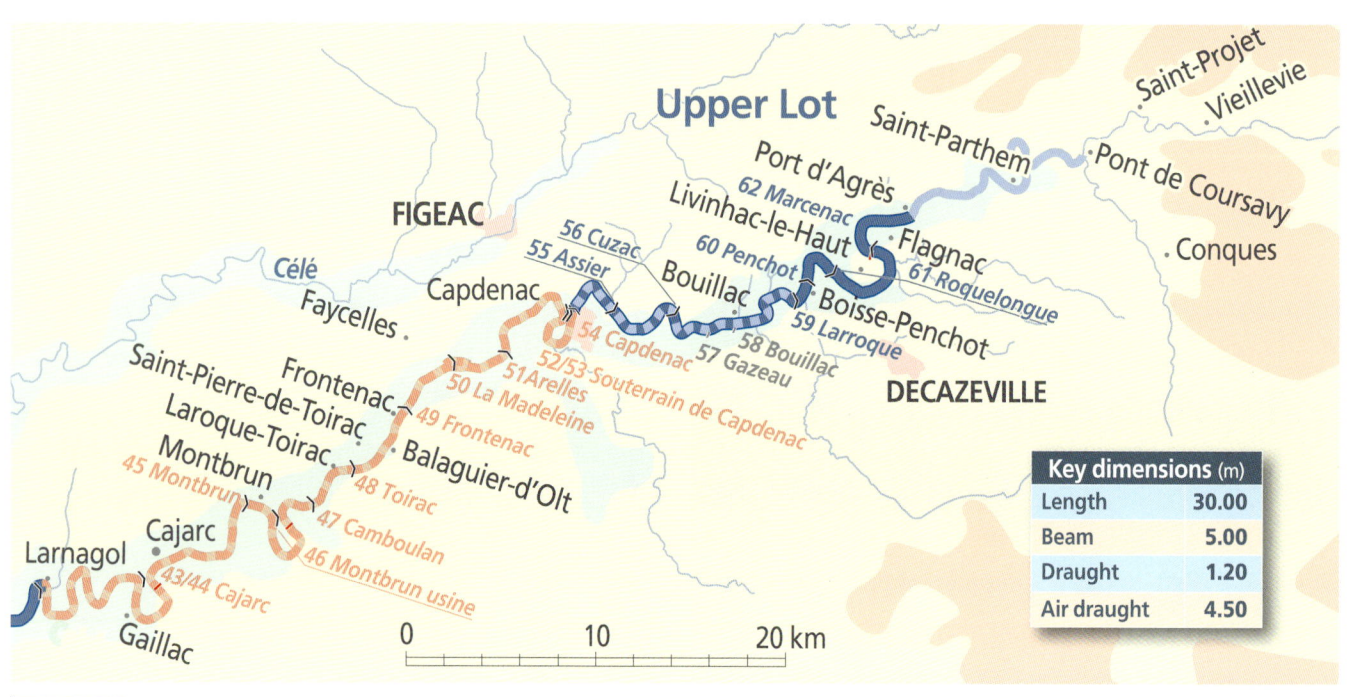

| Key dimensions (m) | |
|---|---|
| Length | 30.00 |
| Beam | 5.00 |
| Draught | 1.20 |
| Air draught | 4.50 |

# River Lot

## Locks
On completion of Cuzac lock, there will be 5 working locks on this section, with navigable dimensions of 30m by 5.00m. They are equipped for do-it-yourself operation, with winding gear in place on the locks. A windlass is needed to operate Marcenac lock. Arrangements for operation of the new lock at Cuzac/Floirac are not yet known.

## Draught
The lock-cuts and all structures, especially lock sills, are designed in principle for an effective draught of 1.60m, but as a precaution the maximum authorised draught is limited to 1.20m.

## Headroom
The maximum authorised air draught is 4.50m, corresponding to the minimum headroom above the highest navigable water level.

## Authority
Conseil Départemental de l'Aveyron, avenue Général de Gaulle, 12000 Rodez 05 65 53 40 00

*The bucolic basin at Penchot and the electric passenger boat L'Olt.*

## Route description, Capdenac to Port d'Agrès

The Upper Lot is expected to be navigable by around 2026 from Capdenac, thanks to current projects for a new lock at Assier and a multi-purpose dam at Cuzac. The section to become navigable is dotted on the map, left.

- PK **241.2** Capdenac bridge, mooring d/s r/b, restaurant
- PK **241.5** Railway bridge (Toulouse-Brive line)
- PK **244.3** Assier lock (rise 2.54m) new lock projected adjacent to hydro-power plant r/b
- PK **244.3** Assier hydropower plant, lock projected
- PK **245.9** Overhead power line
- PK **247.4** New Cuzac lock (rise 3.75m) in lock-cut r/b
- PK **247.7** End of lock-cut, new hydropower plant and weir
- PK **250.1** Site of former Gazeau lock, l/b (weir removed for channel)
- PK **251.1** **Bouillac** bridge, mooring below lock entrance l/b
- PK **251.2** Site of Bouillac lock l/b in lock-cut, navigation in river

Bouillac should have been accessible when the initial phase of restoration works was completed in 2010, but in the absence of a solution for disposing of the contaminated sediments to be dredged downstream of the lock, restoration of this lock had to be put on hold. The higher gated weir projected at Cuzac resolves this issue.

- PK **253.9** **La Roque Bouillac** village r/b
- PK **254.6** Larroque lock (rise 2.30m) in lock-cut l/b
- PK **254.8** End of lock-cut, navigation re-enters river
- PK **255.0** Bridge (D840)
- PK **255.5** Penchot bridge
- PK **255.9** Penchot lock (rise 2.30m) l/b, disused factory r/b
- PK **255.9** **Penchot** basin l/b

This small square-shaped basin makes an ideal mooring and picnicking area, despite the rough stone edge, requiring caution in deploying the boat's fenders.

- PK **257.9** Roquelongue lock (rise 2.30m) in lock-cut l/b
- PK **258.2** End of lock-cut, navigation re-enters river

*The lock at Roquelongue was restored after demolishing a water treatment plant which had been built on its foundations beyond the girder bridge.* ©JOHN RIDDEL/EDITIONS DU BREIL

- PK **259.1** **Livinhac** bridge (D21), campsite and moorings u/s r/b, slipway, Livinhac-le-Haut village 600m r/b, Decazeville with all services 4 km l/b (but 120m climb over hill)
- PK **259.2** Site of former Livinhac suspension bridge
- PK **260.0** Former coal loading quays and limit of navigation (Port Bouquiès) l/b

It is hard to believe how important this was as a coal loading port, since the site has returned to its bucolic natural state with hardly a trace of any such activity.

- PK **262.7** Marcenac lock (rise 5.00m) l/b, adjacent to modern hydropower plant r/b
- PK **264.1** **Flagnac** moorings adjacent to campsite l/b

Attractive grass-edged timber-pile mooring, close to Flagnac, where there is an *épicerie* and a tourist office. Boat trips in an electric passenger boat are operated from here.

- PK **266.0** **Port d'Agrès** bridge, limit of navigation, moorings d/s r/b, hotel-restaurant du Pont, Flagnac 1200m l/b

# VII – Southwest France

## 64. River Garonne and Gironde Estuary

The river Garonne rises in the Pyrenees and drains a large part of the Aquitaine basin. It is navigable as a tidal river from Castets-en-Dorthe to Bec d'Ambès (the confluence of the Dordogne), where it becomes the Gironde estuary.

For the 5km long section in Toulouse, see under the **Canal de Garonne**, and for the 5km section from the confluence with the Baïse at Saint-Léger to the junction with the Lot outlet canal at Nicole, see under **Garonne Crossing** (sections 59 and 62). From Nicole to Castets-en-Dorthe, the shifting channel presents numerous obstacles to navigation and depths vary considerably. Navigation is possible only during moderate floods or in light craft.

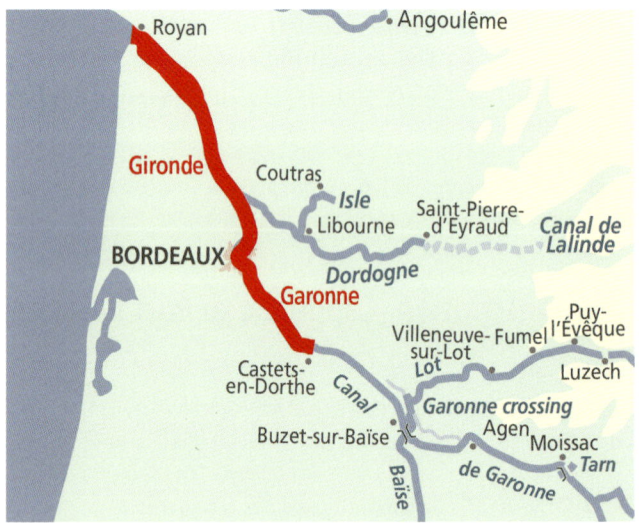

*Commercial navigation extended upstream of Toulouse from the Middle Ages, but the river was never regulated with weirs and locks. Only a short length was made navigable through Toulouse after the weir at Le Bazacle mill was raised to supply water to the Canal de la Garonne. Now navigation is effectively limited to the tidal river.*

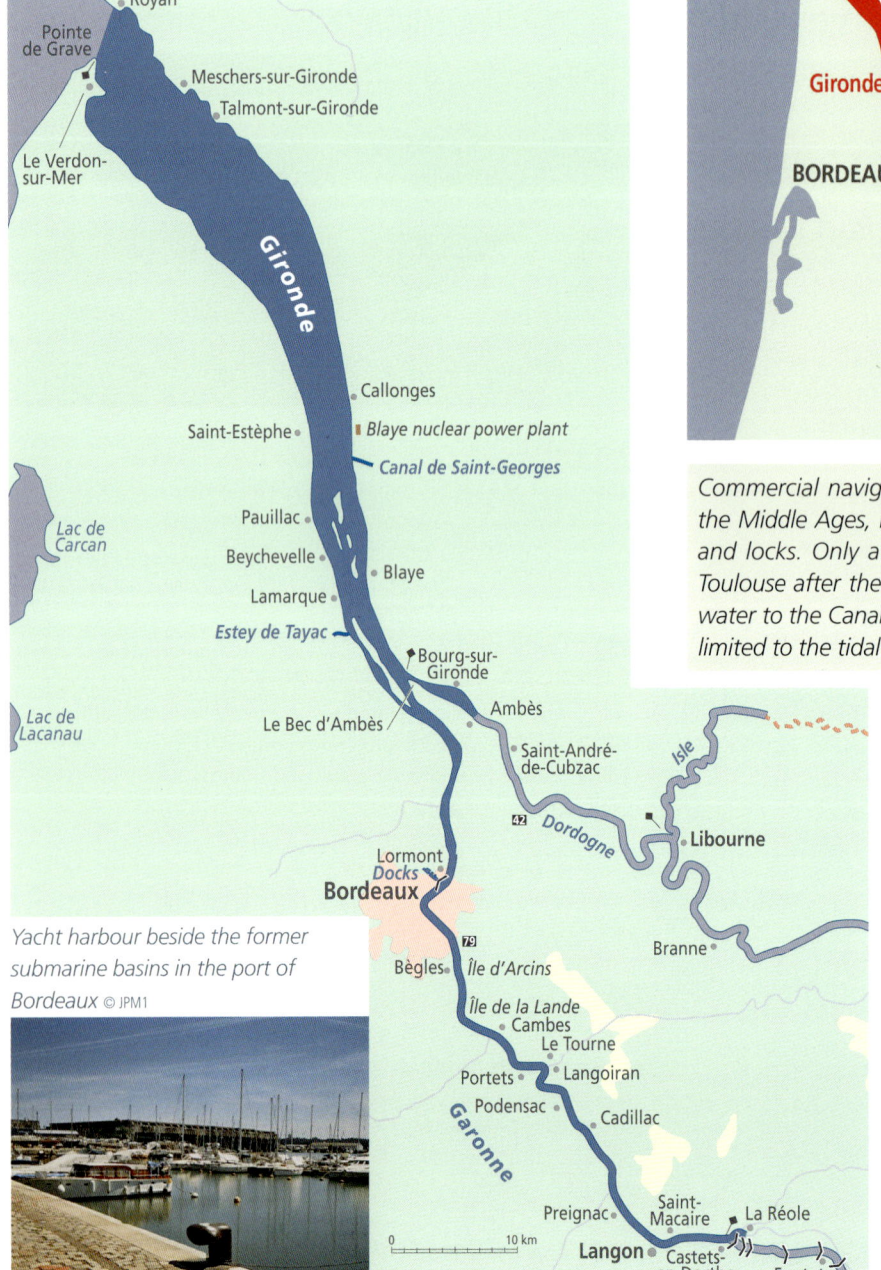

Yacht harbour beside the former submarine basins in the port of Bordeaux © JPM1

From Castets downstream the river forms part of the main route across southern France from the Atlantic to the Mediterranean. The Pont de Pierre in Bordeaux marks the beginning of the maritime waterway. At Bec d'Ambès the Dordogne enters on the right bank, and the two rivers form the Europe's biggest estuary, the Gironde. From Castets-en-Dorthe to Bordeaux is 54km, Bec d'Ambès is a further 25km downstream and the length of the Gironde from Bec d'Ambès to the sea is 71km.

### Navigation

Navigating the tidal stream presents no exceptional difficulty, but careful attention is required and one of the guides covering this river should be used.

# Garonne and Gironde

A bore (*mascaret*) sometimes forms during low flow periods over a distance of 30km upstream from Bordeaux. The most delicate passage is the Pont de Pierre in Bordeaux, with its tricky arches, especially at high tide, or when a strong ebb flow is combined with a river flood. A strong tidal flood flow can be just as difficult. If the tidal stream is properly worked, navigation is greatly facilitated. Putting into the various ports and quays along the estuary will need careful planning, however, and use of the Breil guide No 16 *Estuaire de la Gironde* is recommended. The Royal Cruising Club Pilotage Foundation's *Atlantic France* by Nick Chavasse (Imray) also covers the Gironde up to Bordeaux.

## Draught
Depths are variable and subject to the tides. Local advice should always be obtained, but vessels drawing up to 1·80m (the maximum authorised draught on the lateral canal) are generally able to make the passage between Bordeaux and Castets-en-Dorthe without difficulty.

## Headroom
The bridges leave a minimum headroom of 6·50m above the highest navigable water level.

## Authority
VNF Sud-Ouest – Unité rivière de Cadillac
- 12, rue Adolphe Homeau, 33410 Cadillac 05 56 62 66 50 (PK 0-49) subdi.aquitaine@vnf.fr

## Route description

*Continuation of Mediterranean-Atlantic route, east to west*

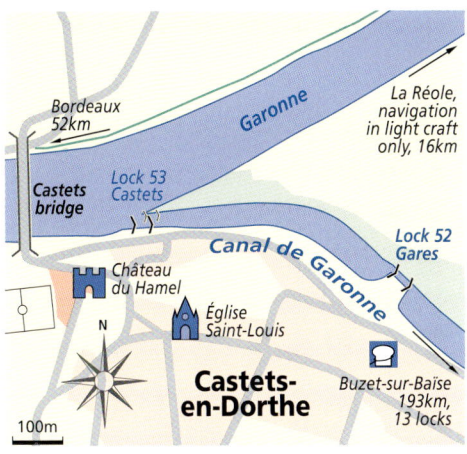

PK 17.3 **Junction with Canal de Garonne**, Castets-en-Dorthe entrance lock l/b

The Garonne is theoretically navigable for a further 17km upstream to beyond La Réole, but the changing river morphology now makes this unfeasible except for light craft. Take the rising tide up from Castets for this adventure. After 2-3km, keep to the outside of the first bend in the river (opposite Caudrot), as there are rocks in mid-channel. The only mooring at La Réole is a rowing club pontoon. Boats reaching this exotic destination may feel obliged to return to Castets without attempting to moor.

PK 17.6 **Castets-en-Dorthe** bridge, village l/b

River waiting pontoon just downstream of the bridge. The lock-keeper on the Canal de Garonne is a valuable source of advice and information on the river, regarding tides, the *mascaret* and mooring places.

PK 20.3 Quay (Mondiet) r/b
PK 23.7 **Saint-Macaire** slipway r/b, village 800m
PK 25.0 Small basin l/b

This basin was built to moor barges carrying where the Airbus parts were unloaded from their barge, for onward road transport to Toulouse, but this traffic has now stopped.

PK 25.6 **Langon** halte managed by Sud-Gironde district, 25m long, Barge Party trip boat, 2 or 3 visitor moorings depending on draught (1m on inside of pontoon), night €10.80, water and electricity included, book by email to escalelangon@gmail.com, small town with all services l/b

A welcome new facility close to the centre of the small town.

PK 26.0 Former bridge piers
PK 26.1 New road bridge (D1113)
PK 26.2 Railway bridge, quay d/s l/b
PK 29.5 Slipway (Garonnelle) r/b
PK 30.9 **Preignac** slipway l/b, village 500m, limit of *mascaret*
PK 32.4 **Barsac** slipway l/b, village 1·5 km
PK 37.1 **Cadillac** bridge, pontoon u/s r/b, night €10, water, electricity, shower, slipway, village 500m r/b

Good mooring, but best avoided at spring tides. Pleasant historic village.

PK 38.1 Quay (Cérons) l/b
PK 38.8 New road bridge (D13)
PK 40.5 **Podensac** village l/b
PK 44.7 Quay (Lestiac) r/b
PK 45.9 Quay (Arbanats) l/b
PK 49.3 Bridge, pontoon moorings d/s r/b, **Langoiran** 300m
PK 50.6 **Portets** slipway l/b, village 700m
PK 55.1 Slipway (Baurech) r/b
PK 56.6 **Cambes** pontoon r/b used by fishermen, village 300m
PK 57.9 Slipway (Esconac)
PK 58.9 River divides (Île de la Lande), navigation in r/b arm
PK 59.3 La Ferme Exotique animal park pontoon l/b in l/b arm
PK 60.5 Downstream tip of island
PK 62.2 La Maison du Fleuve pontoon and restaurant r/b
PK 62.6 Private pontoons, r/b
PK 64.8 Former slipway (Port de l'Homme) r/b
PK 65.5 Upstream tip of island (Île d'Arcins), navigation l/b arm
PK 66.4 **Bègles** port de plaisance l/b, 48 berths, 5 visitor moorings, 05 56 93 93 56, night €20, water and electricity included, showers, fuel, crane 12t, slipway, repairs port@mairie-begles.fr

Visiting boats will be allocated outside pontoon positions, further out into the current. Keep the bow towards the flood tide. Supermarket and other shops nearby, and good transport connections into Bordeaux.

PK 67.1 D/s tip of island

# VII – Southwest France

PK **67.3** Bridge (François Mitterrand), ring road (N230),
PK **71.0** Railway bridges, old Eiffel bridge and new bridge
PK **71.1** Bridge (Pont Saint-Jean), former wharves d/s l/b
PK **72.1** Bridge (Pont de Pierre), limit of inland waterway

Take one of the three central arches. It can be difficult to maintain steerage through the bridge, whether going with the flow or against it. The flood tide is much stronger than the ebb, particularly in the hours HW-4 to HW-3. There are strong eddies on the inland side because the bridge tends to hold back the tidal current. The tidal turn from a strong ebb flow to a strong flood flow occurs very rapidly.

PK **72.5** **Bordeaux** pontoon (Ponton d'Honneur) for all boats l/b, 05 56 10 28 26 or 06 44 18 87 37, 155m long, u/s 50m reserved for passenger vessels

The *Ponton d'Honneur* is the first option for mooring in Bordeaux and a spendid location, close to the city centre.

*Visitor's pontoon below the Pont de Pierre in Bordeaux,* PK *72.*

PK **75.5** New bridge (Pont Jacques Chaban-Delmas) with lifting span
PK **75.7** Entrance lock to docks, l/b, Conservatoire International de Plaisance (museum) in second basin, 05 56 90 58 00 or VHF 12, 9 or 16, 5 berths, crane, repairs, restaurant

This second option for mooring is in a corner of the extensive commercial harbour, via a very large lock, only accessible from HW-1.5 to HW+0.5.

PK **77.6** **Lormont** quay and village (Bordeaux suburb) r/b
PK **77.9** Bridge (Aquitaine suspension bridge, ring road A630), yacht harbour (*halte nautique*) u/s l/b, 06 77 17 91 83

The *halte nautique* by the high suspension bridge is the third possibility for mooring in Bordeaux. The strong river and tidal currents at this point do not make for comfortable berthing. Yacht club pontoon and a riverbus pontoon for Lormont on the opposite bank.

PK **81.6** Bassens wharves r/b
PK **92.3** Oil refineries and power station r/b, wharves
PK **93.5** Tip of island, channel r/b side (danger, submersible dyke)
PK **97.6** Bec d'Ambès, confluence of Dordogne, river changes name to Gironde

Tidal currents and conditions must be taken into account in planning an upstream or downstream passage. The downstream ebb flow occurs for approximately two thirds of the cycle, the upstream flood for one third. This means that the flood tide is much stronger than the ebb, particularly in the hours HW-4 to HW-3. Approximate high water times compared to high water at Pointe de Grave are: Pauillac +1 hour, Bordeaux +2 hours, and Castets +4 hrs. Times can be modified by wind strength and direction.

PK **106.9** **Lamarque** ferry terminal l/b beyond tip of island
PK **109.1** **Blaye** ferry terminal and town r/b (wharves u/s), mooring for 6 boats, free, water, electricity, showers, *halte-nautique@tourisme-blaye.com*
PK **118.6** **Pauillac** quays and town l/b, 06 21 86 48 93, mooring for 130 boats, 7 visitor moorings, night €28, water and electricity included, showers, wifi, crane 15t, slipway

*A favourite mooring in the estuary is Pauillac, where the harbour breakwater serves as a mooring for the cruise ships.* © PATRICK MIRAMONT

Pauillac is ideal for mast stepping or re-masting (the alternatives are Royan and Port Medoc). Optimal access is at HW slack. Pauillac is about 3 hours from Bordeaux. Heading upstream it is advisable to stem the last of the ebb tide for an hour or two, to arrive at the Pont de Pierre just after the turn, thus carrying the upriver flood, but before it becomes uncomfortably strong passing through the bridge arches.

PK **121.9** Oil refinery, tanker berths l/b
PK **124.9** Nuclear power plant (Blayais), r/b
PK **126.6** **Saint-Estèphe** quay l/b, village 1 km
PK **132.8** **Saint-Sorlin-de-Conac** (Port de Vitrezay) r/b, moorings for 41 boats, 1 visitor mooring, 06 22 88 28 25, night €19.50 (first night free), water, electricity, shower, slipway, wifi at restaurant
PK **138.2** **Saint-Christoly** l/b (former quay)
PK **147.3** **Mortagne-sur-Gironde** *port de plaisance* r/b, accessible high tide, 60 berths, 10 visitor moorings, 06 43 48 91 93, night €21.80, water, electricity, showers €1.50, wifi, crane, slipway, pump-out, repairs, village 1200m
PK **150.7** Lighthouse (Phare de Richard) l/b
PK **161.1** **Meschers-sur-Gironde** municipal port r/b accessible high tide, 06 15 11 23 10, 265 berths, 12 visitor moorings, night €20, water, electricity, shower, slipway, pump-out, repairs
PK **163.1** **Le Verdon-sur-Mer** (Port-Médoc) l/b, 950 berths, 40 visitor berths, night €28, water and electricity included, fuel, showers, crane 45t, slipway, pump-out, repairs, restaurant, wifi *port-medoc.com*
PK **167.0** Port-Bloc ferry terminal l/b
PK **168.1** **Royan** ferry terminal r/b, tourist resort, marina opposite the Pointe de Grave l/b, limit of sea, 05 46 38 72 22, *port-royan.com* , night €24.45, fuel, water, electricity, showers €2, crane 24t, slipway €3, repairs

# 65. River Dordogne

THE RIVER DORDOGNE WAS FORMERLY navigable from Bergerac weir to its confluence with the Garonne at Bec d'Ambès. However, navigation is now impossible over the first 14km below the weir and officially begins at Saint-Pierre-d'Eyraud, 12km upstream of the small town of Sainte-Foy-la-Grande. This is a free-flow navigation, with the difficulties that entails, down to Castillon-la-Bataille (PK 39). From here the river is tidal. The distance from Saint-Pierre-d'Eyraud to the confluence with the Garonne is 118km. There are pontoon moorings at the most towns and villages on the river.

*Plans to canalise the Dordogne were never completed. As well as mills and fish farming ponds, a serious obstacle throughout the 17th and 18th centuries was the series of rapids at La Gratusse, upstream of Bergerac. These were finally bypassed by the remarkable Canal de Lalinde, with its triple staircase locks, built in 1838-1844. The canal was in use until 1945. Restoration of Grand-Salvette lock in Bergerac, along with this canal, would open up navigation up to the spectacular Trémolat meander.*

## Navigation
The tidal flow should be used to proceed up the river, especially up to Libourne but even beyond. The possibility of mooring at most of the quays indicated depends on the state of the tide, but they are generally historic 'beaching' quays rather than conventional alongside-mooring quays. Pontoon moorings are rare, and generally dedicated to small craft. This makes the Dordogne experience quite an adventure for larger craft, which should not proceed beyond Branne.

## Draught
Above Branne (PK 56), the river bed is very irregular, and the depth may fall to 0.30m in low flow periods, making navigation virtually impossible. Below Branne there is generally ample depth for navigation. The tidal range increases progressively downstream, with 2.00m below Libourne at low water neaps and as much as 4.80m at high water neaps. Local advice should be sought if it is planned to proceed far up the river.

## Headroom
Above Libourne the fixed bridges leave a minimum headroom of 10m above mean water level, reduced to 5.50m above the highest navigable water level. The bridges below Libourne leave a minimum headroom of 19.85m above the highest water level.

## Authority
VNF Sud-Ouest, Unité rivière de Libourne,
61 cours des Girondins, 33500 Libourne
05 57 51 06 53    subdi.aquitaine@vnf.fr

| Key dimensions (m) | |
|---|---|
| Length | – |
| Beam | – |
| Draught | – |
| Air draught | 5.50 |

# VII – Southwest France

## Route description

PK **117.6** *Confluence with the Gironde*, Bec d'Ambès lighthouse l/b
PK **117.0** Ambès oil terminal and refinery, industrial quays l/b
PK **113.9** **Bourg-sur-Gironde** *halte* on pontoon r/b, night €10, water and electricity included

Historic small town, with a fine château just level with the pontoon. Water can be choppy in the broad estuary.

PK **111.7** Overhead power lines
PK **110.6** **Ambès** *halte* on pontoon 50m long, capacity 8 boats, night €20, water and electricity included, restaurant, slipway, village l/b
PK **105.3** **Saint-André-de-Bubzac** *halte* run by boat club on 130m pontoon r/b, 06 85 53 08 08, 1 visitor mooring, free (maximum 24 hours), water and electricity on pontoon, slipway (Plagne)
PK **102.8** Railway bridge
PK **102.2** **Cubzac-les-Ponts** *halte* on pontoon r/b for 19 boats, €30 for one month, water and electricity included, slipway, village 1.5 km r/b
PK **101.9** Bridge (Eiffel)
PK **100.9** Motorway bridge (A10)
PK **98.3** **Cavernes** *halte* on pontoon 120m long l/b, 1 visitor mooring, free (maximum 24 hours), water and electricity on pontoon, slipway, **Saint-Loubès** 2.6km
PK **96.0** Asques slipway, village r/b
PK **85.6** Saint-Pardon quay and village l/b (access poor)
PK **84.0** Vayres quay and village l/b
PK **82.7** Arveyres l/b
PK **77.7** Fronsac quay and slipway, village r/b
PK **76.4** Motorway bridge (A89)
PK **75.3** *Confluence of River Isle* r/b
PK **75.0** **Libourne** bridge, municipal *port de plaisance* d/s r/b and on river Isle, capacity 15 boats, night €13, water and electricity on pontoon, slipway, town centre r/b

Libourne alone justifies the detour up the Dordogne. Proudly located at the confluence of the river Isle, the town has a long history as a garrison town and commercial port, even rivalling Bordeaux during certain periods in history. For the boater, the pontoon mooring below the Pont de Pierre is tempting, but is reserved for cruise ships and passenger boats. Mooring on the main pontoon in the river Isle is recommended.

PK **74.0** Railway bridge (Libourne)
PK **69.4** Quay (Génissac) l/b
PK **65.0** Bridge (D1089 Libourne bypass)
PK **64.5** Slipway (Carré) r/b, poor condition
PK **59.7** Moulon quay l/b, village 500m
PK **56.1** **Branne** bridge, *halte* on pontoon d/s l/b for 2 boats, free, water, electricity, village l/b

Upstream limit of navigation with comfortable depths on the tide. Continuing upstream with a deep-draughted boat should only be envisaged after confirming the state of the river and the available depths. Shallow-draught vessels may continue as far as they can, and will enjoy glorious river landscapes and many attractive towns and villages.

*The 'Pont de Pierre' in Libourne, PK 75.* © PÈRE IGOR, WIKIPEDIA

PK **52.7** Vignonet quay and village r/b
PK **50.5** Cabara quay and village l/b
PK **49.5** **Saint-Jean-de-Blaignac** bridge, quay and village u/s l/b
PK **45.7** Sainte-Terre, mooring r/b, village 500m
PK **43.8** Island, d/s tip, access to Civrac in l/b arm
PK **43.2** **Civrac-de-Dordogne** quay and village l/b (access from d/s)
PK **42.6** Islands, navigation in middle arm
PK **40.1** Bridge (D15)
PK **39.3** **Castillon-la-Bataille** bridge, quay, village u/s l/b

*Castillon-la-Bataille, PK 39* MICHEL CHANAUD

PK **38.5** Confluence of Lidoire, r/b
PK **33.7** **Lamothe-Montravel** quay and village r/b
PK **30.8** **Flaujagues** quay and village l/b
PK **27.2** **Pessac-sur-Dordogne** bridge, quay, village l/b
PK **22.2** Quay (Saint-Avit) l/b
PK **20.8** **Saint-Aulaye** quay and small village r/b
PK **18.3** **Eynesse** quay and small village l/b
PK **13.6** Bridge (D936 Sainte-Foy bypass)
PK **12.9** Railway bridge
PK **12.6** Bridge
PK **12.3** **Port-Sainte-Foy** bridge, quay d/s r/b, village r/b
PK **11.9** **Sainte-Foy-la-Grande** quay l/b, small town
PK **6.9** **Le Fleix** bridge, quay d/s r/b, village r/b
PK **0.0** **Saint-Pierre-d'Eyraud**, head of navigation (limit of département of Gironde, l/b), village r/b

# 66. River Isle

The river Isle was formerly navigable over a distance of about 144km upstream from its confluence with the Dordogne at Libourne to Périgueux. However, all the structures were abandoned after the decline of commercial navigation, leaving only the tidal navigation, covering a distance of 31km from Libourne to the first lock (40) at Laubardemont. Beyond the tidal navigation the first three locks were restored and are regularly used by a trip-boat. This adds 10km to the previously navigable length, up to the weir and lock at La Pauillade, but in the absence of formal arrangements for maintenance and operation, private boats are not authorised to use the waterway. Further restoration is nonetheless projected, inspired no doubt by the success of the River Lot, the eventual aim being to restore the river navigation up to the historic limit of navigation at Périgueux.

*Navigation to the town of Périgueux was blocked by a series of watermills, and it was decided in 1768 to make the river navigable with weirs and locks. The entire project was completed by a private company under a concession granted in 1820. This was one of the ambitious projects initiated under the Becquey programme for financing public works. It was inaugurated in 1837 from the Dordogne up to Périgueux, with 40 locks, mostly 24.25 by 4.50m, although some were narrower (3.60m). Only a few at the lower end were given the 'Becquey' dimensions of 30m by 5.20m.*

## Navigation
Use the tidal flow to proceed up the river. The possibility of mooring at most of the quays indicated depends on the state of the tide.

## Locks
The locks are 30.00m long by 5.20m wide. They are operated by the trip boat crew only.

## Draught
There is a depth of 0.30m at low water neap tides rising to between 0.80 and 1.60m at high water neap tides (at Laubardemont). The maximum authorised draught in the canalised river is 1.40m.

## Headroom
The bridges leave a clear headroom of 3.80m at high water neaps (more restricted dimensions on the canalised river).

## Authority
VNF Sud-Ouest, 61 cours des Girondins, 33500 Libourne
05 57 51 06 53

## Route description

|  | |
|---|---|
| PK 0.0 | **Confluence with Dordogne** (PK 75) |
| PK 0.7 | **Libourne** bridge, quay u/s l/b, pontoon moorings d/s l/b, town centre 700m |
| PK 3.4 | Motorway bridge (A89) |
| PK 4.1 | Motorway bridge (A89) |
| PK 5.5 | Motorway bridge (A89) |
| PK 7.6 | **Saillans** r/b, village 1200m |
| PK 11.3 | Bridge (D18) |
| PK 16.6 | **Savignac-de-l'Isle** bridge, quay d/s r/b, village 400m r/b |
| PK 20.7 | **Saint-Denis-de-Pile** bridge, quay and village l/b |
| PK 22.1 | Quays l/b (Fleix) |
| PK 28.1 | Bridge (D901e1, Guîtres bypass) |
| PK 28.6 | **Guîtres** bridge, quay and village r/b |
| PK 31.1 | Lock 40 (Laubardemont), in 650 m lock-cut, head of tidal navigation, **Coutras** 2.5 km u/s on Dronne (light craft only), trip boat only from here upstream |
| PK 31.6 | Bridge, disused factory r/b |
| PK 31.8 | End of lock-cut, Isle weir on r/b, bridge (D674) |
| PK 33.0 | Railway bridges (Paris-Bordeaux main line) |
| PK 34.8 | **Abzac** bridge (D17), village 700m l/b, **Coutras** 1800m r/b |
| PK 35.1 | Lock 39 (Abzac) in short cut r/b, weir |
| PK 38.6 | Lock 38 (Penot) in short lock-cut r/b, weir |
| PK 41.1 | Lock 37 (La Pauillade) in short lock-cut r/b, weir, limit of navigation |

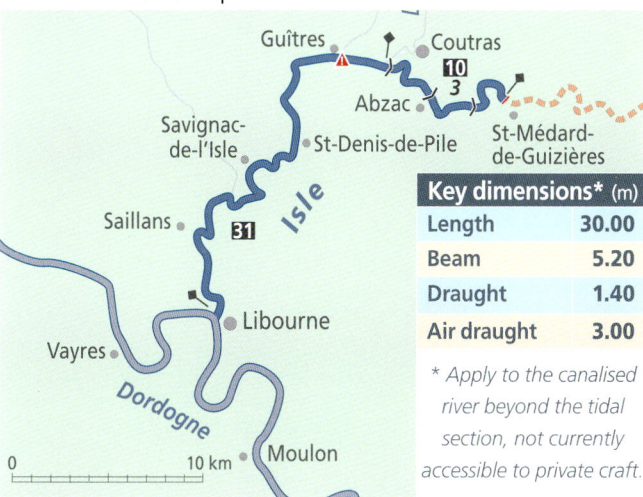

# VII – Southwest France

## 67. Adour and tributaries

THE ADOUR AND ITS TRIBUTARIES form a fascinating and attractive cruising area, despite their isolation from the main waterway network. Until 1979, the river was officially navigable from Saint-Sever to its mouth in the Bay of Biscay near Bayonne, a distance of 133km. However, in view of the uncertainty of navigable conditions in the upstream reaches (especially above the limit of tidal influence), the river has been downgraded over the 101km from Saint-Sever to the confluence with the Gaves-Réunis at Bec-du-Gave. This means that navigation above PK 101 is at the risk and peril of users, with no maintenance and no channel markings are available. On the other hand, downstream of Bec-du-Gave, the minimum conventional waterway markings and signs are in place (down to the Pont Saint-Esprit in Bayonne). Traffic is limited to the professional fishing boats and two trip boats Le Bayonne and La Hire.

Free-flow navigation formerly continued up the Adour and its tributary, the Bidouze, to the ports at Saint-Sever and Mont-de-Marsan respectively, but the channel in these sections has long been abandoned, and there has been no maintenance on these upstream reaches since 1979. Already above the Luy (PK 79) and especially above Dax (PK 67), the limited draught generally precludes navigation during low-flow periods, in other words from June to October inclusive. Moreover, a natural sill has formed on the river just downstream of the bridge (Pont Vieux) in Dax, so that navigation through Dax is only possible when the river is in spate. Above Pontonx, the flow is reduced in dry summers to a modest trickle between the sandbanks.

The route description below gives the official distances, counting from zero at Saint-Sever, but starting at the practical limit of navigation at Pont-du-Pouy.

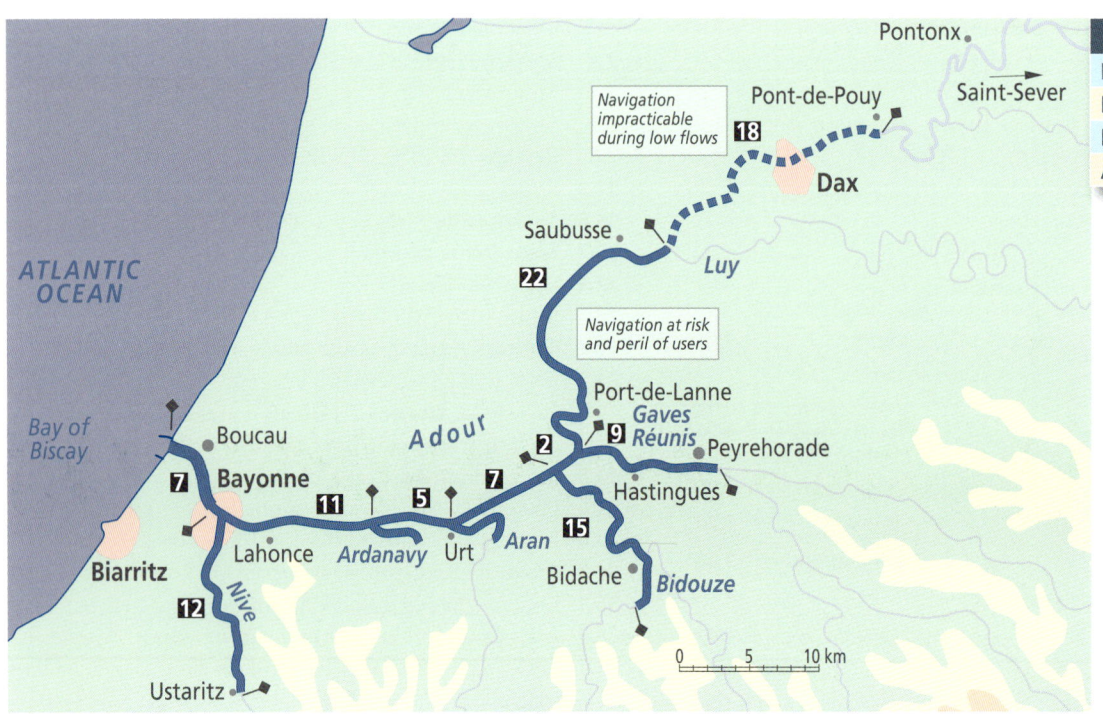

*Since the Adour is a tidal or free-flow navigation, the history of its use and improvement over the centuries is not related to canalisation works, but to channel dredging and clearing as required after major floods. Such works were often difficult to fund because riparians were reluctant to bear the cost. A major project was carried out in 1775, with works on the navigable channel, also providing a towpath between Dax and Port-de-Lanne. During the 19th century, however, the quality of the navigation rapidly deteriorated and traffic declined. The deep tidal waters from the Gaves Réunis down to Bayonne continued to carry substantial traffic until 1920. This isolated waterway network is little used by recreational boaters, but the Basque region and culture are uniquely attractive, and well worth making this southerly detour, for sea-going or trailed craft.*

## Navigation

Tides are critical to navigability of the Adour. Spring tides of high coefficients are felt up to Dax and exceptionally to Pont-de-Pouy (PK 61) or more rarely Pontonx (PK 42), a distance of more than 90km. Regular tides are felt up to Vimport (PK 77, upstream of the Luy), a distance of 56km from the sea, and the rise and fall is quite substantial, varying according to the coefficient from 1 to 4.2m at the mouth and from 1 to 3m at Urt (PK 111).

From Dax (PK 67) to the confluence with the Luy (PK 79), great care is necessary to avoid shoals and the numerous groynes which extend out into the channel. From the Luy to the confluence with the Gaves Réunis depths are greater, especially at high tide, but it is generally advisable to follow the outside of the bends. From the Bec-du-Gave to Bayonne there are no obstructions. In the centre of Bayonne, however, passage through the old bridge (Pont Saint-Esprit) is to be avoided during a strong ebb flow (see below under headroom). Heading upstream from the mouth (or the yacht harbour at Anglet-Blancpignon), passage is always to be preferred on the flood tide, or at high-water or low-water slack.

The passage between Bayonne and Dax is much easier if the tidal stream is properly worked. Propagation time from the mouth to Vimport is approximately four hours. Heading upstream, it is advisable to leave Bayonne two to three hours after low water, but local advice should be sought, either from the authorities or from the harbour-master in the port of Anglet (addresses below). On account of the shifting banks in the Adour estuary below Bayonne, use of the appropriate marine charts is recommended.

Several tributaries of the Adour are also navigable for a short distance upstream from their confluence. These are the Gaves Réunis, navigable for 9km to the town of Peyrehorade, the Bidouze and a short length of its tributary, the Lihoury, giving access to the hilltop village of Bidache (16km), the Aran (6km), the Ardanavy (2km) and the Nive, which is navigable through the centre of Bayonne and upstream over a distance of 12km. Like the Adour, these are all tidal rivers and navigation is easier if the tidal stream is used.

The rivers are free-flow, partly tidal navigations, relatively undeveloped (especially upstream of Saubusse), free of commercial traffic and with very little boat traffic. There is no hire boat activity. The banks are densely wooded and impracticable through much of the length.

## Draught

The available depth varies considerably. Between Dax and the Luy it is normally about 1.00m. From the Luy to the Gaves Réunis it is 1.50m, depending on the state of the tide. From the Gaves Réunis to Bayonne it is 2.00m. The mean depths of each of the tributaries, and the tidal rise and fall in cm, are as follows: Gaves Réunis 1.60m (±40), Bidouze 2.90m (±90), Lihoury 0.90m (±60), Aran and Ardanavy 1.20m (±60) and Nive 1.75m (±75).

## Headroom

The minimum headroom under the fixed bridges at high spring tides is as follows (the figures in brackets indicate the increased headroom available at low tide): Adour 4.30m (8.50m*), Gaves Réunis 3.00m (5.00m), Bidouze 3.50m (5.30m), Lihoury 4.70m (6.00m), Aran 3.60m (4.80m), Ardanavy 3.00m (4.20m) and Nive 0.40m (4.20m). The only problem for most boats is on the Nive at Bayonne, where the bridges should be cleared at low tide before proceeding upstream.

* According to the local navigation regulations, the clearance is 6.50m above the mean water level, which is +2.40m on the datum of the marine charts, not taking into account the higher level which may be caused by flood flows.

## Towpath

The former towpath has been converted into a public road along the left bank for much of the river's length.

## Authority

Direction Départementale des Territoires et de la Mer des Landes
– 351 Bd Saint-Médard, BP 369, 40012 Mont-de-Marsan
05 58 51 30 00   ddtm@landes.gouv.fr (PK 0-40)

Direction départementale des Territoires et de la Mer des Pyrénées-Atlantiques, Délégation à la Mer et au Littoral
– 6, quai de Lesseps, 64107 Bayonne Cedex
05 59 50 31 50 (PK 40-72 and tributaries).

## Route description

| | |
|---|---|
| PK 0.0 | **Saint-Sever** bridge, historic limit of navigation |
| PK 31.6 | Le Hourquet, confluence of river Midouze |
| PK 42.0 | **Pontonx** bridge |
| PK 61.0 | **Pont-de-Pouy** bridge |

This is the effective upstream limit of navigation, but can only be reached when the river is in spate, or with an exceptionally high tide.

| | |
|---|---|
| PK 66.0 | Bridge (des Arènes) |
| PK 66.7 | Bridge (D947) |
| PK 67.0 | **Dax** bridge, quay d/s l/b, town centre l/b |
| PK 67.9 | Railway bridge |
| PK 77.0 | Bridge (Vimport), quay u/s l/b |

This is the 'normal' upstream limit of navigability.

## VI – Southwest France

PK **79.0** Confluence of Luy (unnavigable), l/b
PK **81.0** Quay (Carrère) l/b
PK **83.0** **Saubusse** bridge, quay and village r/b, water
PK **87.0** Bridge (La Marquèze), quay u/s r/b
PK **91.0** Former quay (Gelez) r/b
PK **94.1** Former quay (Rasport) l/b
PK **96.5** **Port-de-Lanne** *halte* on pontoon l/b, for 15 boats, up to 4 visitor moorings, 06 31 13 17 95, free (maximum 48 hours), water, electricity, slipway (high tide), village 1 km
PK **97.7** Bridge (D817)
PK **101.0** Bec du Gave, confluence of Gaves Réunis , l/b

*The splendid Château du Bec du Gave commands the confluence of the Adour (left) and the Gaves-Réunis (right), PK 101.* © BERTRAND MARTIN

PK **101.4** Public quay (Sames), l/b
PK **103.4** Bec de la Bidouze, confluence of Bidouze , l/b
PK **104.9** Former quay (Sainte-Marie-de-Gosse) r/b
PK **110.3** Former quay (Saint-Laurent-de-Gosse) r/b
PK **110.8** Confluence of Aran , l/b
PK **110.9** Bridge (Eiffel)
PK **111.1** Urt quay l/b, pontoon moorings, village 800m l/b

*High tide on the Adour at Urt (PK 111) looking across to Montpellier château on the right bank.* © MICHEL CHANAUD

PK **113.5** Auberge Baladour, l/b (private quay)
PK **115.8** Confluence of Ardanavy , l/b
PK **116.5** Former quay (Urcuit) l/b
PK **118.0** Entrance to Lahonce arm, l/b
PK **119.8** **Lahonce** boat harbour (*Port de Plaisance* de l'Aiguette) l/b, 05 59 31 60 17, 100 berths, water, electricity, €3.90-7.70, village 1800m
PK **119.8** Downstream entrance to Lahonce arm, l/b
PK **124.0** Quay (Mouguerre) l/b
PK **124.4** Motorway bridge (A63)
PK **125.5** Road bridge (Saint-Frédéric, N117)
PK **125.7** Railway and road bridge (Eiffel)
PK **126.6** **Bayonne** bridge (Pont Saint-Esprit), quays d/s, town centre l/b
PK **126.7** Confluence of Nive , l/b (moorings for Bayonne)

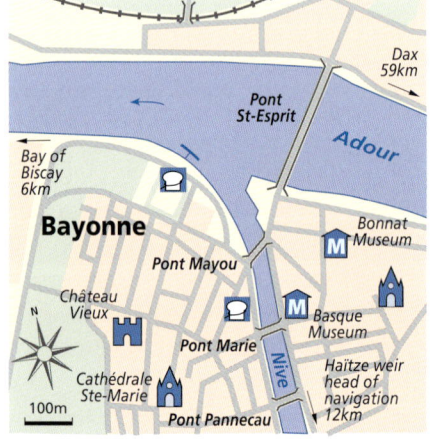

PK **127.5** Pontoon moorings r/b
PK **127.6** Bridge (Henri Grenet, ring road)
PK **130.7** Boucau port (Port de la Cale), small town r/b
PK **132.1** **Anglet** *port de plaisance* (Port du Brise-Lames) l/b, 05 59 63 05 45, 425 berths, 45 visitor moorings, night €25.60, water and electricity included, fuel, showers €2, pump-out, crane 25t, slipway, repairs, restaurant
PK **133.3** Semaphore (Tour des Signaux) l/b, limit of sea

*For continuing coastal passages*, refer to the Royal Cruising Club Pilotage Foundation's *Atlantic France* by Nick Chavasse (Imray).

# Adour tributaries

## Gaves Réunis
- PK **0.0** *Confluence with Adour* (PK 101)
- PK **2.1** Sames quay l/b, stables
- PK **3.0** Railway bridge
- PK **3.9** **Hastingues** quay and village l/b
- PK **6.8** Municipal boat harbour in basin l/b
- PK **7.0** Bridge (A641)
- PK **8.0** **Peyrehorade** bridge, quay d/s r/b, municipal boat harbour in basin reopening 2010, village r/b
- PK **9.4** Confluence of Gave de Pau and Gave d'Oloron, head of navigation

## Bidouze and Lihoury
- PK **0.0** *Confluence with Adour* (PK 103), bridge (D261)
- PK **0.7** Railway bridge
- PK **1.1** Motorway bridge (A64)
- PK **1.7** **Guiche** bridge, quay d/s l/b, small village
- PK **6.2** Former quay (Cassous) l/b
- PK **11.4** **Bidache** bridge, mooring l, b, village 600m l/b
- PK **14.7** Confluence of Lihoury, l/b (navigation continues on Lihoury)
- PK **15.5** Bridge (D936), weir (barrage de la Baignade), head of navigation, Bidache 200m l/b

## Aran or Joyeuse
- PK **0.0** *Confluence with Adour* (PK 111), bridge (D261)
- PK **4.3** Railway bridge, quay u/s r/b
- PK **6.2** Bridge (Larroque), head of navigation, former quay (Bardos) d/s l/b

## Ardanavy
- PK **0.0** *Confluence with Adour* (PK 116), bridge (D261)
- PK **2.0** Private quay (Hayet) r/b
- PK **2.4** Railway bridge, head of navigation

## Nive
- PK **0.0** *Confluence with Adour*, **Bayonne** (PK 127)
- PK **0.3** Bridge (Pont Mayou)
- PK **0.4** Bridge (Pont Marengo)
- PK **0.6** Bridge (Pont Pannecau)
- PK **0.7** Bridge (Pont du Génie), quay l/b, town centre l/b
- PK **0.9** Bridge (ring road)
- PK **1.4** Railway bridge
- PK **2.1** Footbridge (Pont Blanc)
- PK **3.9** Motorway bridge (A63)
- PK **9.5** Footbridge
- PK **11.1** Quay (Compaïto) r/b, **Villefranque** 2 km r/b
- PK **12.3** Weir (Haïtze), head of navigation

# CHAPTER VIII – WEST

The description west is here stretched for convenience all the way down the coast from Brittany to encompass the navigable waterways of the Pays de la Loire (not merged with Brittany in the recent reform of the regions) and the northern part of Aquitaine. The most charming and improbable waterways of France are to be found within this network, now entirely devoted to tourism and fascinating for the region's cultural traditions and unbelievable hospitality.

The backbone of the network – the canal from Nantes to Brest – is sadly no longer navigable throughout, and even if it were, it is hard to imagine huge numbers of boats wanting to cruise throughout from Châteaulin to Nantes: 236 locks in 360km! Such was the ambition of Napoleon Bonaparte, who first conceived the route.

This is small boat territory (see key dimensions). Some adventurous yachtsmen still enter the Brittany canals or the Charente, but compared with the early days of waterway tourism 40 to 50 years ago, yacht sizes have increased significantly, and those who are intent on navigating far afield will generally have to rule out crossing Brittany inland. For motor boats it is a similar story. The comforts that most boatowners buy into mean that seaworthy motor boats will generally be too high or too deep for this region's waterways. So our advice is very straightforward: choose a boat that will squeeze into these locks and through these bridges, because otherwise these idyllic destinations will have to be ruled out. Trailboaters are all the more welcome in Brittany.

*The port of Dinan on the river Rance viewed from the viaduct* © KADER BENFERHAT

# VIII – Western France

## 68. Rance maritime and Canal d'Ille-et-Rance

THE RANCE ESTUARY IS FAMOUS for its Vauban citadel at the port of Saint-Malo commanding its entrance, and for its tidal power station opened in 1967. The barrier makes the estuary a genuinely inland waterway, despite the strong tidal currents and the possibly disconcerting rise and fall. Above the barrier, the estuary gradually narrows, until Le Châtelier lock is reached. This marks the beginning of the Canal d'Ille-et-Rance which extends 85km to Rennes, crossing the watershed between the Rance and the Vilaine. This duo of waterways forms part of the English Channel/Atlantic Ocean link which has long been used by yachtsmen, but has also become increasingly popular as a cruising waterway in its own right. Several hire firms are based on the canal or its connecting waterways.

The canal has a summit level 7km in length, at an altitude of 65m, and in times of drought some restrictions may have to be imposed on the use of locks.

*A canal across Brittany from the Rance estuary to the Vilaine at Rennes was suggested in the 17th century, but the first serious plans were drawn up in 1736. They were incorporated in a project for three canals in the Province, but nothing was done until Napoleon ordered implementation of all three schemes in 1804. Works started, but were interrupted after his defeat. A private company took up the concession to build the canal and started work in 1822. The canal was opened in 1834.*

### Navigation
This route inland from the English Channel comprises two very different sequences, first the estuary, which is sheltered water behind the tide barrier, albeit with considerable tidal flood and ebb currents, then straightforward canal navigation through to Rennes. For information about navigation on the Brittany coast see the Royal Cruising Club Pilotage Foundation's *Channel Islands, Cherbourg Peninsula and North Brittany*, Peter Carnegie (Imray).

### Locks
There are 48 locks, of which 28 rise from the Rance estuary to the summit and 20 fall towards the Vilaine. Their dimensions are 27.10m by 4.70m. The tide lock at Le Châtelier (also called La Hisse) has larger dimensions, 30.80m by 8.00m. This lock and lock 47 (Léhon) are fully electrified. The others have electrically-operated paddles, but manual gates with balance beams or winding gear, except in Rennes. All the locks are worked by the resident lock-keepers, except for lock 2 (Saint-Martin) which is electrically operated and controlled by lights. Operating hours are 08:30 to 19:30 during summer time (end March to end October), with a break from 12:30 to 13:30. During winter hours navigation closes at 1800. Operating hours at Le Châtelier lock are between 0600 and 2100 subject to the tide (which must be +8.50m downstream of the lock).

### Draught
The maximum authorised draught is 1.40m.

### Headroom
The lowest fixed bridges offer a headroom of 2.70m in the centre of the arch and 2.50m at the sides. This is more than the previously indicated 2.50m, which related to the bridges at Dinan and Léhon, when tides topped the weir at Le Châtelier. The estuary's regime with the tidal power plant means that such high tides no longer occur. Boats can now therefore count on the 2.70m being available.

### Towpath
There is a towpath throughout on the canal only, inland from Dinan.

### Authority
Région Bretagne – Service des Voies Navigables
Subdivision Vilaine – Canal d'Ille-et-Rance
– 33 rue Armand Rébillon, 35000 Rennes  02 99 84 47 60
svn-vir@bretagne.bzh (contact for all public moorings along the Canal d'Ille-et-Rance)

# Rance and Canal d'Ille-et-Rance

## Route description

### Rance Estuary

[Note: distances relate to the centre line of the estuary]

PK **0.0** **Saint-Malo** harbour entrance r/b (Sablons), 02 99 81 71 34, *saint-malo.fr*, 1196 berths, night €26.30, fuel, water, electricity, showers, crane 2.5t, quay, ship lock for access to inner harbour (Vauban), 02 99 56 51 91, *port.saintmalofougeres.cci.fr*, 50 berths, night €35, fuel, water, electricity, showers, crane 2t, slipway

PK **0.9** Moulinet point, seaward limit of Rance estuary
PK **1.2** **Dinard**, l/b, quay, 02 99 46 65 55, fuel, water, electricity, slipway, ferry for Saint-Servant/Saint-Malo
PK **1.3** Rocks (Ras de la Mercière)
PK **1.8** Rocks (La Mercière), beacon, Pointe de La Cité
PK **2.2** Prieuré or Dinard bay l/b, Solidor bay r/b, mooring buoys
PK **2.7** La Vicomté point l/b, Bizeux island r/b (beacon)
PK **3.8** Rance tidal barrage, lock on l/b side, 02 99 16 37 33, lift bridge, (D168)

The lock is open on the hour from 4.5 hours before high tide to 4.5 hours after. Operation outside these times may be possible, as long as there is 4m available depth on the seaward side. The lock is operated by EDF.

PK **5.3** **La Richardais** bay l/b, boatyard, moorings, water, crane, slipway, no overnight mooring
PK **5.7** Cancaval promontory l/b, beacon
PK **5.9** Tour des Zèbres beacon r/b
PK **6.1** Le Montmarin bay l/b
PK **6.7** Slipways (Jouvente l/b, Passagère r/b), ferry
PK **6.9** Pierre et Paul (reef, dries at low water, no beacon)
PK **7.3** Island (Île Chevret), beacon
PK **8.3** Langronais promontory l/b, L'Écrais promontory r/b (beacon)
PK **8.6** Island (Île aux Moines)
PK **8.7** **La Landriais** bay l/b, boatyard, mooring, slipway
PK **8.9** Promontories (Thon l/b, Bay du Put r/b)
PK **9.7** Promontory (Garel), La Landriais windmill l/b
PK **10.8** Rocky promontories with beacons r/b
PK **11.1** **Saint-Suliac** jetty and beaching ground r/b
PK **12.1** **Langrolay** slipway l/b, village 800m
PK **13.1** Promontory (Pointe de Garo) r/b
PK **14.4** Promontory (Pointe de la Haie) l/b
PK **15.4** Overhead power lines
PK **15.5** Main road bridge (N176)
PK **15.7** Saint-Hubert suspension bridge, slipways of former ferry, moorings
PK **16.8** **Plouër-sur-Rance** harbour l/b, 02 96 86 83 15, *plouer-sur-rance.fr*, 240 berths, night €30.45, water and electricity included, wifi, showers, pumpout, slipways, restaurant 200m, village 1200m
PK **18.5** Tower (Chêne-Vert) l/b
PK **18.9** Mordreuc jetty and slipway r/b, moorings
PK **19.2** Rocher des Moulières beacon r/b
PK **21.2** Rocher du Galetier, beginning of stakes marking channel to Le Châtelier
PK **21.5** Lessart railway viaduct
PK **22.6** Le Châtelier tide lock (02 96 39 55 66) moving bridge (D57) and submersible weir, bridge, navigation continues in Canal d'Ille-et-Rance

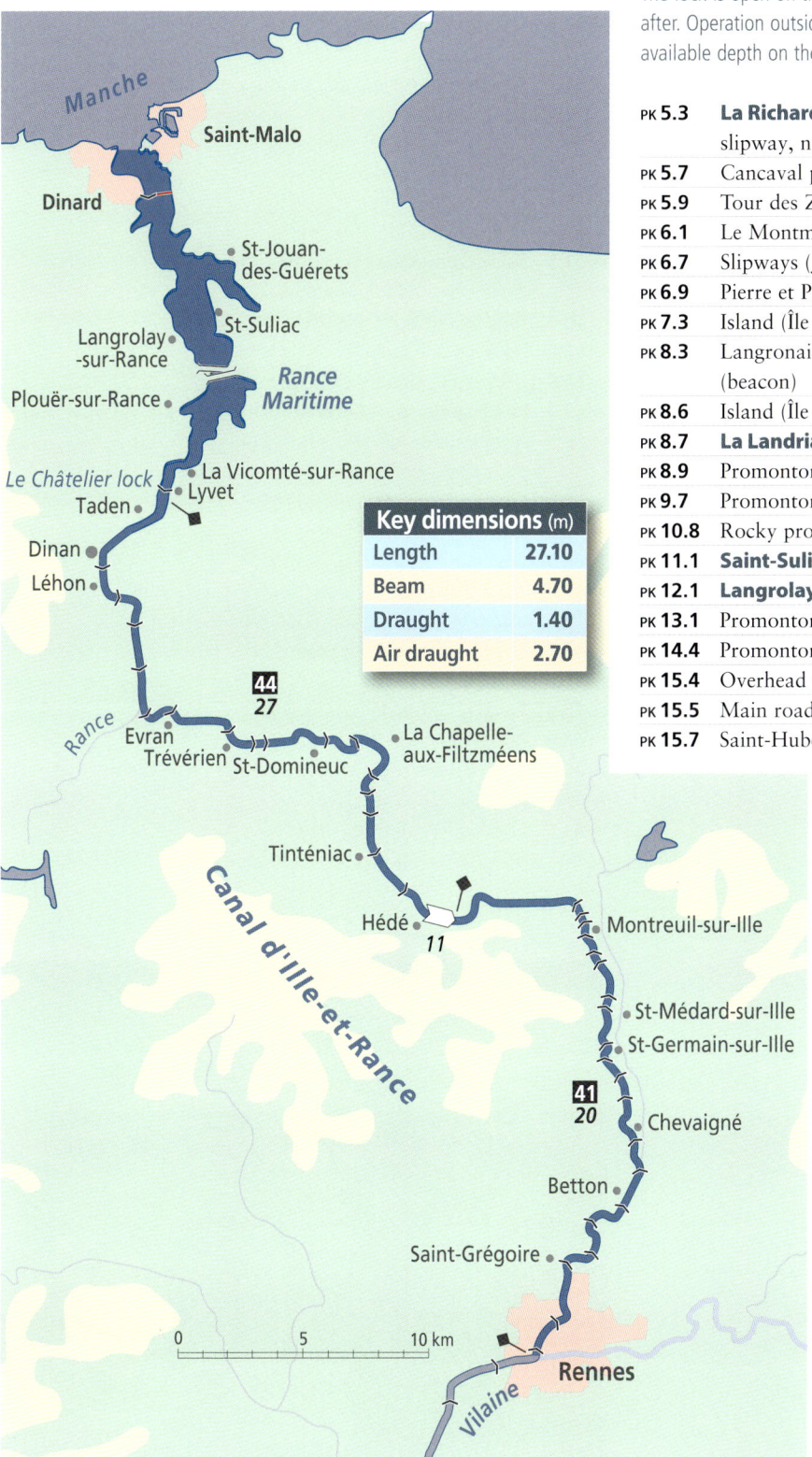

## VIII – Western France

*Le Châtelier is one of the busiest locks on the Brittany canals, since it is used by many sailing boats as well as small motor yachts taking the inland route across Brittany.* © KADER BENFERHAT

## Canal d'Ille-et-Rance

- PK 84.8 Tide lock 48 (Le Châtelier)
- PK 84.2 **Lyvet** quay r/b, moorings for 25 boats, 3 visitor moorings, 02 96 83 35 57, night €21, water, electricity, showers, slipway, restaurant, village 2.5 km
- PK 83.8 Quay (Petit-Lyvet) l/b, **Saint-Samson-sur-Rance** harbour, 150 moorings on buoys, night €12.12, water and electricity included
- PK 83.4 Le Châtelier quay r/b
- PK 82.4 Taden quay l/b, village 700m
- PK 81.5 Quay (Étra or Asile du Pêcheur) l/b
- PK 78.8 Lanvallay quay r/b
- PK 78.6 **Dinan** bridge (Vieux Pont), u/s limit of tides, boat harbour d/s l/b, 02 96 39 56 44, 30 visitor berths, night €18 including water/ electricity, showers, crane 400kg, slipway, restaurant, town 500m

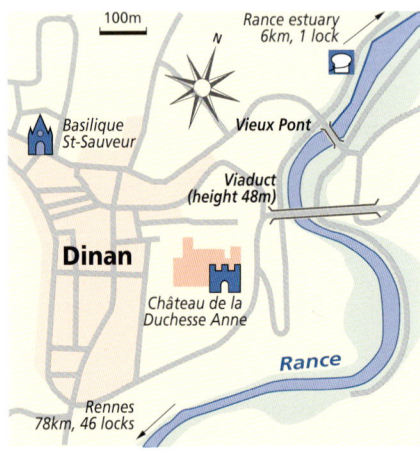

Dinan is a lively town, with restaurants along the attractive quayside, and shops large and small in the town centre, a 75m climb from the river via the pretty cobblestone rue du Petit Fort.

- PK 78.5 Dinan viaduct (D795)
- PK 76.8 Lock 47 (Léhon)
- PK 76.3 Léhon bridge (Vieux Pont), quays, village l/b
- PK 74.1 Lock 46 (Pont-Perrin), bridge,
- PK 73.1 Quay (Vaugré) r/b
- PK 71.8 Lock 45 (Boutron), swing bridge
- PK 71.6 Bridge (Grand Boutron)
- PK 70.0 Lock 44 (Mottay), bridge
- PK 68.2 Bridge (Pont des Planches)
- PK 67.8 Lock 43 (Roche), bridge
- PK 67.0 Turning basin
- PK 66.4 Lock 42 (Evran), bridge
- PK 66.3 **Évran** *halte* r/b, visitor moorings for 4 boats up to 26m long, free (maximum 72 hours), water, electricity, wifi, slipway, village l/b
- PK 65.1 Footbridge (St. Judoce)
- PK 62.4 Lock 41 (Les Islots)
- PK 62.2 Turning basin
- PK 61.7 **Trévérien** bridge, *halte* on quay and turning basin u/s r/b, free (maximum 72 hours), water, slipway, village l/b
- PK 60.9 Lock 40 (La Butte Jacquette)
- PK 60.5 Lock 39 (Gacet), bridge
- PK 58.8 Bridge (Richeville)
- PK 58.7 Main road bridge (D137)
- PK 57.3 **Saint-Domineuc** bridge (Pont de Linon), *halte* on quay d/s l/b, free (maximum 72 hours), water, electricity, slipway, village 700m l/b
- PK 56.6 Lock 38 (Couadan)
- PK 54.6 Lock 37 (Calaudry), bridge
- PK 53.3 **La Chapelle-aux-Filtzméens** bridge, *halte* on quay and turning basin u/s r/b, 2 boats (up to 26m), free (maximum 72 hours), water, electricity, small village 1200m r/b
- PK 50.8 Lock 36 (Pont-Houitte), bridge
- PK 49.9 Lock 35 (Gué Noëllan)
- PK 48.9 Lock 34 (Gromillais), bridge
- PK 47.2 **Tinténiac** *halte* on quay l/b, free (maximum 72 hours), water, electricity, pump-out, village 400m l/b
- PK 47.1 Lock 33 (Tinténiac), bridge
- PK 46.5 Turning basin r/b
- PK 45.4 Lock 32 (Moucherie), bridge
- PK 43.6 Bridge (D795)
- PK 43.5 Lock 31 (La Dialais), beginning of Hédé flight
- PK 43.2 Lock 30 (La Guéhardière)
- PK 43.0 Lock 29 (Petite-Madeleine)

*The Hédé flight of 11 locks.* © GÉRARD (BY KAÏROS)

# Rance and Canal d'Ille-et-Rance

PK **42.8**  **Hédé** *halte*, 02 99 84 47 60, moorings for 15 boats (up to 26m), water, electricity, showers, slipway, pump-out, restaurant, 'Maison du Canal' interpretation centre, small town 1200m l/b

Ascending or descending the Hédé flight of locks is an almost mystical experience, the carefully maintained locks, their wooden balance beams and the grassy lock-sides set against a background of dense forest.

PK **42.7**  Lock 28 (La Madeleine), bridge
PK **42.5**  Lock 27 (La Jaunaie)
PK **42.3**  Lock 26
PK **42.2**  Lock 25 (La Parfraire), bridge
PK **42.0**  Lock 24 (La Charonnerie), water
PK **41.8**  Lock 23 (La Pêchetière)
PK **41.6**  Lock 22 (Malabrie), moorings downstream
PK **41.4**  Lock 21 (La Ségerie), end of Hédé flight, beginning of summit level
PK **40.9**  La Guénaudière bridge
PK **35.5**  La Plousière bridge (D82) and **Guipel** *halte* on quay and small pontoon, free (maximum 72 hours), water, electricity, village 1.5km south
PK **34.2**  Lock 20 (Villemorin), end of summit level, turning basin
PK **33.5**  Lock 19 (Courgalais), bridge
PK **32.8**  Lock 18 (Chanclin)
PK **32.0**  Lock 17 (Lengager), bridge (D221), **Montreuil-sur-Ille** *halte* on quay and turning basin u/s r/b, free (maximum 1 week), water, electricity, pump-out, village 1100m l/b
PK **31.1**  Lock 16 (Haute-Roche)
PK **30.5**  Lock 15 (Ille), bridge
PK **29.0**  Railway viaduct (Bablais)
PK **28.1**  Lock 14 (Dialay)
PK **27.4**  **Saint-Médard-sur-Ille** *halte* on quay l/b, free, water, electricity, village 300m l/b
PK **27.3**  Lock 13 (Saint-Médard), bridge
PK **27.2**  Railway viaduct (Saint-Médard)
PK **26.3**  Railway viaduct (Euzé)
PK **25.7**  Railway viaduct (Bois Marie)
PK **24.8**  Lock 12 (Bouessay)
PK **24.0**  **Saint-Germain-sur-Ille** *halte* on quay l/b, free (maximum 72 hours), water, electricity, shower, village 700m l/b
PK **23.9**  Lock 11 (Saint-Germain-sur-Ille), bridge
PK **21.8**  Lock 10 (Fresnay), bridge
PK **20.4**  Lock 9 (Les Cours)
PK **19.3**  Bridge (Motte)
PK **18.0**  Lock 8 (Grugedaine)
PK **17.8**  **Chevaigné** bridge (Moulin du Pont), village 800m l/b
PK **15.7**  Lock 7 (Les Brosses), bridge, water
PK **13.7**  **Betton** bridge, municipal *halte* on quay, 120m long, d/s r/b, free, water, electricity, showers, village 200m r/b
PK **13.1**  Footbridge
PK **12.6**  Lock 6 (Haut-Chalet)
PK **10.3**  Bridge (Rennais)
PK **9.9**  Lock 5 (Gacet)
PK **9.5**  Bridge (D29)
PK **7.2**  Lock 4 (Charbonnière)
PK **5.6**  Lock 3 (**Saint-Grégoire**), bridge, *halte* on quay u/s l/b, free (maximum 72 hours), water, electricity, showers, shopping centre 500m (crossing at the lock), village 700m r/b across the bypassed river Ille (canoeing course)

PK **5.2**  Footbridge
PK **4.7**  Railway viaduct
PK **4.5**  Bridge (N136, Rennes ring road)
PK **2.8**  Bridge (Boulevard d'Armorique, Rennes inner bypass)
PK **1.4**  Lock 2 (Saint-Martin), bridge, quays u/s, visitor moorings for 6 boats, free (maximum 72 hours), water, electricity, showers, wifi

Alternative mooring for Rennes, just 1km from the centre.

PK **0.9**  Bridge (Legravérend)
PK **0.3**  Bridge (Bagoul or Saint-Étienne)
PK **0.2**  **Rennes** basin (Port du Mail), quay l/b close to centre, visitor moorings for 6 boats, free (maximum 72 hours), water, electricity, showers, wifi

The capital of Brittany is worth a long stay to enjoy all that it has to offer, especially its renaissance parliament building, splendidly restored after the roof was destroyed by a fire some years ago. One of the attractions is the unique diversity of waterscapes along the canal and the river Vilaine, which can be followed upstream from the junction for a few kilometres, through Dupont des Loges lock. This side excursion is available for craft with an air draught of up to 3.30m (see under River Vilaine, section 69).

PK **0.1**  Lock 1 (Mail), bridge, water
PK **0.0**  *Junction with the river Vilaine*

# VIII – Western France

# 69. River Vilaine

THE RIVER VILAINE COMPLETES the waterway route across Brittany from Saint-Malo to the Bay of Biscay, an inland route that was regularly used by yachtsmen long before the boom in inland cruising started in the late 1970s. The river is navigable from Rennes, where it is joined by the Canal d'Ille-et-Rance, to below La Roche-Bernard, where it flows into the Atlantic, a distance of 137km. Below Redon (PK 89) it used to be tidal until a barrage was built at Arzal, 6km inland, incorporating a large lock. This has transformed the estuary into a wide fresh-water lake of more or less constant level and very attractive for yachting as well as inland cruising.

The junction with the Canal de Nantes à Brest is in Redon at PK 89, but in the direction of Nantes it is also possible to enter the canal 7km downstream through the lock at Bellions.

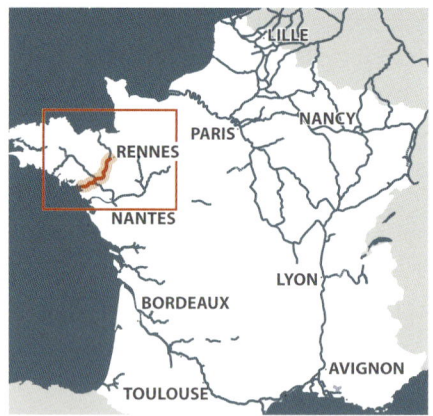

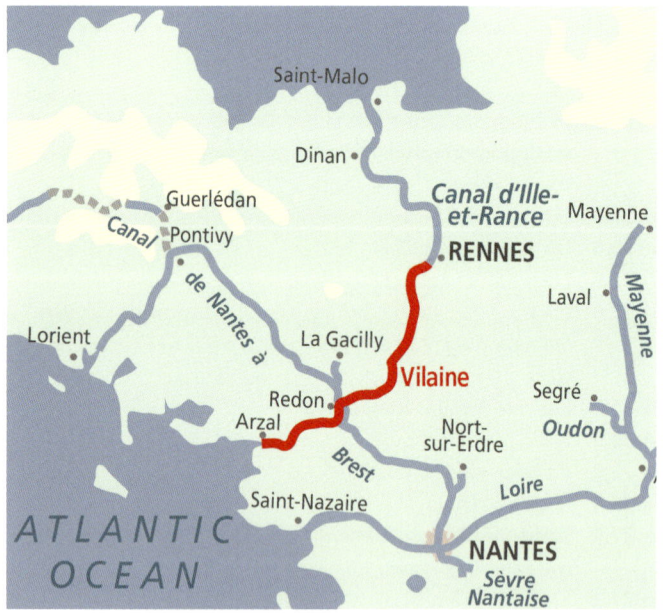

*With its gentle gradient, the Vilaine was one of the first rivers in France to be equipped for navigation with weirs and flash locks built from 1540. A lock was projected in Rennes in 1610, but the overall project was not started until 1784. The waterway was completed in 1834 by the Compagnie des Quatre Canaux, formed in 1821. The river is now entirely under the responsibility of the Brittany region. All operating staff were transferred to the Region in 2010.*

## Navigation
The Vilaine is a delightful cruising river with no particular difficulties, with potential for sailing in the wide sheltered estuary towards the Arzal barrage.

## Locks
There are 12 locks on the river between Rennes and Mâlon (PK 52), with dimensions of 27.10m by 4.70m. The lock at the Arzal barrage is of large dimensions (85 by 12.90m), allowing big yachts and passenger boats to navigate up the river to Redon. There is an intermediate gate which allows a shorter length of the chamber to be used when sufficient. A lift bridge spans the lock.

## Draught
The maximum authorised draught is in principle 1.60m, but this may be reduced to 1.20m between Rennes and Redon by silt deposits on lock approaches. Downstream of Redon the maximum draught is 4.30m.

## Headroom
The bridges leave a minimum clear headroom of 3.20m above normal water level, reduced to as little as 1.80m above the highest navigable water level between lock 13 (Mâlon) and Redon. During floods local enquiries should therefore be made. The nominal headroom is guaranteed through the covered section of the Vilaine in Rennes.

## Towpath
The towpath has been restored from Rennes to Cran bridge (PK 100), with an interruption at Redon, where local roads must be used from the canal basin to south of the Oust confluence.

## Authority
Région Bretagne – Service des Voies Navigables
Subdivision Vilaine – Canal d'Ille-et-Rance
– 33 rue Armand Rébillon, 35000 Rennes
  02 99 84 47 60   (PK 0-90)
  *svn-vir@bretagne.bzh*
Établissement Public Territorial de Bassin La Vilaine
– Boulevard de Bretagne, B.P. 11, 56130 La Roche-Bernard
  02 99 90 88 44   (for maritime waterway PK 90-137)
  *contact@eptb-vilaine.fr*

# Vilaine

The Vilaine in Rennes, and entrance to the Canal d'Ille-et-Rance on the left behind the barges   © KADER BENFERHAT/COMITÉ DES CANAUX BRETONS

| Key dimensions (m) | |
|---|---|
| Length | 26.60 |
| Beam | 4.70 |
| Draught | 1.20 |
| Air draught *above normal water level* | 3.20 |

## Route description

- PK **0.0** Bridge (Pont de Bretagne)
- PK **0.1** Junction with Canal d'Ille-et-Rance, r/b
- PK **0.2** **Rennes** quays, visitor moorings for 8 boats, free (maximum 72 hours), water, electricity, wifi, town centre 500m

Many boaters prefer this mooring for the capital of Brittany, along the attractively landscaped Quai Saint-Cyr, to the moorigs on the Canal d'Ille-et-Rance above lock 1.

The centre is very close. One of the city's attractions is the unique diversity of waterscapes along the canal and the river Vilaine, which can be followed upstream from the junction for a few kilometres, through Dupont des Loges lock. This side excursion is available for craft with an air draught of up to 3.30m.

See the detailed map of Rennes on the next page.

- PK **0.7** Bridge (Abattoir)
- PK **0.9** Skew bridge (Robert Schuman)
- PK **1.0** Confluence of Ille, r/b
- PK **1.3** Railway bridge, former industrial quays d/s
- PK **1.9** Lock 2 (Comte) in short lock-cut l/b, swing bridge
- PK **2.5** Bridge
- PK **2.6** Road bridge (N136, Rennes bypass)
- PK **4.2** Meander cutoff r/b
- PK **5.5** Lock 3 (Apigné) in short lock-cut l/b, bridge
- PK **9.3** Bridge (Chancors), weir r/b, entrance to lock-cut l/b
- PK **9.7** Bridge (D34)
- PK **11.0** Lock 4 (Cicé), lift bridge, navigation re-enters Vilaine
- PK **13.9** Entrance to lock-cut l/b, confluence of Meu, r/b
- PK **14.1** Bridge (Mons), quay d/s l/b, **Bruz** 2 km l/b
- PK **14.3** Lock 5 (Mons)
- PK **14.5** Bridge (D177)
- PK **14.8** Navigation re-enters Vilaine
- PK **17.8** Lock 6 (Pont-Réan), l/b, and weir
- PK **18.0** **Pont-Réan** bridge, *port de plaisance* d/s r/b for 17 boats, free, water, electricity, slipway, village r/b
- PK **20.3** Confluence of Seiche, l/b
- PK **20.5** Railway viaduct (Cahot), moorings d/s l/b
- PK **21.0** Lock 7 (Boël), r/b, and weir

# VIII – Western France

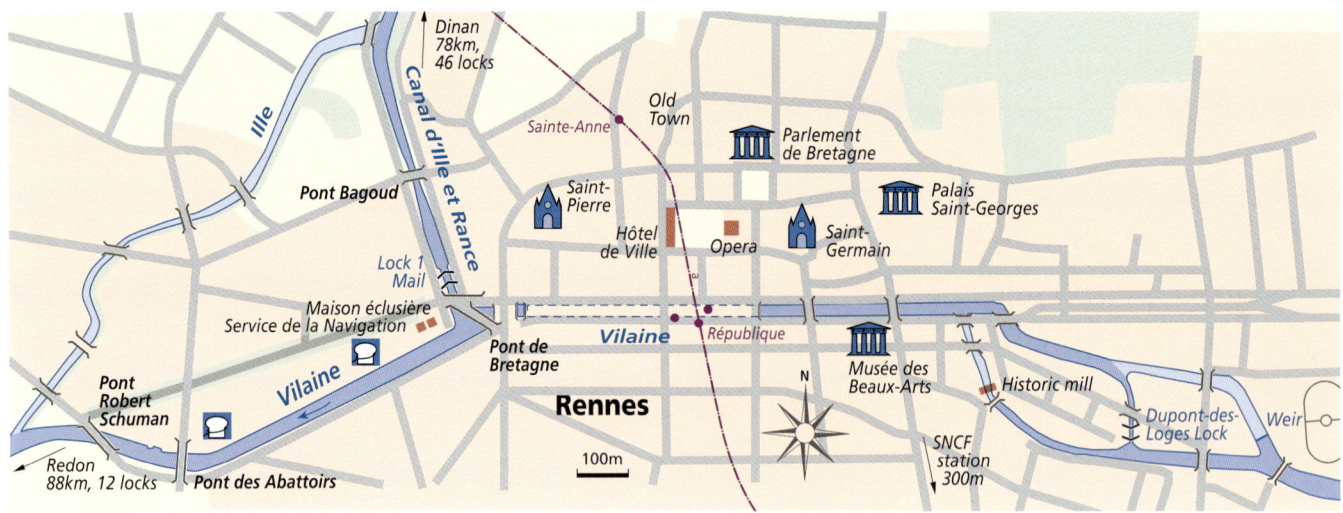

|  | |
|---|---|
| PK 23.7 | **Laillé** bridge, boat moorings d/s r/b, water, electricity, mooring free, village 2.5km l/b, **Guichen** 3600m r/b |
| PK 26.8 | Lock 8 (Bouëxière), r/b, and weir |
| PK 27.9 | Bridge (D38) |
| PK 28.5 | Bridge (Glanret), quay d/s r/b, 1800m l/b |
| PK 30.2 | Lock 9 (Gailieu), r/b, and weir, **Bourg-des-Comptes** *halte* on quay u/s l/b for 5 boats, free, water, electricity €3 for 10 hours (€1 coin in slot at meter), showers at camp site (200m) |
| PK 33.8 | Lock 10 (Molière), r/b, and weir |
| PK 35.3 | Bridge (Charrière), **Pléchâtel** 1km l/b |
| PK 37.3 | Railway viaduct (Cambrée) |
| PK 39.9 | Bridge (Macaire), moorings d/s l/b |
| PK 40.6 | Lock 11 (Macaire), r/b, and weir |
| PK 46.9 | **Messac** *port de plaisance* and Le Boat hire base in basin l/b, 02 99 34 61 32, 166 berths, 6 visitor moorings on pontoon facing harbour entrance, night €8, water and electricity included, showers, slipway, fuel, pump-out, crane 10t, repairs |
| PK 47.6 | Lock 12 (Guipry), r/b, and weir |
| PK 47.7 | **Guipry** bridge, municipal *halte* on quay d/s r/b, 4 boats, free (maximum 72 hours), water, slipway, Guipry-Messac centre 1.5km r/b, Messac 1300m l/b |
| PK 48.5 | Railway bridge (Messac) |
| PK 52.0 | Lock 13 (Mâlon), r/b, and weir, shoals d/s |
| PK 55.0 | Bridge (Saint-Marc), entrance to gorge |
| PK 56.7 | Railway viaduct (Corbinières) |
| PK 62.2 | **Port de Roche** bridge, municipal *halte* on quay u/s r/b, free (overnight mooring), water, slipway, end of section in gorge, small village r/b, **Langon** 2.5km |
| PK 63.5 | **Sainte-Anne-sur-Vilaine** *halte* on pontoon l/b, 4 boats, water and electricity (on request), slipway |
| PK 66.4 | Confluence of Chère, l/b |
| PK 67.6 | Railway viaduct (Droulin) |
| PK 69.3 | **Beslé** bridge, public quays u/s both banks, 30m pontoon d/s l/b, water, electricity, slipway, village 500m l/b |
| PK 71.3 | **Brain-sur-Vilaine** quay and village r/b |
| PK 73.0 | Ferry |
| PK 74.3 | Bridge (Ilette), quay u/s r/b |
| PK 76.5 | Lake (Lac de Murin) beyond left bank |
| PK 79.3 | Bridge (Painfaut), small village 300m r/b |
| PK 84.0 | **Sainte-Marie** bridge (Pont du Grand-Pas), 25m pontoon u/s r/b for 3 boats, free, water, electricity, slipway |
| PK 85.9 | Main road viaduct (D177/D164, Redon bypass) |
| PK 88.8 | Railway viaduct (Redon) |
| PK 89.1 | Redon bridge (Pont de Saint-Nicolas), quay u/s r/b, town centre r/b |
| PK 89.2 | **Crossing of Canal de Nantes à Brest** in centre of Redon |
| PK 89.3 | Quays r/b |
| PK 89.4 | Site of former weir (Grand Vannage) |
| PK 89.7 | **Redon** basin (Grand Bassin) r/b, *port de plaisance*, **additional junction with Canal de Nantes à Brest** at end of basin, Les Canalous hire base, 10 visitor moorings, 07 77 88 23 22, night €22, water, electricity, showers, diesel, pump-out, crane 13t (up to 15m) **capitainerie@redon-plaisance.fr** |

*The charming port of Guipry, downstream of the lock*
SYNDICAT D'INITIATIVE DE MESSAC

Redon is the first of the two major canal cross-roads in Brittany, and is a charming small town, ideal for short stays, for meeting with crew from afar (thanks to the excellent train services), or even for over-wintering, thanks to the boatyards and other services in the extensive port, managed by Redon district (Redon Agglomération Bretagne Sud).

# Vilaine

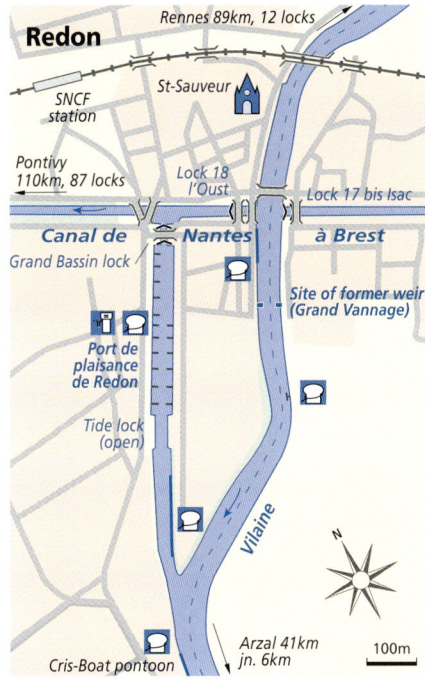

*The extensive port de plaisance at La Roche Bernard* © LEHIBOU

PK 90.1  Former commercial quay for seagoing vessels r/b, Cris'Boat hire base, pontoon moorings
PK 90.9  Confluence of Oust, r/b
PK 96.1  Junction with Canal de Nantes à Brest, l/b, through Les Bellions lock
PK 96.7  **Rieux** municipal *halte* on two pontoons r/b, capacity 20 boats, night €13, water and electricity included, showers and wifi at campsite in season, slipway
PK 100.0  Confluence of Isac, l/b
PK 101.8  Bridge (Cran) with swinging span l/b, opens at fixed times for boats requiring more than 5.8m headroom, pontoon moorings u/s and d/s l/b, restaurant
PK 103.8  Ferry (Passage Neuf)
PK 115.3  **Folleux** *port de plaisance* r/b, managed by Compagnie des Ports du Morbihan, 02 99 91 80 87, VHF 9, 370 berths, pontoon for visiting boats r/b, night €28, water, electricity, showers (with code), wifi (24 hour pass), **Béganne** 4.5km  *port-folleux.com*

This attractive marina spread across both banks and into a charming inlet on the right bank has received a gold award from The Yacht Harbour Association.

PK 120.9  Boat moorings l/b
PK 121.1  Main road bridge (N165)
PK 122.0  Suspension bridge (D765)
PK 122.6  **La Roche-Bernard** *port de plaisance* (Port du Rhodoir) l/b, moorings and boatyard (Atelier Naval de la Couronne) 02 99 90 62 17, 560 berths, 54 visitor moorings, night €28, water, electricity, showers, pump-out, crane 13t, slipway, repairs, wifi, restaurants, village 500m up hill l/b
  *roche-bernard@compagniedesportsdumorbihan.fr*

PK 130.8  **Arzal-Camoël** *port de plaisance* l/b, 1200 berths, 02 97 45 02 97, visitor moorings for 57 boats, night €34.00, fuel, water, electricity, showers, crane, pump-out, repairs (Marinarzal, *marinarzal.com* and Méca Nautique, *mecanautique.bzh*, wifi, restaurants 150m  *arzal.camoel.com*
PK 131.0  Arzal dam, lock r/b, lift bridge
PK 131.2  Slipway (Vieille Roche) l/b
PK 136.6  **Tréhiguier** quay and boat harbour l/b, 4 berths, former ferry
PK 137.0  Discharge into the Atlantic, Pointe du Moustoir r/b, Pointe du Scal l/b

## Branch through Rennes

PK 0.0  Rennes bridge (Pont de Bretagne)
PK 0.1  End of tunnel
PK 0.5  Entrance to tunnel (covered section of Vilaine)
PK 0.6  Footbridge
PK 0.8  Bridge (Pasteur), Musée des Beaux Arts
PK 1.0  Bridge (Richemont)
PK 1.2  Entrance to lock-cut
PK 1.3  Lock (Dupont-des-Loges), head of navigation for small craft

*The Vilaine in Rennes, upstream of the covered section (in the background)...* JOHN RIDDEL/EDB

# 70. Canal de Nantes à Brest

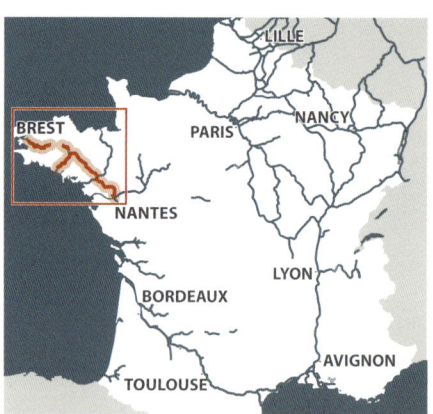

THE CANAL DE NANTES À BREST was a truly epic achievement by all engineers and workers who built it in the early 19th Century, to fulfil a Napoleonic dream, and is without doubt in the author's top five waterways in France. It is formed by canalised rivers and three canal sections built to cross three successive watersheds: between the rivers Loire and Vilaine, the rivers Oust and Blavet and finally from the Blavet to the river Hyères, a tributary of the river Aulne. This was the most ambitious canal project ever completed in France, 360km long with no less than 218 locks! The canal was closed as a through route in 1920, when a section was submerged by Guerlédan dam (PK 227), a short distance west of the junction with the canalised river Blavet at Pontivy. The entire length of waterway west of Guerlédan was officially closed in 1957, and the 21km length from Pontivy to Guerlédan also subsequently fell into disuse. At the same time, the disappearance of all commercial traffic (in 26m long barges carrying up to 140 tonnes) resulted in the gradual silting up of the canal section between Rohan and Pontivy, reducing the available depth to 0.90m or less.

*The Canal de Nantes à Brest was built between 1804 and 1836 as a strategic link between the two seaports, thus securing military supplies in case of a blockade of Brittany's ports by the British. Works and operation were conceded in 1822 to the Compagnie des Quatre Canaux under the Becquey prigramme, with a new funding mechanism. The waterway never carried much commercial traffic. Recreational traffic has also been limited because of the 'barrier' of the watershed section of the Nantes-Brest canal east from Pontivy, with its countless locks, and the real barrier of Guerlédan Dam to the west. However, recreational use of the towpath has developed spectacularly in recent years, also on the unrestored lengths, and is now one of the arguments for completing restoration end to end, as promoted for 50 years by the Comité des Canaux Bretons. The canal's new owner, Brittany Regional Council, is considering the options.*

The situation was greatly improved thanks to substantial investments made when the entire canal system was transferred to Brittany Region. Dredging works were completed throughout the navigable lengths, and the isolated western section was extended up to Goariva. This was a 'second restoration', after floods damaged the structures restored in the 1980s. The potential of the Brittany canals for cruising and tourism is recognised by local authorities throughout the region, thanks in no small measure to the campaigning efforts of the *Comité des Canaux Bretons*, the oldest waterway association in France, which has been absorbed into a new regional association *Escales Fluviales de Bretagne*. The complete length of the waterway is given in the route description, distinguishing navigable and non-navigable sections as follows:

- **Eastern section**, Nantes to Guerlédan 225km, 116 locks, navigable, although the last 21km to Guerlédan, with 11 locks, remains to be restored,
- **Guerlédan bypass**, presumed to be a canal and boat lift about 800m long (bypassing 19 locks of the original canal),
- **Middle section**, Guerlédan to Mellionec 26km, 10 locks, navigable,
- **Missing link**, Mellionec to Goariva 27km, 45 locks, unnavigable, but restoration of the locks is in an ongoing project,
- **Western section**, Goariva to Port Launay 81km, 41 locks, navigable.

It should be noted that the unnavigable sections are available for small boats and canoes, and that the towpath is available throughout for walkers and cyclists, except along the Erdre and around the Guerlédan reservoir.

In recent years there has been a serious threat to integrity of the canal because of a drive to demolish the weirs on the canalised river Blavet west of Pontivy, as well as on the canalised river Aulne in the canal's western section. The main advocates of weir demolition are the angling community and their representative organisations, who want to encourage migrating fish species to return to the rivers. After careful study of the impacts of weir removal, the idea has thankfully been abandoned as unfeasible.

Studies showed in particular that significant negative environmental effects could follow removal of the weirs.

### Eastern section, Nantes to Pontivy
The Canal de Nantes à Brest, 225 km in length from Nantes to Guerlédan, offers two alternative routes to the Bay of Biscay from the English Channel, in addition to the direct route via the river Vilaine. The navigator reaching the Brittany waterway crossroads at Redon may turn south-east towards Nantes, a distance of 95 km from the entrance lock at Redon. Over the last 22km navigation is in the river Erdre, which is wide and almost estuarine in character, and one of the most picturesque rivers in France. From Nantes the Loire estuary gives access to the Atlantic at Saint-Nazaire.

The alternative route is north-west to the Pontivy cross-roads (111km from Redon). From here the Canal du Blavet leads down to the sea at Lorient.

The summit level section from Rohan to Pontivy was closed for many years because of recurrent failure and eventual closure of the 63km long Hilvern feeder from Bosméléac reservoir. This was overcome by building a pipeline from the Blavet near Pontivy to the summit which can supply up to 450 litres per second.

### Navigation
A truly delightful waterway throughout, with no particular difficulty apart from the hard work going through all the locks between Josselin and Pontivy.

### Locks
From Nantes to Redon there are 18 locks, minimum dimensions 26.50m by 4.70m. The first, Saint-Félix, gives access from the Loire to the river Erdre (then lock-free). It is open from 3 hours before to 3 hours after high tide. Six more lead up to the summit level at 19.80m above sea level. There are 10 locks down to the Vilaine, this section incorporating the canalised river Isac. The Vilaine is entered at Redon or 6km before Redon is reached, through Bellions lock (17).

From Redon to Pontivy there are 90 locks, of slightly smaller dimensions (25.70m by 4.60m), distributed as follows:
- 35 to Rohan, this section being made up essentially of the canalised river Oust,
- 26 (in a length of 6.6km) to the summit level, at an altitude of 129.60m,
- 29 from the summit down to Pontivy.

The section from Pontivy to the projected Guerlédan boat lift, gradually being restored, has 11 locks, of which 4 are currently operational.

### Draught
The maximum authorised draught on the canal is 1.20m from Quiheix to Redon and 1.40m from Redon to Pontivy.

### Headroom
The maximum authorised air draught is 3m, reduced to 2.20m under the highest navigable water level).

### Towpath
There is a well-maintained towpath along the canal sections, but not along the river Erdre, nor along the river Vilaine from Bellions lock to Redon.

### Authority
**Conseil Départemental de Loire-Atlantique**
Service des Infrastructures Maritimes et Voies Navigables
- 23-25 rue Pitre-Chevallier, 44000 Nantes
  02 40 99 15 05 (PK 0-95)

**Région Bretagne** - Service des Voies Navigables, Institution d'Aménagement de la Vilaine
- 1 quai amiral de la Grandière, 35600 Redon
  02 99 72 35 35 (PK 95-105)

Subdivision Blavet-Canal de Nantes à Brest
- 1 avenue du Commandant Ameil, 56140 Malestroit
  02 97 75 12 45  *svn-bnb@bretagne.bzh* (PK 105-227)

### Guerlédan bypass
The long-term goal of restoration of the complete waterway would be served by the construction of a bypass canal including two or more locks and a boat lift to transfer boats from the canal to the Guerlédan reservoir. A feasibility study commissioned by the Brittany Regional Council in the 1990s proposed several possible solutions with estimated costs, but no decision was taken. The project is now being actively promoted by the local district (see p.113).

### Middle section, Guerlédan to Mellionec
The département of Côtes d'Armor restored a section of the canal from the head of the Guerlédan reservoir to an isolated chapel (La Pitié) in the commune of Mellionec, near Rostrenen, a distance of 26km. The first 10km is in the Guerlédan reservoir, which submerged 16 locks. The remainder is the restored canal, with 10 locks, the last (Coat-Natous) being the only double staircase lock in Brittany.

### Missing link, Mellionec to Goariva
This section is mentioned for reference. It is 27km long, with 45 locks, of which 13 rise from Coat-Natous to the summit level, the other 34 falling to Goariva, which marks the limit of the Finistère département.

### Western section, Goariva to Châteaulin
The western section is the entire length of the canal in the Finistère *département*, a distance of 81km from Goariva, near Carhaix-Plouguer, to Châteaulin. This waterway has suffered heavily from flood damage in the past, and is still under threat from vigorous campaigning by the angling community, supported by environmental groups, in favour of abandoning the navigation and demolishing all the weirs. As on the Blavet section towards Pontivy, the idea of restoring free-flow conditions has to date been rejected by the decision-makers in favour of maintaining the waterway as multi-use heritage.

Downstream of Châteaulin the Aulne is a maritime navigation, although there is a tide lock at Guily-Glaz, 4km downstream. For convenience an approximate route

## VIII – Western France

description is given for navigation between Châteaulin and Brest, although nautical works should be consulted for crossing the Brest roadstead.

## Locks
There are 45 locks (numbered 192 to 236 on the original canal), of which 12 are on the canal section down to Port-Triffen, 6 are on the canalised river Hyère and the remaining 27 on the canalised river Aulne. Their dimensions are 25.70m by 4.65m. The locks are unmanned, and have to be worked by the boat's crew using a windlass, supplied against a deposit of €50. An instructions leaflet is issued to all boaters. The tide lock at Guily-Glaz is 40m long and 10m wide, allowing large vessels to reach Châteaulin. Boat owners reaching Châteaulin from the sea and intending to proceed up the Aulne may be supplied with a windlass by the Guily-Glaz lock-keeper. This lock is operated from 2 hours before to 2 hours after high tide.

## Draught
On the inland waterway down to Châteaulin the maximum authorised draught is 1.20m. Châteaulin is accessible to vessels drawing up to 3m.

## Headroom
The fixed bridges leave a minimum headroom of 3m.

## Towpath
There is a towpath throughout this section from Gouarec to Châteaulin, developed as a popular cycling itinerary.

## Authority
Conseil départemental Loire-Atlantique, Service Infrastructures Voies Navigables, 3 quai Ceineray, 44141 Nantes, 02 40 99 15 05 (PK 0-95)
Région Bretagne, Direction des Voies Navigables, Subdivision Canal de Nantes à Brest et Blavet
– 1 avenue du Commandant-Ameil, BP24, 56140 Malestroit 02 97 75 12 45 (PK 95-360)
Conseil Départemental du Finistère
Direction de l'Aménagement, de l'Agriculture, de l'Eau et de l'Environnement
– 32 boulevard Dupleix, 29000 Quimper 02 98 76 26 54 (tidal river and locks 236 and 237)

## Route description

| | |
|---|---|
| PK 0.0 | Junction with river Loire |
| PK 0.1 | Lock 1 (Saint-Félix), footbridge, water |
| PK 0.2 | Bridge (Tbilissi), basin u/s (Saint-Félix) |
| PK 0.6 | Road bridges and railway bridge |
| PK 0.7 | Entrance to tunnel Saint-Félix, under boulevards |
| PK 1.4 | **Nantes**, basin at northern tunnel entrance, moorings close to city centre |
| PK 1.5 | Bridge (Saint-Mihiel) |
| PK 1.7 | D/s entrance to *port de plaisance* (Port de l'Erdre) r/b access to long-term moorings only |
| PK 1.8 | Footbridge (Île Versailles), park on island |
| PK 2.0 | **Nantes** *port de plaisance* u/s entrance, r/b, (Port de l'Erdre) access to long-term moorings only, 20 visitor moorings on pontoon in main channel, 02 40 37 04 62, night €18.50, fuel, water, electricity, showers, slipway, wifi, repairs, restaurant *ports-nantes.fr* |
| PK 2.3 | Bridge (Général de la Motte-Rouge) |
| PK 3.1 | Bridge (Tortière) |

# Canal de Nantes à Brest

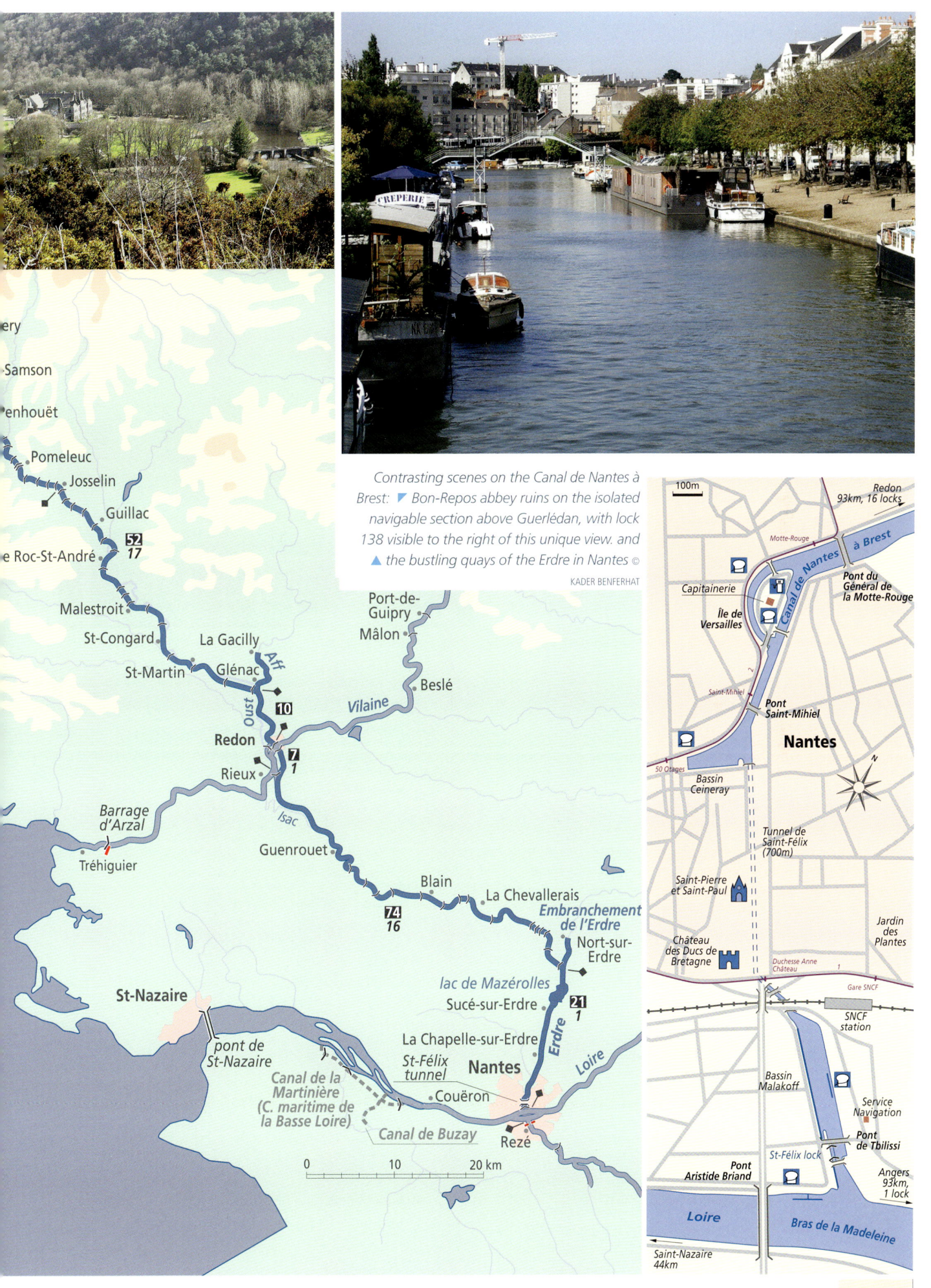

*Contrasting scenes on the Canal de Nantes à Brest:* ▼ *Bon-Repos abbey ruins on the isolated navigable section above Guerlédan, with lock 138 visible to the right of this unique view. and* ▲ *the bustling quays of the Erdre in Nantes* ©

KADER BENFERHAT

## VIII – Western France

| | |
|---|---|
| PK 5.2 | **La Jonelière** quay r/b |
| PK 5.5 | Railway bridge (La Jonelière) |
| PK 5.6 | Road bridge (La Beaujoire), N844 Nantes ring road |
| PK 5.9 | Water sports centre l/b |
| PK 8.0 | Motorway bridge (A11) |
| PK 9.0 | **La Chapelle-sur-Erdre** quay r/b, village 2.5 km |
| PK 10.5 | **Carquefou** quay l/b, village 3 km |
| PK 15.1 | **Sucé-sur-Erdre** bridge, municipal *port de plaisance* d/s r/b, managed by Bretagne Fluviale, 15 visitor moorings, night €14 (maximum 1 week), water, electricity, pump-out, slipway, additional moorings d/s r/b, repairs by Bretagne Fluviale, crane 15t, boats up to 14m **bureauduport@suce-sur-erdre.fr** |
| PK 27.7 | Bridge (Plessis), **Nort-sur-Erdre** 2.5 km l/b |

For Nort-sur-Erdre, see the branch at the end of this section.

| | |
|---|---|
| PK 28.9 | Lock 4 (Rabinière), bridge (Rocher, D164) |
| PK 29.9 | Lock 5 (Haie Pacoret) |
| PK 30.9 | Lock 6 (Cramezeul) |
| PK 31.5 | Bridge (Rouziou) |
| PK 32.3 | Lock 7 (Pas d'Héric), beginning of summit level |
| PK 33.0 | Bridge (Coudrais), quay |
| PK 35.4 | Pipeline crossing |
| PK 35.9 | Bridge (Saffré) |
| PK 38.2 | Bridge (Bout-de-Bois), quay |
| PK 38.5 | Motorway bridge (Glanet), N137 |
| PK 39.9 | Bridge (Remaudais) |
| PK 40.7 | Lock 8 (Remaudais), end of summit level |
| PK 42.3 | **La Chevallerais** bridge, quay d/s r/b, 02 40 79 10 12, village 600m l/b |
| PK 43.4 | Bridge (Gué de l'Atelier) |
| PK 43.8 | Lock 9 (Gué de l'Atelier) |
| PK 43.9 | Canal becomes canalised river Isac |
| PK 45.3 | Lock 10 (Terrier) |
| PK 45.6 | Bridge |
| PK 45.9 | Bridge (D164) |
| PK 48.7 | Lock 11 (Blain) |
| PK 50.0 | Footbridge |
| PK 50.2 | **Blain** quay r/b, *halte nautique* for 20 boats, 10 visitor moorings, night €13 (first two nights free), water and electricity included, shower, pump-out, town centre 500m |
| PK 50.3 | Bridge (Pont de la Croix Rouge) |
| PK 50.5 | Disused railway bridge |
| PK 51.5 | Lock 12 (Paudais) |
| PK 56.2 | Lock 13 (Bougard), bridge, quay u/s r/b |
| PK 59.5 | Lock 14 (Barel) |
| PK 59.6 | Bridge |
| PK 61.9 | Lock 15 (Touche) |
| PK 63.5 | Bridge (Pont-Nozay), D3, quay d/s l/b |
| PK 65.9 | Lock 16 (Melneuf) |
| PK 66.1 | Bridge (Melneuf) |
| PK 69.3 | Château de Carheil r/b |
| PK 72.8 | **Guenrouët** bridge (Saint-Clair), municipal *halte* on quay d/s l/b, capacity 14 boats, free (maximum 48 hours), water, electricity, shower, slipway, village 800m l/b |
| PK 80.0 | Navigation enters Thénot diversion canal, r/b |
| PK 81.7 | Bridge (Catée) |
| PK 83.5 | Bridge (D773, Fégréac bypass) |
| PK 83.7 | **Fégréac** bridge (Pont-Miny), municipal *halte* on quay u/s l/b, 4 boats, free, water, electricity, shower €1, wifi at Maison du Canal interpretation centre, village 1.5 km r/b |
| PK 85.5 | Railway bridge (Trouhel) |
| PK 86.0 | Bridge (Trouhel) |
| PK 88.5 | Bridge (Saint-Jacques) |
| PK 88.6 | **Junction with river Vilaine**, through lock 17 (Bellions), alternative route to Redon via the Vilaine is 700m longer than by the canal |
| PK 90.8 | Footbridge |
| PK 91.7 | Bridge (Le Tertre) |
| PK 92.5 | Bridge (Quinssignac) |
| PK 93.1 | **Saint-Nicolas-de-Redon**, bridge, village r/b |
| PK 94.7 | Lock 17 (Isac, or La Digue), lift bridge and footbridge |
| PK 94.9 | **Redon**, **Vilaine crossing**, quays, town centre 200m |

*Vilaine crossing in Redon, Lock 17bis (Isac) on the far side.* © PHILIP COOK

| | |
|---|---|
| PK 95.0 | Lock 18 (Oust or Redon), bridge and moving bridge |
| PK 95.1 | **Junction with Redon basin** through Grand Bassin lock, lift bridge (see under River Vilaine) |

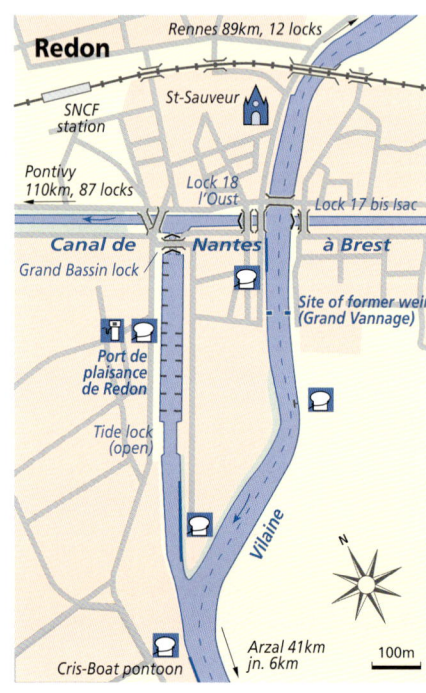

| | |
|---|---|
| PK 95.2 | Road and rail swing bridge, entrance to large basin r/b |
| PK 95.7 | Suspension bridge (Guichardais) |
| PK 96.1 | Bridge |
| PK 96.4 | Bridge (Codilo) |

# Canal de Nantes à Brest

PK **96.5** Railway bridge
PK **97.3** Bridge (Courée)
PK **99.4** Bridge (Marionnette), D764
PK **101.4** Suspension bridge (Potinais)
PK **101.7** Navigation enters river Oust, turning right (u/s), weir left
PK **103.7** Island (Île aux Pies), beauty spot
PK **104.1** **Saint-Vincent-sur Oust** *halte* on quay and two landing stages r/b, free (maximum 72 hours), water, electricity, shower at camp site

This is the mooring beside the famous beauty spot of the Île aux Pies. The quay used to load limestone from the former quarry.

PK **105.2** Confluence of river Aff l/b
PK **105.3** Lock 19 (Maclais, or Painfaut), navigation enters lock-cut
PK **107.0** Bridge (Prévotais)
PK **108.7** Bridge (Bilaire)
PK **109.8** Lock 20 (Limur), bridge
PK **109.9** Navigation re-enters river Oust
PK **112.0** **Peillac** *halte* r/b, hard quay (40m) and boardwalk (120m) moorings, free (maximum 72 hours), water, electricity, shower at camp site, slipway, village 2 km r/b
PK **112.5** Bridge (Pont-d'Oust)
PK **112.5** **Peillac** bridge (Pont-d'Oust)
PK **116.6** Lock 21 (Le Gueslin)
PK **117.5** **Saint-Martin-sur-Oust** bridge (Le Gueslin), municipal *halte* on 70m pontoon with fingers d/s l/b, up to 6 visitor moorings stern-to, free (maximum 72 hours), additional pontoon u/s, water, shower (€2), village 800m l/b
PK **120.4** Lock 22 (Rieux)
PK **121.8** **Saint-Gravé** quay r/b, village 5500m
PK **123.7** **Saint-Congard** bridge, quay, small village r/b
PK **125.5** Lock 23 (Beaumont) in short lock-cut r/b
PK **129.6** Lock 24 (Foveno) in short lock-cut r/b
PK **132.0** Footbridge
PK **132.2** **Malestroit** bridge (Pont Neuf), quay and timber jetty d/s r/b, mooring free (maximum 72 hours), water, sanitary building, village 300m

Malestroit is a delightful small town, proud of its history as a river port dating back to the 16th century.

PK **132.3** Bridge (Aristide-Briand) over entrance to lock-cut r/b
PK **132.6** Lock 25 (Malestroit), bridge
PK **134.4** Lock 26 (Lanée), bridge
PK **135.4** Lock 27 (Lanée), permanently open, bridge, navigation re-enters Oust
PK **137.2** Motorway bridge (N166)
PK **137.6** Railway bridge
PK **139.7** Lock 28 (Ville-aux-Fruglins)
PK **141.0** **Le Roc-Saint-André** bridge, mooring d/s r/b, 5 berths, free (maximum 72 hours), water, electricity, shower at camp site in season, village r/b
PK **141.5** Railway bridge (Hungleux)
PK **143.7** Lock 29 (**Montertelot**), bridge, quay u/s l/b for 7 boats, mooring free (maximum 72 hours), water, electricity €2), slipway, village l/b

One of most delightful moorings and villages of the canal.

PK **145.0** Railway bridge (Deux-Rivières)
PK **146.2** Lock 30 (Blon)
PK **148.0** Bridge, quay u/s r/b
PK **149.0** Lock 31 (**Guillac**), village 1 km l/b
PK **152.1** Lock 32 (Carmenais)
PK **153.7** Bridge (Saint-Gobrien)
PK **154.1** Lock 33 (Clan)
PK **155.3** Railway bridge (disused)
PK **155.6** Lock 34 (Saint-Jouan), bridge
PK **157.3** Lock 35 (Josselin), visitor centre and facilities
PK **157.5** **Josselin** municipal *halte* on 80m pontoon l/b (under the château des Rohan), for up to 10 boats, free (maximum 72 hours), water, electricity, shower, pump-out, small town 300m l/b

*The Renaissance-style 'Château des Rohan', completed in 1520, towers over the river Oust in Josselin.* © JOHN RIDDEL/EDITIONS DU BREIL

Josselin is the most emblematic site of the river Oust, and the château des Rohan is a sumptuous residence dating from the 14th century but completely renovated after the Rohan family recovered the property in 1850.

PK **157.7** Bridge (Sainte-Croix)
PK **157.9** *Halte* on pontoon r/b, additional mooring for Josselin
PK **158.4** Lock 36 (Beaufort) in short lock-cut l/b
PK **158.8** Bridge
PK **159.7** Motorway bridge (N24)
PK **159.8** Lock 37 (Caradec) in short lock-cut l/b, bridge
PK **161.4** Lock 38 (Rouvray)
PK **163.1** Lock 39 (Bocneuf)
PK **164.6** Bridge (D764)
PK **164.7** Bridge (Bocneuf)
PK **165.6** Lock 40 (Pomeleuc) in lock-cut r/b
PK **165.9** Lock 41 (Tertraie), bridge
PK **167.2** Lock 42 (Tertraie), permanently open, bridge, navigation re-enters Oust
PK **169.8** Lock 43 (Cadoret) in short lock-cut r/b, bridge
PK **170.9** Lock 44 (Lié) in lock-cut r/b
PK **171.2** Access to **Les Forges** harbour, 800m l/b, pontoon, water
PK **172.4** Lock 45 (Griffet) in lock-cut l/b, bridge (Perrin)
PK **173.3** Lock 46 (Grenouillère)
PK **174.1** Navigation enters canal section l/b
PK **174.2** Lock 47 (Trévérend), bridge
PK **175.4** Lock 48 (Penhouët), bridge
PK **176.4** Lock 49 (Lille), bridge

## VIII – Western France

PK **178.4** Lock 50 (Timadeuc), bridge, Timadeuc abbey 600m l/b
PK **179.1** Navigation re-enters Oust
PK **180.5** Lock 51 (Quengo)
PK **181.4** Lock 52 (Rohan)
PK **181.5** **Rohan** bridge (Pont Notre-Dame), *port de plaisance* d/s r/b, 27 berths, free (maximum 72 hours) including water and electricity, showers, crane on request, slipway, pump-out, village r/b

*The hotel barge* Duchesse Anne *heads upstream out of Rohan lock, where the vast majority of boats call it a day and head back downstream..* © JOHN RIDDEL/EDITIONS DU BREIL

PK **181.9** Bridge (Pont d'Oust)
PK **182.3** Footbridge
PK **182.4** **Saint-Samson** *port de plaisance* r/b, village l/b
PK **183.6** Lock 53 (Saint-Samson) in lock-cut r/b, bridge
PK **184.2** Footbridge
PK **184.8** Lock 54 (Le Guer), bridge

*Lock 54, Le Guer, PK 185.* © KADER BENFERHAT

PK **185.7** Navigation leaves Oust for last time, r/b
PK **185.8** Lock 55 (Coëtprat), bridge
PK **186.8** Lock 56 (Kermelin), bridge
PK **187.2** Lock 57 (Sablière)
PK **187.5** Lock 58 (Kériffe)
PK **187.8** Lock 59 (Boju), bridge, quay, **Gueltas** 1200m r/b
PK **188.0** Lock 60 (Parc-Coh)

PK **188.2** Lock 61 (Goiffre)
PK **188.5** Lock 62 (Goirball)
PK **188.8** Lock 63 (Guernogas)
PK **189.0** Lock 64 (Branguily)
PK **189.2** Lock 65 (Neau-Blanche)
PK **189.4** Lock 66 (Pont-Terre)
PK **189.5** Lock 67 (Forêt), bridge
PK **189.7** Lock 68 (Menn-Merle)
PK **189.9** Lock 69 (Toulhouët)
PK **190.1** Lock 70 (Ville-Perro)
PK **190.2** Lock 71 (Gouvly)
PK **190.4** Lock 72 (Saint-Gonnery), bridge
PK **190.6** Lock 73 (Kervezo)
PK **190.8** Lock 74 (Douaren)
PK **190.9** Lock 75 (Grand-Pré)
PK **191.1** Lock 76 (Hilvern), bridge, **Saint-Gonnery** 1.5 km l/b
PK **191.2** Lock 77 (Pépinière)
PK **191.4** Lock 78 (Bel-Air), beginning of summit level, Hilvern feeder (disused) enters canal
PK **193.5** Motorway bridge (D768)
PK **194.9** Bridge (Brou)
PK **195.6** Quay (Saint-Gérand)
PK **196.3** Lock 79 (Kéroret), end of summit level, bridge, **Saint-Gérand** 700m l/b
PK **196.4** Lock 80 (Er Houët)
PK **196.5** Lock 81 (Kérivy)
PK **196.7** Lock 82 (Parc er Lann)
PK **196.8** Lock 83 (Kerihoué)
PK **196.9** Lock 84 (Parc Lann Bihan)
PK **197.1** Lock 85 (Lann Vras)
PK **197.2** Lock 86 (Parc Buisson)
PK **197.3** Lock 87 (Couëdic), bridge
PK **198.2** Bridge (Kergouët)
PK **199.1** Railway bridge
PK **199.4** Bridge (Saint-Caradec)
PK **199.7** Lock 88 (Joli-Cœur)
PK **199.8** Lock 89 (Parc-Lann-Hir)
PK **199.9** Lock 90 (Parc-Lann-Ergo)
PK **200.0** Lock 91 (Parc-Bihan)
PK **200.1** Lock 92 (Kerponer)
PK **200.3** Lock 93 (Restériard)
PK **200.4** Lock 94 (Tri-parc-lann-favilette)
PK **200.6** Lock 95 (Parc-bras)
PK **200.7** Lock 96 (Ros), bridge
PK **200.8** Lock 97 (Guerlaunay)
PK **201.1** Lock 98 (Bohumet)
PK **201.3** Lock 99 (Kervégan), bridge
PK **202.0** Lock 100 (Tren-deur-ros)
PK **202.3** Lock 101 (Kerveno)
PK **202.8** Lock 102 (Parc-Lann-hoarem)
PK **203.5** Lock 103 (Haie), bridge
PK **204.0** Lock 104 (Villeneuve)
PK **204.5** Lock 105 (Kerdudaval)
PK **205.1** Lock 106 (Kervert)
PK **205.5** Lock 107 (Ponteau), bridge
PK **205.9** **Pontivy**, *junction with Canal du Blavet*, quays, town centre 400m
PK **206.0** Bridge
PK **207.1** Lock 108 (Cascade)
PK **209.4** Lock 109 (Guernal)

# Canal de Nantes à Brest

*Guerlédan dam, PK 227.* © KADER BENFERHAT

PK **212.2** Lock 110 (Porzo)
PK **213.6** Bridge (Lenvos), Neuillac 1.5 km l/b
PK **214.5** Lock 111 (Trescleff)
PK **216.6** Lock 112 (Auquinian)
PK **218.7** Lock 113 (Stumo), bridge
PK **220.4** Lock 114 (Boloré), bridge
PK **221.8** Navigation enters canal section l/b
PK **222.0** Lock 115 (Saint-Samson)
PK **222.4** Lock 116 (Poulhibet), bridge
PK **223.9** Lock 117 (Kergoric), bridge
PK **224.3** Lock 118 (Quénécan), bridge, quay, **Saint-Aignan** 1 km r/b, **Mûr de Bretagne** (part of **Guerlédan**) 3 km l/b

## Guerlédan bypass

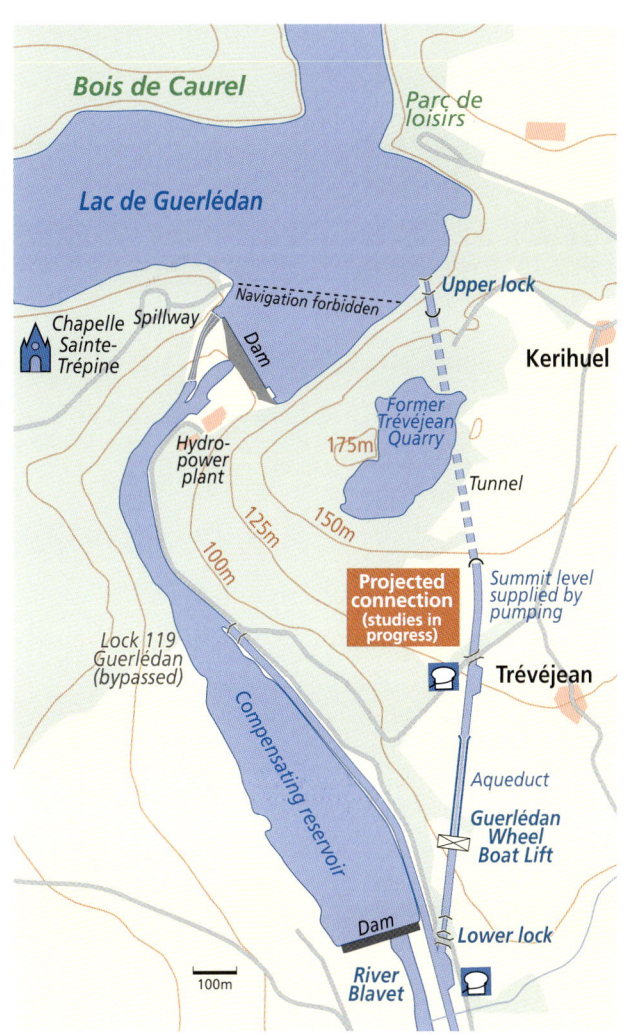

The plan below left gives an indication of the possible layout of the Guerlédan bypass canal, as promoted by the local district (Loudéac Communauté Centre Bretagne) and the new commune of Guerlédan. The project is based on a boat lift inspired by the Falkirk Wheel in Scotland, associated with two or more locks, needed for technical and operational reasons. The canal will enable boats to bypass the Guerlédan dam which has interrupted navigation since 1927. Overall, it is estimated that the site could attract at least 400 000 visitors per year.

PK **225.3** Entrance to new cut l/b
PK **225.7** Guerlédan boat lift (projected), height 35m
PK **226.0** Bridge at end of lift's upstream aqueduct
PK **226.3** Southern entrance to tunnel, 550m long
PK **226.8** Northern entrance to tunnel
PK **226.9** New Guerlédan lock, drop depending on reservoir level, navigation enters Lac de Guerlédan 400m upstream of dam (clear of the forbidden area on dam approach)
PK **227.3** Entrance to arm (Anse de Landroanec) l/b
PK **230.3** Mooring for trip boat l/b
PK **230.0** Camp site, beach and moorings in entrance to arm l/b
PK **231.8** Entrance to arm (Anse de Sordan) r/b, pontoon moorings, 02 97 27 52 36, 15 berths, showers at camp site, slipway, restaurant

The actual distance covered between Lock 118 and Lock 137 through the new Guerlédan bypass canal and the Lac de Guerlédan is 11km, while the original distances on the canal total 12.8km in this section. The original distances are shown from here westwards.

PK **237.1** Lock 137 (Les Forges)
PK **239.1** Lock 138 (Bon-Repos), bridge, Bon-Repos abbey ruins d/s l/b
PK **240.9** Lock 139 (Saint-Hervé)
PK **243.7** Canal enters the river Dore
PK **243.6** Bridge
PK **244.0** **Gouarec** bridge, village l/b
PK **244.1** Lock 140 (Gouarec)
PK **246.3** Lock 141 (Kerlouët)
PK **247.5** **Plélauff** bridge, village r/b
PK **247.6** Lock 142 (Plélauff)
PK **250.0** Lock 143 (Guendol)
PK **250.8** Lock 144 (Pont-Even), bridge (D764)
PK **252.0** Lock 145 (Kerlan)
PK **252.2** Double lock 146 (Coat-Natous)
PK **252.4** La Pitié chapel r/b, moorings, current limit of navigation

# VIII – Western France

## Section to be restored

The canal in this section is under the responsibility of the Agence Technique Départementale in Rostrenen, which is responsible for all restoration works:
**atdguingamp-rostrenen@cotesdarmor.fr**

PK **253.0** Lock 147 (Restouel), bridge
PK **254.7** Lock 148 (Stang-an-Dour)
PK **256.1** Lock 149 (Cosquer)

*Coat-Natous double staircase lock* © KADER BENFERHAT

PK **257.2** Lock 150 (Bonen), bridge
PK **258.3** Lock 151 (Kerjégu)
PK **258.5** Bridge (D23)
PK **259.5** Turning basin
PK **259.8** Lock 152 (Pont-Auffret), bridge (D790)
PK **261.3** Lock 153 (Kériou), bridge
PK **262.2** Lock 154 (Kerisloyet)
PK **262.8** Lock 155 (Pont-Yannic)
PK **263.2** Lock 156 (Tréhu-Moron)
PK **263.5** Lock 157 (Cosquérou)
PK **263.6** Lock 158 (Ménez-ar-Faouët)
PK **263.9** Lock 159 (Quitinic), beginning of summit level
PK **264.0** Reservoirs (Pont-Len and Mézouet) on south side
PK **264.6** Glomel bridge (D3), village 2.5 km south-west
PK **265.1** Entrance to cutting, narrow section
PK **267.0** Bridge
PK **267.8** End of cutting, canal opens to reservoir on south side (Créharer)
PK **268.0** Lock 160 (Créharer), footbridge
PK **268.1** Lock 161 (Stang-Jean)
PK **268.2** Lock 162 (Quinquis)

*Lock 162, near the non-navigable summit level, is in remarkably good condition.* © YATTITUDE

PK **268.4** Lock 163 (Saint-Péran), bridge
PK **268.5** Lock 164 (Ty-Lostec)
PK **268.7** Lock 165 (La Chapelle)
PK **268.8** Lock 166 (Menguen)
PK **269.0** Lock 167 (Kergicquel)
PK **269.1** Lock 168 (Kermarerhquer)
PK **269.2** Lock 169 (Kerlerès)
PK **269.4** Lock 170 (Trémalvézen)
PK **269.6** Lock 171 (Kergudon)
PK **269.9** Lock 172 (Kergiador)
PK **270.1** Lock 173 (Kérangal)
PK **270.4** Lock 174 (Prat Marc'h)
PK **270.8** Lock 175 (Dauwlas), bridge
PK **271.2** Lock 176 (Cajan)
PK **271.5** Lock 177 (Kerdelan)
PK **271.8** Lock 178 (Rosquelven)
PK **272.3** Lock 179 (La Pie), bridge (D11) d/s, Paule 2300m r/b
PK **272.6** Lock 180 (Keriffaut)
PK **272.9** Lock 181 (Lestrou)
PK **273.2** Lock 182 (Tronjoly), bridge
PK **273.8** Lock 183 (Kerbernès)
PK **274.0** Lock 184 (Moulin de Tronjoly)
PK **274.8** Lock 185 (Lansalaünn), bridge d/s
PK **275.4** Lock 186 (Saint-Éloy)
PK **276.3** Lock 187 (Stang-ar-Dour)
PK **276.7** Lock 188 (Moulin de Stang-ar-Dour)
PK **277.5** Lock 189 (Stang-ar-Vran), bridge
PK **278.0** Lock 190 (Moustoir)
PK **278.5** Lock 191 (Kerhun)

## Western section, Goariva to Châteaulin

PK **279.1** Goariva bridge (D83), limit of départements of Finistère and Côtes d'Armor
PK **279.4** Lock 192 (Goariva)
PK **280.1** Lock 193 (Kervoulédic)
PK **280.5** Lock 194 (Prat-ar-Born)
PK **280.8** Bridge
PK **281.0** Lock 195 (Pellerm)
PK **281.7** Lock 196 (Kergouthis)
PK **282.4** Lock 197 (Pont d'Auvlas)
PK **282.6** Bridge, Carhaix-Plouger 3 km r/b
PK **283.2** Lock 198 (Rochaër)
PK **283.8** Lock 199 (L'Île)
PK **284.2** Bridge, basin d/s
PK **284.3** Lock 200 (Pont-ar-Brost)
PK **284.8** Former railway bridge
PK **284.9** Lock 201 (Kergaden)
PK **285.8** Lock 202 (Kerdugnès)
PK **286.3** Port-de-Carhaix bridge (D769), quay u/s l/b
PK **286.4** Bridge
PK **286.7** Lock 203 (Kergoat)
PK **287.3** Navigation enters canalised river Hyère
PK **287.6** Lock 204 (Coz-Castel), bridge (used by footpath GR 37)
PK **289.1** Lock 205 (Kergoff)
PK **291.2** Lock 206 (Stervallen)
PK **292.4** Bridge, Cléden-Poher 2300m r/b
PK **293.4** Lock 207 (Le Ster)
PK **295.7** Lock 208 (Lesnévez)
PK **297.2** Lock 209 (Pont-Triffen)
PK **297.3** Bridge (D17), Landeleau 2.5 km r/b

# Canal de Nantes à Brest

PK 297.3 Confluence with river Aulne (canalised from this point), 'Maison du Canal' interpretation centre r/b, moorings, water, slipway
PK 299.1 Lock 210 (Pénity)
PK 301.7 Lock 211 (Roz-ar-Gaouen)
PK 303.3 Lock 212 (Méros)
PK 305.3 Lock 213 (Rosily)
PK 307.3 Lock 214 (Lanmeur)
PK 307.6 Bridge (Pont du Stang, D117)
PK 309.9 Lock 215 (Voaquer)
PK 310.2 Bridge, Saint-Goazec 1 km l/b
PK 311.8 Lock 216 (Moustoir)
PK 314.5 Lock 217 (Boudrac'h)
PK 316.3 Lock 218 (Bizernic)
PK 316.8 **Châteauneuf-du-Faou** bridges (Pont du Roy and new bridge), quay u/s r/b, *port de plaisance*, 02 98 73 40 31, water, showers

*Châteauneuf-du-Faou* © HERBYTHYME

PK 316.9 Quay r/b, Aulne Loisirs Plaisance hire base, 02 98 73 28 63, night €5, fuel (on demand), shower, crane, repairs, restaurant
PK 318.0 Lock 219 (Châteauneuf)
PK 319.9 Lock 220 (Kerboaret)
PK 321.8 Lock 221 (Kersalig)
PK 322.4 Bridge (Pont-Pol-ty-Glas)
PK 322.7 Bridge (D72)
PK 325.6 Lock 222 (Prat-Pourrig)
PK 328.2 Lock 223 (Ménez)
PK 329.7 **Pont-ar-c'hlan** quay r/b
PK 330.9 Lock 224 (Rosvéguen)
PK 331.9 Bridges (D41), moorings d/s r/b, water
PK 334.2 Lock 225 (Buzit)
PK 336.3 Lock 226 (Saint-Algon)
PK 336.8 **Pont-Coblant** bridge, quay u/s l/b, 02 98 26 68 11, water, electricity, shower, slipway, village l/b
PK 338.1 Lock 227 (Stéréon)
PK 340.9 Lock 228 (Coat-Pont)
PK 343.4 Lock 229 (Lothey)
PK 345.7 Lock 230 (Trésiguidy)
PK 348.7 Lock 231 (Le Guillec)
PK 350.6 Lock 232 (Aulne), quay u/s r/b, water, shower, slipway
PK 351.8 Main road bridge (N165)
PK 353.4 Lock 233 (Prat-Hir)
PK 356.2 Lock 234 (Toularodo)
PK 357.8 Lock 235 (Coatigrac'h)

PK 360.0 **Châteaulin** bridge
PK 360.4 Lock 236 (Châteaulin), bridge, municipal *halte* d/s r/b, 20 berths, 02 98 86 10 05, free (maximum 30 days), water, electricity, shower (key to be requested at the *mairie*)

This historic port marks the end of the inland waterway. Navigation continues in the tidal river Aulne.

## Navigation in tidal river Aulne

PK 0.0 **Châteaulin** bridge
PK 0.4 Châteaulin Lock 236 (Châteaulin)

Since the tidal river Aulne is considered to start at Châteaulin bridge, the first 400m overlaps with the end of the Canal de Nantes à Brest.

PK 0.5 Viaduct
PK 2.9 **Port-Launay** quays, 800m, 20 visitor berths, free, water, electricity, showers (all services charged), 06 88 46 33 20, pumpout, slipway
PK 3.9 Guily-Glaz railway viaduct
PK 4.3 Lock 237 (Guily-Glaz), operated between 2 hours before and 2 hours after high tide
PK 10.0 Confluence of the Douffine r/b
PK 27.0 **Landévennec** l/b

The estuary opens into the Brest roadstead, and the port is a further 24km.

## River Erdre branch

PK 0.0 *Junction with Canal de Nantes à Brest* d/s of lock 2
PK 5.0 Quay (Port Mulan) r/b
PK 6.0 **Nort-sur-Erdre** bridge, head of navigation, quay, Le Boat hire base and municipal *port de plaisance*, 06 86 38 60 99, 30 berths, 4 visitor moorings, night €17 (first two nights free), water, electricity, showers, pump-out, crane on request, slipway, repairs, village r/b

## River Aff

PK 0.0 *Junction with Canal de Nantes à Brest* (PK 105.2)
PK 0.7 Access to Glénac, basin, quays, Bretagne Fluviale hire base, 5 berths, water, slipway
PK 2.0 Bridge
PK 4.9 Bridge
PK 8.3 **La Gacilly** bridge, head of navigation, quays r/b, 02 99 08 21 75, 10 berths, free (maximum 72 hours), water, electricity, slipway

La Gacilly is a charming market town which has become famous for its annual open-air photo festival from June to September.

# 71. Canal du Blavet

THE CANALISED RIVER BLAVET is one of the links in the Brittany canal system. It connects with the Canal de Nantes à Brest at Pontivy (PK 206) and runs to Hennebont, a distance of 60km. From the last lock at Polvern, 2km short of Hennebont, the river is tidal and considered as a maritime waterway, giving access to the seaport of Lorient and the Atlantic Ocean (a further 14km beyond Hennebont). Major repairs were required to locks and weirs on this canalised river following major floods in 1996 and 2001. A comprehensive programme of rehabilitation works was conducted from 2002 to 2005, and the river navigation is now again fully operational. The navigation is operated and maintained by the *département* Morbihan, under concession from the Brittany Regional Council and with financial support.

## Navigation
A delightful and straightforward river navigation except when the Blavet is in flood.

## Locks
There are 28 locks, 26.30m by 4.70m.

## Draught
The original maximum authorised draught of 1.40m has been restored thanks to a substantial programme of dredging works on the lock approaches.

*The canalisation works were carried out by order of Napoleon in 1802 to provide access to the strategic military town of Pontivy. Like the entire Brittany canal network, its raison d'être was military defence in case of a naval blockade of the coast by the 'perfidious Albion'. Works began in 1804 and were completed in 1825. The waterway has little recreational traffic because of the 'barrier' of the watershed section of the Nantes-Brest canal east from Pontivy, with its countless locks, and the real barrier of Guerlédan Dam to the west.*

*Pontoon mooring and quay on the Blavet at Pontivy* © KALB

## Headroom
The least headroom under the fixed bridges is 3.00m, reduced to 2.40m above the highest navigable water level. The two bridges on the tidal river at Hennebont need to be negotiated at half tide, since headroom is only 50cm at a high tide of coefficient 100, while there is hardly any depth at low tide. On either side of these bridges pontoon moorings are available, where boats can wait for the right conditions. It is preferable to proceed against the current, which is strong at half tide.

## Towpath
The towpath is practicable throughout most of the length of the canalised river.

## Authority
Région Bretagne - Service des Voies Navigables Subdivision Canal de Nantes à Brest et Blavet – 1 avenue du Commandant-Ameil, 56140 Malestroit
02 97 75 12 45   *svn-bnb@bretagne.bzh*

# Canal du Blavet

## Route description

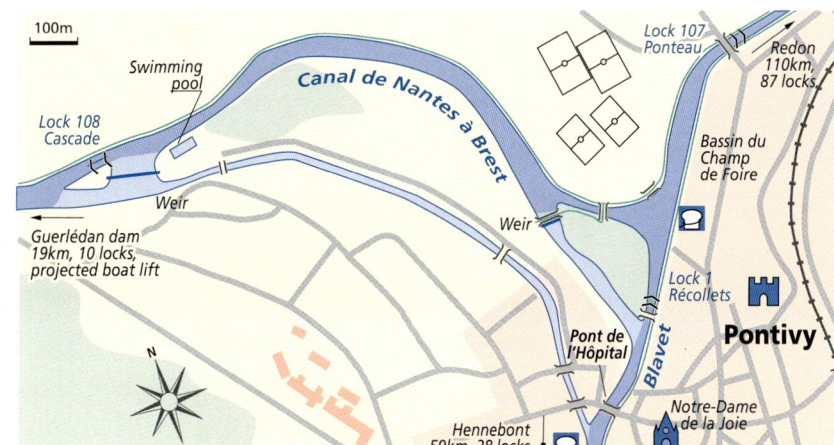

| | |
|---|---|
| PK 0.0 | **Pontivy** basin (Bassin du Champ de Foire), *junction with Canal de Nantes à Brest* (PK 205.9), moorings, town centre 300m |
| PK 0.1 | Lock 1 (Récollets), bridge, navigation enters river Blavet, quay l/b |
| PK 0.3 | Bridge (Pont de l'Hôpital), municipal *halte* d/s r/b, mooring free (maximum 72 hours), water, electricity, town centre 300m |

Pontivy is Brittany's second major waterway junction after Redon. Its potential as a cruising destination will be considerably improved on completion of the connection to Guerlédan Lake and the Canal de Nantes à Brest heading west to Gouarec and Rostrenen.

| | |
|---|---|
| PK 0.7 | Bridge (Pont de la Caserne) |
| PK 1.4 | Bridge (Pont Neuf) |
| PK 1.6 | Railway bridge, quay l/b |
| PK 2.4 | Lock 2 (Lestitut) |
| PK 2.7 | Bridge |
| PK 3.2 | Bridge, private quay d/s l/b |
| PK 4.3 | Lock 3 (Signan or Saint-Michel) |
| PK 4.5 | Bridge (Rhin-Danube) |
| PK 7.2 | Lock 4 (Roch) |
| PK 9.6 | Loch 5 (Divit) |
| PK 11.8 | Lock 6 (Rimaison) |
| PK 11.9 | Bridge |
| PK 13.9 | Lock 7 (Kerbecher) |
| PK 15.8 | Lock 8 (Guern) |
| PK 16.5 | Railway bridge |
| PK 17.3 | Railway bridge |
| PK 17.5 | Lock 9 (Saint-Nicolas-des-Eaux) |

| Key dimensions (m) | |
|---|---|
| Length | 26.30 |
| Beam | 4.70 |
| Draught* | 1.40 |
| Air draught | 2.40 |

## VIII – Western France

PK **17.8** **Saint-Nicolas-des-Eaux** bridge, moorings u/s l/b on 100m-long pontoon, free (maximum 72 hours), water, electricity, pump-out, small village

A favourite mooring place, in a village offering basic shops and services.

*The charming village of Saint-Nicolas-des-Eaux, PK 18, with its grass bank and opposite, a 100m-long pontoon.* © SABOTIÈRE

PK **19.6** Lock 10 (Couarde)
K **20.2** Railway bridge
PK **21.1** Lock 11 (Camblen)
PK **23.0** Lock 12 (Moulin-Neuf)
PK **25.0** Lock 13 (Boterneau), quay l/b
PK **25.2** **Saint-Rivalain** bridge, village 1.5 km r/b
PK **26.6** Lock 14 (Tréblavet)
PK **28.6** Lock 15 (Talhouët)
PK **30.5** **Saint-Adrien** bridge, small village 300m l/b
PK **30.6** Railway bridge
PK **30.9** Lock 16 (Saint-Adrien), quay r/b
PK **34.2** Lock 17 (Trémorin)
PK **34.4** Railway bridge
PK **36.4** Lock 18 (Sainte-Barbe)
PK **37.0** **Pont-Augan** bridge, pontoon moorings (30m) d/s l/b, free (maximum 72 hours), water, electricity, village r/b
PK **39.4** Lock 19 (Minazen)
PK **44.6** Lock 20 (Maneruen)
PK **46.5** Bridge (Pont Neuf), quay d/s r/b
PK **47.2** Lock 21 (Rudet)
PK **49.3** Lock 22 (Trébihan)
PK **50.9** Lock 23 (Kerousse)
PK **51.2** Overhead power lines
PK **52.3** Lock 24 (Quellenec), private quay u/s l/b
PK **54.3** Lock 25 (Lochrist) in l/b arm
PK **54.6** **Lochrist** bridge, halte d/s, 35m pontoon, free (maximum 72 hours), water, electricity, village r/b, Langroix l/b
PK **55.0** Railway bridge (disused)
PK **56.0** Lock 26 (Grand Barrage)
PK **56.3** Lock 27 (Gorets)
PK **57.3** Lock 28 (Polvern), private quay u/s r/b
PK **59.6** Footbridge (Hennebont)

PK **59.8** **Hennebont** bridge, junction with Blavet maritime, pontoon moorings for 10 boats d/s r/b managed by local association, 06 70 92 88 09, night €20, water and electricity included, slipway, small town l/b
PK **60.3** Railway viaduct, quay and pontoon moorings d/s r/b
PK **62.3** Viaduct (N165)
PK **65.7** Bridge (Pont du Bonhomme, D194)
PK **67.8** **Saint-Guénaël** halte on pontoon r/b
PK **71.5** **Lorient** port de plaisance r/b, 370 berths on pontoons, 50 visitor moorings, night €37, water and electricity included, showers, wifi *port-lorient@sellor.com*
PK **73.1** **Locmiquélic** port de plaisance l/b, VHF 9, 607 berths on pontoons, 30 visitor moorings, night €16, water and electricity included, showers, pump-out, slipway *locmiquelic@compagniedesportsdumorbihan.fr*

The Blavet maritime is a tidal estuary well covered by nautical charts and guides.

*The railway viaduct in Hennebont is just 500m down the estuary from the bridge that marks the end of the inland waterway.* © JOHN RIDDEL/ÉDITIONS DU BREIL

# 72. River Loire

THE MAJESTIC RIVER LOIRE, THE LONGEST RIVER in France, was formerly navigated upstream as far as La Noirie, level with Saint-Étienne, 880km from the sea, but its extreme flow regime makes it the least navigable of all France's major rivers. The flow is relatively small throughout much of the year and wanders about over a wide bed. In many reaches the depth drops to no more than 25cm. During floods, the river rises rapidly, and the fast current makes navigation dangerous as soon as depths of about 2m have been reached. For this reason all navigation has long ceased on the upper and middle courses of the river, except at two places where the water is held back by weirs: at Roanne there is access to a short navigable length of the river from the Canal de Roanne à Digoin, but the link is no longer used for navigation, while at Decize the river is navigable for 1.7km from the Decize branch of the Canal latéral à la Loire to the Canal du Nivernais.

The river is navigable from its estuary to its confluence with the river Maine at Bouchemaine. It thus links the the Canal de Nantes à Brest in Nantes to the Maine and its navigable tributaries (Mayenne, Oudon and Sarthe), a distance of 84km. The total distance from the sea at Saint-Nazaire to the confluence at Bouchemaine is 138km.

*In 1700 the port of Nantes numbered more inland waterway craft than any other port in France. This statistic alone testifies to the historic importance of navigation on France's longest river. Shallow-draught gabares and other river craft continued to transport goods into the industrial era, including coal from Saint-Étienne loaded onto barges in Orléans. However, the hazardous free-flow navigation and limited tonnages meant that railways killed off the surviving traffic from the 1850s. In 1894 a company was set up to promote improvements to the navigation from Nantes to Briare. The works were authorised in 1904 and carried out in two phases from Angers to the limit of tides at Oudon. These works, with groynes and submersible embankments, survive and contribute to the limited navigability under present-day conditions.*

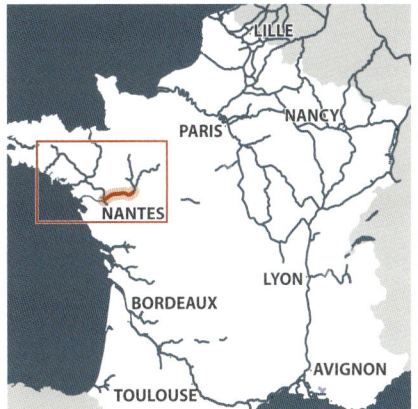

## Navigation

The information here applies only to the inland waterway section upstream of the Pont Anne de Bretagne in Nantes. For navigation in the estuary, the maritime chart SHOM N° 7396L should be used. The whole length from Nantes to Bouchemaine comprises numerous narrow passages and fast-flowing sections, not to mention the many side arms to be avoided, some of which are much wider and would appear to be the obvious choice of route. Channel markers are in place, and are to be followed carefully (see under *Draught*). According to the Breil guide *Pays de la Loire*, there are sections where the flow can reach 12km/h.

| Key dimensions (m) | |
|---|---|
| Length | – |
| Beam | – |
| Draught* | 1.50 |
| Air draught | 4.50 |

*\* Less in certain sections at low water*

In order to meet the regulation minimum speed over the ground of 3.6 km/h, considerable engine power is needed. Few inland craft are capable of 16 km/h.

Major works are to be carried out in the bed of the river Loire at a cost of €42 million. The gradual lowering of the river bed by erosion created an unsatisfactory situation, not only for navigation under low water conditions, but also for the environment. Secondary channels and arms of the river became disconnected and dried out, threatening biodiversity in what should be aquatic environments. The first works are planned for 2021 in the Ingrandes/Montjean sector. In 2022, the sector between Anetz and Oudon will be treated, to remove several shoals. The works at Sainte-Luce will begin in 2023. There is a marked break in the river's gradient here, between the deep Loire with its tidal rise and fall, and the free-flowing Loire upstream. The project aims to smoothen the transition here by recreating a structure called a *duis* (a riprap dyke, permanently under water) in two parts, placed parallel with the current. This submerged dyke, located on the left bank, will connect to the natural rocky sill. The part diverting the current will be 300 m long. This constantly submerged *duis* will have an effect at low water and at low tide, channeling the flows and raising the upstream water level as far as Oudon, 18 km upstream. At low water levels, this will provide an additional depth of 1.80 m. At high tide, the *duis* will be submerged and will have no effect. One of the objectives of the project is not to increase the flood water level, and this essential prerequisite is satisfied.

## Draught

From Bouchemaine to Nantes a channel 100 to 150 m wide is defined by means of submersible dykes and groynes. The channel is marked by buoys, red on the left-bank side and green on the right-bank side. At low water the navigable channel is marked by 4.50 m high stakes driven into the sand, those on the left-bank side having their tops partly broken and hanging down. In principle a depth of 1.50 m is maintained at medium low water, but there may be marked variations, with as little as 0.35 m over certain sills in the channel at exceptional low water levels. Spring tides may be felt as far upstream as Champtoceaux. In low water periods enquiries should be made at the VNF office (address below) before making the passage. Use of the detailed Breil guide *Pays de la Loire* is recommended.

## Headroom

The bridges on the inland waterway section leave a minimum headroom of 4.50 m above the highest navigable water level (7.00 m above the mean water level).

## Towpath

There was never a conventional towpath along the river, but a cycle route has been laid out through the valley, often using paths on flood embankments affording superb views of the river, and has become a popular cycling itinerary, the *Loire à Vélo*.

## Authority

Port Autonome de Nantes-Saint-Nazaire
– 18 quai Ernest Renaud, 44186 Nantes Cedex 4
02 40 44 20 20 (PK 138-86)
VNF Direction territorial du Bassin de la Seine - UTI Loire
– 10 bd Gaston Serpette, 44036 Nantes Cedex 1
02 40 67 26 01  **uti.loire@vnf.fr** (PK 86-0)

## Route description

*From the sea to Bouchemaine*

PK **138.0** **Saint-Nazaire** suspension bridge (D213) limit of sea (port entrance a further 3 km d/s)
PK **130.0** **Donges** port, r/b
PK **125.0** **Paimboeuf** quay and small town l/b
PK **114.0** **Cordemais** power station, coal unloading quay r/b
PK **103.5** La Martinière quay l/b (in entrance to former ship canal)
PK **101.0** Le Pellerin quay and village l/b, ferry
PK **99.0** **Couëron** *port de plaisance* in small basin r/b (access 2 hours before to 2 hours after high tide), 02 40 37 04 62, 36 berths, 3 visitor moorings, night €16.50, water, electricity, slipway, restaurant, repairs and maintenance **alumarine-shipyard.com**, small town r/b

*A refreshing welcome at the port of Couëron* © RAYMOND GRELET

PK **95.0** Basse-Indre quay, village r/b, Indret quay l/b, ferry
PK **93.0** Quay (Haute-Indre) r/b, d/s limit of port of Nantes
PK **90.3** Motorway bridge (Cheviré), N844 Nantes ring road
PK **88.4** Shipyard Pôle Nautique Loire Estuaire r/b, 02 40 43 94 94, maintenance, repairs, slipway 60 m by 10 m, crane 12 t, up to 12 m, covered dry dock
PK **87.8** **Trentemoult** *port de plaisance* in small basin l/b, (access 2 hours before to 2 hours after high tide), 02 40 37 04 62, 24 berths, no visitor moorings, water, electricity, showers, wifi, slipway, restaurant

This delightful former fishermen's village is worth visiting despite the lack of welcome at the *port de plaisance*. It can be reached by waterbus from the centre of Nantes.

PK **87.3** River divides into two arms, Madeleine arm left (r/b), Pirmil arm right (l/b)

# River Loire

## La Madeleine arm

**PK 86.3 Nantes** *halte* on 'Belem' pontoon r/b, 20 visitor moorings, draught 3m at low tide, night €34, water, electricity, showers, pump-out. The 100m pontoon (Ponton des Chantiers) on the l/b is less convenient, night €30, water, electricity   les3ports@nge-nantes.fr

The 'Belem pontoon' is ideally situated in the city centre. Former capital of Brittany and major seaport from the 17th to the 19th century, Nantes is worth staying several days, but moorings on one of the connecting waterways, the Erdre (Canal de Nantes à Brest) to the north or the Sèvre Nantaise to the south may be more comfortable than on the Loire.

*Arriving in Nantes, you have to hope that the 'Belem pontoon' is not totally occupied as here by the cruise ship Loire Princess*

- PK 86.1  Bridge (Anne-de-Bretagne), limit of maritime waterway, mooring d/s r/b, shipyards l/b
- PK 85.8  Footbridge (Victor Schoelcher)
- PK 85.3  Bridge (Haudoudine)
- PK 84.9  Bridges (Général Audibert, tram lines 2 & 3)
- PK 84.3  Bridge (Aristide Briand), Nantes city centre r/b
- PK 84.0  **Junction with Canal de Nantes à Brest** (navigable river Erdre), r/b, waiting pontoon 120m just downstream of the entrance
- PK 83.7  Bridge (Willy Brandt)
- PK 83.6  Railway bridge (Résal)
- PK 83.2  New bridge (Pont Éric Tabarly) for public transport, cyclists, pedestrians
- PK 82.4  Railway bridge (Pont de la Vendée)
- PK 82.2  Tip of island, arms merge

## Pirmil arm

- PK 86.3  Bridge (Trois Continents)
- PK 85.5  Railway bridge (Pornic)
- PK 85.3  **Confluence of Sèvre-Nantaise**, l/b
- PK 84.9  Bridges (Pirmil), tram lines 2 & 3
- PK 84.3  **Nantes** bridge (Georges Clémenceau), town centre 1700m r/b
- PK 83.5  Bridge (Léopold Sédar Senghor)
- PK 82.4  Railway bridge (Pont de la Vendée)
- PK 82.0  Tip of island, arms merge, La Madeleine arm r/b, Pirmil arm l/b
- PK 78.4  Bridge (Belle-Vue), N844 Nantes ring road
- PK 73.2  Bridge (Thouaré)

**PK 69.0 La Chapelle-Basse-Mer** (Port de la Pierre Percée) municipal port in basin off river l/b, 02 40 03 60 73, for 50 boats, up to 3 visitor moorings on outside pontoon, water, electricity, pump-out, slipway

**PK 67.8 Mauves-sur-Loire** bridge, village 700m r/b

**PK 62.4 Le Cellier**, floating pontoons for 3 boats, water, electricity, slipway, château de Clermont r/b

**PK 58.6 Oudon** municipal *port de plaisance* in basin off river r/b (through railway bridge, limited air draught), 02 40 83 65 69, 30 boats, 2 visitor moorings on 18m pontoon on river, free (maximum 72 hours), water and electricity on Loire pontoon, shower €2 at campsite, slipway, village 200m

**PK 57.9** Bridge (Pont de Champtoceaux)

**PK 56.1 Champtoceaux**, mooring in backwater l/b, village 800m

*The channel meanders between groynes upstream from Champtoceaux, while the northern arm (left) is almost dry.*

**PK 49.6 Ancenis** suspension bridge, municipal *halte* for 18 boats u/s r/b, 4 visitor moorings, free (maximum 72 hours), water, electricity, slipway, small town and château, r/b

**PK 37.4** River divides, Batailleuse island, navigation in l/b arm

**PK 36.9 Saint-Florent-le-Vieil** bridge (l/b arm), municipal *halte* on pontoon for 4 boats u/s l/b, draught 1.10m, free (on request to Mairie, stflorentlevieil@mauges-sur-loire.fr), water, electricity, slipway

**PK 29.0 Le Fresne-sur-Loire** municipal *halte* r/b, capacity 10 boats on pontoon, night €1.30, water and electricity charged, showers at campsite

*A slipway and grassy bank at Le Fresne, a typical 'informal' mooring on the Loire.* © COMATA

## VIII – Western France

| | |
|---|---|
| PK **28.1** | **Ingrandes** suspension bridge, quay for 10 boats u/s r/b, night €1, water, village r/b |
| PK **23.6** | **Montjean-sur-Loire** suspension bridge (D15), quay d/s l/b, village l/b |

*The former Mayenne barge Cap Vert is the main exhibit at the Cap Loire visitor centre at Montjean-sur-Loire*

| | |
|---|---|
| PK **22.6** | Bridge (Passerelle de Montjean), VNF operations centre u/s l/b |
| PK **14.6** | **Chalonnes-sur-Loire** bridge, quay u/s l/b |

*Canoes and kayaks are more frequently encountered craft on the Loire, here having just passed under the suspension bridge at Montjean.*

| | |
|---|---|
| PK **11.3** | Tip of Chalonnes island, two arms merge |
| PK **10.9** | Railway bridge (Alleud) |
| PK **7.8** | **La Poissonnière** quay r/b, village 400m r/b |
| PK **5.1** | Bridge (Béhuard), **Savennières** 1km r/b |
| PK **4.6** | Béhuard r/b (on island) |
| PK **0.4** | **La Pointe Bouchemaine** r/b, pontoons, water, slipway |
| PK **0.0** | **Confluence of Maine**, r/b |

Head close into the right bank to enter the river Maine, as the Loire groynes extend over two thirds of the width of the river at the confluence.

# Sèvre Nantaise/Petite Maine

## 73. Sèvre Nantaise and Petite-Maine

The Sèvre Nantaise, a partly tidal river, is navigable over a distance of 21.5km from its confluence with the Loire at Pont-Rousseau (a suburb of Nantes) to Monnières bridge. Its tributary, the Petite Maine, although much narrower, is navigable over a distance of 6km up to the first (disused) lock at Pont Caffino, in the village of Chateauthébaud. The two rivers are ideal for cruising, offering many attractive moorings in the heart of the Muscadet wine-growing area. For convenience, the route is described proceeding upstream from its confluence.

*This tributary of the Loire, with its gentle gradient, lent itself to canalisation to give the local population convenient access to Nantes and to transport stone for building in the city. The weir (Chaussée des Moines) and lock were built at Vertou in the late 19th century, and passenger steamers operated until the 1930s. The half-tide weir at the confluence was built in the 1980s, replacing the impractical earlier sluice-gates. The navigation belongs to the* **département** *Loire Atlantique, but is managed by a local river authority (***syndicat de rivière***).*

### Navigation
This is a delightful navigation, once through the restricted entrance from the river Loire. Access to the Sèvre Nantaise is via a half-tide sluice 200m in from the confluence (Pont-Rousseau), which is open from one hour before to one hour after high tide.

### Locks
On the river Sèvre there is just one lock, situated at Vertou, with a length of 31.50m and a width of 5.50m.

### Draught
From the confluence with the Loire to Vertou lock the river is tidal, but the rise and fall is minimal following construction of the Pont-Rousseau tide-sluice at the confluence. Depths are generous compared to the maximum authorised draught of 1.20m.

On the Petite-Maine the maximum authorised draught is 0.90m.

### Headroom
There are several fixed bridges. The lowest headroom is at the Pont-Rousseau sluice structure, which limits access to boats with an air draught of 4.00m.

### Towpath
There is no towpath.

### Authority
Conseil départemental Loire-Atlantique, Service Infrastructures Voies Navigables, 3 quai Ceineray, 44141 Nantes, 02 40 99 15 05 (manages the navigable lengths of the Sèvre Nantaise and Petite-Maine)

## Route description

| PK 0.0 | **Confluence with the Loire** (PK 85.3) |
| PK 0.2 | Rézé tidal sluice |

The sluice (central passage) is to be passed between 1 hour before and 1 hour after high tide. There is a 12m long waiting pontoon on the left bank just inside from the confluence, 130m before the sluice gates.

| Key dimensions (m) | |
|---|---|
| Length | 31.50 |
| Beam | 5.50 |
| Draught | 1.20 |
| [Petite Maine] | 0.90 |
| Air draught | 4.00 |

*Modern flap gates replaced the inadequate sluice structure at Pont-Rousseau in the 1980s, making the Sèvre Nantaise much easier to enter from the Loire (in the background, with the Béghin-Say sugar factory on the far bank).* © LUMINEM

# VIII – Western France

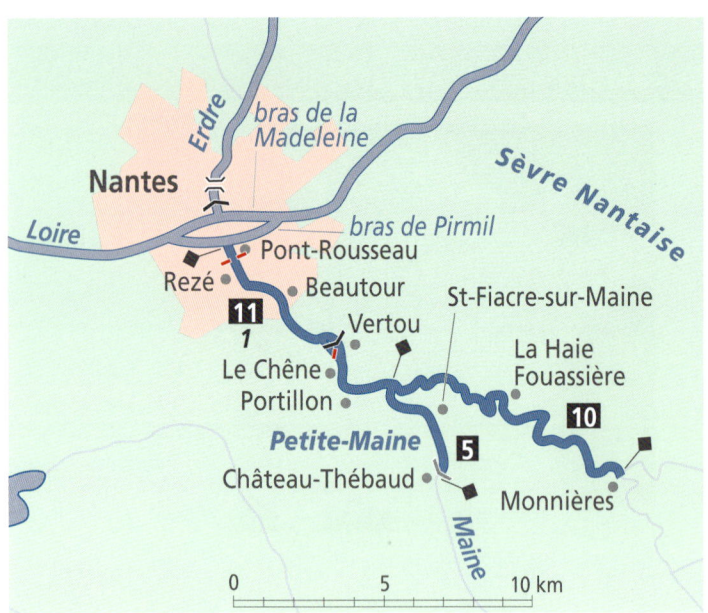

| PK 0.2 | **Pont-Rousseau** quay l/b |
|---|---|
| PK 0.3 | New bridge (Pont-Rousseau) |
| PK 0.3 | Old bridge (Pont-Rousseau), moorings u/s l/b, trip boat |
| PK 2.0 | Bridge (La Morinière) |
| PK 2.1 | Port des Lys pontoon moorings l/b |
| PK 2.5 | Bridge (des Bourdonnières) |
| PK 2.8 | Overhead power lines |
| PK 3.1 | Bridge (motorway spur to Nantes town centre) |
| PK 3.5 | **Beautour** quay r/b |
| PK 4.1 | Bridge (N844, Nantes ring road) |
| PK 4.5 | Overhead power lines |
| PK 5.2 | Château (Portereau), l/b |
| PK 6.7 | **Vertou** lock and weir (lock in r/b arm) |

The lock was restored and its approaches improved in 2021. The restaurant 'L'Écluse' right beside the lock is one of many in this very popular weekend retreat for the people of Nantes. The weir, called the Chaussée aux Moines, winds across the broad river and during low flow periods is used as a ford to walk across. The river becomes even prettier upstream from Vertou.

| PK 7.1 | **Le Chêne** bridge, moorings d/s l/b, water, electricity, Vertou 1km r/b |
|---|---|
| PK 4.5 | **Portillon** bridge, moorings u/s l/b |
| PK 11.1 | *Confluence of Petite-Maine* l/b, navigable upstream 6.0km to Chateau-Thébaud |
| PK 11.6 | Bridge (Ramée), D59 |
| PK 15.0 | La Cantrie moorings l/b |
| PK 16.1 | **La Haie Fouassière** bridge, moorings d/s r/b, water, village 1 km |
| PK 21.0 | **Port Domino** quay r/b |
| PK 21.5 | **Monnières** bridge, head of navigation |

The stone bridge marks the end of the waterway.

## Petite-Maine

| PK 0.0 | *Confluence with Sèvre Nantaise* |
|---|---|
| PK 0.3 | Château (Le Coin), r/b |
| PK 4.3 | **Saint-Fiacre-sur-Maine** bridge, moorings u/s r/b |
| PK 5.9 | **Château-Thébaud** bridge (Pont Caffino), quay d/s r/b, village 500m l/b |
| PK 6.0 | Disused lock (Pont Caffino), head of navigation |

*The upper gates of Vertou lock and the Chaussée aux Moines, more ford than weir during the summer.* © LUMINEM

*The stone bridge at Monnières carries the only navigation sign to be seen on the river (apart from the Pont-Rousseau sluice): the no-entry sign indicating the end of the waterway.* © FRÉDÉRICK

*The château du Coin, just 300m up the Petite-Maine, showing the potential navigational hazard of tree trunks.* © JEAPIL

# 74. Rivers Mayenne-Maine and Oudon

THE MAYENNE IS ONE OF the delightful river navigations of the Anjou region, long abandoned by commercial traffic but increasingly popular as a cruising waterway. It was conceded by the State to the Pays-de-la-Loire region, allowing development of the river as a cruising waterway and tourist asset. The Mayenne is navigable from Mayenne to its confluence with the Loire at Bouchemaine, a distance of 134km. For many years the upstream 26km section to the town of Mayenne was no longer navigable, but the 17 locks and weirs in this section were restored in 1986-1990 by the region and *département*. Note however that only boats with limited air draught can proceed upstream of Laval (see under *Headroom*).

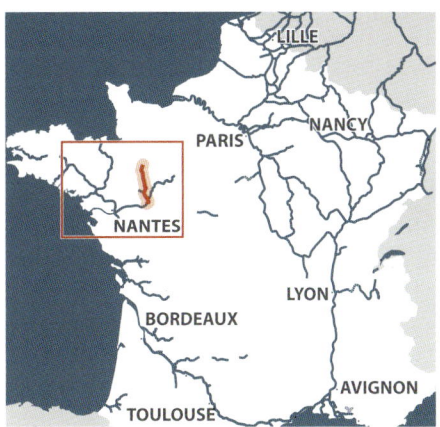

Just above the town of Angers the Mayenne is joined by the Sarthe, and from this point it takes the name of Maine. The development of pleasure cruising (especially with deep-draught boats) was long hindered by the severely limited draught during summer drought periods on the lower free-flowing (i.e. unregulated) sections of both the Mayenne and the Maine. This situation was remedied by construction of a new weir and lock downstream of Angers. A secondary channel, known as the Vieille-Maine, forms a cross-link with the Sarthe downstream of Montreuil-Belfroy (see plan). For craft passing from one river to the other, use of this link saves 5km by comparison with the route via the confluence, although most navigators will probably prefer to visit Angers for the facilities offered in the town.

The river Oudon, a right-bank tributary of the Mayenne, is navigable upstream from the Mayenne to the small town of Segré, a distance of 18km, where a *port de plaisance* has been established near the head of navigation.

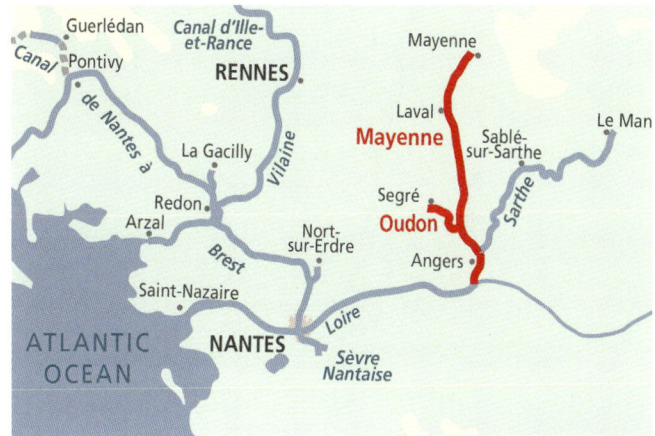

| Key dimensions (m) | |
|---|---|
| Length | 31.00 |
| Beam | 5.20 |
| Draught | 1.50 |
| Air draught* | 4.40 |
| [above Laval | 2.80] |

*The Mayenne was navigable in its natural state up to Château-Gontier. Above here, flash locks were built from the mid-16th century, and trade developed up to Laval. Economic expansion in the 17th and 18th centuries justified canalisation, not only to Laval but also upstream to Mayenne. This extension, with 20 locks and weirs, was built at the same time as about 40 flash locks were replaced by 25 weirs and locks, some in short lock-cuts, between 1853 et 1878. The river Oudon was also made navigable with locks and weirs in the 1850s, to link the market town of Segré to Angers and the Loire. At this time it was planned to build a watershed canal north from Mayenne to the tidal river Orne at Caen, but the project was abandoned as railways became the preferred carrier of freight. The navigation was abandoned after World War II, but restored from the 1970s as a cruising waterway. The upstream section was completed in the early 1990s. The **départements** remain concessionaries from the State until ownership is transferred outright to the Region Pays de la Loire.*

\* *Air draught at normal water levels.*

## Locks

There are 45 locks between Mayenne and Montreuil-Belfroy. The first 37 are 31.00m by 5.20m, the last eight being slightly longer (33m). Signs on the locks distinguish the different situations which boaters will encounter:

*Château overlooking the river in Mayenne.* © DANIEL LELOUP

## Navigation

The Mayenne-Maine and the Oudon are placid rivers flowing in wide gently-sloping plains, making them easy to navigate, except during floods.

## VIII – Western France

- Red disk: lock closed, passage forbidden.
- Yellow disk: lock in operation, and worked by the lock-keeper (whether resident or posted temporarily).
- Blue disk: lock in operation, to be worked by the boat's crew (but forbidden at night, also in stormy weather).

All locks up to Laval are normally worked by lock-keepers, while upstream to Mayenne lock operation is do-it-yourself. During the high season (April to September) a maintenance team supervises this section of the river and is available to provide assistance as necessary. Operating hours are 9:00 to 12:30 and 14:00 to 20:00 (17:00 in March and November). There are three locks on the river Oudon, overcoming a difference in level of 3.50m. Their dimensions are 33.00m by 5.20m. They are manually operated by lock-keepers, with the same operating hours as the Mayenne.

### Draught
The maximum authorised draught is 1.40m, increased to 1.80m from Angers to the confluence with the Loire. On the river Oudon, the maximum authorised draught is 1.50m, although in times of drought boats drawing more than 1.00m may have difficulty.

### Headroom
Above Laval the air draught is restricted by the limited headroom under the Pont de l'Europe, 2.80m above normal water level and 2.10m above the highest navigable water level. From Laval to the confluence with the Sarthe the bridges offer a minimum headroom of 4.10m above normal water level, reduced to 3.40m above the PHEN. On the Maine the normal headroom is 6.40m. On the river Oudon, the least headroom under the bridges is 4.60m above normal water level, reduced to 3.60m above the highest navigable water level.

### Towpath
There is a crushed gravel cycle path throughout, with metalled sections near the locks, recently laid out and signposted as a long-distance cycle route.

### Authority
Conseil départemental Mayenne, Direction routes et rivière
- 39 rue Mazagran, CS 21429, 53014 Laval cedex 09, 02 43 59 93 60 (PK 0-86)

Conseil départemental Maine-et-Loire, Service Rivières et Domaine Public Fluvial
- Place Michel Debré, CS 94104, 49941 Angers cedex 09, 02 41 86 65 00 (PK 86-134 and river Oudon)

## Route description

| | |
|---|---|
| PK 0.0 | Bridge (MacRacken), head of navigation |
| PK 0.2 | Bridge (Pont Neuf) |
| PK 0.4 | **Mayenne**, *halte fluviale* on quay l/b (extending upstream of Pont Neuf in front of tourist office), capacity 42 boats, free, water (hose from tourist office), electricity, showers, wifi, slipway |

Small town with all facilities, and several notable sites, including the fine medieval *château* overlooking the river

| | |
|---|---|
| PK 0.7 | Bridge |
| PK 0.8 | Lock 1 (Mayenne) |

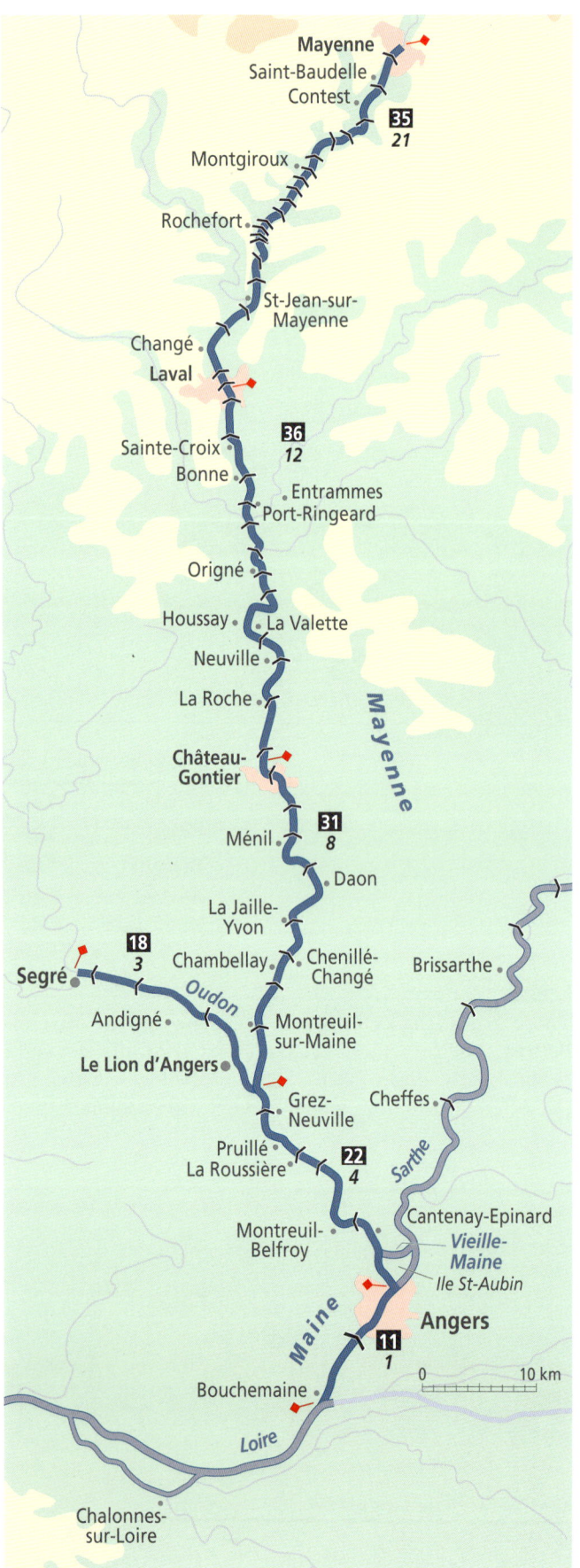

# Mayenne/Maine and Oudon

- PK **3.4** **Saint-Baudelle** bridge, village 300m r/b
- PK **3.6** Lock 2 (Saint-Baudelle)
- PK **5.2** Le Val, hamlet and chapel, l/b
- PK **7.5** Lock 3 (Grenoux), r/b
- PK **9.5** Lock 4 (La Roche)
- PK **10.5** Lock 5 (Boussard)
- PK **13.1** Lock 6 (Corçu), La Giraudière, small village l/b
- PK **14.3** Lock 7 (Bas-Hambert)
- PK **14.5** **Montgiroux** bridge, *halte* for up to 15 boats, managed by boat club, May-September, free, water, electricity, showers, wifi, **Martigné-sur-Mayenne** 4km l/b, **Saint-Germain-d'Anxure** 2.5km r/b
- PK **14.7** Lock 8 (Communes), Montgiroux castle r/b
- PK **15.9** Lock 9 (Port)
- PK **17.3** Lock 10 (Nourrière), castle on hillside l/b
- PK **18.3** Lock 11 (Verrerie)
- PK **19.2** Lock 12 (Richardière)
- PK **19.8** Lock 13 (Fourmondière supérieure)
- PK **20.0** Bridge (Rochefort), **Andouillé** 3km r/b
- PK **20.1** Lock 14 (Fourmondière inférieure)
- PK **20.9** Lock 15 (Moulin Oger)
- PK **23.9** Lock 16 (Ame)
- PK **24.7** Lock 17 (Maignannerie)
- PK **26.3** **Saint-Jean-sur-Mayenne** bridge, municipal *halte* on quay for 6 boats d/s l/b, night €10, water, electricity, showers, village r/b
- PK **27.1** Lock 18 (Boisseau), l/b and weir
- PK **28.9** Motorway bridge (A81)
- PK **29.9** Lock 19 (Belle-Poule) l/b and weir
- PK **31.0** **Changé** bridge, village r/b
- PK **32.4** Bridge (Pritz, D900, Laval ring road)
- PK **33.5** Lock 20 (Bootz) l/b and weir
- PK **34.0** Railway viaduct and footbridge
- PK **34.3** **Laval** bridge (Pont de l'Europe), halte on quays u/s and d/s r/b, Anjou Navigation hire base, 07 54 32 99 87, capacity 12 boats, 4 visitor moorings, night €8, water and electricity included, showers, slipway, pump-out, restaurant

Town centre on both banks.

*This view of tranquil river in the evening sun was captured from a TGV crossing the viaduct upstream of Laval.* © RAIMO KETOLAINEN

- PK **34.7** Bridge (Pont Neuf)
- PK **34.8** Lock 21 (Laval) l/b and weir
- PK **35.0** Bridge (Pont Vieux)
- PK **35.6** Boat moorings (base nautique) l/b
- PK **35.9** Lock 22 (Avenières) l/b and weir
- PK **36.0** Bridge (Pont d'Avenières, D57, Laval ring road)
- PK **38.7** Lock 23 (Cumont) r/b and weir
- PK **39.3** Saint-Pierre-le-Potier l/b
- PK **42.3** Lock 24 (Bonne) r/b and weir
- PK **43.9** Lock 25 (Port-Ringeard) r/b and weir
- PK **44.0** **Entrammes** bridge (D103), *halte* on pontoons d/s l/b, for 30 boats, 6 visitor moorings, night €4.50, water and electricity included, slipway, village 1800m l/b
- PK **44.1** Boat moorings l/b
- PK **45.0** Lock 26 (Persigand) r/b and weir
- PK **48.5** Lock 27 (Briassé) r/b and weir
- PK **51.2** Lock 28 (Bénâtre) r/b and weir, **Origné** halte on two pontoons and picnic area d/s managed from lock cottage, free, water, showers, wifi (when restaurant open), village 800m r/b
- PK **53.2** Lock 29 (Fosse) r/b and weir
- PK **58.2** **La Valette** bridge (D4), mooring and picnic area, castle u/s l/b, **Houssay** 1km r/b
- PK **59.4** Lock 30 (Rongère) r/b and weir, castle u/s r/b
- PK **62.1** **Saint-Sulpice** boat moorings for 2 boats, water, shower
- PK **62.2** Lock 31 (Neuville) r/b and weir
- PK **65.8** Lock 32 (Roche-du-Maine) r/b and weir, picnic area d/s r/b
- PK **68.4** Lock 33 (Mirvault) r/b and weir, slipway
- PK **70.5** **Château-Gontier** bridge, quay d/s r/b, *port de plaisance* 200m u/s l/b, three jetties with catways and one pontoon for mooring stern-to, *capitainerie* 02 53 68 50 11, night €5 (first two nights free), water, electricity, showers, wifi

Small town listed in the 100 most attractive towns in France for its built heritage, its environment (floral decor) and its quality of life. Many historic buildings to visit, and the park amusingly called the Jardin du Bout-du-Monde, on the other side of the river from the moorings.

- PK **71.1** Bridge (N162, Château-Gontier ring road)
- PK **71.7** Lock 34 (Pendu) r/b and weir
- PK **71.9** Disused railway viaduct
- PK **72.4** **Azé** l/b
- PK **75.9** Lock 35 (Bavouze) r/b and weir, recommended restaurant
- PK **76.6** Entrance to lock-cut, r/b
- PK **77.4** Bridge
- PK **77.8** Lock 36 (**Ménil**), moorings for 2 visiting boats u/s r/b, night €4, water and electricity included, showers €2 (at campsite), wifi, slipway, end of lock-cut, weir l/b
- PK **78.0** Ménil ferry
- PK **81.6** U/s tip of island, navigation r/b arm
- PK **82.1** Lock 37 (Fourmusson) r/b
- PK **83.5** **Daon** *halte* managed by association in front of campsite l/b, 27 berths, 6 visitor moorings (up to 15m), night €5 (one night free), 06 29 06 90 31, water, electricity €2.50, shower, slipway, village and leisure park 'Au Fil de l'Eau'
- PK **83.8** Bridge (Daon), village 300m l/b
- PK **85.4** Limit of *départements* Mayenne and Maine-et-Loire, l/b
- PK **86.1** Limit of *départements* Mayenne and Maine-et-Loire, r/b
- PK **88.0** Lock 38 (**La Jaille-Yvon**) r/b and weir, small village r/b
- PK **90.5** Lock 39 (Chenillé-Changé) in short cut, r/b

## VIII – Western France

**PK 90.6 Chenillé-Changé** l/b, Canalous Plaisance hire base, 06 60 49 78 30, moorings on two pontoons, 30m and 12m, subject to availability, free for one night, water, electricity, showers (at campsite), slipway

Another delightful village with its preserved mill 'Grand Moulin', right by the moorings at the hire base.

- **PK 92.1 Chambellay** bridge, mooring for 4 boats, water, slipway, village r/b
- **PK 93.6** Lock 40 (Roche-Chambellay) in short cut, r/b
- **PK 96.8** Lock 41 (Montreuil-sur-Maine) r/b and weir
- **PK 96.9 Montreuil-sur-Maine** municipal *halte* on pontoons for 8 boats, free, water, electricity, slipway, village r/b
- **PK 98.0** River divides, keep to r/b arm
- **PK 99.0** Bridge (Pont de l'Aubinière, D770), **Le Lion d'Angers** 2 km r/b
- **PK 101.0 Confluence of Oudon**, r/b
- **PK 101.8** Entrance to lock-cut, r/b
- **PK 102.7** Lock 42 (Grez-Neuville) r/b and weir, end of lock-cut
- **PK 102.9 Grez-Neuville** bridge, quay, Anjou Navigation hire base u/s r/b, 02 43 95 14 42, 15 boats, 3 visitor moorings, night €5 (first night free), water and electricity €5/day, slipway, village 200m l/b
- **PK 106.3 Pruillé** r/b (ferry), municipal *halte* managed by association, capacity 50 boats on pontoons, stern-to, 2 visitor moorings, night €4 (first 2 nights free), wifi at campsite, slipway, repairs and maintenance, Griffnautic, *griffnautic.com* **Longuenée-en-Anjou** 3km
- **PK 107.3** Lock 43 (La Roussière) r/b and weir
- **PK 107.4** La Roussière château and quay r/b
- **PK 108.9** Entrance to lock-cut, r/b
- **PK 109.4** Lock 44 (Sautré), end of lock-cut, weir l/b
- **PK 110.4** Port-Albert quay l/b, **Feneu** 1300m
- **PK 113.1** Bridge (Juigné-Béné), quay d/s r/b
- **PK 115.6** Lock 45 (Montreuil-Belfroy) in cut, r/b, weirs l/b (cruising information available here and at lock 44)
- **PK 118.2 Cantenay-Épinard** bridge (heading u/s take r/b arm), municipal *halte* for 3 boats, free (maximum 72 hours), water, slipway, village 700m l/b
- **PK 118.9** River divides, **Vieille-Maine l/b leads to Sarthe**
- **PK 120.9** Ferry
- **PK 122.5 Confluence of Sarthe**, l/b, Mayenne becomes Maine
- **PK 122.6** Railway bridge
- **PK 122.7** Motorway bridge (Viaduc de la Maine, A11)
- **PK 123.0** Bridge (Jean-Moulin), inner ring road
- **PK 124.1** Tramway bridge (Confluences), also for pedestrians/cyclists
- **PK 124.4** Bridge (Pont de la Haute-Chaîne), quays l/b
- **PK 124.9** New bridge (Pont des Arts et Métiers) opened 2019
- **PK 125.0** Bridge (Pont de Verdun)
- **PK 125.3 Angers** *port de plaisance* in basin r/b opposite château and town centre, trip boats, 43 berths, 14 visitor moorings, night €8 (one night free, maximum 2 weeks), water and electricity included

*Grez-Neuville is one of many pretty villages along the Mayenne.* © MANFRED HEYDE/WIKIMEDIA

*Municipal port in Angers, with the château des Ducs d'Anjou and Saint-Maurice cathedral in the background*

# Mayenne/Maine and Oudon

Very attractive former provincial capital with a proud 'city' feel to it, remarkable for its château of the Ducs d'Anjou, residence of François I, and home of the largest tapestry ever created, depicting the apocalypse, reinterpreted in the context of the 100 Years War. For those renting boats, hence not allowed on to the river Loire, traditional trip boats go from the *port de plaisance* to various sites on the river, excursions highly recommended.

- PK **125.5** Bridge (Pont de la Basse-Chaîne), quay (Éric Tabarly) d/s r/b
- PK **126.5** Road bridge (Pont de l'Atlantique, N23)
- PK **126.7** Lock (Angers) l/b and weir
- PK **127.2** U/s tip of island (Robinson), navigation in l/b arm, commercial quay l/b
- PK **127.7** D/s tip of island, navigation in l/b arm
- PK **128.1** Basin l/b
- PK **129.4** Bridge (Pruniers, formerly rail)
- PK **131.7** Railway bridge
- PK **132.4** **Bouchemaine** suspension bridge, village r/b
- PK **132.9** Former oil tanker quay r/b
- PK **133.7** *Confluence with Loire*, navigable d/s only

## Vieille Maine
- PK **0.0** *Junction with river Mayenne* at PK 118.9
- PK **3.0** *Junction with river Sarthe* at PK 128.3

## River Oudon
- PK **0.0** *Confluence with river Mayenne* (PK 101), Bec d'Oudon, bridge
- PK **2.0** **Le Lion-d'Angers** bridge, quay d/s r/b for 20 boats, 02 41 95 30 16, water, electricity, moorings free for 2 nights, village r/b

The village is famous for its national horse-breeding centre and race course.

- PK **4.0** Bridge (N162)
- PK **8.0** Lock 3 (Himbeaudière) l/b and weir
- PK **8.8** Bridge (Pont du Port-aux-Anglais), **Andigné** 1 km r/b
- PK **14.0** Lock 2 (**La Chapelle-sur-Oudon**) l/b and weir, village r/b
- PK **16.9** Bridge (D775)
- PK **17.0** Lock 1 (Maingué) l/b and weir
- PK **17.1** Railway bridge
- PK **18.0** **Segré**, head of navigation (Moulin de la Tour), *port de plaisance* d/s at former quay, managed by Club Nautique Segréen, capacity 32 boats, free (maximum 48 hours), water, electricity, showers (code from tourist office), pump-out, slipway

Small town with all services.

## VIII – Western France

# 75. River Sarthe

THE SARTHE IS NAVIGABLE FROM the Barrage d'Enfer, a weir situated in the town of Le Mans, to its confluence with the Mayenne upstream of Angers, a distance of 132km. Over the first 113km down to the lock at Cheffes the river is canalised. The remaining 18km is free-flow navigation, offering restricted depths during summer drought periods. This problem has been solved by the construction of a new weir and lock on the Maine downstream of Angers (see under Mayenne-Maine). Together with the Mayenne and Oudon, the Sarthe forms the Anjou river system, a delightful cruising network where several hire bases have been established.

*With its gentle gradient the river was naturally navigable up to Malicorne. Flash locks were built in the Middle Ages to enable boats to reach Le Mans, but by the 16th century were no longer in use. The town actively promoted canalisation from the early 18th century and works were let to a private company in 1741. The project was shelved, to be revived at the same time as that for the Mayenne, in the mid-19th century. The flash locks were replaced by a reduced number of weirs and locks, some of them in lock-cuts. The navigation was abandoned after World War II, to be revived from the 1970s after the successful campaign by the Brittany Canals Committee, which also covered the rivers of Anjou.*

## Navigation
The channel is well marked and navigation is straightforward, excepting the risk of shoals in certain sections.

## Locks
There are 20 locks. The first 16 (down to the limit of Sarthe and Maine-et-Loire) are 30.85m long and 5.20m wide. The last four are 33.00m long and 5.15m wide.

## Draught
The maximum authorised draught is 1.40m, but in practice there is only 1.10m between Le Mans and Sablé during low flow periods, and little more in the free-flow section downstream of Cheffes lock.

## Headroom
From Le Mans to PK 86 the bridges offer a minimum headroom of 3.90m (reduced to 3.40 above the highest navigable water level). Over the rest of the waterway the least headroom is 4.40m (4.00m above HNWL). It should be noted that access to the moorings at Malicorne, on the weir stream at PK 47, is through a bridge offering very restricted headroom (2.35m).

## Towpath
A riverside cycle path has been laid out along the river.

## Authority
Direction Départementale des Territoires de la Sarthe
– 12 rue Ferdinand de Lesseps 72013 Le Mans Cedex 2
 02 43 50 46 00

## Route description

| | |
|---|---|
| PK 0.0 | Weir (Barrage d'Enfer), limit of navigation in Le Mans |
| PK 0.5 | Bridge (Pont Yssoir) |
| PK 0.8 | Bridge (Pont Perrin) |
| PK 0.9 | Bridge (Pont Gambetta), quay d/s r/b, tram line |
| PK 1.4 | **Le Mans** *port de plaisance* r/b for 22 boats, 4 visitor moorings, night €6 (first night €1), maximum 2 weeks, 02 43 23 39 43, water, electricity, showers €1.50, wifi, crane on request, pump-out, slipway *portdumans.com* |

Excellent location and all facilities in the town centre. Le Mans was built on a former Roman settlement and has many attractions, apart from the famous 24-hour race south of the town.

*The* port de plaisance *in Le Mans* © JEAN-PIERRE POURCINES

130

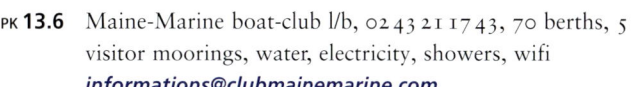

# Sarthe

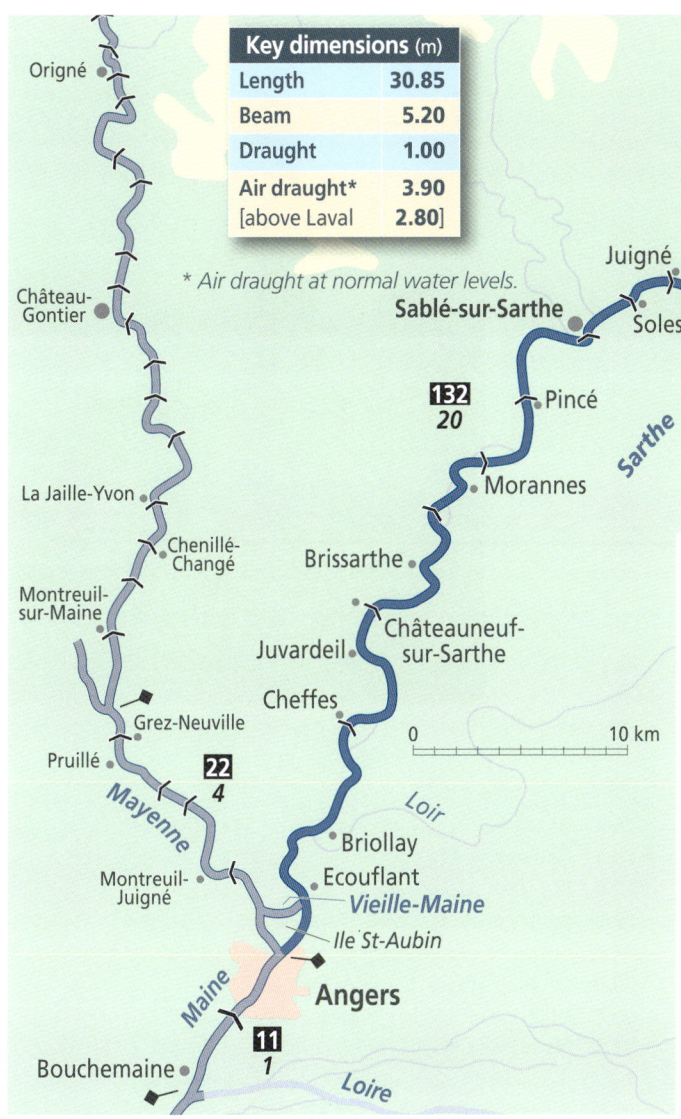

| Key dimensions (m) | |
|---|---|
| Length | 30.85 |
| Beam | 5.20 |
| Draught | 1.00 |
| Air draught* | 3.90 |
| [above Laval] | 2.80 |

* Air draught at normal water levels.

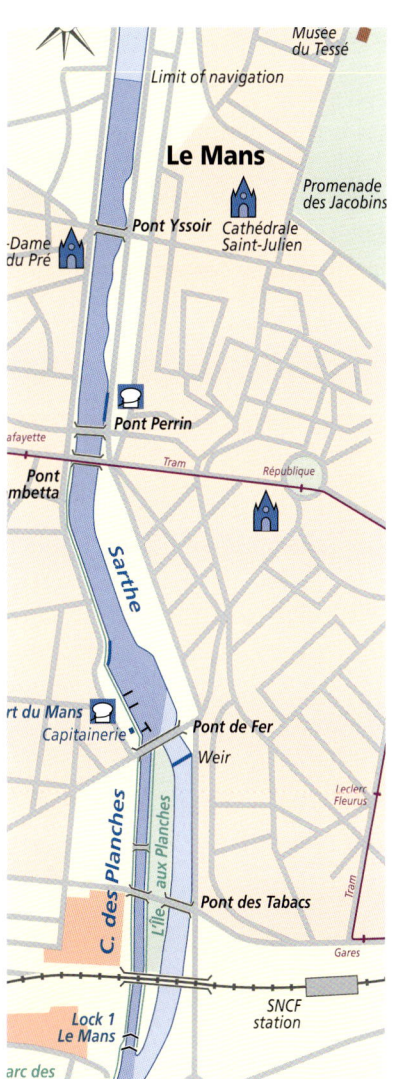

| PK 13.6 | Maine-Marine boat-club l/b, 02 43 21 17 43, 70 berths, 5 visitor moorings, water, electricity, showers, wifi *informations@clubmainemarine.com* |
|---|---|
| PK 13.9 | Main road bridge (D323) |
| PK 14.2 | Entrance to lock-cut, l/b, bridge |
| PK 14.5 | **Spay** bridge, village 600m r/b |
| PK 15.4 | Lock 4 (Spay), end of lock-cut |
| PK 17.4 | **Fillé-sur-Sarthe** bridge, village r/b, municipal *halte* on pontoons d/s r/b for 6 boats, 02 43 87 14 25, water, electricity |

| PK 1.5 | **Le Mans** bridge (Pont de Fer), weir l/b, entrance to lock-cut r/b |
|---|---|
| PK 1.8 | Bridge (Pont d'Eichtal or des Tabacs) |
| PK 2.0 | Railway bridge |
| PK 2.1 | Lock 1 (Le Mans), end of lock-cut |
| PK 2.3 | Site of projected new *port de plaisance* |

The new facility at the Parc des Lavandières is designed to replace the port at PK 1.4, which is to be developed as a new park for the city

| PK 2.7 | Footbridge (des Sables d'Or) |
|---|---|
| PK 3.0 | Confluence of Huisne, l/b |
| PK 3.2 | Foot and cycle bridge (des Riffandières) |
| PK 3.3 | Road bridge (D338, Le Mans ring road) |
| PK 4.0 | Railway bridge |
| PK 4.4 | Entrance to lock-cut, l/b, weir r/b |
| PK 4.7 | Bridge (Pont Rouge) |
| PK 5.2 | Lock 2 (Raterie), end of lock-cut |
| PK 5.4 | Bridge (D147e) |
| PK 5.9 | Footbridge (Chahoué) |
| PK 6.2 | Weir l/b |
| PK 6.5 | Lock 3 (Chahoué) |
| PK 8.8 | Footbridge (Passerelle de la Gêmerie) |
| PK 9.3 | Bridge (Pont de la Gêmerie, D326) |
| PK 10.3 | **Arnage** l/b |
| PK 11.3 | Island, keep to right-hand arm |

## VIII – Western France

| | |
|---|---|
| PK 17.7 | Entrance to lock-cut, r/b |
| PK 17.9 | Flood gates, bridge |
| PK 20.3 | Bridge (Cheneaux) |
| PK 22.2 | Lock 5 (Roëzé), end of lock-cut |
| PK 23.4 | **Roëzé-sur-Sarthe** bridge, village r/b, municipal *halte* on pontoon d/s l/b, free, water, shower at campsite, slipway |
| PK 26.0 | Bridge (D23) |
| PK 26.8 | **La Suze-sur-Sarthe** bridge, municipal *halte* on pontoon u/s r/b, 6 boats, free water €2 on tap at campsite, village l/b |
| PK 26.9 | Entrance to lock-cut, r/b |
| PK 27.1 | Railway bridge |
| PK 27.3 | Lock 6 (La Suze), end of lock-cut |
| PK 33.1 | Fercé-sur-Sarthe bridge, village 200m r/b |
| PK 33.3 | Lock 7 (Fercé) l/b and weir |
| PK 40.1 | Railway bridge |
| PK 40.3 | **Noyen-sur-Sarthe** municipal *halte* on pontoon and quay r/b for 11 boats, water, electricity, pump-out, slipway, village r/b |
| PK 40.4 | Entrance to lock-cut, l/b |
| PK 40.6 | Bridge |
| PK 41.8 | Lock 8 (Noyen), end of lock-cut |
| PK 47.0 | Entrance to lock-cut, r/b |
| PK 47.2 | **Malicorne-sur-Sarthe** bridge, village 300m l/b, municipal *halte* on weir stream, access from u/s, managed by Aventure Nautique, 06 52 04 18 72, capacity 10 boats, free (maximum 48 hours), water, electricity |
| PK 47.4 | Lock 9 (Malicorne), end of lock-cut |
| PK 51.8 | Motorway bridge (A11) |
| PK 52.9 | **Dureil** small village with church, l/b |
| PK 54.7 | Château r/b (Château de Pêcheseul) |
| PK 56.0 | Entrance to lock-cut, r/b |
| PK 56.4 | Lock 10 (Ignères), end of lock-cut |
| PK 58.8 | Entrance to lock-cut r/b, quay l/b, water, slipway |
| PK 59.1 | **Parcé-sur-Sarthe** bridge, quay d/s l/b, village 200m |
| PK 59.3 | Lock 11 (Parcé), end of lock-cut |
| PK 61.7 | **Avoise** municipal *halte* on pontoon for 4 boats r/b, free, water, electricity €3.60, showers €2.50 |
| PK 63.5 | Entrance to lock-cut, r/b |
| PK 64.1 | Lock 12 (Courtigné), end of lock-cut |
| PK 65.4 | Confluence of Vègre, r/b |
| PK 69.3 | Lock 13 (**Juigné-sur-Sarthe**) r/b and weir, village r/b, municipal *halte* on pontoon u/s r/b, free, water, electricity |
| PK 70.3 | **Solesmes** bridge, pontoon u/s r/b, slipway, abbey l/b |

The neogothic abbey of Saint-Pierre-de-Solesmes towers above the river, just opposite the entrance to the lock-cut, and is one of the major attractions of the river Sarthe, best visited from the *port de plaisance* at Sablé 3km downstream.

| | |
|---|---|
| PK 70.5 | Entrance to lock-cut r/b |
| PK 71.0 | Lock 14 (Solesmes) in short cut, r/b, end of lock-cut |
| PK 72.2 | Railway bridge (Port-Étroit), quay r/b |
| PK 72.9 | Bridge (D306) |
| PK 73.2 | **Sablé-sur-Sarthe** bridge, quay d/s l/b, Anjou Navigation hire base, 02 43 95 14 42, 30 boats, 5 visitor moorings, first week free, water and electricity €6.15/day, showers, small town r/b   *anjou-navigation.fr* |
| PK 73.5 | Lock 15 (Sablé), weir stream enters l/b |
| PK 75.3 | Island, channel in r/b arm |

*Port de plaisance and church at Sablé-sur-Sarthe, PK 73.* © JEAN-CHARLES SÉBILLET

| | |
|---|---|
| PK 76.7 | Island |
| PK 78.1 | Railway viaduct |
| PK 81.6 | Entrance to lock-cut r/b |
| PK 82.0 | Lock 16 (Beffes), end of lock-cut |
| PK 87.6 | Entrance to lock-cut r/b, weir and mill l/b |
| PK 88.0 | Lock 17 (Pendu), end of lock-cut |
| PK 90.5 | Island, channel in r/b arm |
| PK 91.3 | **Morannes** bridge, *halte* on pontoon d/s l/b, 24 boats, 4 visitor moorings, night €9, water, electricity, pump-out, slipway, village l/b |
| PK 94.0 | Entrance to lock-cut, r/b |
| PK 94.2 | Lock 18 (Villechien), weir and hydropower station l/b, end of lock-cut |
| PK 98.3 | **Brissarthe** quay and village r/b |
| PK 100.2 | Le Porage, railway station, l/b |
| PK 103.9 | Lock 19 (Châteauneuf-sur-Sarthe) r/b and weir |
| PK 104.1 | **Châteauneuf-sur-Sarthe** bridge, quay d/s r/b, village r/b, boat harbour l/b (pontoons) |
| PK 106.7 | **Juvardeil** quay and village r/b |
| PK 109.8 | River divides, navigation in r/b arm |
| PK 111.6 | (Boats heading u/s) river divides, navigation in r/b arm |
| PK 113.5 | Weir (Cheffes) l/b |
| PK 114.1 | Bridge (D74) |
| PK 114.3 | **Cheffes-sur-Sarthe** r/b, *moorings* for 27 boats, 5 visitor moorings, night €9, water and electricity included, showers at camp site, slipway   *servicetourisme@ccals.fr* |
| PK 114.4 | Lock 20 (Cheffes) l/b and weir |
| PK 121.1 | **Briollay** bridge, village d/s l/b, moorings d/s l/b, water |
| PK 123.4 | Confluence of Loir, l/b (Bec du Loir) |
| PK 127.9 | **Écouflant** l/b |
| PK 128.3 | **Confluence of Vieille-Maine** (3km navigable arm connecting with Mayenne) r/b, pontoon l/b, water, slipway |
| PK 130.6 | Island, pass on r/b side |
| PK 132.6 | **Confluence with Mayenne and Maine** (3km u/s of Angers) |

# 76. Rivers Charente and Boutonne

The Charente, one of the most beautiful cruising waterways in France, is navigable over a distance of 164km from the sea to Angoulême. The first 24km up to the small coasting port of Tonnay-Charente is tidal estuary. Above this point the waterway is maintained and operated by the *départements* Charente and Charente-Maritime, to whom the waterway was conceded in 1952 and 1963. Convenient and attractive moorings have been provided at many towns and villages. Several hire firms operate on the river, in addition to trip boats at the main towns, and recreational use of the waterway is developing despite the disadvantage of the river's isolation from the rest of the waterway network.

An attractive tributary, the Boutonne, is theoretically navigable over a distance of 29km from its confluence with the Charente at PK 128 to the small town of Saint-Jean-d'Angély, with four locks. These were restored in the 1980s, and one of the passes of the Carillon tide barrier (near the confluence) was provided with a raised footbridge to allow boats to pass when the levels of the two rivers permit. The cumbersome procedure is dissuasive, and few boats have taken advantage of this possibility. However, construction of a new lock is projected to bypass this barrier, and the Boutonne would doubtless then attract many more boats.

From the sea to PK 134 the river is considered as an entrance channel to the ports of Rochefort and Tonnay-Charente. Boats must leave the main channel clear for ships, and anchoring is forbidden.

Upstream from Tonnay-Charente, speed is limited to 12km/h in Charente-Maritime (up to PK 67) and to 10km/h in Charente. There are local restrictions to 6km/h.

## Navigation

The slow, lazy river Charente is an ideal cruising waterway, and the only difficulty will be shoals, especially approaching the limit of navigation at Angoulême.

*Pontoon mooring in Cognac, PK 59* © F-W

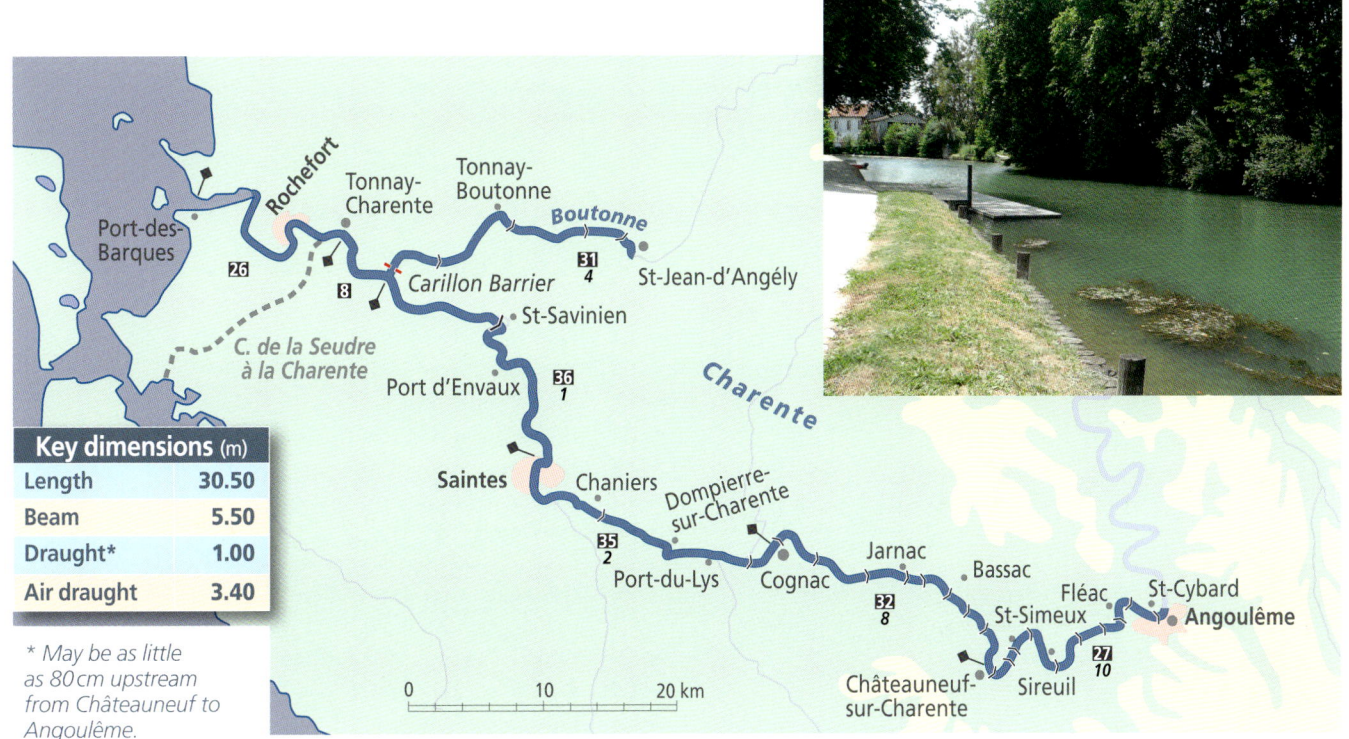

| Key dimensions (m) | |
|---|---|
| Length | 30.50 |
| Beam | 5.50 |
| Draught* | 1.00 |
| Air draught | 3.40 |

\* May be as little as 80cm upstream from Châteauneuf to Angoulême.

## VIII – Western France

*The river was described by François I as 'la plus belle rivière du royaume', and was navigable in its natural state until mills were erected at many locations in the 14th century. Some locks were built but through navigation remained impossible for centuries. Improvements to the navigation were projected by the engineer Trésaguet under Louis XVI in 1772, but work was interrupted by the Revolution. The project was revived under the Restoration and canalisation completed in 1835. The waterway above Cognac was abandoned in 1926 and the rest in 1957. The* départements *took over operation under concessions in 1963, and transfer of ownership to the Nouvelle Aquitaine region is under discussion.*

### Locks
There are 21 locks, the minimum dimensions of which are 34.00m by 6.30m. Saint-Savinien lock (48.50m by 8.00m) was built in 1968 as part of a multipurpose river improvement and flood control scheme. Most of the other locks are unattended, and users have to lock through themselves, using the straightforward paddle winding gear and gate winches. A clear instruction leaflet in English is issued by the waterway authority (addresses below).

The locks on the Boutonne are 30.50m by 5.50m. To pass through the Carillon tide barrier on the Boutonne, advance notice is to be given to the authority at Rochefort, for manual operation of the gates. Passage is possible whenever the tide coefficient is greater than or equal to 70. The authority will send an itinerant lock-keeper to lock boats through, but these arrangements are understood to be no longer in place, and in any case not for boats from the Charente.

### Draught
In the tidal estuary, the least depth available at low tide is 3.00m. Upstream as far as Cognac, the least depth is 1.50m at low water, but during the summer, when the gates of the weirs at Saint-Savinien and La Baine are closed, the minimum water levels maintained are such that 2.50m may be counted on. The available depth decreases progressively working upstream, with 1.50m around Jarnac, and 0.80 to 1.00m between Châteauneuf and Angoulême.

### Headroom
The fixed bridges offer a minimum headroom of 3.55m above the highest navigable water level. This is the headroom under the railway bridge (Pont de la Cèpe) at PK 133, where the mobile span is now no longer in operation. The second lowest bridge is at Vibrac (PK 32), with a headroom of 3.72m.

### Towpath
The towpath has long fallen into disuse.

### Authority
Direction Départementale des Territoires de Charente
- 43 rue du Docteur Duroselle, BP1374, 16016 Angoulême cedex, 05 17 17 37 37 (PK 0-67)

Direction Départementale des Territoires et de Mer de Charente-Maritime
- 89 avenue des Cordeliers, 17018 La Rochelle cedex 1 05 16 49 61 00 (PK 67-138)

Port de Rochefort
- Quai Lemoine de Sérigny, 17300 Rochefort 05 46 83 99 96, *port.plaisance@ville-rochefort.fr* (PK 138-163)

## Route description

PK **0.0** Bridge (Saint-Antoine), river may be navigated 3.2km upstream to Chalonne mill (but beware of shoals)

PK **0.3** Footbridge

PK **0.5** **Angoulême** quay l/b (Port l'Houmeau), capacity 15 boats, 06 10 38 39 67, night €5, water €2, electricity €2, shower, slipway, town centre 1km, *angouleme-developpement.com*

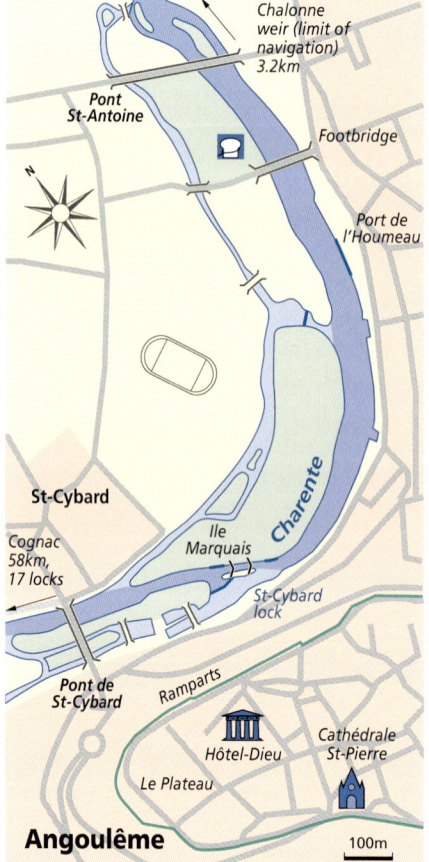

Angoulême

PK **1.1** Lock (Saint-Cybard) r/b (against island)
PK **1.3** (U/s boats) river divides, take l/b arm
PK **1.5** Saint-Cybard bridge
PK **2.1** Bridge (inner ring road)
PK **2.8** Island, navigation l/b
PK **3.2** New road bridge (N10 Angoulême by-pass)
PK **3.8** Footbridge
PK **4.5** Lock (Thouérat), r/b, opposite gunpowder factory
PK **5.6** (U/s boats) river divides, keep to r/b
PK **6.3** Islands, navigation l/b, Fléac r/b
PK **7.7** Bridge (Basseau), island d/s, take r/b arm
PK **7.9** Lock (Basseau) r/b, weir
PK **9.6** Lock (Fleurac) r/b

# Charente and Boutonne

| | |
|---|---|
| PK **10.0** | D/s end of Fleurac islands (u/s boats keep to r/b) |
| PK **10.9** | Islands, navigation l/b |
| PK **12.1** | Lock (La Mothe) l/b |
| PK **13.2** | Bridge, Nersac 1 km l/b, islands d/s, channel r/b |
| PK **16.0** | Islands, navigation r/b |
| PK **17.5** | **Sireuil** bridge, Inter-Croisières hire base, 06 18 09 29 05, night €5, water and electricity (coin-operated), wifi €2, showers, slipway, *intercroisieres.com* |
| PK **17.8** | Lock (Sireuil) l/b |
| PK **18.6** | D/s end of island (u/s boats keep to l/b) |
| PK **20.5** | River divides, navigation in r/b arm |
| PK **21.4** | Lock (La Liège) |
| PK **21.6** | (U/s boats) river divides, take r/b arm |
| PK **23.1** | Lock (**Saint-Simeux**) l/b, access to village via weir stream r/b |
| PK **23.8** | Bridge (u/s boats turn into l/b arm above bridge) |
| PK **24.1** | Entrance to lock-cut r/b (visible at last minute) |
| PK **24.3** | Lock (Malvy) |
| PK **24.6** | (U/s boats) river divides, take r/b arm |
| PK **25.8** | Island (Île des Groles), navigation r/b |
| PK **27.0** | Lock (Châteauneuf) in short lock-cut r/b, weir l/b, canoe pass l/b side of weir |
| PK **27.2** | End of lock-cut (u/s boats take r/b arm) |
| PK **27.5** | **Châteauneuf-sur-Charente** bridge, *halte* on both banks, free, water, electricity, small town 200m l/b |
| PK **28.9** | Island (Île Muguet), navigation r/b |
| PK **29.8** | Entrance to backwater (Brassour) l/b |
| PK **31.0** | River divides, navigation in l/b arm |
| PK **31.5** | (U/s boats) river divides, navigation in l/b arm |
| PK **31.9** | Entrance to lock-cut (middle of three channels), bridge |
| PK **32.1** | Lock (Vibrac), one side slopes, the other has a step |
| PK **32.2** | End of lock-cut |
| PK **33.9** | **Saint-Simon** *halte*, village r/b (u/s boats take l/b arm), *village-gabarier.com*, restaurant La Petite Gabarre |
| PK **34.6** | Juac bridge, small village r/b |
| PK **35.0** | Lock (Juac) in lock-cut l/b, weir |
| PK **37.8** | Entrance to lock-cut r/b (visible at last minute) |
| PK **38.1** | Lock (Saintonge), **Bassac** 1 km r/b |
| PK **38.2** | End of lock-cut |
| PK **39.0** | Bridge (Vinade), **Bassac** 1 km r/b |
| PK **41.6** | Weir (Gondeville) l/b, keep to r/b |
| PK **41.7** | Lock (Gondeville) |
| PK **42.1** | Weir streams l/b, keep to r/b |
| PK **42.6** | Bridge (N141) |
| PK **43.0** | Island, navigation l/b |
| PK **43.9** | Entrance to lock-cut l/b |
| PK **44.1** | Lock (Jarnac), end of lock-cut |
| PK **44.3** | **Jarnac** bridge, quay and Le Boat hire base u/s r/b, 05 45 36 59 98, visitor moorings for 5 boats, night €20 including water/electricity, diesel, showers, crane 10t, slipway, small town r/b, *leboat.com* |
| PK **47.6** | Entrance to lock-cut r/b |
| PK **47.9** | Lock (Bourg-Charente) |
| PK **48.0** | End of lock-cut |
| PK **48.7** | **Bourg-Charente** bridge, capacity 4 boats, water, village l/b |
| PK **52.5** | Lock (Garde-Moulin) l/b, weir |
| PK **53.7** | Island, navigation l/b |
| PK **54.0** | Bridge (D15), **Saint-Brice** village, castle 600m r/b |
| PK **54.8** | Small island, navigation l/b |
| PK **55.6** | Island, navigation l/b |
| PK **56.0** | Island, navigation l/b |
| PK **56.6** | Entrance to Solençon backwater r/b (no access) |
| PK **57.3** | Bridge |
| PK **59.0** | Entrance to lock-cut (mill stream l/b) |
| PK **59.1** | Lock (Cognac) |
| PK **59.3** | End of lock-cut (u/s boats take l/b arm) |
| PK **59.4** | **Cognac** bridge, quays d/s, Canalous Plaisance hire base, capacity 10 boats, 05 45 82 93 12, night €14.10 including water/electricity, showers during office hours only, crane to order, slipway, pump-out, repairs, town centre and distilleries l/b |

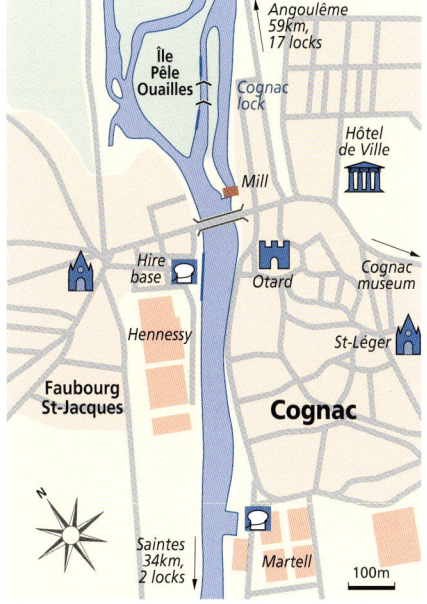

| | |
|---|---|
| PK **60.7** | Bridge |
| PK **61.1** | Bridge (N141 Cognac by-pass) |
| PK **61.3** | Island, navigation l/b |
| PK **61.8** | Island, navigation r/b |
| PK **62.8** | Lock (Crouin) in short lock-cut r/b |
| PK **66.0** | Bridge (D144), **Saint-Laurent-de-Cognac** 1.7 km r/b |
| PK **67.2** | Limit of Charente and Charente Maritime *départements* l/b |
| PK **67.4** | Quay (Port-du-Lys) l/b, boat club moorings, floating pontoons, slipway |
| PK **68.3** | Limit of Charente and Charente Maritime *départements* r/b |
| PK **72.2** | **Brives-sur-Charente** bridge, quay, small village 800m l/b |
| PK **76.7** | **Rouffiac** municipal *halte*, water, electricity, shower, slipway, l/b, *rouffiac17.com* |
| PK **77.4** | **Dompierre-sur-Charente** ferry, municipal *halte*, pontoon moorings, water/electricity €3.50/day in season, slipway, village 500m r/b |
| PK **80.5** | Bridge (D134) and railway bridge (Beillant) |
| PK **82.0** | River divides, navigation in r/b arm |
| PK **82.4** | Entrance to lock-cut l/b |
| PK **82.7** | Lock (La Baine) |
| PK **82.8** | End of lock-cut (u/s boats take middle of three channels) |
| PK **83.6** | **Chaniers** ferry, municipal *halte* u/s r/b, water, electricity, small village 300m r/b, *chaniers.fr* |
| PK **86.8** | Port-Hublé slipway, r/b |
| PK **89.8** | Saint-Sorlin r/b |
| PK **91.7** | Bridge (N141 Saintes by-pass) |

## VIII – Western France

| PK | |
|---|---|
| **91.8** | Railway bridge (Lucérat) |
| **93.5** | Road bridge (Saintonge), quay l/b (Quai des Roches) |
| **94.1** | Footbridge |
| **94.4** | **Saintes** bridge (Pont de Palissy), quayside moorings d/s r/b, water, electricity, slipway, town centre l/b, railway station 1 km r/b |

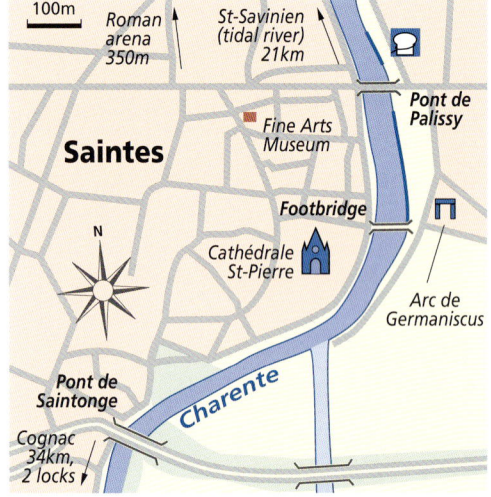

| PK | |
|---|---|
| **95.2** | Pontoon moorings (Saintes boat club - Port Larousselle) l/b, water, electricity, crane 12t, pump-out |
| **97.0** | Courbiac castle l/b, race track r/b |
| **99.2** | Bussac castle r/b |
| **104.9** | Quay (Port-la-Pierre) r/b |
| **105.6** | Motorway bridge (A10) |
| **106.8** | Taillebourg bridge, quay and village r/b |
| **109.5** | **Port-d'Envaux** quay and village l/b (former ferry), pontoon moorings for 5 boats, 06 07 13 20 13, night €14.30, water, electricity, shower, slipway, *portdenvaux.fr* |
| **116.1** | Navigation enters lock-cut l/b, straight on for **Saint-Savinien** *port de plaisance* 200m d/s on river, 25-30 berths but none available for passing boats, *halte* 800m, d/s of bridge l/b, free, water, electricity, slipway, pump-out, restaurant, village r/b, *saint-savinien.fr* |

*Pontoon mooring at Saint-Savinien* © F-W

| PK | |
|---|---|
| **116.7** | Lock (Saint-Savinien), bridge |
| **117.1** | End of lock-cut |
| **120.9** | Motorway bridge (A837) |
| **127.0** | Bridge (Pont de l'Houmée), Bords 2 km r/b |
| **128.0** | **Confluence of Boutonne** r/b, navigable to Saint Jean-d'Angély |
| **133.4** | Railway bridge (Pont de la Cèpe) |
| **136.1** | Bridge (D137 Tonnay-Charente bypass) |
| **137.4** | *Halte* managed by local club, 2 berths for boats up to 7m, 1 night free including water/electricity |
| **137.7** | **Tonnay-Charente** suspension bridge, quays for coasters and small town d/s r/b, municipal *halte* d/s r/b, 8 berths, free 48 hours, then €10/night, *tonnay-charente.fr* |
| **139.0** | Saint-Gobain factory, quay r/b |
| **140.2** | **Junction with Canal de la Charente à la Seudre** (disused) l/b |
| **143.6** | Commercial port basin (3) through lock r/b |
| **144.1** | **Rochefort** basins 1 and 2 through lock, r/b, *port de plaisance* 40 visitor berths up to 18m by 6m, night €28.80, third night free, 05 46 83 99 96, water, electricity, showers, crane 13t, pump-out, repairs, town centre 300m (see plan), *ville-rochefort.fr*. JS Marine boatyard, repairs/services, 05 46 87 52 08 |

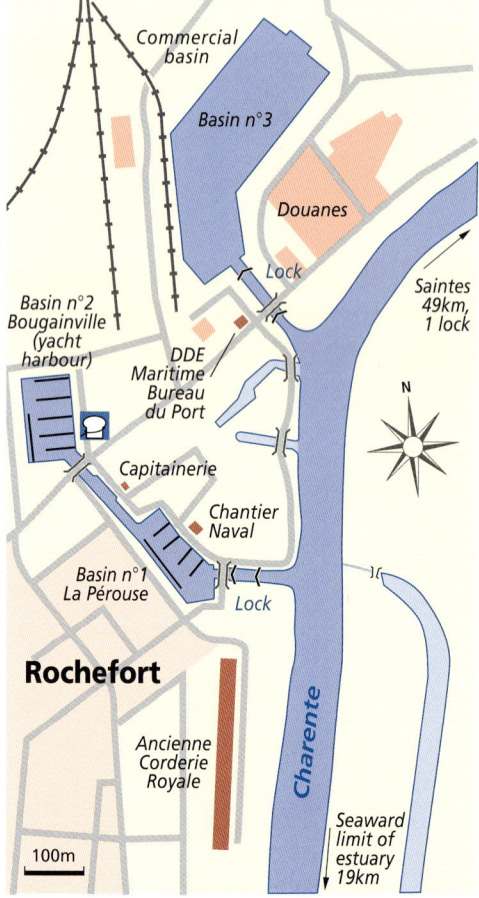

| PK | |
|---|---|
| **144.2** | Quay (Quai de l'Artillerie) with pontoon moorings, r/b |
| **147.5** | Former transporter bridge (Martrou) |
| **147.7** | Site of a former lifting road bridge |
| **147.9** | Road bridge (Martrou-Rochefort, D733) |

# Charente and Boutonne

PK **151.7 Soubise** l/b, *port de plaisance*, 05 46 84 49 32, night €21 on pontoon including water/electricity, diesel, shower, slipway, repairs, restaurant, former ferry, *port-adhoc.com*

PK **157.5** Entrance to Canal de Charras r/b (no access)

PK **162.0 Saint-Nazaire-sur-Charente** *port de plaisance* l/b, water, electricity, shower, *port-adhoc.com*

PK **163.5 Port-des-Barques** l/b, limit of sea, boat harbour, night €10.60, fuel, water, electricity, showers, slipway €3.50, *ville-portdesbarques.fr*

*Bernouet Lock, PK 28, the last before Saint-Jean-d'Angély, in far too good condition to be so little used.* © F-W

## River Boutonne

| | |
|---|---|
| PK **0.0** | **Confluence with Charente** PK 128 |
| PK **0.2** | Bridge (Carillon) |
| PK **0.4** | River divides, keep to r/b arm to pass through tide barrier (possible future lock in l/b arm) |
| PK **0.7** | Carillon tide barrier (practically impassable at present) |
| PK **1.1** | Railway bridge |
| PK **1.3** | Motorway bridge (A837) |
| PK **3.6** | Overhead power lines |
| PK **5.8** | Entrance to lock-cut, l/b |
| PK **6.0** | Lock (Bel-Ébat) |
| PK **10.5** | Sharp bend |
| PK **13.2** | Footbridge |
| PK **14.0** | **Tonnay-Boutonne** bridge, village r/b |
| PK **15.1** | Junction with Canal Sainte-Julienne (drain), r/b |
| PK **15.7** | Lock (L'Houmée) in short cut, l/b, bridge |
| PK **18.4** | Sharp bend |
| PK **21.2** | **Torxé** bridge, small village r/b |
| PK **24.0** | Lock (Voissay) in short cut, l/b |
| PK **26.4** | Overhead power line |
| PK **27.0** | Motorway bridge (A10) |
| PK **28.1** | Entrance to lock-cut, l/b |
| PK **28.2** | Lock (Bernouet) |
| PK **28.8** | Footbridge, basin (public park) |
| PK **29.2** | Bridge (Les Granges), effective limit of navigability, boat club and moorings d/s r/b, slipway |
| PK **30.7** | **Saint-Jean-d'Angély** bridge (Saint-Jacques), limit of waterway, town centre 600m r/b |

# 77. Sèvre Niortaise and connecting waterways

The Sèvre Niortaise is navigable from the mouth of its estuary in Aiguillon bay (north of La Rochelle) to the historic river port of Niort, a distance of 72km. Much of its course lies in the regional park of the Marais Poitevin, a fenland area ideal for cruising in smaller boats. The waterway may be divided into two distinct sections. The first 18km from the sea to from Marans, is maritime and part of its length is bypassed by a ship canal, the Canal maritime de Marans-au-Brault, by which coastal vessels gain access to the small seaport. The remaining 54km from Marans to Niort is the canalised river Sèvre. Connection is made in this section with the canalised rivers Vieille Autise, Mignon and Jeune Autise. The situation is made clear by the accompanying map. The three navigable tributaries of the Sèvre Niortaise are also described here.

*The first plans for canalisation of the Sèvre and drainage of the marshland were drawn up by Humphrey Bradley in the mid-16th century. Napoleon I took up the project in 1808 but little progress was made before the engineer Évrard designed in 1862 the plans for all the structures and artificial cuts as built. The main purpose of the navigation was to carry timber from the Marais Poitevin to the seaports of Marans or La Rochelle. The ship canal from Marans to Le Brault was started in 1891 and opened at the turn of the century.*

## Canal de la Vieille Autise

The Canal de la Vieille-Autise is the canalised river Autise, and is navigable over a distance of almost 10km from the Sèvre-Niortaise near Damvix (PK 32) to the head of navigation in a small basin at the village of Courdault.

## Mignon

The canalised river Mignon, generally known as the Canal du Mignon, was the longest of the Sèvre tributaries, navigable for boats with limited draught from its confluence with the Sèvre-Niortaise at PK 34.3 to the small town of Mauzé-sur-le-Mignon, a distance of 17km, but the last two locks are now disused, reducing the available length to 11km.

## Autise (Jeune)

Although officially designated a river navigation, the Jeune-Autise is a man-made canal which receives part of the natural flow of the river Autise through a 4.5km feeder canal. It extends almost 9km from a junction with the through route on the Sèvre-Niortaise at Maillé (PK 37.3) to a basin in the village of Souil, the first 1.2km being in

| Key dimensions* | |
| --- | --- |
| | (m) |
| Length | 20.00 |
| Beam | 5.10 |
| Draught | 1.00 |
| Air draught | 2.20 |

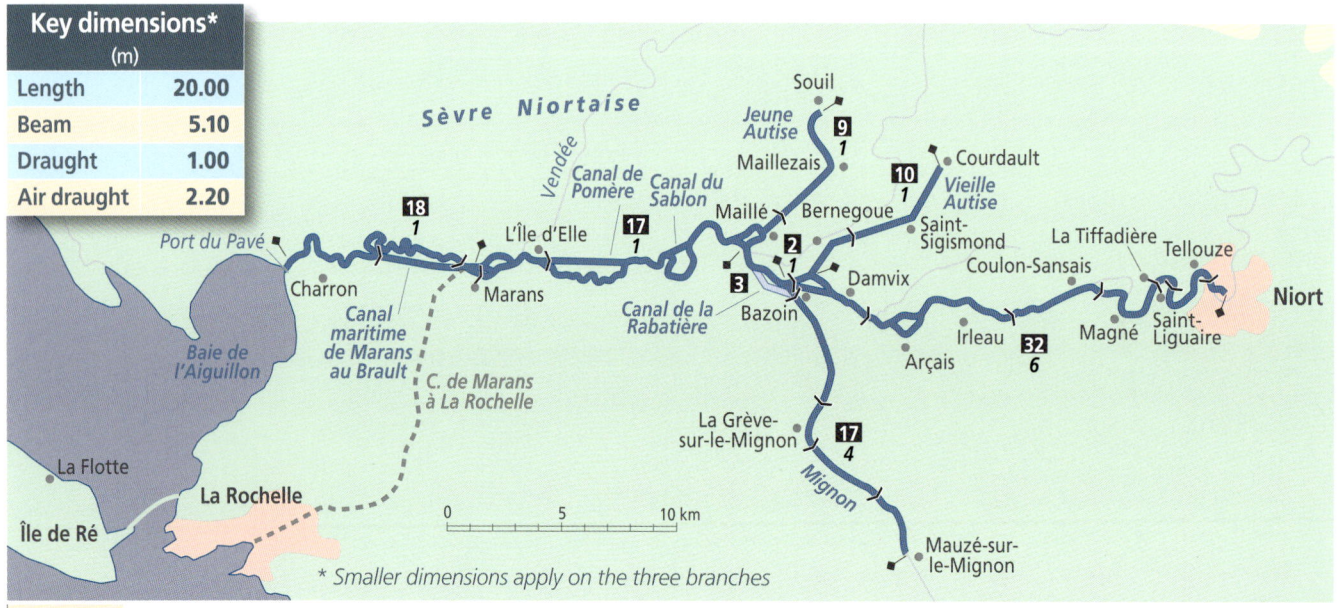

* Smaller dimensions apply on the three branches

a navigable loop of the Sèvre. The original lock here, of very small dimensions (for fishing boats only), has been bypassed by a new lock accessible to craft of up to 12m.

## Navigation

Traffic amounts to no more than 150 to 200 boats per year, one important limiting factor being the draught and headroom in the upper reaches, another being the hostility of the local population to powered boats. Careful navigation is called for, so as not to worsen the situation, and depending on the boat's size and hull shape it may be advisable to cruise at below the maximum permitted speed of 10km/h, especially when passing the countless flat-bottomed river boats which ply the river. However, the greatest difficulty is likely to be weed clogging the propeller.

## Locks

Access from the sea is either via the natural estuary, leading to Enfreneaux lock, measuring 40m by 7m, a short distance downstream of Marans, or via a ship lock 126 by 11m at the seaward end of the Canal maritime de Marans au Brault.

From Marans to Niort there are 8 locks, dimensions 31.50m by 5.20m (minimum), overcoming a total difference in level of 8m. Their use is controlled during the low flow period, which corresponds to the pleasure cruising season (June to October).

The lock on the Vieille-Autise has a length of 31.50m and a width of 5.20m. On the Mignon, there are four locks, offering minimum dimensions of 31.50m by 5.10m. They overcome a difference in level of 4.65m.

On the Jeune-Autise, there is just one lock, at Maillé. It has restricted dimensions of 12.00m by 4.20m.

Locks (and lift bridges) are operated by remote control, to be acquired at one of the three operational centres on the system:

**Niort**  Cale du Port, 1 quai de Belle Île,  79000 Niort, 05 49 09 01 55

**Bazoin**  85420 Damvix, 02 51 87 90 66

**Marans**  52 quai Foch, 17230 Marans, 05 46 01 10 35.

*Trip boat at the quay in Damvix* © MARK C. CAPRIOLI

## Draught

On the tidal Sèvre up to Enfreneaux lock, the depth ranges between 1.00m at low tide and 5.50m at high tide. The port of Marans and the ship canal offer depths of 5.35m (MW)/4.50m (LW). From Marans to Bazoin depths are 2.50m (MW) and 2.00m (LW). Depths in the various bypassed sections of the river between Marans and lock 7 (Bazoin) are 1.50m (mw)/1.00m (lw). From lock 7 (Bazoin) to Niort the mean water depth is 1.60m, reduced to 1.40m during periods of drought. However, there are shoals downstream of locks 3 (Tiffardière) and 4 (Marais-Pin) and at La Barbée (PK 32), where the guaranteed depths are further reduced to 1.20m (mw) and 1.00m (lw).

**Vieille-Autise**  The normal depth of water is 1.20m, but this drops to 0.80m during the summer low water period.

**Mignon**  From the confluence to a short distance upstream of La Grève-sur-Mignon the normal depth of water is 1.20m, falling to 0.60m at low water. In the upper reaches no more than 0.60m may be counted upon in normal conditions, reduced locally to 0.40m at times of low water. It should be mentioned that these depths, although insufficient for large cruisers, are adequate for the local flat-bottomed river boats which ply the Sèvre-Niortaise and its tributaries. On the **Jeune-Autise**, from the Sèvre to the lock at Maillé, the normal depth of water is 2.20m, reduced to 1.70m during the summer low water period. Similar depths are available above the lock, but the lock itself has a very shallow sill, offering a depth of only 0.50m at normal water level, reduced to 0.20m at low water.

## Headroom

Craft aiming to reach Niort should not be higher than 2.20m, which is the least headroom offered at mean water level in the section above lock 5 (Sotterie). At the highest navigable water level the headroom is reduced to 1.10m, but this would be an exceptional occurrence during the cruising season. From Marans to lock 5 the minimum headroom is 2.40m (mw)/1.70m (lw). The new bridge downstream of Brault offers ample headroom.

The minimum headroom under the bridges above normal water levels is 3.05m on the Vieille-Autise, 3.30m on the Canal du Mignon and 2.40m on the Jeune-Autise

## Towpath

There is a rough towpath throughout, but conditions vary widely according to local usage and access to the towpath may be difficult.

## Authority

Institution Interdépartementale du Bassin de la Sèvre Niortaise
– Maison du département - CS 58880 - 79028 Niort
05 49 78 02 60

# VIII – Western France

## Route description

### Sèvre-Niortaise

- **PK 72.0**  Port du Pavé causeway l/b, moorings, Aiguillon bay narrows into Sèvre estuary
- **PK 67.9**  Le Corps de Garde moorings l/b, limit of sea
- **PK 65.6**  Lift bridge (Pont du Brault)
- **PK 64.9**  Entrance to ship canal (Canal maritime de Marans au Brault) through Le Brault lock), l/b (Note: the canal is 5.2km long, while the tidal section of river it bypasses is 9.7km)
- **PK 64.8**  Former moving bridge (Pont du Brault)
- **PK 55.6**  Lock (Enfreneaux) r/b, to tidal Sèvre, bridge
- **PK 55.2**  End of ship canal, navigation re-enters river

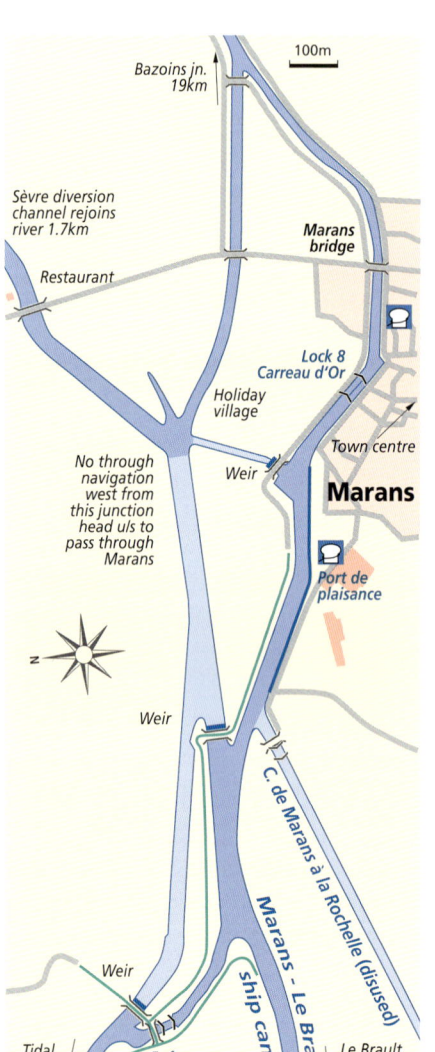

- **PK 55.0**  *Junction with former Canal de Marans à La Rochelle*, l/b (disused)

Restoration of this canal has begun; it would be a remarkable extension to this waterway network, giving access to the port of La Rochelle.

- **PK 54.4**  **Marans**, end of maritime waterway, *port de plaisance*, 06 25 79 16 35, 180 berths, 10 visitor moorings, night €14, water, electricity, showers, wifi (€2 for 24 hours), crane 3.2t, slipway, repairs
- **PK 54.2**  Lock 8 and weir (Carreau d'Or)
- **PK 53.9**  Bridge (Marans), town l/b
- **PK 53.2**  Entrance to outlet drain, r/b (not navigable)
- **PK 52.2**  River divides, take l/b arm
- **PK 50.9**  Confluence of Vendée, r/b (unpowered boats only)
- **PK 50.8**  Railway bridge
- **PK 50.7**  Entrance to Canal de Pomère
- **PK 50.6**  **L'Île d'Elle** bridge, village 1200m r/b
- **PK 45.9**  End of Canal de Pomère, r/b, navigation possible in bypassed section (Contour de Pomère)
- **PK 45.1**  Short meander cutoff, l/b (d/s of yacht club)
- **PK 42.7**  Entrance to meander cutoff (Canal du Sablon) r/b, navigation possible in bypassed section (Contour des Combrands)
- **PK 42.1**  Footbridge
- **PK 41.3**  End of meander cutoff
- **PK 38.9**  Bridge (Sablon)
- **PK 38.2**  Entrance to meander cutoff (Fossé du Loup) l/b, *junction with Canal de la Jeune Autise* via the bypassed loop (Contour de Maillé), bridge

As the plan shows, it is worth making the detour to the village of Maillé or – even better – to continue up the Jeune Autise to the village of Souil, rarther than taking the short cut via the Fossé du Loup.

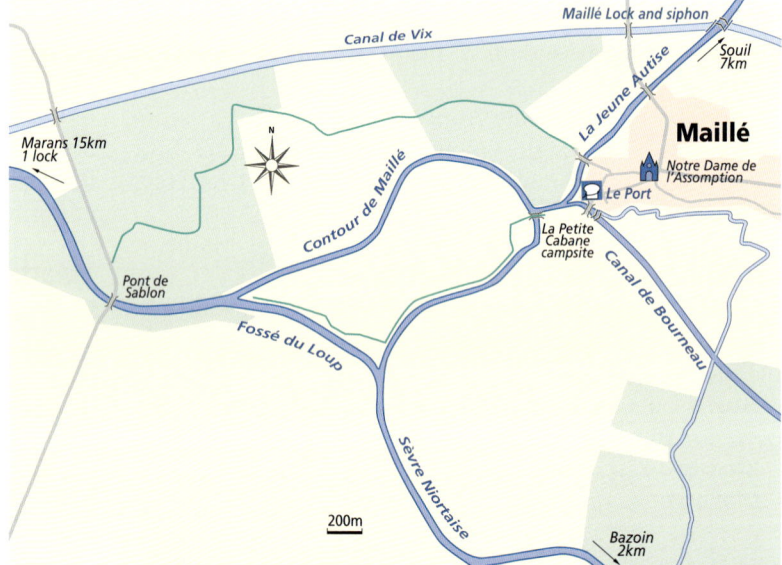

*Maillé village quay*  ©JEAN-PIERRE CASSERON

- **PK 37.3**  End of meander cutoff
- **PK 36.4**  Junction with Canal de la Rabatière, l/b (not navigable)

# Sèvre Niortaise and tributaries

PK 36.2  Rabatière diversion canal, l/b (no interest for navigation)
PK 35.0  Bridge (Croix des Maries)
PK 34.3  Junction with Canal du Mignon, l/b

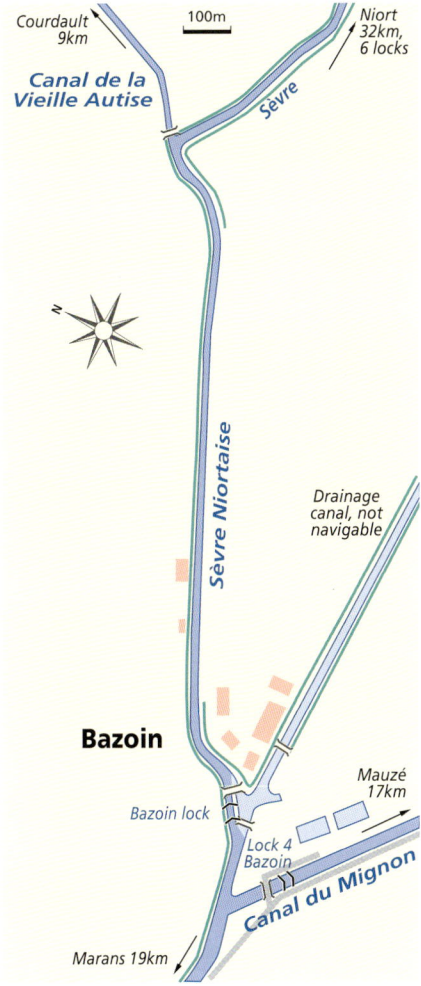

PK 34.0  Lock 7 (sloping sides) and weir (Bazoin), bridge
PK 32.5  Junction with Canal de la Vieille Autise, r/b
PK 32.0  La Barbée, r/b
PK 31.3  Les Loges, r/b
PK 30.1  **Damvix** bridge, moorings and slipway u/s r/b, village r/b
PK 29.2  Confluence of Vieille Sèvre, r/b
PK 28.7  Lock 6 and weir (Bourdettes), lift bridge
PK 27.5  Entrance to Arçais arm, l/b
PK 25.6  End of Arçais arm, l/b (navigation uses r/b arm)
PK 23.7  Footbridge (Cabanes de la Sèvre)
PK 21.2  **Irleau** bridge, village 1 km l/b
PK 19.1  Lock 5 and weir (Sotterie), bridge
PK 16.6  Junction with canal to La Garette, l/b (small boats only)
PK 16.4  Footbridge
PK 16.0  **Coulon-Sansais** bridge, moorings and slipway d/s r/b, small boats for hire, village r/b
PK 13.6  Lock 4 and weir (Marais-Pin)
PK 10.9  **Magné** lift bridge, quay d/s l/b, village l/b

Boaters use the remote control to operate this bridge.

PK 10.1  Sevreau arm l/b (navigable by small boats 500m to Sevreau bridge)
PK 8.3  Railway bridge
PK 8.1  **La Tiffardière** bridge, village r/b
PK 7.6  Lock 3 and weir (Tiffardière), sloping sides
PK 6.8  Lock 2 and weir (La Roussille), bridge

*Charming site of lock 2, La Roussille*   © PATXARAN6

PK 6.0  **Saint-Liguaire** slipway, moorings, village l/b
PK 4.2  Bridge (boulevard Willy Brandt)
PK 2.5  Tellouze castle r/b
PK 1.5  Main road bridge (Niort bypass)
PK 0.9  Lock 1 and weir (Comporté), sloping sides
PK 0.0  **Niort** canal basin, head of navigation, moorings, town centre across river

A splendid town with all shops and services, and possibly a great relief to get there after struggling through thick weeds and other obstructions

*The basin and former commercial harbour at the head of navigation in Niort*  © GSV

## VIII – Western France

### Tributaries of the Sèvre Niortaise

#### Vieille-Autise

| | |
|---|---|
| PK 9.7 | Footbridge (Ouillete), confluence with Sèvre-Niortaise (km 32) |
| PK 8.4 | **Bernegoue** bridge, village 700m r/b |
| PK 7.5 | Bridge (Pont Noir) |
| PK 6.8 | Lock (Saint-Arnault) |
| PK 3.3 | **Saint-Sigismond** bridge, village 200m l/b |
| PK 2.2 | Bridge (Chanceau), Liez 1500 r/b |
| PK 0.0 | **Courdault** basin, head of navigation, village 300m |

#### Mignon

| | |
|---|---|
| PK 17.1 | *Confluence with Sèvre-Niortaise* (PK 34) |
| PK 17.0 | Lock 4 (Bazoin) and weir, bridge |
| PK 16.4 | Entrance to Dérivation de la Rabatière (not navigable) l/b |
| PK 14.9 | Rigole de la Garette drain enters r/b |
| PK 12.4 | Lidon r/b |
| PK 9.9 | Lock 3 (Grève-sur-Mignon) and weir |
| PK 8.7 | **La Grève-sur-Mignon** bridge, village 700m l/b |
| PK 8.6 | Bridge (former railway) |
| PK 6.4 | Bridge (Port des Gueux), quay l/b |
| PK 5.6 | Lock 2 (Sazay) disused, weir, bridge, limit of navigation |

The rest of this former navigation is given for reference.

| | |
|---|---|
| PK 4.2 | Weir |
| PK 4.0 | Footbridge |
| PK 3.6 | Quay (Chaban) l/b |
| PK 2.7 | Lock 1 (Chaban) disused, weir |
| PK 1.0 | Bridge (Moulin-Neuf) |
| PK 0.0 | **Mauzé-sur-le-Mignon** basin, head of navigation, village 1 km |

#### Jeune-Autise

| | |
|---|---|
| PK 8.9 | *Confluence with Sèvre-Niortaise* in Maillé loop (1.2km from main route) |
| PK 8.7 | Junction with Canal de Bourneau, footbridge, access to village of **Maillé**, municipal *halte*, 06 83 52 02 52, 9 visitor berths (up to 15m), free, electricity, showers |

See the plan on p.140.

| | |
|---|---|
| PK 8.5 | Bridge |
| PK 8.0 | **Maillé** bridge (Saint-Nicolas), village 400m l/b |
| PK 7.5 | Lock (Aqueduc de Maillé), bridge |
| PK 3.3 | **Maillezais** bridge, abbey ruins, village 800m l/b |
| PK 1.8 | Bridge |
| PK 1.4 | Bridge |
| PK 1.2 | Bridge |
| PK 1.0 | Weir (Château Vert), limit of navigation |
| PK 0.5 | Feeder enters, l/b |
| PK 0.1 | Bridge |
| PK 0.0 | **Souil** basin, small village 200m |

# Index

Waterway names in bold (excepting historic names and disused waterways)
*Topics (historic or current, including personalities) in italics*

**Aar, river**  6
Abzac  91
**Adour, river**  53, 92-5
**Aff, river**  111, 115
Agde  33, 34, 36-7, 47, 48
Agen  53, 55, 59-60, 66
Aigues-Mortes  25, 27, 29, 30
**d'Aigues-Mortes, Canal de dérivation**  29
Aiguillon (Lot)  71, 72, 74-5
Aiguillon (Sèvre Niortaise)  138, 140
Albas  73, 79
Albi  63, 65
Ambès  90
Ancenis  121
Andigné  129
Andouillé  127
Anetz  120
Angers  119, 125, 128, 130
Anglet  93, 94
Angoulême  133, 134
Anjou river system  130
Aran (Joyeuse)  93, 94, 95
Arcambal  82
Ardanavy  93, 94, 95
**Ardennes, Canal des**  4
Argeliers  39
Argens-Minervois  33, 40
Ariane, Port (Lattes)  28, 31, 32
Arnage  131
Arzal barrage  102, 105
Arzal-Camoël  105
Assier  84
Atlantic (*routes*)  19, 54, 86, 98, 102, 107, 116
Aubencheul-au-Bac  7
Aude  49, 50-51
**Aulne, river**  6, 106, 107-8, 115
*authorities*, 21
  see also start of each waterway
**Autise** see **Jeune Autise**; **Vieille Autise**
*automated locks*  16-17
Aveyron  5, 73
Avignonet-Lauragais  44
Avoise  132
Ayguelèze  65
Azé  127

**Baïse, river**  53, 54, 60, 66-9, 70, 73
**Baïse-Lot connection (Garonne Crossing)**  70-71, 73
*The Barge Association (DBA)*  4, 10, 20
Barques, Port-des-  137
Barsac  87
Bassac  135
Bayonne  92, 93, 94, 95
Bazoin  139, 141, 142
Beaucaire  23, 24, 26
Beautour  124
Bec d'Ambès  86, 88, 89, 90
Bec de la Bidouze  94
Bec-du-Gave  92, 93, 94
Béganne  105
Bègles  87
Bellegarde  27
Belley  6
Bellions  102, 107
Bergerac  89
Bernegoue  142
Bernoy  77
Beslé  104
Bessan  47, 48
Bessières  65
Betton  101
Béziers  33, 37-8
**Bidache, river**  93, 95
**Bidouze, river**  92, 93, 95
Blain,  110
**Blavet, river**  6, 106, 107, 116, 118
**Blavet, Canal du**  19, 107, 112-13, 116-18
Blaye  88
*blue flag rule*  14
*Blue Links project*  5
*boat hire*  12-13
*boat licences* (péage plaisance)  10-11
*boat transport*  11
Boé  59
*bollards at locks*  16
*books*  19-20
Bordeaux  19, 86, 87, 88
Bouchemaine  119, 120, 122, 125, 129
Bouillac  73, 85
Bourg-Charente  135
Bourg-des-Comptes  104
Bourg-sur-Gironde  90
**Boutonne, river**  133-4, 137
Bouziès  82
Bouzigues  25, 30
Brain-sur-Vilaine  104
Bram  42
Branne  89, 90
**Brault, Canal maritime de Marans au**  138, 139
Bray  8
Brégnier-Cordon  7
Bressols  65
Brest  108
**Brest, Canal de Nantes à**  6, 19, 97, 106-115, 119
Briare  119
*bridge signs*  15
**Brienne, Canal de**  46, 54, 62
Briollay  132
Brissarthe  132
Brittany (*through routes*)  19
Brittany Canals  5-6, 97-118

*Brittany Waterways (office)*  21
Brives-sur-Charente  135
Bruz  103
Buzet-sur-Baïse  53, 54, 60, 61, 66, 67, 70

Cadillac  87
Cahors  72, 80, 81
Cahors L'Archipel  81
Caillac  77, 81
Caïx  81
Cajarc  72, 73, 83, 84
Camargue  25
Cambes  87
Campagnac  77
Cantenay-Epinard  128
Cap d'Agde  48
Capdenac  72, 73, 84, 85
Capestang  39
Carcassone  33, 42
Carillon tide barrier  133, 134, 137
Carnon  28
Carquefou  110
Cassafières, Port  37
Casseneuil  77
Castanet  44
Castelfranc  79
Castelmoron-sur-Lot  73, 76
Castelnau  56
Castelnaudary  33, 35, 43
Castelsarrasin  57
Castets-en-Dorthe  53, 54, 62, 86, 87
Castillon-la-Bataille  89, 90
Caumont-sur-Garonne  61
Cavernes  90
Le Cellier  121
Cénevières  83
Cers  37
*certificates of competence*  9-10
Cesse  49
*CEVNI rules*  9, 10
Chalonnes-sur-Loire  122
Chambellay  128
Champtoceaux  120, 121
Changé  127
Chaniers  135
La Chapelle-Basse-Mer  121
La Chapelle-sur-Erdre  110
La Chapelle-aux-Filtzméens  100
La Chapelle-sur-Oudon  129
Charente  97, 133-7
Château-Gontier  125, 127
Château-Thébaud  123, 124
Châteaulin  97, 107-8, 115
Châteauneuf-sur-Charente  134, 135
Châteauneuf-du-Faou  115
Châteauneuf-sur-Sarthe  132
Le Châtelier lock  98, 99
Chautagne  6
Cheffes-sur-Sarthe  130, 132
Le Chêne  124

Chenillé-Changé  128
**Cher, river**  6
Chevaigné  101
La Chevallerais  110
Civrac-de-Dordogne  90
Clairac  75
Coat-Natous  107, 113-14
Cognac  134, 135
Colmar  5
Colombiers  39
*COLREGS*  10
Compiègne  7
Condom  69
Conques  84
Corbarieu  63, 65
Corbières  33
Cordemais  120
Couëron  120
Coulon-Sansais  141
Courdault  138, 142
Coutras  91
*COVID-19*  4
Crégols  72
*cruise planning*  1, 9-20, 21
*Cruising Association (CA)*  20
Cubzac-les-Ponts  90
Cuxac d'Aude  51
Cuzac  84, 85

Damazan  60
Damvix  138, 141
Daon  127
Dax  92, 93
*DBA (The Barge Association)*  4, 10, 20
Decazeville  72
Decize  119
*depths*  13
  see also start of each waterway
**Descente en Baïse**  54, 70
**Descente dans l'Hérault maritime**  34, 36, 47, 48
**Descente en Tarn**  54, 58
Dieupentale  56
**Digoin, Canal de Roanne à**  119
*dimensions, navigable*, 13
  see also start of each waterway
Dinan  100
Dinard  99
*DIY locks*  17
*documentation*  9-11
Domino, Port  124
Dompierre-sur-Charente  135
Donges  120
**Dordogne, river**  53, 86, 89-90, 91
Douai  6
Douelle  81
*draught*  13
  see also start of each waterway
Duravel  79
Dureil  132

Écouflant  132
*Éditions du Breil*  19, 20
English Channel  19, 98, 107
Entrammes  127

# Index

d'Envaux, Port 136
Erdre 106, 107, 115
Escatalens 57
Escaut 6, 8
Étang des Eaux Blanches 25
**Étang de Thau** 23, 24, 25, 29, 30, 33
EU 5-10
*European Boating Association* 10
Evran 100
Eynesse 90

Fégréac 110
Feneu 128
Feugarolles 60, 68
Fillé-sur-Sarthe 131
Flagnac 85
*flags* 9
Flaran 69
Flaujagues 90
La Fleix 90
*Fluviacarte* 19, 20
Folleux 105
Fongrave 77
Fonsérannes 33, 35, 38-9
Fontet 62
Les Forges 111
*formalities* 9-11
Fourques-sur-Garonne 23, 61
Le Fresne-sur-Loire 121
*Freycinet (standard) waterways* 13, 14, 16-17
Frontignan 25, 29
Fumel 4, 73, 74, 78

La Gacilly 115
Gaillac 65
Gallician 27
Gardouch 44
**Garonne, river** 53, 54, 62, 70, 86-8
**Garonne, Canal de** 46, 53, 54-62, 87
**Garonne Crossing (Baïse-Lot connection)** 70-71, 73
Gaves Réunis 92, 93, 94, 95
**Gironde estuary** 53, 86-7, 88, 90
Givet 4
Goariva 106, 107, 114
Golfech 53, 58, 64
Gouarec 113
*grand gabarit (high-capacity) waterways* 13, 16
La Grande-Motte 28
Granges-sur-Lot 75
Le Grau d'Agde 47, 48
Le Grau-du-Roi 25, 30
La Grève-sur-Mignon 139, 142
Grez-Neuville 128
Grisolles 56
Gueltas 112
Guenrouët 110
**Guerlédan dam & bypass** 6, 106, 107, 113, 117
Guiche 95
Guichen 104
*guides & publications* 19-20
Guillac 111
Guipel 101

Guipry 104
Guîtres 91

La Haie Fouassière 124
Ham 7
Hastingues 95
Hauterive 77
*headroom & heights* 13
 see also start of each waterway
Hédé 101
Hennebont 116, 118
**Hérault, river** 33, 34, 36, 47-8
*hire boats* 12-13
Homps 41
*hours of navigation* 18
Houssay 127
Hure 61
**Hyère, river** 106, 108, 114

L'Ile d'Elle 140
**d'Ille-et-Rance, Canal** 98, 100-101, 102
*Imray publications* 19, 20
Ingrandes 120, 122
*Inland Waterways International* 4
*insurance* 9
Irleau 141
Isac 107
**Isle, river** 53, 91
L'Isle-sur-Tarn 65

La Jaille-Yvon 127
Jarnac 134, 135
**Jeune Autise, river** 138, 139, 142
**Jonction, Canal de (La Nouvelle branch)** 49
La Jonelière 110
Josselin 107, 111
**Joyeuse (Aran)** 93, 94, 95
Juigné-sur-Sarthe 132
Juvardeil 132

La Chapelle-Basse-Mer 121
La Chapelle-sur-Erdre 110
La Chapelle-aux-Filtzméens 100
La Chapelle-sur-Oudon 129
La Chevallerais 110
La Fleix 90
La Gacilly 115
La Grande-Motte 28
La Grève-sur-Mignon 139, 142
La Haie Fouassière 124
La Jaille-Yvon 127
La Jonelière 110
La Landriais 99
La Noirie 119
**La Nouvelle branch (Canal du Midi)** 49-51
La Pauillade 91
La Poissonière 122
La Redorte 41
La Réole 62, 87
La Richardais 99
La Robine 40
La Roche-Bernard 102, 105
La Rochelle 138
La Roque Bouillac 85

La Suze-sur-Sarthe 132
La Tiffardière 141
La Valette 127
Lacourt-Saint-Pierre 64
Lafrançaise 65
Lagruère 61
Lahonce 94
Laillé 104
Lalande, Port 76
Lalinde, Canal de 89
Lallaing 6
Lamagdeleine 81
Lamagistère 58
Lamarque 88
Lamothe-Montravel 90
Landévennec 115
La Landriais 99
Langoiran 87
Langon (Garonne) 87
Langon (Vilaine) 104
Langrolay 99
Lanne, Port-de- 93, 94
Larnagol 80, 83
Laroque-des-Arcs 81
Larroque-Toirac 83
Lasserre 68
Lattes 23, 31, 32
Laubardemont 91
Launay, Port 106, 115
Lauragais, Port 43
Laval 125, 127
Lavardac 68
Le Cellier 121
Le Châtelier lock 98, 99
Le Chêne 124
Le Fresne-sur-Loire 121
Le Grau d'Agde 47, 48
Le Grau-du-Roi 25, 30
Le Lion d'Angers 128, 129
Le Mans 130-31
Le Mas d'Agenais 61
Le Roc-Saint-André 111
Le Ségala 43
Le Someil 40
Le Temple-sur-Lot 74, 76-7
Le Verdon-sur-Mer 88
Les Forges 111
Les Onglous 25, 30, 33, 36
**Lez, river** 24, 31-2
**l'Hérault maritime, Descente dans** 34, 36, 47, 48
**Liaison Dunkerque-Escaut** 8
Libourne 89, 90, 91
*licences* 9-11
*lights* 15
Lihoury 93, 95
L'Ile d'Elle 140
Le Lion d'Angers 128, 129
L'Isle-sur-Tarn 65
Livinhac 85
Lochrist 118
*locks* 16-17
 see also start of each waterway
Locmiquélic 118
Loire 19, 107, 119-22, 129
**Loire, Canal latéral à la (Decize)** 119
**l'Oise, Canal de la Sambre à** 4
Longuenée-en-Anjou 128
Lorient 107, 116
Lormont 88
**Lot, river** 4-5, 53, 66, 70-85

Luy 92, 93
Luzech 72, 73, 79, 80, 81
Lyon 6
Lyvet 100

Magné 141
Maguelonne Abbey 28
Maillé 138, 139, 140, 142
Maillezais 142
**Maine, river** 119, 122-25, 128
 see also **Mayenne-Maine; Petite Maine; Vieille Maine**
Malause, 58
Malestroit 111
Malicorne-sur-Sarthe 130, 132
Malpas 33, 39
Le Mans 130-31
*maps* 19-20, 21
Marais Poitevin 138
Marans 138, 139, 140
**Marans-au-Brault, Canal maritime de** 138, 139
Marcellus 61
Marcenac 84, 85
**Maritime, Canal (Le Grau-du-Roi)** 25, 30
Marmande 61
Marseillan 25, 30
Marseillette 41
Marssac-sur-Tarn 65
Martigné-sur-Mayenne 127
Le Mas d'Agenais 61
*mast manoeuvres* 11, 19
Mauves-sur-Loire 121
Mauzé-sur-le-Mignon 138, 142
**Mayenne, River** 119, 125-6, 129, 130
**Mayenne-Maine, river** 125-9
Mediterranean (*routes*) 8, 19, 24-5, 34, 51, 54, 86
Meilhan-sur-Garonne 61
Mellionec 106, 107
Ménil 127
Mercuès 81
Meschers-sur-Gironde 88
Messac 104
Mèze 25, 30
**Midi, Canal du** 9, 23, 25, 33-46, 47, 49
**Mignon (Canal du Mignon)** 138, 139, 142
Minervois 33
Mirepoix 65
Moissac 53, 54, 55, 58
Moncrabeau 68
Monnières 123, 124
Mont-de-Marsan 92
Montauban 53, 54, 63, 64, 65
Montbéliard à la Haute-Saône, Canal de 8
Montbrun 72, 73, 83
Montech 55, 56-7, 57, 63
**Montech, Canal de** 53, 54, 63-4
Montertelot 111
Montesquieu-Lauragais 44
Montgiroux 127
Montgiscard 44
Montjean-sur-Loire 120, 122

144

# Index

Montpellier 23, 31, 32
Montreuil-Belfroy 125, 128
Montreuil-sur-Ille 101
Montreuil-sur-Maine 128
*mooring* 11, 18, 21
Morannes 132
Mortagne-sur-Gironde 88
**Moselle, river** 8
Mulhouse 8
Mûr de Bretagne 113

Nantes 19, 97, 107, 108-9, 119, 120, 121
**Nantes à Brest, Canal de** 6, 19, 97, 106-115, 119
Narbonne 23, 49, 51
Naurouze 43
*navigable dimensions* 13
  *see also start of each waterway*
*navigation signs & signals* 15
Nérac 68
Neuville-Day 4
Nicole lock 70-74, 86
Nîmes 27
Niort 138, 139, 141
**Nive, river** 93, 94, 95
**Nivernais, Canal du** 119
Nogent 8
La Noirie 119
Nord, Canal du 7
Nort-sur-Erdre 110, 115
*North Sea-Mediterranean link* 8
**La Nouvelle branch (Canal du Midi)** 49-51
Noyen-sur-Sarthe 132

**Oise, river** 4, 7, 8
l'Oise, Canal de la Sambre à 4
Les Onglous 25, 30, 33, 36
Orb, river 33, 37-8
Origné 127
**d'Orléans, Canal** 6
**Oudon, river** 119, 120, 121, 125-6, 128, 129, 130
**Oust, river** 106, 107, 110, 111-12
*overtaking* 14

Paimboeuf 120
Palavas-les-Flots 28, 32
Paraza 40
Parcé-sur-Sarthe 132
Parnac 81
Pauillac 88
La Pauillade 91
Peillac 111
Penchot 85
Penne, Port-de- 77
Périgueux 91
Pessac-sur-Dordogne 90
**Petit-Rhône, river** 23, 24
**Petite Maine, river** 123, 124
Peyrade, Canal de la 25
Peyrehorade 93, 95
*planning a cruise* 1, 9-20, 21
Pléchâtel 104
Plélauff 113
Plouer-sur-Rance 99
Podensac 87
Poilhes 39
Pomère, Canal de 140

Pommevic 58
Pompignan 56
Pont-Augan 118
Pont-ar-c'hlan 115
Pont-Coblant 115
Pont-du-Pouy 92, 93
Pont-Réan 103
Pont-Rousseau 123, 124
Pontivy 19, 106, 107, 112, 116, 117
Pontonx 92, 93
Port d'Agrès 72, 73, 84, 85
Port Ariane (Lattes) 28, 31, 32
Port Cassafières 37
Port Domino 124
Port Lalande 76
Port Launay 106, 115
Port Lauragais 43
Port de Roche 104
Port-des-Barques 137
Port-d'Envaux 136
Port-de-Lanne 93, 94
Port-la-Nouvelle 35, 49, 51
Port-de-Penne 77
Port-Saint-Foy 90
Portets 87
Portillon 124
Portiragnes 33, 37
Pradines 81
Preignac 87
*priority rules* 14
Pruillé 128
Puichéric 41
Puy-l'Evêque 5, 74, 79

Rabastens 65
*radio telephone ship licence* 9
Ramonville 44
**Rance, Canal d'Ille-et-** 98, 100-101, 102
**Rance maritime** 98-9
Redon 19, 102, 104-5, 107, 110
La Redorte 41
*registration documents* 9
*Registry of Shipping & Seamen (Cardiff)* 9
*regulations* 9-11
Rennes 98, 101, 102, 103, 105
La Réole 62, 87
**Rhin, Canal du Rhône au (Northern Branch)** 5
Rhine-Rhône waterway 6, 8
**Rhône, river** 6-7, 24, 25
**Rhône à Sète, Canal du** 7, 23, 24-30
La Richardais 99
Rieux 105
*Riquet, Pierre-Paul* 33-4, 43
Roanne 119
**Roanne à Digoin, Canal de** 119
La Robine 40
**Robine, Canal de la (La Nouvelle branch)** 49-51
Le Roc-Saint-André 111
Roche, Port de 104
La Roche-Bernard 102, 105
Rochefort 133, 134, 136
La Rochelle 138

Roëzé-sur-Sarthe 132
Rohan 106, 107, 112
La Roque Bouillac 85
**Roubaix Canal** 5
Roubia 40
Rouffiac 135
*routes (through routes)* 19
  *see also* Atlantic; English Channel; Mediterranean
*Royal Yachting Association (RYA)* 9, 10
Royan 88
*rules & regulations* 9-11
*rules of the road* 14-16

Sablé-sur-Sarthe 132
Saillans 91
Saint-Adrien 118
Saint-Aignan 113
Saint-André-de-Bubzac 90
Saint-Armand-les-Eaux 6
Saint-Aulaye 90
Saint-Baudelle 127
Saint-Brice 75, 135
Saint-Christoly 88
Saint-Cirq-Lapopie 80, 83
Saint-Congard 111
Saint-Denis-de-Pile 91
Saint-Domineuc 100
Saint-Estèphe 88
Saint-Fiacre-sur-Maine 124
Saint-Florent-le-Vieil 121
Saint-Foy, Port 90
Saint-Gérand 112
Saint-Germain-d'Anxure 127
Saint-Germain-sur-Ille 101
Saint-Géry 82
Saint-Gilles 23, 24, 27
Saint-Gonnery 112
Saint-Gravé 111
Saint-Grégoire 101
Saint-Guénaël 118
Saint-Jean-d'Angély 133, 137
Saint-Jean-de-Blaignac 90
Saint-Jean-sur-Mayenne 127
Saint-Jean-Poutge 66
Saint-Jory 56
Saint-Laurent-de-Cognac 135
Saint-Léger 66, 67, 70, 71
Saint-Liguaire 141
Saint-Loubès 90
Saint-Macaire 87
Saint-Malo 19, 98, 99, 102
Saint-Martin-Lalande 43
Saint-Martin-sur-Oust 111
Saint-Médard-sur-Ille 101
Saint-Nazaire (Loire) 107, 119, 120
Saint-Nazaire-sur-Charente 137
Saint-Nicolas-des-Eaux 118
Saint-Nicolas-de-Redon 110
Saint-Pierre-d'Eyraud 89, 90
Saint-Pierre-Toirac 83
Saint-Porquier 57
Saint-Rivalain 118
Saint-Samson (Oust) 112
Saint-Samson-sur-Rance 100
Saint-Savinien 134, 136
Saint-Sever 92, 93
Saint-Sigismond 142
Saint-Simeux 135

Saint-Simon 135
Saint-Sorlin-de-Conac 88
Saint-Suliac 99
Saint-Sulpice 127
Saint-Sylvestre 77
Saint-Vincent-sur-Oust 111
Saint-Vite 74
Sainte-Anne-sur-Vilaine 104
Sainte-Foy-la-Grande 89, 90
Sainte-Livrade 77
Sainte-Luce 120
Sainte-Marie 104
Saint-Vite 4
Saintes 136
Sallèles-d'Aude 49, 50
Salvagnac-Cajarc 83
**Sambre à l'Oise, Canal de la** 4
**Saône, river** 8
**Sarthe, river** 119, 125, 128, 129, 130-32
Saubusse 93, 94
Savennières 122
**Savières, Canal de** 6
Savignac-de-l'Isle 91
**Scarpe inférieure, river** 6
*seasons* 18-19
Sedan 4
Le Ségala 43
Segré 125, 129
**Seine, river** 8
**Seine-Nord Europe Canal** 7, 8
Sérignac-sur-Garonne 60
Sète (port) 7, 19, 23, 24, 25, 29
**Sète, Canal du Rhône à** 7, 23, 24-30
**Sèvre Nantaise, river** 121, 123-4
**Sèvre Niortaise, river** 138-42
*ship's radio licence* 9
*signs & signals* 15, 16
Sireuil 135
*Small Ships Register* 9
Solesmes 132
Le Someil 40
*Somerville, Robert* 17-18
**Somme, Upper Canal de la** 7
Soubise 137
Souil 138, 142
*sound signals* 15
Spay 131
*speed limits* 16
Strasbourg 5
Sucé-sur-Erdre 110
La Suze-sur-Sarthe 132

**Tarn, river** 53, 54, 55, 58, 63-5
*taxes* 9
Le Temple-sur-Lot 74, 76-7
*temporary import* 9
Thau *see* Étang de Thau
La Tiffardière 141
*time of day* 18
*time of year* 18-19
Tinténiac 100
*tipping* 17
Tonnay-Boutonne 137
Tonnay-Charente 133, 136
Tonneins 61
Torxé 137
Toulouse 19, 23, 33, 45-6, 53, 54, 55-6, 62

145

# Index

Touzac  79
*towpaths see start of each waterway*
Trèbes  41
Tréhiguier  105
Trentemoult  120
Trévérien  100
*turning*  16

Valence d'Agen  58
Valence-sur-Baïse  66, 69
La Valette  127
*VAT documentation*  9
Ventenac d'Aude  40
Le Verdon-sur-Mer  88
Vers  82
Vertou  123, 124
Vianne  68
Vias  37
Vidourle  24, 28, 30
Vieille Autise  138, 139, 142
Vieille Maine  125, 128, 129
*vignettes*  10-11
**Vilaine, river**  19, 98, 101, 102-5, 106, 107
Villebrumier  65
Villefranque  95
Villemur-sur-Tarn  65
Villeneuve-lès-Bèziers  37
Villeneuve-sur-Lot  73, 74, 77
Villepinte  43
Villesèquelande  42
Villeton  61
Vimport  93
VNF (Voies Navigables de France)  1, 3-11, 21

*waterway categories*  13-17
*weather*  18
*websites*  19, 20